RELIGIOUS PLURALISM
AND
WORLD COMMUNITY

STUDIES
IN THE HISTORY OF RELIGIONS

(SUPPLEMENTS TO *NUMEN*)

XV

RELIGIOUS PLURALISM AND WORLD COMMUNITY

LEIDEN
E. J. BRILL
1969

RELIGIOUS PLURALISM AND WORLD COMMUNITY

INTERFAITH AND INTERCULTURAL COMMUNICATION

EDITED BY

EDWARD J. JURJI

LEIDEN
E. J. BRILL
1969

Copyright 1969 by E. J. Brill, Leiden, Netherlands

All rights reserved. No part of this book may be reproduced or translated in any form, by print, photoprint, microfilm or any other means without written permission from the publisher

PRINTED IN THE NETHERLANDS

CONTENTS

	Page
Preface	v
EDWARD J. JURJI, Introduction	1
HUSTON SMITH, Identification of Problem	21

Part One
PROFILES OF RELIGIOUS PLURALISM

K. S. MURTY, History, Historical Consciousness and Freedom	35
K. N. JAYATILLEKE, Buddhist Relativity and the One-World Concept	43
LOUIS FINKELSTEIN, The Jewish Vision of Human Brotherhood	79
A. H. ABDEL KADER, The Islamic Involvement in the Process of History	93

Part Two
INVOLVEMENT OF THE RELIGIONS IN MODERN SOCIETY

WING-TSIT CHAN, The Historic Chinese Contribution to Religious Pluralism and World Community	113
HAJIME NAKAMURA, The Indian and Buddhist Concept of Law	131
ANNEMARIE SCHIMMEL, Islam in the Modern World	175
H. C. GANGULI, Religion and the Population Explosion	193

Part Three
DESEGREGATION OF RELIGIONS AND CULTURES: GUIDELINES

S. G. F. BRANDON, A New Awareness of Time and History	225
C. J. BLEEKER, Methodology and the Science of Religion	237
FAZLUR RAHMAN, The Impact of Modernity on Islam	248
R. E. WHITSON, The Situation of Theology	263
Epilogue	297
Index	309

PREFACE

Princeton Theological Seminary was the first American institution of comparable stature to recognize the history of religions as a field of study conducive to interfaith and intercultural communication in scholarly depth. Included in the celebration of its Sesquicentennial in 1963 was a conference on "The Significance of Comparative Religion in Modern Culture." Among the participants were scholars of the humanities and behavioral sciences as well as theologians and historians of religions.

Thanks to the munificence of Edward F. Gallahue of Indianapolis, two conferences were held in 1964 and 1966. The topic of the former was "The Phenomenon of Convergence and the Course of Prejudice;" its proceedings appeared in the Graduate Journal of the University of Texas, Vol. VII, 1966, Supplement. The latter conference was convoked under the general theme, "Religious Pluralism and World Community." Papers then introduced form the substance of the present symposium.

The purpose of this book is largely documentary. History of religions perspectives here reflect universal elements of dramatic conflict. These happen to be set against the background of philosophical divergence, political and economic tensions no less than the familiarly ingrained theological ferments of our age. Also noted are certain major profiles of world religions. Both the desegregation and involvement of religious structures are envisioned in the light of the historical process and the trend toward world community.

The contributing cast comprises specialists of Great Britain and India, of France, Germany, and Japan, of Holland, the U.A.R. and the United States of America, as well as of Ceylon, Pakistan, and Vatican City. As the table of contents reveals, the principal cultures of mankind are involved in direct though tentative dialogue. It is our hope that the volume will not only serve as a tool useful in the history of religions and related fields of study and research, but that it will further commend itself to all those who are responsive to the potentialities of a common mind transcending barriers of creed, culture and ideology in the modern world.

None of these strides and ideals could have been implemented but for the enthusiastic vision, indefatigable support, and keen judgment of

James I. McCord, President of Princeton Theological Seminary. In addition to impressive services as chairman, Dr. McCord rendered a statesmanlike contribution in relating the venturesome enterprise to the integral academic and curricular structure of a first-rate seminary.

In the preparation of the manuscript for publication, an attempt was made to preserve the integrity of each author's style and diction. Several persons gave liberally of their time and talent in facilitating the editorial task. Among these, special credit is due Professor C. J. Bleeker of the University of Amsterdam for invaluable advice and suggestions. His gracious consent to admit the volume into the distinguished Numen Supplement Series is gratefully acknowledged. Mr. James E. Andrews, Assistent to the President and Director of Information at the seminary, gave most assiduously of his attention in the execution of the conference schedule upon which the eventual correlation of materials incorporated in this work was necessarily dependent.

Insofar as the mechanics of the volume were concerned, Mrs. William S. Dunifon was not only responsible for the typescript but proved ingeniously adept in effecting the necessary literary improvements in the text.

To all these, and particularly to my wife, Ruth Guinter Jurji, without whose counsel and encouragement the project as a whole might never have been completed, my deep appreciation is hereby recorded.

E. J. J.

INTRODUCTION
RELIGIOUS PLURALISM AND WORLD COMMUNITY

BY

EDWARD J. JURJI
Princeton

Amidst a sequence of lively and moving events, intriguingly organized to strike a happy balance between what is festively intellectual and sociably relaxed, Princeton Seminary's experience with conferences on world religions hit an all time high in May, 1966. At not a few points in the course of an eight-day session, moments of unforgettable drama flashed across the scene.

There was an episode, for instance, too melodramatic and subtle to be described in words. It broke out when a participant, youthful El-Biali—an Egyptian assistant director of the Islamic Center, Washington, D.C.—took the floor. He asked Rabbi Louis Finkelstein, speaker of the afternoon, a pertinent question. Speaking with unfeigned candor and trust, El-Biali wanted to know whether Jewish restiveness could possibly have originated in the kind of historically adverse setting to which Jewry had long been exposed. What seemed to stun the plenary was the wonder of the questioner's complete abandon with not a hint of acrimony.

In launching a second Gallahue Conference, May 4-11, 1966, and proposing "Religious Pluralism and World Community" for a theme, the Seminary took a resolute step in its historic role of service to American and world scholarship. It joined hands in an enterprise with leading United States and other institutions as more than fifty eminent scholars from practically every representative culture area of the globe concerted their efforts on a crucial frontier.

A primary aim was to establish—for the benefit of all concerned—a focus of world scholarship, research, and interchange. This was envisaged within an overall framework of religious pluralism and world community, of academic and spiritual values. Advanced study, dialogue, and irenic conversation were deemed a necessary prelude to deeper consciousness and sensitive confrontation within the order of an inclusive polarity.

The conference was avowedly hospitable to every shade of religious and philosophical persuasion. This general outlook followed the guidelines of a phenomenology requiring that each religious entity be manifest through its own exponents precisely as it appears on the world stage. Muslim conferees thus stated the case for Islam's involvement in the process of history and modern culture. Hindu scholars likewise reflected on the problem of religion and the population explosion.

Two distinguished Buddhist scholars, the one a dean of the University of Tokyo, the other a ranking philosopher of the University of Ceylon, defined the Indian and Buddhist views of relativity vis-à-vis the one-world idea. Responsible Western scholars had a golden opportunity to listen and understand, to deliver papers, and to contribute toward realization of authentic dialogue.

I

Problem Identified

Inevitably, many an issue was touched upon that was vital to present-day political and existential thinking. In the keynote address, Huston Smith urged the faiths to develop what he described as their "irenic potential" by building mankind's confidences in them, by strengthening their mutual ties, and by giving careful attention to the way they relate themselves to political conflicts. He noted that religious differences historically have exacerbated political divisions more than they have tempered them. To document this, Professor Smith added that we do not have to go back to the Crusades or other wars of religion. In our own life-span there is evidence to spare.

In order to identify the problem more precisely, Huston Smith posed a number of pertinent questions. Would Pakistan be partitioned from India today if Hinduism and Islam were not disparate? Would there be 600,000 refugees in Jordan (1,300,000 in Arab states as a whole) if Judaism were not a historic community distinct from Islam? Recalling Cardinal Newman's words, "Oh, how we hate one another for the love of God!", he formulated the problem this way: How can we keep our religious differences from exacerbating political conflicts? He had a dynamic concept of the task before the conference: Can our religions, despite their differences, help to resolve political conflicts that endanger us? Can religion in our time be a force for the taming of the nations? Does it have an irenic potential?

The odds are that Wilfred Cantwell Smith was incredibly sound in his "summation" when he hurled at the conference the challenge that it failed. Its failure was the outcome, he said, of reluctance to tackle deep-seated differences. But he did understand that the conference had not sought "clear conclusions," "agreed-upon solutions," or "nicely defined questions." Its main achievement, he said, was that it had "educated its participants to a truer, more intimate, and more personal awareness of what the problems are; of where we differ; of what directions our thinking and striving must take if we are to aspire to world community across religious frontiers."

No one could say, however, that the central issue of our time, Marxism, was a subject quietly forgotten. Huston Smith reproduced an extraordinary stance on Marxism suggested by an Oxford scholar and conference participant, Professor R. C. Zaehner (*Matter and Spirit*, New York, Harper and Row, 1963, p. 17-18.) Instead of focusing on its irreligious features, Zaehner saw Marxism as an eruption in our day of an age-old essentially religious dream of human solidarity. From the beginning, he wrote, there have been, within religions, two tendencies in dialectical tension with each other—the one drawing the individual ever deeper into himself, down into the "kingdom of God" that is "within you," and the other integrating him ever more closely with religious community.

In modern times, according to Zaehner, the latter tendency has re-emerged in the Marxian hope of an infinitely perfectible world which is to come into being once the last of the social contradictions has been surmounted and man is no longer exploited by man. He regarded Marxists and Christians at one in affirming "a power that is greater than man, greater than nations, and greater than individual religions, the power that Marx identified with matter itself, and which a Christian would identify with the Spirit of God that moved upon the face of the waters before the world began, the Spirit which is ever busy kneading mankind into a coherent mass, however much individual men may kick against the pricks."

Further light on the problem was shed by the nature of religious pluralism.

II

Profiles of Religious Pluralism

Etched on broad canvas, the complex of religious pluralism projected profiles of philosophy, relativism, chosenness, and dogmatism. These were dealt with by Murty of India, Jayatilleke of Ceylon, Finkelstein of the U.S.A., and Abdel Kader of the U.A.R., respectively.

1. In professor K. S. Murty of Andhra University, India, the Conference discovered at the final scheduled session a perceptive philosopher. He illumined the theme of the conference and sought to tackle the central problem posed. His paper on "History, Historical Consciousness, and Freedom" constituted a singular profile of religious pluralism as it is envisaged by a top-flight Indian thinker. Historical reality is the past with a living message. He declared it is like Indus civilization which did not exist for the contemporary world till excavations begun in 1922 at Mohenjodaro and Harappa brought it to light. The ultimate aim of history is to understand human existence.

The proper key for the interpretation of human history, Murty went on to say, is man as he was, is, and shall be. Such an historical consciousness liberates us. In fleeting moments, man can grasp that history is grounded in the Absolute, that is, glory is fragmentarily manifested in history. Now and then man falls an easy prey to the illusion that the Transcendent has been or is found in a particular person or event or thing. Others are not quite thrilled to relate themselves to the Transcendent. They desire to become it, or reduce it to an historical existence. A cat, however, may never become a tiger. It is not wise to try to become sugar instead of remaining content with tasting it.

Murty's reflections yielded a contribution to the problem in terms of a favored withdrawal to a philosophy that was disposed to find the light of history in man—a polymorphic being with infinite potentialities for experience. World community and social responsibility could then fall by the wayside. This could easily be the deduction to be drawn from Murty's insight that human history is the exhibition of man's failure to convert the world into heaven and himself into deity.

Murty could draw upon his knowledge of Hindu and philosophical formulations. He portrayed human history as a record of ideas and passions. One's own historical judgement liberates him from the irony cf history. It is historical consciousness itself that provides freedom from history. An awareness of one's historicity leads to communion with the transhistorical, and harmonious living-together of free men becomes a worthy rational ideal. Since men are not wholly rational, however, nor can become wholly free, this freedom is never fully realized. Nevertheless, such an ideal does serve as a beacon light to humanity and should inspire perhaps some to strive for it.

2. From Hindu philosophy we pass on to Buddhist relativity as a second profile in the complex of religious pluralism. Professor K. N. Jayatilleke, chairman of the Department of Philosophy, University of

Ceylon, suggested that the Buddhist concept of relativity with its emphasis on oneness and spirituality constituted a formidable contribution to world community. Its permissive interpretative technique is an object lesson, he said, to other religions which tend to stress their exclusivity to the point where they fail to see what they have in common with one another.

Jayatilleke further maintained that Buddhism is up-to-date. It is compatible, in his judgement, with contemporary scientific cosmology. Earlier Buddhist texts spoke of the "thousands of suns, moons, and inhabited worlds, thousands of heavenly worlds of varying grades." He did not indicate, however, whether Buddhism thus equated with scientific rationalism ought to abandon its traditional spirituality.

He further observed that Buddhist scholars had anticipated Marxist philosophy. They taught that the maldistribution of goods was responsible for the loss of values and ultimately a cause of war. They advocated welfare systems to curtail poverty and unemployment. Indicative of a distinct preference for self-government moreover, was Buddhism's emphasis on equality and respect for the individual. In his exposition of Buddhist relativity, Jayatilleke adverted to the class of Buddhist doctrines and practices which he described as attractive to people of diverse conditions across many centuries. Those were tenets and acts, in his opinion, which made no exclusivist claim whatever.

Jayatilleke went on to profess that early Buddhism was by no means atheistic in the materialist and Marxist sense. He dismissed as utterly commonplace the contrast often drawn between an original atheistic Buddhism and a developed theistic variety of the so-called Mahayana school where allegedly the concept of a cosmic Buddha emerged. His contention was that both the primitive and Mahayana types were atheistic in that they knew nothing of a personal God. Parenthetically he noted that a universe created in time by an omniscient and omnipotent deity could not but figure as a rigged cosmos. If at all construed, the will of any such deity, he said, should tend to denigrate manhood, reducing man's status to that of a puppet. Any effective attempt to resolve the problem of evil and free will should then prove futile.

The distinction was, however, made that ever since its inception, Buddhism was theistic in inculcating the validity of moral and spiritual experience. It also subscribed to an impersonal, transcendent, and ultimate reality beyond time, space, and causality. In this sense, it is perfectly in order for a Buddhist to embrace a conception of God beyond theism.

Be that as it may, it was anything but self-explanatory that the central core of Buddhism as the speaker asserted had not been appreciably changed, nor was his argument less precarious that a hard core of theism had accompanied this faith since its most pristine beginnings.

3. "Chosenness" was not exactly the title of the paper given by Chancellor Louis Finkelstein of the Jewish Theological Seminary of America, but it might serve to describe his significant contribution. Rabbi Finkelstein dealt with his formal subject, "The Jewish Vision of Human Brotherhood" in an objective and impressive manner. In contemplation of Jewish source material and procedural documentation, the presentation was both learned and lucid. Commendable restraint was exercised in stating the case for the Shammaitic and Hillelite wings of Pharisaism, with their chauvinistic and universalists norms, respectively.

In thus investigating Judaic concern with the "in" and the "outside" groups, Dr. Finkelstein rendered a service to students of pluralism and its relation to world community. One wondered, however, whether the idea of progress and the concomitant concept of human perfectibility were to be taken integrally or not with the vision of messianic brotherhood at the end of time.

Finkelstein won his audience by dint of personal charm. Departing not infrequently from the prepared text, he succeeded in making the incredible credible. This he achieved by force of allusion and anecdote as well as a category of illustrative technique all his own. He traced the concept of the chosen people mainly with reference to the Pentateuch. (Professor Charles T. Fritsch of Princeton raised the question of whether Wisdom and Prophetic literature, too, should not be considered.) But Chancellor Finkelstein had actually included Second Isaiah and the Jewish Prayer Book—"the most significant tract of Jewish theology." In all these writings, the selection of Israel was translated into a command, said Finkelstein. Israel had been chosen for specific tasks and responsibilities. At the very beginning of literary prophecy, Amos informed Israel that it was no different before the Lord than the nations of the Ethiopians, Philistines, or Arameans. Mans' hunger for primacy is given satisfaction. But the primacy to be achieved is in service, not in power.

4. Dogmatics would quite logically come up in any sampling of profiles having to do with the nature of the problem under study. Directly to the point was the paper on "The Islamic Involvement in the Process of History," offered by an al-Azhar theologian, Dr. Ali

Abdel Kader, presently Director of the Islamic Center, in Washington, D.C. Aware of the menace, reportedly described as "fissiparous" tendencies by the late Jawaharlal Nehru, the conference strategy had aimed at creation of a dialogue situation through certain oblique hints spelled out in themes and sub-themes.

The maneuver proved surprisingly successful. Dr. Abdel Kader minced few words in stating the case for Islamic dogmatics along lines of exegesis and hermeneutics, even of straight apologetics. His central assumption was on this order: Islam has a comprehensive nature, intrinsically capable of setting forth guidelines for society. It is equally well-equipped to guide the individual Muslim toward God, his fellow believers, and human society generally.

Kader specified that Islamic involvement in the process of history cannot be adequately grasped apart from the Koran, its primary legislative source. His analysis confirmed the Koran as the "infallible word of God which gave rise to the first Muslim state within the confines of the Arabian Peninsula." Working through historical and juridical material, he arived at five principal conclusions: 1) that Islam is both religion and state, 2) that the division of the world into an abode of Islam and an abode of war is the invention of later Muslim jurists, an invention uncritically swallowed by Orientalists (his own contention being that Islam is not a religion of war but of peace), 3) that the Koran is a formidable source of legislation imparting support and meaning to Islamic intellectual life, 4) that Islamic jurisprudence derives from the Koran and meets twentieth-century requirements, 5) that secularism in the Muslim world is a sign of intellectual incompetence to project a new Muslim personality in the context of modern history.

An unanswered question was just what such a refurbished Islam proposed as a platform for communication-dialogue and improved understanding with other religions. Dr. Arend T. van Leeuwen of the Kerk en Wereld Institute, Driebergen, the Netherlands, in the course of a detailed commentary, inquired whether a post-Muslim phenomenon, on the order of the so-called post-Christian era, was anywhere predictable.

III

Involvement of the Religions in Modern Society

Whatever light these profiles might have shed on the problem, they did unveil a medley of religions and cultures wrapped up in the political, juridical, and social institutions of world civilization. Four such patterns of involvement in regional and global ethos were singled out for special examination. Each pattern was expertly analyzed by an authority in a non-western field who was simultaneously conversant with the western cultural tradition.

In each instance, the topic had a worldwide significance transcending particularist relevance. There was, firstly, the case of Chinese pluralism. It was ably assessed by Professor Wing-tsit Chan of Dartmouth College. Secondly, there was an evaluation of the Asian concept of law by Professor Hajime Nakamura of Tokyo University. Thirdly, Professor Annemarie Schimmel of Bonn University cited a pattern of involvement consisting of the confluence of western and Islamic cultural streams. A fourth and last category of involvement of religion in social and demographic affairs was introduced by Professor H. C. Ganguli of New Delhi University on the subject of population explosion.

1. Professor Chan expounded the involvement of religious pluralism in today's monolithic Chinese structure. He took cognizance of the same phenomenon in the over-all cultural heritage of China. He referred to the so-called "Let One Hundred Flowers Bloom and Let One Hundred Schools Contend" movement of 1957, adding that while the one hundred flowers may not be blooming at the present, the one hundred schools are still contending.

What has China contributed to religious pluralism? Simply the fact, he replied, that religion (Confucianism, Taoism, and Buddhism, as well as the latecomers, Christianity and Islam) can flourish together. One can profess all of the first three at the same time. What made this possible, he observed in passing, was emphasis on similarities rather than differences. When China shall once more take her place in the world community, he continued, her pluralistic character will once more come to grips with western religions. Past experience has taught us, he reasoned, that trouble can be avoided if religions do not serve political and economic interests. Such issues as God as personal, original sin, immortality, and the cycles of life and death, can perhaps be resolved through discussion.

Chan enlarged upon this theme of the involvement of religion in China's total record. "Coexistence or even synthesis" of religions was a "shining example of the amiable relationships" possible among religions. He noted furthermore, that China had been relatively free from religious persecutions. Even where these arose they had lasted only for a short time. The reason was that such religious outbreaks were at bottom economic and political rather than spiritual or ethical.

Basic to China's experience of relative religious concord was the conviction that religion is not to be made a tool for conquest or conversion. Its primary purpose was to preach a good way of life. Chan described the anti-Christian movement of the twentieth century as having had "more of the nature of anti-imperialism than anything else," although an element of "anti-foreignism" also existed. He maintained that the Chinese attacked Christianity not as a particular religion but chiefly as "an instrument of western imperialistic encroachment on Chinese sovereignty" and as a beneficiary of "unequal treaties that bound China in a semi-colonial status."

Returning to the more strictly religious dimension, the involvement of China's religions in society prompted Chan to observe that differences in doctrine are not easy to avoid. A basic source of conflict is the claim of a given religion to be all-inclusive and supreme, on the one hand, and, on the other, China's peculiar concept of religious pluralism. Logically, he declared, one cannot be two, and two cannot be one. Fortunately, he quipped, logic has seldom led to solutions of religious problems.

Perhaps the very desire to live together, he counseled, might show us the way. It was nowhere certain, however, that China's pattern of involvement, impressive and historic though it be, had ever been implemented on an international scale outside her territorial borders. Although Professor Chan's assumption left open the possibility of China's ultimate involvement in world community, the idea had a purely conjectural ring.

2. Involvement through impact of law was elaborately developed and documented by Professor Hajime Nakamura. Utilizing Sanskrit and Pali, as well as Chinese and Japanese sources, he traced the Indian-Buddhist concept of *dharma* (law). Nakamura exhibited all along more than casual acquaintance with the collateral western apparatus. Despite outward similarity between the concept of *dharma* and that of *logos,* he drew a sharp line of demarcation between them. He argued that *dharma* tended to be subjective, controlling human behavior; whereas *logos* tended to be objective controlling the world of nature which forms the environment of mankind.

There was a conclusion to which Nakamura said his studies inescapably led: the societies of eastern and southern Asia evolved out of small, localized farming communities. Asians did away with nomadic life, he said, at an early stage. They settled on rice fields. He observed, furthermore, that people who throve on rice tended to settle permanently in one spot. In such societies through long generations, genealogies and kinships acquired established norms and took on the spectacle of unified families. In such a setting, Nakamura saw individuals closely knit together in an exclusive human nexus. Asians thus were schooled to adjust themselves to such a type of familial organization, an expression of a way of life that met their needs.

Indo-Europeans, in contrast, nomadic and engaged for the most part in hunting, found themselves at close quarters with alien peoples. Human relations accordingly were bound to be those of fierce rivalry and suspicion. Consistently, a rational plan or a strategem of some sort had to be improvised. Such a trait, Nakamura interjected, survives in the present-day western world. It was extremely difficult, he had to concede, to draw a sharp juridical line between east and west. He made no secret of his own personal opinion that humanity essentially is one. He went on to explain that, if he had detected certain differentials of Hindu and Buddhist cultures, his aim could only be to serve the cause of mutual understanding between east and west.

3. Further illumination emanated from the paper on "Islam in the Modern World" read by Professor Annemarie Schimmel. The subject was altogether germane to the involvement of religion in twentieth-century ideas and political configurations. "Confluence" has been suggested as preferable to "impact" in depicting the influence of western culture abroad. Professor Schimmel drew upon firsthand knowledge of Islamic civilization in defining the nature of such confluence. Her purview encompassed crucial facets of the total Islamic *Leitbild*. The treatment thus embodied an analytical critique of Islam: the concept of a personal God, prayer, preaching, alms-giving, pilgrimage, holy war, the Koran, the person of Muhammad. Other pivotal Islamic issues examined were those centered in the Hadith-tradition, emancipation of women, and Sufi-mysticism. Scientific evidence obviously contradicts Lord Cromer's celebrated dictum that "Islam reformed is Islam no more."

Almost every Muslim intellectual exults in the belief that a perfect unity of *dīn* and *dawla,* religion and the socio-political order, is prescribed in the Koran. Since the two form facets of an identical reality, the Muslim esteems the validity of a teaching true to human experience and progress. In a world disarrayed by the basic anomaly of division between the sacred and profane such an involvement carries essential weight. It is calculated to temper such alienation of religious sanctities as the primacy of our secular age breeds.

Confrontation with modern science did occasionally stir certain theologians to fix on Koran 55:33 as an allusion to Sputnik and on 81:6 as a forecast of the A-bomb. Behind such claims was a frenzied yearning to exalt the integrity of God-given revelation in the face of formidable rivals. Yet, as Professor Schimmel intimated, the Koran has an adequacy all its own, sufficient for it to outlive the keenest competition. This is probably quite accurate. Yet the spirit of the Koran is strictly anti-classical. It is incompatible with such Greek philosophical, rational and esthetic motifs as made both Renaissance and Enlightenment real.

4. If any doubt lingered that taken singly or in aggregate the religions are profoundly involved in the destiny of mankind, Professor Ganguli's treatment of "Religion and the Population Explosion" shattered it. He urged that the religions "not only tolerate fertility control in the best interest of the future generations but propagate it, and give it all the weight of their authority." The only way to do this, he held, was for the religions to adopt a Protestant ethic that considers marriage beneficial in itself and not primarily a means for procreation. Ganguli reckoned that most religions, with the exception of the Roman Catholic Church, agree that a curb needs to be placed on present population trends. None of the other great religions has taken a negative attitude toward the use of contraceptive devices. He regarded Roman Catholic approval of the "rhythm method" a "very good compromise attempt between total abstinence advocated by Mahatma Gandhi and the permissive Protestant disposition." But he maintained that the latter compromise has meant sacrifice of intellectual vigor and practicality.

Strangely, however, Ganguli's own researches in the field did not jibe with his conclusion in holding the Roman Catholic Church reprehensible for delay in promotion of birth control. He did bolster his thesis with a statistical analysis of population trends. He was fully aware, moreover, that the rate of population growth tends to run on an average of seventy per cent higher in the less developed countries.

Professor Bernard J. Cooke, S.J., of Marquette University, emphasized that the Roman Catholic Church was in the throes of rapid change in her official attitude toward birth control. Under study by a Vatican Commission appointed by Pope Paul VI, the issue is not basically a problem of sex morality, Father Cooke advised the conference. It is rather an issue of the continuity or discontinuity of basic Catholic doctrine.

The irony of it all is that discussants at this session never got down to the present-day problem of over-population. In their zeal and concern for the remote future of the race, participants ruled out by default any substantial interest in the demographic situation in some overpopulated regions where intolerable conditions prevail. There can be no serious consideration of world community, and the involvements of the world religions, apart from an awareness of the disease, hunger, and degradation which threaten social stability. Political and economic, as well as ethical, involvements run neck and neck with the central theology of the problem. This might have been the vital intent of Professor Joseph M. Kitagawa's thougtful commentary on the Ganguli statement which was read in his absence by Professor Willard G. Oxtoby of Yale.

IV

DESEGREGATION OF RELIGIONS AND CULTURES: GUIDELINES

With the problem thus set forth and substantiated through the several profiles as well as in the involvements to which the conference addressed itself, the response of a qualified participant needs to be interposed. Dr. Fazlur Rahman, offical representative of the Government of Pakistan, offered a written commentary which said in part:

"For the first time in the history of the world, the world has felt the need for and is striving to build a world community since World War II. The question of religious pluralism in a world community is a complementary counterpart of national pluralism in a world community. Interreligious and intercultural dialogue and understanding is a human need which as imperatively challenges man as does the need for political understanding. Without stretching the religious and political parallel too far, one may simply state that whereas man has been willing to found and belong to a United Nations, a United Religions organization has not yet come into existence.

"Yet a conference like the present one is, to this writer, quite encouraging. Although the problems of religious pluralism have yet to be fully stated and faced, particularly in terms of ongoing religious tradition, the proceedings of the conference have made it clear that leaders of thought in these traditions are actually conscious of the needs for a meaningful coexistence. General statements may have been more or less individual in character rather than representing the tradition to which an individual belongs—and again—some may have been rather apologetic than realistic. Nonetheless, the statements in themselves were significant.

"I think, however, that the coexistence potential of religious traditions still needs to be further explored in a scholarly and objective manner, not merely to give us a true picture of the past of these traditions, but in order to assess, on scientific basis, as to how this potential may be strengthened in each case. I basically support the formulation of the task of such a conference by Professor Huston Smith. This would involve a scientific examination of the major relevant factors in each tradition at different levels—doctrinal as well as concrete attitudes—and in different phases, including the modern age which itself is continually developing and unfolding itself.

"Again, the traditions and systems are not to be restricted to what are called 'religious' and 'theistic' traditions but should include all the major cultural systems and ideologies existing in the world. Only thus can we do justice to this problem as a human problem. In this I support and welcome the thesis of Father Whitson, that theology is grounded in human experience."

Providing general background for a "desegregation" of religions and cultures were papers by Professor S. G. F. Brandon of the University of Manchester on "A New Awareness of Time and History," of Professor C. J. Bleeker of the University of Amsterdam on "Methodology and the Science of Religion," of Dr. Fazlur Rahman on "The Impact of Modernity on Islam," and of Professor Robley E. Whitson of Fordham University on "The Situation of Theology."

1. Professor Brandon offered a definition of religion as the expression of man's instinctive quest for security resulting from the sense of insecurity triggered by a consciousness of time. However, if religion originates from a time-sense common to all mankind, this sought-after security from insecurity has been conceived of in a multiplicity of forms. Both extinct and living religions show how varied, and often strange, have been the fashions in which such security parades.

The pyramid texts of ancient Egypt, Iranian and Indian sacred writings, gnosticism, and other relics of religious antiquity were masterfully tested by Dr. Brandon in the course of his investigation. He granted that technical examination of source material reveals a totally different conception of time in the theologies of Judaism, Christianity, and Islam. Here a linear rather than cyclic conception of time arises. Such a divergence in the concept of time has left an impress on the *Weltanschauung* of the western world.

Out of this Judaeo-Christian conception of time sprang a normative western doctrine of man. According to this, the individual soul was especially created for a single incarnate life in this world. It was a life construed as a proving ground for eternity. Created by the omnipotent God, the universe has a beginning and an end in divine purpose. During the eighteenth-century Enlightenment, supernatural sanctions were rejected. Yet the secularized idea of progress owed its inception to the Christian valuation of history.

Although such a valuation is no longer tenable, Brandon was convinced that its ghost continues to haunt western thought and culture. To this anomaly he ascribed the malaise which afflicts contemporary western thought. We are unable to discern any purpose or pattern in history, he said, but he agreed, nonetheless, with Alfred North Whitehead "that that religion will conquer which can render clear to popular understanding some eternal greatness incarnate in the passage of mortal fact."

2. Professor Bleeker's paper, "Methodology and the Science of Religion," projected another dimension for a world community of desegregated religions and cultures. Many of the blunders in national and international politics and economics could be averted, he surmised, if statesmen took into account the religious emotions and ideas involved by their decisions. He was convinced that the principal insights of the science of religion, particularly phenomenology, serve to substantiate harmony for the still nebulous pursuits of interfaith and intercultural understanding.

Dr. Bleeker saw world community realized through rapid modern communication. He dispelled any assumption, however, that differences among world religions would soon fade out giving way to a world religion. He urged that all undertakings to study the problem of relations among world religions be conducted in line with the scientific methods and findings reflected in the phenomenology of religion. Necessary clarifications and implications, said Bleeker, are contingent upon the phenomenological approach and procedure. His explications of the nature and purpose of phenomenology went straight to the core of his thesis.

The phenomenology of religion has successfully developed since its introduction in 1887 by the Leyden historian of religion, P. D. Chantepie de la Saussaye. Professor Bleeker also reminded the conference of the twin principles of phenomenology: (a) *epoché*, the suspension of judgement till a given religious phenomenon has been fully sustained; and (b) the *eidetic* vision, that is, an understanding of religious essentials displayed by the phenomenon under investigation. He further referred to another Leyden scholar, W. B. Kristensen, who once said: "Let us not forget that there is no other religious reality than the faith of believers... Not only our religion, but every religion is according to the faith of the believers, an absolute unity and can only be understood under this aspect."

To the foregoing, Bleeker added his own incisive judgement: "It must be remembered that the believer keeps a secret which he cannot and does not wish to reveal to non-believers and believers in another faith. Nevertheless, it is possible to attain by factual knowledge, and by religious intuition, insight into what is unique in the forms of the religion one is studying." It is the task of the phenomenology of religion, he concluded, to make religiously understandable what is humanly not understandable.

3. Professor Fazlur Rahman's paper, "The Impact of Modernity on Islam," raised certain issues of common reformation importance. Of his insights, a number might serve to elucidate the general problem of the desegregation of religions and cultures in world community. With the possible exception of Turkey (and even there secularism among the country folk is far from whole-heartedly understood or accepted), the Muslim world's citizenry and officialdom vie with one another in lauding Islam as a complete way of life. Yet what is deprecated as bifurcation of society into sacred and secular is the order of the day in most Islamic states.

Versatile Pakistani reformer that he is, Fazlur Rahman had serious misgivings about any such bifurcation. Vexing his task, as it were, was the fact that although dedicated to a Koran-based society, he at the same time found himself a modernist and an avid rationalist. He could scarcely steer a course removed from the strategy of demythologizing and isolated from philosophical reconception. As a wrestler with traditional Islam, the posture he chose to take could never be other than that of radical Islamic theology.

Such a vision of thoroughgoing reform was impeded and jeopardized in Pakistan by the dearth of intellectual talent. In the teeth of a fundamentalist theology, only the state seemed redoutable enough to institute effective measures in support of such reforms as those of women's education, co-education, updating an archaic banking system, and the liberalization of religious law.

Ernst Troeltsch maintained that the Protestant Reformation did not effect a fresh start until it had successfully detached itself from medieval Christendom and taken the Enlightenment as a point of departure. In a somewhat similar vein, Fazlur Rahman contended that Islamic reform could not get started until a return to Koran and Sunna carried convictions of a responsible reformation rooted in a dynamic and meaningful reinterpretation of the faith.

4. Professor Whitson's address on "The Situation of Theology" revealed the need for a comprehensive sensitivity in the field. He noted that participants in world religions gatherings talk *to* rather than *with* one another. The several religions are now being challenged, he said, to move into dialogue, seeking that universal convergence toward which "we now seem to be drawn."

Father Whitson went further to speak of the values of new communities formed by new institutions. They could in fact enable scholars of different religious and cultural backgrounds to develop shared experience, for "knowledge occurs within community." But this process is not only the exchange of ideas, said Father Whitson. It is an experience in the shared formation of ideas. All this will involve a situation of unity as the convergence of major areas of knowledge must significantly produce.

Whether the Roman Catholic Church is prepared to engage in such an undertaking was a question posed during the animated discussion that followed. While speaking for himself, Father Whitson replied that the Roman Catholic Church regarded the ecumenical situation as "maximal." Now implicitly, and more and more explicitly, it regards the religious situation as universal. Concern with those of other faiths, he thought, had led to the establishment of the Vatican Secretariat for Non-Believers. The destiny of the human race seems to be the move toward union.

Father Whitson's extensive document peered into many a major phase of religious culture and thought. Embraced were Confucian and Taoist, Hindu and Buddhist, Zoroastrian and Jewish, Christian and Muslim components. Far from being an eclectical trial balloon, the treatment attempted a theological synthesis under a novel definition of theology: the systematization of man's experience of definitive relationships grounded in the *theos* and *logos* category. But in its assessments of other faiths the investigation went far beyond the imperatives of phenomenology.

Actually, as in the cases of Hinduism and Islam, the evaluation was surprisingly inattentive to the findings of the history of religions. Some rather antiquated judgements in the field were perpetuated. Yet profound and refreshing were the radical and revolutionary tenets of Father Whitson's essay. Whereas his concept of knowledge-shared-in-community apparently leaves us meager scope for maneuver in personal initiative, save on fringes of the problem, it does capitalize on an essential guideline. Such a guideline was conspicuously drawn out in a flair for the intellectual potential. Above all, it was embedded in Father Whitson's understanding of "involvement" in its humanist valuation.

Postscript

In the last analysis, a theological critique of such a religious pluralism set in a one-world context is likely to engender an awareness of the need today for a theology of involvement. But if theological correlation at this juncture is to have a meaningful future, the enterprise, of necessity, must transcend certain aspects of nineteenth-century field reconnaissance and twentieth-century exploration.

For the sake of argument, nineteenth-century theological insights into the field of pluralism may be telescoped under a design bestowed upon them by Ernst Troeltsch. His call for an encounter, geared to the concept of the cross-fertilization of cultures and interacting humanist ideals and values, was conceived within the framework of an already ebbing missionary hypothesis. The twentieth century came up with superseding dicta betraying an unmistakable cultural messianism. Such new dicta were to be read under the cupola of a balance of terror. Subsidiary ramifications of the new outlook could boast many things: Examples might include political, democratic alignment, or non-alignment, the United Nations, social change and functionalism, economic strategies of interdependence, technology, civil rights, and the urge either to converge or to perish—all under an invisible dome of nuclear over-kill power.

On the merits of its pioneer effort in this area, Princeton Seminary may or may not have won a world-religions championship. Indubitably, it came quite near to setting a record in the fact that the specific achievement was wrought in the province of interfaith and intercultural dialogue.

There was, to begin with, a Sesquicentennal Celebration conference, January 18-19, 1963, devoted to a preparatory topic, "The Significance of Comparative Religion in Modern Culture." Next, through the munificent wisdom and vision of Edward F. Gallahue of Indianapolis, a series of two interrelated meetings were sponsored bearing the donor's name. The first Gallahue Conference of October 27-29, 1964, pursued the same goal. Participants representing the four major American groupings: Protestants, Catholics, Jews, and humanists discussed the theme, "The Phenomenon of Convergence and the Course of Prejudice." A proceedings volume was published by the Graduate Journal of the University of Texas in Austin. (Vol. VII, 1966, Supplement.) As noted above, the second Gallahue Conference, dealt with here, was structured on a broader international scale.

What these three modest frontier operations meant was that a new departure in this critical domain was at hand. Whereas the three gatherings were conducted outside the pale of ecumenicity, and indeed implied a post-ecumenical development, they would have been utterly unthinkable apart from twentieth-century ecumenical spadework.

As regards *intentionality,* the conferences were geared to the assumptions of the education of man. Proceedings, researches, and scholarship were bound to elicit a response in consciousness of congregation, parish, sangha, synagogue and mosque, order and fraternity, or whatever the counterpart of a "local church" may happen to be called. If conferees at times felt caught up in a cul-de-sac of no exit, hemmed in, as it were, from before and behind, the reason was not far to seek. Such an immobility was reckoned awfully healthy in an encounter between as many shades of metaphysical doctrine, all the way from pre-modern to post-Christian. The cleavage dividing Europe from America, even Asia from the West, failed to set off damaging fireworks. Sharp discrepancies instead cut across barriers of language and creed. Muslim disagreed with Muslim and occidental with occidental. Intimated were four "unlosable" findings that might be deemed essential in any serious concern with formulation of a theology of involvement.

Firstly, the *interpenetration* of religion and culture was set in bold relief by a classical folk dichotomy. Almost everywhere in the world, the phenomenon of interplay of orthodoxy with its folk counterpart was explicit. The great religions almost invariably constitute merger between academic and popular strains. John Clark Archer of Yale once advanced a symbol of such symbiosis. It took the form of the letter X, on its side, as the Romans wrote it to signify the number 1000. Thus one stroke stood for mythical folklore and sundry visible elements of mass religion as they appear in rite and cult, festival and ceremony. The other stroke represented classical, conceptual, and scriptural norms of faith and order.

These two strokes of the symbol suggest twin historical streams flowing down from high antiquity. Intersecting at a specific point in time, they form a so-called traffic circle affording both transit and interchange of further direction. Therefore, study of religions on both the classical/metaphysical and popular/individualistic sides may be construed as requisite. Conference deliberations and follow-up discussions confirmed the inevitability of correlation between religion and society in the classical as well as the folk dimension.

Secondly, it was hard to miss the inadequacy of *apologetic* as the believers in other faiths struggled to implement their own religious defences. Such a deficiency was even more obvious in the theologically-oriented religions such as Christianity and Islam. If at times the apologetic of Asia tended to appall us, one had only to imagine how offensive his own brand of apologetic might be as it fell on Asian ears. Professor Gustave E. von Grunebaum of the University of California had a pungent word for Eastern apologetic. It was, he said, the sort of *monologisch* required by the nature of new-old cultures aroused to the consciousness of an exceedingly competitive modern world.

Thirdly, it was made abundantly clear that radical theological reform was contingent upon *integrity*. To go beyond nineteenth-century and twentieth-century criteria and presuppositions in a post-ecumenical, post-Christian setting demands a clear-cut break with current methodologies. Certain cherished contemporary approaches are obsolete already. Before any breakthrough in dialogue can arise, there must emerge a desire for mutual understanding. Yet even this awaits prior reckoning with understanding as such.

In order to understand, we must organize the data of religious and cultural phenomenology. That is only another way of saying that a theology of involvement will take infinite pains to wrestle with the history of religions. In anticipation of such a newness of thought and faith, contemplation of traditionally particularist symbols hopefully will lead us to a discovery: that the meanings of such symbols, if depreciated, may be redeemed through the metaphors of a world come of age.

Fourthly, a theology of involvement keeps faith with a relevant vision of reality. It strives for a world community transcending religious pluralism. Such a theology is nurtured by the *truth*. That is, a truth hammered out on the anvil of inclusive rather than exclusive polarity. The time of God and the time of man draw individuals and societies, cultures and faiths, institutions and symbols, in an ambivalence of perceptive harmony and fruitful interchange of knowledge.

This is a transaction of mind and spirit making for unity in diversity. It is an understanding that the Word becomes flesh in the victories of courage amid doubt, of strength over weakness, and of hopeful creativity of fulfillment in a word of dark conflict and chaos. The implications for the mind and the spirit are reform and convergence now, liberation through the desegregation of cultures and religions in our time.

In short, no one has as yet devised a technique to recapture moments of truth as they tick off in all their dramatic eloquence and imperturbable logic at a confrontation of brilliant minds with a fantastic repertoire of knowledge, sophistication, tradition, and vision. The parable of the Tower of Babel, with its caution against illusory utopianism, seemed to have been mastered in essence if not in form. If there were any longings to erect a citadel of concord, they were more than matched by a sober trend toward prophetic expectation.

IDENTIFICATION OF PROBLEM: THE IRENIC POTENTIAL OF RELIGION

BY

HUSTON SMITH

Massachusetts Institute of Technology

What did the conveners of this conference have in mind when they decided that it should focus on the problem of "Religious Pluralism and World Community"? Something, I think we would all assume, like this: The greatest danger man faces at this historical moment arises from political pluralism, for nations possess now the power to mash one another in minutes. Religion today is likewise plural: the affiliations represented in this conference make its roster read like a religious version of the United Nations. Historically, religious differences have exacerbated political differences more than they have tempered them. To document this, we do not have to go back to the Crusades or other wars of religion. In our own life spans there is evidence to spare. Would Pakistan be partitioned from India today if Hinduism and Islam were not disparate? Would there be 600,000 refugees in Jordan today (1,300,000 in Arab lands as a whole) if Judaism were not an historic community distinct from Islam? "Oh, how we hate one another for the love of God!"—with Cardinal Newman's cry still ringing in our ears, the fundamental problem for this Gallahue Conference is clear. Modestly conceived, the problem is: How can we keep our religious differences from exacerbating political conflicts? Ambitiously conceived, it is: Can our religions, despite their differences, help to resolve the political conflicts that endanger us? Can religion in our time be a force for the taming of the nations? Does it have, *can* it have, what I shall call irenic potential?

I

The question shapes up differently for different kinds of religions. the first class I shall call political religions. Tillich would call these quasi-religions; others might call them pseudo-religions or idolatries inasmuch as they involve, in Toynbee's phrase, "the worship of human collective power." No matter, they command today more final loyalties, more martyrs, than do the religions *we* represent, so operationally they deserve to be considered religions. A political religion considers the political plans of existence as more important than all others. It absolutizes one of its possible structures, and it widens the scope of politics to include all of life. It can be positivistic (in which case no claims are made for its objective superiority or metaphysical sanctions, and the religion boils down to passionate patriotism), or it can be metaphysical (in which case the political structure in question *is* thought to be objectively superior and cosmically backed). Political religion can be national (as instanced by some of the emerging African states, for example, Ghana under Nkrumah) or international (as instanced by international communism). Its "god" can be an existing regime or a future possibility currently envisioned as an ideology. In the latter case, international communism is again the conspicuous example. The varieties of political religion need not concern us, for they all stand in a single and simple relation to our problem. Their irenic potential is nil. If anything, they intensify political conflicts by infusing them with religious fervor.

What about the so-called "high" religions: Buddhism, Christianity, Hinduism, Islam, Judaism, and the like? These admit of distinctions, two of which might bear on our problem. The first is the distinction between ethnic and universal religions. Ethnic religions (of which Hinduism, Judaism, and Shinto are the usual examples) deliberately mesh religion with heredity, social customs, and geography. Universal religions (Buddhism, Christianity, and Islam) claim to transcend such particularities. The second standard way of dividing the major religions is into prophetic (Semitically originated Judaism, Christianity, and Islam) and mystical (Hinduism, Buddhism, and Taoism).

I say these two sets of distinctions look, at first glance, as if they might be relevant to our topic. One's presumption is that ethnic religions, involved as they are with things like land and ancestry,—things that nations, too, are concerned with—are likely to get more embroiled with politics than are universal religions. Facts, however, support no such logic. Note the three most religiously-charged conflicts since World War II. In the Israel-Arab conflict, Israel is an ethnic religion, and Islam is a universal one. In the India-Pakistan showdown, India has an ethnic religion, and Islam (as noted), a universal one. On Cypress, two universal religions, Islam and Christianity, throw themselves at each other. In no instance did the universal religions display a greater capacity to rise above the patriotic, martial passions that were excited. The same equivalence holds for the prophetic and mystical religions. Prophetic religions have been more aggressive than have the mystical ones and have been more guilty of invoking the sword to back the cross and the crescent. But they have also displayed a greater capacity to *criticize* their governments and hold raw chauvinism in check.

It seems that no distinctions can be drawn among the high religions regarding their irenic potential. Their theologies provide no basis for predicting how they will behave politically. Their behavior seems to be dictated far more by exigencies of time and place than by their theologies.

Vietnam provides the immediate case in point. The Buddhists have political power, and they are using it. But this has nothing to do with the kind of religion Buddhism is, or with its religious dimensions at all. Vietnamese Buddhism has no political program and no native propensity to get politically involved. But ninety per cent of the Vietnamese are Buddhists. They are unhappy with the way things are going, and, lacking a political opposition party to champion their discontents, they lodge their complaints with the most important existing alternative to the ruling regime. This alternative just happens to be the Buddhist church. One cannot say that religion either compounds or eases the political problems of Vietnam. Vietnamese Buddhism has become political because it has been drawn into a political vacuum. Awkwardly, gropingly, it is making like a political party because a *bona fide* party representing majority sentiments is needed, but lacking.

To get back to the point, no claim that a single high religion, or class of high religions, possesses greater irenic potential than do the others appears valid. This fact carries a moral, if only a negative one. It indicates a blind alley. It tells us that the way for religions to contribute to world peace does not lie through spotting the religion (or type of religion) most conducive to peace and proposing that the other religions model themselves after it (or them), for no such "most irenic religion" (or type) exists. We must proceed in a different, more egalitarian, direction by noting, first, that *all* high religions have irenic *potential,* then asking how this irenic potential can be increased.

II

The religious experience, as Father Robley E. Whitson points out in his paper for this conference, "seems always to insist upon an absolute involvement of everything which actually constitutes man, and hence man's social situation precludes a purely individualistic significance for religion. Thus, theological systems inevitably express involvement of man in the broadest posisble terms, reflecting an irreducible human interrelationship which somehow has ultimate significance." We can propositionalize this statement as follows:

    a. Religion involves in an absolute way everything that makes man what he is.

    b. Man is made, in important part, by society.

    c. Religion must, at some point, find itself concerned with society.

To these propositions we can add:

    d. Religion is anchored in hope. Its gaze is fixed on the ideal, on perfection.

    e. Applied to society, the ideal stipulates harmony, some form of just peace.

Conclusion? High religions have the hope of peace built into their very make-up.

Questions arise at once. Granted that religions have peace built into their inner logics, do they differ in what they see as its prerequisite? Mystical religions stress love. Prophetic religions stress justice. Why the prophetic religions came to take such a lively interest in social justice is not fully known. Was it because the prophetic passion for righteousness got processed through Greek rationalism and Roman law, giving rise thereby to ideology? Or (and?) was it because the prophetic religions have been more interested in history and its messianic consummation? Do religions that stress love as the prime condition of peace lend themselves more to supporting immediate peace, while prophetic religions (stressing justice as prerequisite for *enduring* peace) stand more willing to sacrifice immediate peace for the sake of a future peace which they hope will be more lasting? These are interesting and important questions, but they are subsidiary. The point that is *not* subsidiary is that all the high religions have embedded within them a peace potential. This sets the stage for asking: Are there principles that can guide us toward maximizing the peace potential in our several faiths?

I propose three.

1. *The first way to augment the irenic potential in our faiths is to be careful about how we relate them to political conflicts.* Once nations go to the mat in war, it is too much to expect religions to

provide much of a counterpoise: *ahimsa* and "resist not evil" are alike tabled or casuistically circumvented, and peace churches (Friends, Mennonites) are tolerated only because of numerical insignificance. But before conflicts come to a showdown, before tensions reach the point where to attempt to throw a bridge to the adversary appears treasonable, religions can involve themselves with politics in a variety of ways. Let me be concrete and cite two recent proposals that link religion to politics, one of them exemplary, the other carrying, I suggest, certain dangers.

The negative example is taken from an essay entitled "Buddhism and Christianity as a Problem of Today," which appeared in *Japanese Religions,* III, 1-2, 1963, and which was written by the distinguished professor of philosophy and religion at Nara College of Liberal Arts, Dr. Abe Masao. In this two-part article, Professor Abe proposes that Buddhism and Christianity join ranks in opposing "scientism, Marxism, and nihilism," these being the "major *anti-religious* powers" of our time. Of the three proposed adversaries, I single out Maxism, it being the one that has explicit political implications.

There is, of course, some logic in this proposal. As against Marxism, Buddhism and Christianity share a higher regard for the transcendent and more concern for human inwardness, that is, for problems that do not admit of solution via social reform. Being *for* transcendence and inwardness, they have no alternative but to be against the planks in Marxism which deprecate these things. But to be against Marxism itself is another matter. For Marxism contains other planks, some of which are exemplary, for instance, concern for justice, appreciation of the importance of life's physical base, resolution of alienation, and the dream of a classless society. So to oppose Marxism in toto puts one in the awkward position of opposing these virtues. Moreover, Marxism is the professed ideology of nations and parties. Unlike "scientism" and "nihilism", the word is capitalized. Consequently, to oppose Marxism involves pitting oneself against nations or parties whose nature is constituted only in fraction by their indifferences to inwardness and transcendence. Our opposition is imprecise. We begin by opposing irreligion and end by opposing, on religious grounds, political and economic programs whose validity has not been weighed. Nations and parties who challenge us in other than religious areas should be opposed, if they are to be opposed, on other than religious grounds.

I may have misunderstood Dr. Abe, but if I have not, I suggest that this proposal could have ramifications detrimental to his deep concern that religions be approached, today, "from the situation where we find ourselves now," which involves keeping one eye on the burning question: "How can we establish...world order?".

Professor R. C. Zaehner has also taken a religious look at Marxism, and in *Matter and Spirit* (alternatively titled *The Convergent Spirit*) proposes a different stance toward it. Instead of focusing on its irreligious features, Professor Zaehner see Marxism as an eruption, in our time, of the age-old, essentially religious dream, of human solidarity. "From the beginning," he writes, "there have been, within religions, two tendencies in dialectical tension with each other—the one drawing the individual ever deeper into himself, down into the 'kingdom of God' that 'is within you,' and the other integrating him ever more closely with the religious community... In modern times (the latter tendency) has re-emerged in the Marxian hope of an infinitely perfectible world which is to come into being once the last of the social contradictions has been surmounted and man is no longer exploited by man." (p. 17) Furthermore, whereas Professor Abe sees Marxism "negating the transcendent, suprahistorical aspect of religion and reducing it to an immanent principle... 'the law of history,'" Zaehner sees Marxists and Christians at one in affirming "a power that is greater than man, greater than nations, and greater than individual religions...the power that Marx identified with matter itself and which (a Christian) would identify with the 'Spirit of God' that 'moved upon the face of the waters' before time began, the Spirit that is ever busy kneading mankind into a coherent mass however much individual men may kick against the pricks." (p. 18)

I am sure that the importance of Professor Zaehner's analysis is evident. An invitation to reconciliation, it seeks to bridge the most dangerous spiritual chasm of our time—that which divides communism from the west. To the extent that it succeeds, it provides a passage over which religious sentiments can flow to reduce this yawning aperture.

2. *A second way to augment the irenic potential of our religions is to strengthen their ecumenical spirit.* Every religion, as Wilfred Cantwell Smith reminds us, contains forces making for openness and forces making for closure. Sufism and philosophy keep Islam open, while legalism, fundamentalism, and the Muslim Brethren work to hold it shut. In Hinduism, communalism as represented by the Hindu Mahasabha, the Rashtriya Swayamsevak Sangh, the Ram Rajya Pari-

shad, and the Jana Sangh turn narrowly inward, [1] whereas Vedanta, Radhakrishnan, Indian philosophy, and the Ramakrishna Mission look outward in openness. Daisetz Suzuki and Zen generally represent Japanese Buddhism at its most open. Soka Gakkai, if it represents Buddhism at all, represents it at its fanatical worst. Examples could be multiplied. The point is simply that there exist in every religion elements which can be used to build bridges and elements which can be used to dig moats. Bridge-building is a way to increase irenic potential.

The time is ripe for doing so. "Ecumenism" is in the air. The way that word has jumped to prominence is evidence of man's growing sense of both the need for, and the possibility of, a truly planetary man. "Ecumenism" expresses a mood, a disposition. It is, as George Williams has pointed out, "a word of the atomic age, of the jet age, of the age of unprecedented social and international mobility, opportunity, and peril." [2] It reaches out to experience the primordial unities of unexpected togetherness in today's turmoil, and to tap the reservoirs of love and power impounded and stagnated in ethnic, class, national, confessional, and communal divisions within the family of a mankind so long prone to bitterness and belligerency. "Ecumenism" acknowledges spiritual proximity, a deeper sense of community that does not repudiate, though it may reconstruct or recast, former continuities and loyalties.

Specialists in conflict resolution tell us that the most effective way to unite dissident factions is to confront them with a common enemy. If this is true, it augurs well for religious unity, for all the high religions face, today, a common adversary. Call it scientism or secularism, [3] this adversary considers science the only valid index of truth, and technology the prime resource for human fulfillment. The differences that divide the world's religions are as nothing compared with the gulf that separates them all from this secular mind-set. As Professor Jayatilleke points out in his paper prepared for this conference, "The problem of the great religions today is not so much whether this or that religion is true or false, but that the religious conception of man

---

[1] Cf. Donald Eugene Smith, *India as a Secular State*, (Princeton University Press, 1963), pp. 454-83.

[2] George Williams, "Dimensions of Roman Catholic Ecumenism," International Association for Religious Freedom Papers on Religion in the Modern World, Number 1, p. 1.

[3] use the word philosophically, not politically, where (as in India today) it refers to a state pledged to treat all religions equally.

and the universe has been greatly undermined by...science and technology." Since not only science and technology, but the outlook which absolutizes these, are rapidly blanketing the globe, spokesmen for the various faiths are going to find themselves increasingly driven to common cause: how to defend the transcendent (which they all affirm) against naturalism's claims to exclusive adequacy.

Fortunately, at the very moment that we are pressed by galloping secularism into a common defense, the way opens for us to see objectively (pressured or not) the extent to which our cause *is* a common one. We see this by virtue of our increased understanding of symbols. We know now that because persons use different symbols they are not necessarily at odds. The *meanings* these symbols express may be much more alike than the symbols themselves. From this, one cannot conclude that on the meaning level we are all saying, religiously, the same thing. It *does* follow that we find ourselves happily faced with a new method for discovering where our real differences lie. And it looks as if we are going to discover along the way that our differences are smaller in ratio to the things that unite us than we had supposed.

We could document how far we have already travelled in this direction by taking a swing around the globe and pointing out recent signs of openness in each of the religions represented in this conference, but time does not allow. I shall limit myself to a single example: "The Declaration on Non-Christian Religions" which emerged from Vatican II. Following a moving introduction (Section One) on the common task of promoting unity and love among men and nations in light of the common origin and destiny of mankind, Section Two canvasses appreciatively the moral and spiritual values of all religions and expressly Hinduism and Buddhism. Section Three spells out the common ground of Christian and Muslim monotheism and calls for a mutual forgetting of historical hostilities in order, for the benefit of all mankind, to work for mutual understanding and social justice. Section Four covers much the same ground with respect to Judaism; and though the statement on Jewish innocence in the Crucifixion is less forceful than many wish, anti-Semitism is unequivocally condemned. Finally, a firm conclusion (Section Five) exhorts all men to foster universal brotherhood as children of the Father of all to the end of eliminating every form of discrimination and harassment stemming from race, color, conditions of life, or *creed*. The document is earnest of a quiet and controlled revolution in institutional charity. Never before has an official document of the Christian Church gone so appreciatively into the meaning of religiousness outside the Christian fold. And though some of our Asian colleagues may view Christianity as "Johnny-come-lately" in this matter, this does not diminish the step that has been taken.

3. *The third way to increase the irenic potential of our faiths is to strengthen our confidence in them.* Unity is not enough. It is conceivable that secularism might pressure the religions into sensing how much they have in common while simultaneously eroding their confidence that this common religious factor is valid, that it has hold of something important which secularism, to man's detriment, omits. If this confidence *is* eroded, religion is not going to prompt *any* kind of distinctive conduct, irenic or other. The point can be expressed in a formula: no distinctive sense *of* the world, no distinctive behavior *in* the world. The fact that Jesus was able to act in love was not unrelated to the fact that he was convinced that those who so acted would be fulfilled, absolutely and completely, in the immanent Kingdom of God.

We just noted the possibility that secularism will undermine the confidence of all religions in the validity of their perspectives. But the opposite possibility is open also. Reasoning together and in dialogue with secularism, the great religions may come to see more clearly (a) what the distinctive religious stance on life *is,* and (b) what it has to offer beyond secularism.

Not that we are about to discover the eternal essence of religion. That is a hope as vain, perhaps, as the hope of defining the essence of life. But the challenge of technology may help us to see some things about religion more clearly. As a colleague of mine, Samuel Todes, puts the mater, it can make us see that it is not religion's job to relieve life's specific distress such as poverty, disease, pain, drudgery, and the like. That's technology's job. Secularism is right in saying that whereas religion *promised* to relieve life's distress, technology does the job. To see this is a great gain, for it means that once technology comes into the picture, religion can withdraw from the business of trying to relieve distress. It can turn that job over to technology.

What's left? What technology seems unable to supply is the positive. It can relieve distress, but it cannot deliver happiness or, even better, fulfillment. The reason seems to have something to do with the fact that man is by nature agent as well as patient, and for this reason fulfillment cannot be given him. It must be won. Enter religion with its irreducible existential emphasis, telling us that eternal life can never be conferred, it must be achieved. After everything possible is done *for* man, he has still to work out his own salvation "with diligence," said the Buddha, "in fear and trembling," say voices closer to home. This salvation requires its own world. It follows that, since fulfillment has to be *won,* its world, too, must be forged. It cannot be passively taken over. Religion always brings news of another world, but it is not a world that is ready-made. It is a world every man must make for himself. As Luther put it, every man must do his own believing, as he must do his own dying.

The contours of the world, or rather, the worlds, of faith we shall not attempt to sketch. By definition they differ from the worlds of common sense and science which are accessible to all. The point is that unless the religions have such worlds of faith to counterpose to the worlds of common sense and science, the actions of the "religious" will not be distinctive. If the "religious" get to the point where they are *of* the world as well as *in* it, their behavior will be indistinguishable from the behavior of the worldly. We return to restate our third principle: The irenic potential of a faith increases with confidence in its distinctive perspective.

III

We live in a time when the problems that confront us are so vast and so complex that not only individuals but whole disciplines and institutions wonder if they can do anything about them. So with us gathered here. We are led to wonder at the close of this evening whether what goes on in religion makes any difference one way or the other, really, to the way the world goes. We have reason to wonder. Yet, before we conclude in the negative, we should listen to two informed opinions from *outside* the field of religion. The first is from a political scientist. "One difference between religion and other forms of thought," writes David Apter, "is that religion has more power. So fundamental is its power that one cannot examine individual conduct or desires without reference to it. In that sense religion cuts into human personality in a way in which ordinary ideological thought rarely does." [1] The second statement is by a man of affairs, James Wechsler, editor of *The New York Post.* "Perhaps," Wechsler wrote two months ago, "the ultimate irony of history is that, if there is to

---

[1] David Apter, "Political Religion in the New States," *Old Societies and New States,* ed., C. Geertz, (Glencoe, Ill.), 1963, p. 64.

be any escape from the entrapment in which modern man finds himself, the architects of the new beginning will be the world leaders of the Roman Catholic Church—Pope John and now Pope Paul—and a modest Buddhist named U Thant who heads the United Nations... I do not know of any better prospect...It is time...that we begin to look beyond the battlefields of Vietnam and ask far more reflective questions about man's destiny." [1]

---

[1] James Wechsler, *The Progressive,* XXX, 3, March, 1966, p. 14.

I
PROFILES OF RELIGIOUS PLURALISM

HISTORY, HISTORICAL CONSCIOUSNESS AND FREEDOM

BY

K. SATCHIDANANDA MURTY

Andhra University

The self, says the *Aitareya Aranyaka* (II 3-1-5), gradually develops in man. It is because of this that man can cognize, recognize, recollect, and express in language. One of the most important human capacities is the ability to discriminate and differentiate from each other the past, present, and future. Man alone, says this forest book, "knows what is to happen tomorrow." The historical approach begins when man becomes aware of the problem of time, when, without confining himself to the narrow circle of immediate desires and needs, he inquires into the origin of things and events. We have history when we ideally connect opposite poles of time and get a sense of unity and continuity of individuals, things, and institutions. History is a way of ideally organizing phenomena in an unbroken succession of related events, stages, or things differentiated into those that were, are, and will come to be. History is what happens as well as the consciousness of what happens. All things have history, but man alone can reflect on his history. It is the consciousness of his historical life that differentiates man from animals.

Man can become aware of contemporaneity as a totality in which he is involved. The deepening of this awareness is the self-consciousness of the present of which he is an integral part. Man can also stand aloof from contemporaneity and contemplate it as a flow of events which confronts him. The first is subjective history, consciousness of one's present situation only, and the second is objective history, the totality of the past which is transforming itself into the present. These supplement each other, for unless one knows the past one does not know to what one belongs and cannot understand one's present situation and fully participate in the present. If we are not inspired by objective history, we lack foundations and have to live from day to day, for then we do not have any memory by which we live. As it is the idea of the past that shapes the mode of experiencing the present, it is the interpretation of history that develops in man a sense of what he is living for and shapes his will. But unless one knows oneself to be a present historical existence, a being involved in time, the past as a whole has no meaning for one. We have to relate the present to the past through remembrance and find in phenomena a continuity, thus injecting into them significance and worth. Memory of the past, of humanity's passage through the ages—tradition, must be transmuted by reflection into present possession. What was and has been become thus ingredients in what is and what will be. Otherwise time becomes mere repetition, and what is going on becomes disjointed and rootless, a mere flux.

Nothing temporal is perfect. History is a movement which never reaches a final conclusion or goal. Everything in the world has a history and is involved in history, because everything is finite and imperfect and so must always become something different from what it is. Nowhere in history do absolute truth, fullness of life, perfect happiness, and plenitude of peace emerge. Truth, life, happiness, and peace are present in history but are not consummated in it. If anything were perfect and absolute, it would not have any history. It is imperfection and contingency, mutability and mortality, that constitute historicity. What is not exactly repeated or duplicated, what is not common and universal, and what is not a type, is the unique and singular. The more unique and singular any being is, the more historical it is, and since it is a human being who is especially so, he is historical existence par excellence, Also, because only man can become aware of the Transcendent *(Brahmavedanam)* and realize his relationship to it, he alone can attempt to go beyond history, though as an historical existence he does not completely succeed. But this awareness and realization are possible because he is in time. The ancient scripture says, "Man knows the visible and invisible worlds. By means of the mortal he desires the immortal."

I

Historical existence is neither the immutable eternal, nor the nonexistent *(sadasadvilakshana)*. It is a compound of the true and the fasle *(satyanrta mithuna)*. It is a continuous temporal flow not describable as Being or non-Being *(tattvanyatvabhyam anirvacaniya)*, for, while it is not Being, it has no foundation other than in Being and has no existence apart from it. History reveals Being, but does not contain it. It is an alternation *(vikalpa)* of the infinite and finite in the sense that is a movement in which man lays hold of the eternal, but does not become the eternal nor come to possess it permanently. It is neither self-explanatory nor self-sufficient and is negated in time *(traikalika badhyam)*, i.e., it is and becomes not. Individual historical existences begin and end, but historical existence as a whole has neither a beginning nor an end. No existence which is a part of history can know why there is history.

Man is an historical being. History is located in man. Between these two is a deep and somewhat mysterious relationship. Historical existence is the only concrete reality, coherent no doubt, but contingent. A particular type of relationship to historical reality, achieved through reflection on one's situation and the past, makes one aware of the implied conflict in history between eternity and time. Such a reflection becomes possible when man knows himself in his concrete fullness and the various forces that act on him, and if he has a sense of history as "his." One is a part of history, so one's destiny is tied up with the destiny of mankind, of the universe. While man can contemplate history as the other, he has no existence apart from it. If we know ourselves to be in the totality of history, we derive from it a foundation and a goal which give meaning to life. Awareness of one's historicity leads to a communion with the transhistorical. If we know we are imperfect and dependent, we develop a sense of what is not so.

II

The proper key for the interpretation of human history is man as he was, is, and shall be. Any individual, by meditation on himself, finds himself to be thinking, doing, striving, suffering, and enjoying. Men of the past similarly thought and did, suffered and enjoyed; so are all men in the present thinking, doing, suffering, and enjoying. Other people's thinking, doing, enjoyment, and suffering must become now one's knowledge as does one's own experience. Then is history revealed in the depths of one's own being and in the spirit of man as involved in time and yet reaching out to eternity illuminated. The real individual man, who is expressed through his acts, speech, etc., is the true subject matter of the understanding of history or historical consciousness. By the light of history, we discover man in all his grandeur and insignificance, and his life presents itself as a drama with all its tensions, hopes, illusions, torments of passions, and moments of thrill and peace. Man as revealed by history is a polymorphous being with infinite potentialities for experience. He is an agent and enjoyer, changeful and mortal, who hankers after the Absolute, and can relate himself absolutely to it if he wills. Reflection on history and one's own situation awakens this consciousness, which transforms and liberates man. History makes us aware of universal human bondage, as well as of freedom, and widens our knowing and feeling selves.

This needs further elucidation. The realities of life bind and determine man. An individual's own nature, upbringing, development, and circumstances impose limits on the possibilities open to him. Historical consciousness liberates him to some extent from these. Possibilities inherent in one are opened out when one meditates upon the paths traversed by other men in earlier situations. Historical consciousness enables us to visualize a situation in a vivid manner, such that we can re-create for ourselves a similar situation, in which we can reproduce in ourselves the experience which another person had in the original situation. What happened in another man thus passes through our consciousness. We rethink in our own minds what another thought while writing something or doing something. We ourselves re-experience what another experienced in a certain situation. To give an example, we can read Caitanya's life and his sayings, with productive empathy, and go through the experiences which he had by projecting ourselves into his situation, and can achieve contemporaneity with him. Then the drama of Caitanya's life is re-enacted in our own. We come to possess his experience, thinking, his thoughts and feelings, as he did. As a result of this, an extraordinary development of religious sensibility takes place in us, and there opens out to us a spiritual world in which it is possible for men to live. Except through historical consciousness, we would be blind to experiences of such eruptive power as Caitanya had, and to possibilities in men's lives such as he had. In this way we are freed from the limitations imposed on us by our circumstances and course of life, and we realize certain human possibilities, thus enriching ourselves. Historical consciousness constantly brings back man to himself, enabling him to apprehend the many-sidedness of human existence, which liberates him from individual and momentary passions and prejudices.

III

There is another sense in which historical consciousness liberates us. The past in the form of tradition encompasses us, for we are not only the products of the past but are immersed in the illusions, hopes, fears, values, and ideals that are bequeathed by it. The judgement of the world—history—binds and weighs upon us. We think and act only in the ways in which our ancestors and neighbors did and do. But if we study what happened, analyze its causes, and know its sequence, historical existence is thereby illumined and our understanding informed. Tradition—norms, customs, and institutions—which shapes and canalizes our instincts, in ways approved by convention and morality, is then transformed into an object of historical consciousness which gives us fresh inspiration to form our own historical judgement. Untrammelled by the past, yet related to it, we are thus in a position to decide what ought to and can be done and to fix practical purposes for ourselves. We will thus be in a position to formulate new ways of action or to consciously relive another person's experience, and, in either case, to move towards a life of our own. During the course of such a life may emerge new values and goods, for which the striving may open out still further ways of realizing possibilities undreamt of before, as well as ways of interpreting the past with a fresh insight. One's own historical judgement liberates one from history, or, to put it in another way, through historical consciousness lies freedom from history.

It may be asked why it becomes necessary for each individual to form his own historical judgement. It is true that history is concerned with objective events which happened in the past, but objectivity implies a process of judgement, and what happened is what we are obliged to believe on the basis of present evidence. History is not actual past events which are made objects of present cognition. It is a new intellectual synthesis, an ideal reconstruction on the basis of the analysis of materials now available, interpreted as living messages from the past. It is the organization of one's present ideas derived from an interpretation of present evidence. It is impossible to separate the "given" from its interpretation. This is not to deny that there was a past, but we know only the past as it is experienced now. The past which does not speak to us through what remains of it now is dead and finished. Through discovery of fresh evidence, a past which did not exist for a particular generation may become historical reality for the next generation. The Indus civilization did not exist for the contemporary world until the excavations begun from 1922 at Mohenjodaro and Harappa brought to light its remains. Historical reality is the past with a living message. Narration of events and facts in chronological order is only the skeleton of history, while interpretation of human works and deeds, which are the residues of actual human existence, is its flesh and blood. The ultimate aim of history is to understand human existence. Human works are kept enduring through historical memory, which is kept alive by their constant restoration, renewal, and repeated interpretation. An individual can truly grasp historical reality only by studying, analyzing, and interpreting the evidence of what happened in the context of his own experience. All historical understanding is from a perspective. Thus, only the individual can criticize the judgement of the world and form his own judgement to serve as the basis of his life, so that he can achieve to the best of his capacity a self-centered and self-contained existence.

In a sense it may be said that all knowledge of any actual man is historical, for we can truly understand a man only when we relive as he did, putting ourselves in his situation. But we cannot do this externally by keeping aloof and studying him as an object (i.e., scientifically). Achievement of contemporaneity is the core of historical understanding. A man is more or less what he experiences, what he thinks, feels, and does. If we can experience all that another experiences, we will fully understand him, but this is never completely possible. We can understand what Kautilya thought in so far as we can project ourselves into his situation and think as he thought; and to the extent that we can visualize the situation in which Samudragupta was and the ways of thinking and acting which were open to him and discover the meaning of his deeds and works, we can understand him. Subjectivity (*jnatrtva*) is the essence of human existence. One is a subject only for oneself. For others one is an "other," a "he" (never an "I"). But even in the case of oneself, as soon as one tries to know oneself, one objectifies oneself. What is known is never the "I".

So every human being remains an enigma for himself and to others as well to some extent. While the secret of human existence is impenetrable by scientific understanding, the historical way of understanding is more useful. It is by envisaging the context in which the Manusmrti was written and by rethinking what its author thought that we can know his mind, and by a similar process alone can one know what one's friend meant when he expressed himself in certain words. What made Clive establish a robber state in Bengal? What is the meaning of Gandhi's Satyagraha? If we go through the biographies, contemporary accounts and the writings and speeches of Clive and Gandhi, projecting ourselves into their circumstances, we can partly at least experience what they experience, and reproduce in ourselves their mental lives. This leads to an historical understanding of them.

It is by a similar process that even a contemporary man can be understood. If this is the historical way of understanding, it is thus that we gain a knowledge of any man. But this has its limitation. No individual can cease to be himself, completely abandon his own perspective, totally forget his own situation and achieve identity with another. So the historical way of understanding is never perfect, and one can never be sure that one is not superimposing on the object of such an understanding attributes and activities which it never possessed. It is also clear that only a human being can be sought to be understood in this way, and not an animal or a thing. Of course an insane man may think he is a poached egg or God.

IV

As already said, we do not know why there is history, nor is there any demonstration that it had a beginning or that it would end. In fleeting moments man can, however, grasp that history is grounded in the Absolute, that its glory is fragmentarily manifested in history. But this is an act of faith, though this can be criticized and clarified by reason. Now and then man falls a prey to the illusion that the Transcendent has been or is found in a particular historical person, event, or thing. Some men are not satisfied with relating themselves to the Transcendent, they wish to become it or to reduce it to an historical existence. A cat can never become a tiger, and it is not wise to try to become sugar instead of remaining content with tasting it. Human history is the exhibition of man's failure to convert this world into heaven and himself into Deity. Man has ideas and passions. Ideas have a place only in our thinking. Passions give them actual existence. By man's will translated into activity, ideas are realized. Human history is a history of ideas and passions. It is, however, impossible to realize some ideas. But these ideas may continue to haunt men, making them undertake certain activities or lead a certain kind of life. Thus, these too make history, though they are never actualized.

One of the finest ideas man has thought of is that of freedom, to be a self-centered and self-contained existence. *Atmani eva atmana sthitah*. Only by knowing oneself is this possibility opened out, and by one's will and activity this may be realized. Through historical consciousness this possibility is revealed, for history is a form of self-knowledge. Freedom is an idea consciously conceived by a few great men, some of whom have sought to realize it in their lives. There is no evidence that the implicit aim of all history, let alone human history, is the realization of this idea. History is not merely the story of liberty, but of bondage and liberation. A harmonious living together of free men is a worthy, rational ideal, but inasmuch as men are not wholly rational, nor can become wholly free, this ideal will never be completely realized. But it can serve as a beacon light to humanity, inspiring at least some men to strive for it. Establishment of an absolute relationship to the Transcendent is much more than freedom. Release *(Mukti)* is something higher than aloneness *(Kaivalya)*.

BUDDHIST RELATIVITY AND THE ONE-WORLD CONCEPT

BY

KALATISSA NANDA JAYATILLEKE

University of Ceylon

The hope that science and technology would usher in a world of peace, plenty, and happiness has been shattered somewhat by two world wars and the grim prospect of a third, which may destroy the greater part of humanity. In the meantime, there is nothing that science and technology has not affected from the ways of thought to the ways of life of men in the remotest corners of the globe, which has itself shrunk in size in the minds of men with the annihilation of time and distance.

The findings of science and the scientific outlook, which is inseparable from the pursuit of science, have profoundly affected religion and philosophy as well. The developments in logic and mathematics, the better understanding of language, the advances made in the natural sciences as compared with the sterility of metaphysics have made first the Logical Positivists and later the Analysts, the dominant school of philosophy in the English-speaking world, doubt whether factual truths can be found outside the realm of the verifiable facts and hypotheses of the natural sciences. The result is that serious thinkers have ceased to speculate unlike the philosophers of old about the traditional problems concerning the nature and destiny of man in the universe. The Existentialists, who have also discarded classical metaphysics for yet other reasons (for example, its lack of relevance for life) themselves confine their discussions to the interpretation and evaluation of personal experience, aware of the subjectivist tenor of their thought.

Modern youth, brought up with a scientific outlook and educated in the techniques of experimental science, are not prepared to accept the myths and dogmas of religion (whatever the religion may be) at their face value. They ask for evidence and proof of the kind that is adduced in support of prevailing scientific theories. They are more inclined to accept psychoanalytical and sociological explanations of these myths and dogmas and are less inclined to believe in them as a basis for a religious life.

While the religious basis of traditional morality tends to be undermined, ethical relativists have questioned the objectivity of moral judgements, and modern philosophers tell us that ethical propositions cannot be deemed to be either true or false. Yet the need for all that was for all practical purposes sound and fruitful in religion and morality was never so great in the world as it is today when the peoples of the world, grown up from their childhood in the past and aware of the doings and misdoings of their fathers and forefathers, confront each other and realize the need to live together in one small world with each other's help rather than face the alternative of committing mass suicide.

Freudians may tell us that man is fooling himself with his religious illusions (whether they be true or false) and Marxists may assert that men are also fooling others with religious beliefs, which are the opium of the masses and the ideological weapons of the imperialist powers and the ruling classes. Whatever the worth of these criticisms may be, the decline of faith in religious beliefs and values has certainly made man's life less meaningful and has alienated him to a great extent from his environment and his fellow beings. Yet, although expediency may take the place of sound moral principles in dealings between men and nations, even those who resort to such tactics cannot help but pay lip-service to the principles on which the U.N. was formed, and even some of the political ideologies which are presented as substitutes for religion cannot help but utilize and appeal to the moral concepts and values of the religions that have been or are to be discarded. This does not mean that all the ages of belief were by any means perfect ones since the religious attempts to glorify a chosen race or a chosen caste or to sanctify social injustice and curtail freedom were no more genuinely religious than the attempt to glorify a chosen class, the proletariat, and to found the new society under its alleged leadership.

I

In this paper, I propose to talk about the contribution that Buddhism could make in the context of religious pluralism in order to make the concept of the world community a feasible and tangible one in the hearts and minds of at least some people on earth. For it is becoming increasingly clear that, despite the changing temperatures of the cold war and the rifts within the Communist camp, the peace of the world cannot last for long on the slender threads of diplomatic maneuvers or the balance of power or terror. There seems to be no alternative now but to beat our swords into plowshares, and our spears into pruning hooks and bring about universal disarmament at least by stages and establish truly effective institutions for the prevention of war. The days when wars could be won with the aid of war gods or the blessings of priests is over, and if men of good will all over the world truly intend to bring into existence a world in which there would be both material and spiritual well-being, this will not obviously come about with the help of our nuclear armory. For if the world is as it is described in the scriptures of the Buddhists and the Christians, then "a conquerer would always find another to conquer him," and those who rise by the sword shall surely perish by the sword.

What hinders the establishment of the legislative, executive, and judicial institutions, which are necessary to maintain world order, and what obstructs the diversion of the enormous expenditure on armaments towards the eradication of poverty and disease on a worldwide scale is our collective greed, hatred, and ignorance. Many people, some of whom feel that they are emancipated from the religious superstitions of bygone ages, want to liberate the world either from imperialism or communism, as the case may be, when the only hope of salvation in an individual or national sense seems to lie in genuine cooperation in a world which has become increasingly interdependent economically and culturally. It is greed, hate, and ignorance again, which prevent humanity from seeing itself as a single family as a result of which we have created artificial barriers between us on the basis of race, caste, or color, or on the basis of our allegiance to our respective nation-states rather than to humanity, or on the basis of the religious and political ideologies, to which we cling. It is this same greed, hatred, and ignorance, which, according to the message of both schools of Buddhism, prevents us from getting out of our self-centered shells and living as vibrant, useful, happy, and contented individuals.

It may seem strange at the outset that a religion, which appears to be divided into two great camps with several sects in each, can be a unifying force in the modern world. But this division is more apparent than real. For on the one hand when we today survey the past history of Buddhism, we see that not a drop of blood has been shed in the propagation of any form of Buddhism, and on the other there has been widest internal tolerance of views concerning the Buddha and his teaching. History records that the members of the two great schools of Buddhism have lived together within the precincts of the same monastery, and, except in very rare and exceptional circumstances, there has been no persecution of views considered to be heretical.

The unity of Buddhism is not so much the unity of strictly orthodox beliefs for Buddhism never sought to inculcate such orthodoxies and curb the free spirit of inquiry in man. It is rather the unity of the fruits of a genuinely religious life—peace, harmony, and happiness flowing from wisdom and compassion. But a common core of doctrine is not lacking, and the differences on the whole are differences of presentation or emphasis. Hiuen-Tsiang, an ancient pilgrim traveler in Buddhist lands, notes the similarity and difference as follows: "In agreement with the mysterious character of this doctrine the world has progressed in its higher destiny; but distant peoples coming to interpret the doctrine are not in agreement. The time of the Holy One is remote from us and so the sense of the doctrine is differently expounded, but as the taste of the fruit of different trees of the same kind is the same, so the principles of the schools as they now exist are not different." [1] A knowledgeable twentieth-century traveler speaks in the following strain of the qualities that, despite its history and ramifications, makes Buddhism one religion: "Not so obvious, perhaps, are those persistent characteristics which help to make it, in all its ramifications and all its history, still one religion...What I mean is that there are certain qualities of character and feeling, of point of view, conduct and belief, which may properly be called Buddhist, and that these are not confined to any one school of Buddhism, whether Hinayana or Mahayana, but are to be found in all those who by common consent would be considered typically Buddhist in all the lands we have studied, from southern Ceylon to northern Japan. These qualities, I hold, transcend not only nations but centuries, and unite the earnest follower of the most up-to-date Japanese sect with the earliest disciples of the Founder." [2]

In the contemporary scene, Buddhism, like Christianity of the Eastern Orthodox Church in Russia, has been forced to adopt a subservient role to that of the totalitarian Marxist ideology in China

---

[1] See Samuel Beal's translation of *The Life of Hiuen-Tsiang,* by the Shamans Hwui Li and Yen-Tsung (London, Trubner, 1888), p. 31.

[2] See James Bissett Pratt, *The Pilgrimage of Buddhism and a Buddhist Pilgrimage.* (New York, 1928), p. 709.

and Tibet, where Buddhist values are given a purely social orientation and utilized for purposes of social reconstruction. In Japan there is a resurgence of Buddhist beliefs and values, adapted to the needs of a modern industrial society. In the southeast Asian countries the masses retain their allegiance to the Buddhist view and way of life along with the demand for modern education and social and economic change, despite the organized attempts at subversion on the part of Marxists and of domination by privileged non-Buddhist minorities, who are partly a heritage of colonial rule.

In India, the original home of Buddhism, the attitude to Buddhism on the part of Hindus has been ambivalent. While extremist Hindu orthodoxy has opposed Buddhism, the Vaiṣṇavaites have defied the Buddha as the ninth Avatār (Incarnation) of God and one of the greatest Hindu thinkers, Sankara, has been known as a "concealed Buddhist" (pracchanna-Bauddha) due to the profound influence that Buddhist doctrine has had on his thought. Buddhistm also deeply affected the thought and life of Mahatma Gandhi and Jawaharlal Nehru, and Hinduism claims to have absorbed Buddhism rather than discarded it. Today the minds of many Hindus continue to be drawn by the modernity of Buddhist thought while hundreds of thousands of so-called depressed classes, following their late leader Ambedkar, have consciously embraced Buddhism, attracted by its doctrine of social and spiritual equality.

Buddhism has also attracted a few western thinkers for a variety of reasons, and there are small Buddhist minorities today in several western countries.

II

The term "Buddhist relativity" admits of several interpretations. If we take Buddhist thought as a whole, we find that it has distinguished between literal or absolute truth (*paramārthasatya*) and conventional or symbolic truth (*saṃvṛti-satya*). It has recognized the need for and required that the literal or absolute truth be so presented to hearers as to suit their capacity to receive it, and the skill in doing so has been designated by a special term, *upāya-kauśalya*, i.e., the skillfulness as to the means adopted in teaching the doctrine. Despite this variety in interpretation and presentation, the fruits of the Buddhist way of life, including final deliverance as well as the central core of its view of life, has throughout remained the same on the whole.

Let us take an example to illustrate the difference between literal and conventional or symbolic truth. All schools of Buddhism have recognized that, although we may speak of "persons" as separate entities in a conventional sense, from a literally correct or absolute standpoint, a person is a congeries of ever-changing psychophysical constituents, maintaining a certain individuality in a relative sense in one life or in a succession of lives without any underlying identity or essence. Theravāda Buddhism tries to demonstrate this by a detailed empirical analysis of the personality. In the Mahāyāna texts, the same idea is often conveyed in the form of a paradox: "...the idea of a being or a living being or a person is no-idea... these, Subhūti, are neither beings nor no-beings. And why? Because, O Subhūti, those who were preached as beings, beings indeed, they were preached as no-beings by the Buddha and therefore they are called beings." (Vajracchedikā, XIV, XXI). The intention is to draw our attention to the misleading implications of language, which seem to suggest a world of discrete entities, where in fact there are only interdependent dynamic processes. This does not imply that Buddhism considers persons as automata. Far from it. The Buddhist view is that both moral and spiritual growth, as well as harmonious relations between people, are possible and desirable in the phenomenal world on such a realistic conception of "persons." The tender care and concern that Buddhist ethics recommends in our treatment of others is sufficient proof of the acceptance on the part of Buddhism of what is popularly referred to as "respect for personality or human dignity." [1] But this is an area in which there is misunderstanding between the Buddhist and the Christian, as the following quotation from Paul Tillich would show: "The Buddhist priest asks the Christian philosopher, 'Do you believe that every person has a substance of his own which gives him true individuality?' The Christian answers, 'Certainly!' The Buddhist priest asks, 'Do you believe that community between individuals is possible?' The Christian answers affirmatively. Then the Buddhist says, 'Your two answers are incompatible; if every person has a substance, no community is possible.' To which the Christian replies, *'Only* if each person has a

---

[1] "Thus we gather from the attitude of the Buddha himself that in Buddhism personality is respected above all else. Teaching and expounding of the Dhamma is carried on in the most ideal way, with no trace of indoctrination, without coercion. The pupil gives his free assent, if he so decides, with his mind left in complete integrity." (Professor Kurt F. Leidecker, *Buddhism and Democracy*, Buddhist Publication Society, Kandy, 1963, p. 2).

substance of his own is community possible, for a community presupposes separation. You, Buddhist friends, have identity, but not community." [1]

The recognition of such a difference in the standpoint from which the Dhamma (i.e., the teachings of the Buddha) may be presented naturally has its repercussions in the diversity of presentations suited to people of different temperaments, interests, capabilities, and cultural milieux. Yet, as we have said, the basic principles taught and the fruits of such teachings are considered to be the same. The relativist differences in presentation have ultimately to be justified, explained, and established on the basis of the truth of the literal truths to be found in the original teachings of the Dhamma. We must not forget, however, that much of the non-literal expositions are also to be found in early Buddhism itself. The Mahāyānist writer who quoted Sir Charles Eliot on this subject was quite correct when she said: "These ideas (of Mahāyāna) are all to be found in the Nikāyas, sometimes as mere seeds, sometimes as well-grown plants. But between early Buddhism and the Mahāyāna there is a great difference in emphasis." [2]

This does not mean that every development was legitimate or justified. Certainly the majority of them were. Zen Buddhism was such a legitimate development starting from certain early Buddhist practices in the meditative culture of the mind in which a stage was reached when the mind was "without rational or discursive thinking (*avitakkaṃ avicāraṃ*)." The word "Zen" itself was a development from Pāli "*Jhāna*" (Skr. *Dhyāna*) through Chinese "*Ch'an*." The experience of *satori,* with the cessation of intellection or conceptualization, is a glimpse of the transcendent, carrying with it a feeling of exaltation, an authoritativeness, a noetic quality and an impersonal tone. [3] Such an experience gave meaning to life and made the person more stable, serene, and harmonious in his relations with his environment. But it is also possible that in some of the later traditions we meet with an exaggeration of aspects of the original teaching, emphasizing parts of the truth at the expense of the whole and even accretions, which misrepresent or distort the truth, without sufficient corresponding gains.

---

[1] *Christianity and the Encounter of the World Religions,* (Columbia University Press, New York and London, 1963), pp. 74, 75.

[2] Beatrice Lane Suzuki, *Mahāyāna Buddhism,* with an introduction by Professor D. T. Suzuki, (David Marlowe Limited, London, 1948), p. 17.

[3] See D. T. Suzuki, *Zen Buddhism,* (Doubleday Anchor Books, New York, 1956), pp. 103-108.

The compromises effected by Tantric Buddhism with its use of spells and possibly amoral practices (if such did exist) are such cancerous growths.

The school of idealistic metaphysics (*Vijñāna-vāda*), corresponding to Berkeleian idealism in the history of Christian philosophy, is a departure from the original teachings, which emphatically recognized the material reality of the physical world even though it held that it was changing and lacking in substance. The speculation of this school was motivated by the conviction that if the transcendent reality, which is of the nature of "consciousness" is the ultimate reality, then the material world was somehow dependent upon it. It therefore tries to picture the material world as being the product of the Master Hypnotist, the transcendent consciousness, and gives rational arguments to show that the material world was unreal despite the contention of early Buddhism that such things could not even be proved by mere reasoning.

Another school, which tries to provide a metaphysics for early Buddhism which does not need it, is the relativity school (*Sūnyavāda, Mādhyamika*) of Nāgārjuna, whose fame spread to China and Japan. Professor T. R. V. Murti [1] has tried to suggest that this school faithfully portrays the philosophical stand of early Buddhism and has called it the central conception of Buddhism. This is only partially true, for although it makes use of a great many premises of early Buddhism, it strays from its standpoint in certain respects.

The idealists upheld the doctrine of degrees of truth, which is also found in the relativity school. An imaginary truth (*parikalpita-satya*) is what we would normally call an error, as when we mistake a lamp-post at a distance for a man. All knowledge about the world consists of dependent relative truths (*paratantra-satya*) since this knowledge is a product of our causally-conditioned experience and our spatio-temporal setting. The knowledge of common sense and science would constitute such knowledge. Absolute truth (*paramārtha-satya*) arises from the realization that all such relative knowledge, which is useful for practical purposes, is also defective since it is based on categories of thought which, on analysis, are shown to be self-contradictory. The Buddhist "right view of life" (*samyagdṛṣṭi*), which is also a relative truth in no exception. It is useful up to a point, but since it is itself

---

[1] *The Central Philosophy of Buddhism*, (George Allen and Unwin, London, Second Edition, 1960).

based on concepts such as "causation", which on analysis are shown to be unintelligible, it has to be discarded with the intuition of reality, which cannot be conceptually apprehended or described. The absolute is "described" by the word *sūnyatā* (Voidness), though it is said even such a description is necessarily unsound. This absolute, looked at through thought form (*vikalpa*), is the phenomenal relative dependent world of becoming or *saṃsāra,* but freed from such superimposed thought forms (*nirvikalpa*) is *Nirvāna.* So there is no distinction in principle between the phenomenal world of *saṃsāra* and the noumenal reality of *Nirvāna.*

Nāgārjuna strays from early Buddhism in treating all propositions, verifiable and unverifiable, as equally unintelligible. Early Buddhism considered propositions about the origin and extent of the universe in a special category [1] but held that there were true verifiable propositions about nature. Early Buddhism upheld the regularity theory of causation after rejecting other theories, [2] but Nāgārjuna rejects the very conception of causation as inexplicable. The statement that there is no distinction in principle between *Nirvāṇa* and *saṃsāra* is due to the tacit assumption that, if *Nirvāṇa* were the absolute, it must somehow comprehend *saṃsāra,* but such a conclusion would not be justified according to the stand of early Buddhism or even the logic of Nāgārjuna. The Buddha himself, it is true, argued in the *Brahmajāla Sutta* that the several religious philosophies about the universe, including theism and materialism, were a product of partial knowledge about aspects of reality based on the conditioned experience of the founders of these philosophies. The Buddhist "right view of life" in this respect is claimed to comprehend universal truth, but, in the parable of the raft, the Buddha shows that even the "right view of life" (not to speak of other religious philosophies), which was useful for crossing over, was to be set aside on reaching the threshold of *Nirvāṇa.* Nāgārjuna tries to synthesize all these truths in his critique of metaphysics and reasoning, but, as we have indicated, he departed from the stand of early Buddhism in certain respects.

By "Buddhist relativity" I would primarily refer to the class of Buddhist doctrines and practices which have appealed to people of different times and climes, without being on the whole mutually contradictory in fact and without producing in them exclusivist atti-

---

[1] See K. N. Jayatilleke, *Early Buddhist Theory of Knowledge,* George Allen and Unwin, (London, 1963), pp. 470ff.
[2] See *ibid,* pp. 445-457.

tudes towards each other on the ground that each of them alone was true to the exclusion of all others. I think that this is not without its lessons for the modern world in which different religions by stressing unduly their exclusiveness have failed to see what they have in common, and, in the process, have tended to forget the very essence of religion itself.

The ethics of Buddhism has also been taught to suit the capacities of individuals. It ranges from the voluntary undertaking to keep the five precepts to the practice of the noble eightfold path. But the ten courses of moral conduct, [1] stated both in a positive and negative form, is what frequently occurs in the scriptures of all schools. Their practice is considered to conduce to the stability and well-being of both the individual and the society. Meditative exercises have also been adapted to suit the special needs of individuals according to their temperament, character, and shortcomings, though some of them are recommended as being useful for most individuals, such as the cultivation of watchful self-analysis.

Buddhism also has a social philosophy and a conception of social evolution. The *Singālovāda Sutta* (*Dīgha Nikāya,* XXXI) presents a picture of society as a cooperative enterprise, in which the different classes of individuals such as parents and children, husbands and wives, teachers and pupils, employers and employees, religious leaders and their followers are expected to perform their respective duties with love and concern for the weal and welfare of the entire community. But it conceives of society like all other institutions as undergoing change and the *Cakkavattisīhanāda Sutta* (*Dīgha Nikāya,* XXVI), among others, has a conception of the Just Society, which it believes will come into existence in the future after mankind has learned certain lessons from history, some of which may be very bitter. So it is not correct to say that Buddhism does not have a sense of history. For it does, despite its conception of the immensity of time.

III

I propose in this paper to illustrate aspects of "Buddhist relativity"

---

[1] They are: (1) refraining from killing and causing harm and practicing kindliness, (2) refraining from stealing and being honest and pure of heart, (3) refraining from sexual misconduct and practicing restraint, (4) refraining from falsehood and devotion to the truth, (5) refraining from slander which causes divisions and being a peacemaker, (6) refraining from rude speech and speaking what is pleasant, (7) refraining from gossip and talking sense and to the point (8) refraining from covetousness and being unselfish, (9) refraining from ill will and cultivating benevolence, (10) refraining from false views and acquiring the right view of life.

as I have defined the term, considering their relevance for the main theme of this conference.

It is important for western scholarship to realize that the Theravāda and the Mahāyāna conceptions of reality are not diametrically opposed to each other or mutually exclusivist in outlook. The classical literature of the two schools have often referred to the intrinsic worth of the teachings of the other school though recognizing its limitations from each point of view. A book called "The Path of Purity (*Visuddimagga*), the epitome of orthodox Theravāda, clearly recognizes the superior worth of the Mahāyānist ideal of aspiring to be a Bodhisattva (Buddha-to-be) in order to save all mankind, when it says that "virtue motivated by craving, the purpose of which is to enjoy continued existence, is inferior; that practiced for the purpose of one's own deliverance is medium; the virtue of the perfections (pāramitā), practiced for the deliverance of all beings, is superior." (I. 33) It differs from Mahāyāna in holding that this superior path is not meant for the multitude, but for a few altruistic souls. Most people are egoists, and the most that one can do with most egoists, at least for a start, is to turn them into enlightened egoists.

In the *Saddharma-puṇḍarīka,* a standard Mahāyāna work, the Buddha is represented as the spiritual father and savior of the world of beings, who are represented as his prodigal sons who prefer to play about in the world burning with the fires of greed, hate, and ignorance rather than escape from it by a process of self-evolution. The Buddha exhorts his children to make use of one of three vehicles to come out of this world and speaks as follows: "Betake yourselves to the three vehicles; the vehicle of the disciples, the vehicle of the Pratyekabuddhas, the vehicle of the Bodhisattvas. I give you my pledge for it, that I shall give you these three vehicles; make an effort to run out of this triple world. And to attract them I say these vehicles are grand, praised by the noble ones, and provided with most pleasant things. With such you are to sport, play, and divert yourselves in a noble manner." (III, 38). Here the vehicle of the disciples is no other than the path of salvation taught in the Theravāda or Hīnayāna schools. We see that this way of salvation is not decried or discredited. It has its place in the scheme of things. It attracts certain types of people and is egoistic in its appeal. The exhortation to tread the path of the Pratyekabuddhas also has its attraction for people of independence of judgement, who dislike dependence on teachers and texts. But the Mahāyāna holds that eventually those who have trod both these egoistic paths to self-salvation would change over to the great vehicle. For it is said that the Buddha "by an able device holds forth three vehicles and afterwards leads all to complete *Nirvāna* by one great vehicle." (*Saddharma-puṇḍarīka*, III, 38).

We see from the above that each appears to be justified from each point of view, but each view at the same time is broad enough to recognize the worth of the other. Historically what happened was that, when the members of the Theravāda school appeared to be too self-centered in their quest for salvation, the pendulum swung in the other direction resulting in the birth of the Mahāyānist ideal.

The reconciliation of these two standpoints is to be found in the teachings of original Buddhism contained in the early portions of the Theravāda scriptures. Here it is pointed out that the ideal should be ethical universalism and not ethical egoism or ethical altruism. The Buddha says: "There are these four persons in the world. What four? He who is bent neither on his own welfare nor on the welfare of others, he who is bent on the welfare of others but not on his own, he who is bent on his own welfare but not of others, and he who is bent on the welfare both of himself as well as of others.... He who is bent on the welfare of oneself as well as of others, is of these four persons the chief and best, topmost, highest, and supreme." (*Anguttara Nikāya*, II, 95). Likewise, it is argued that one can save another or help another only to the extent to which one is capable of giving that help. As the Buddha says, "it is not possible for one who is stuck in the mud to help out another, but it is possible for one who is not stuck in the mud to help out another who is stuck in the mud. It is not possible for a man who has not saved himself to save another, but it is possible for a man who has saved himself to save another." (*Majjhima Nikāya*, I, 46). The very means of self-salvation consist in cultivating the virtues of selfless service in place of selfishness or greed, and compassion in place of hate, and this cannot be done unless the egoist is prepared to act, even out of self-interest, with genuine concern for others. Thus the purely egoistic and the purely altruistic ideals are self-stultifying, though we may still grant a difference between a predominantly egoistic and a predominantly altruistic conception of salvation.

There is no doubt about the different emphases between Mahāyāna and later Theravāda, but these differences are not the radical differences that many western scholars of Buddhism have led us to expect. Thus the impression has been created that original Buddhism was atheistic and the historical Buddha was a mere human being, while Mahāyāna is theistic and in it the Buddha is deified. Thus the two appear to be irreconcilable and contradictory points of view, both of which cannot be true.

A close study of the early Theravāda scriptures and the Mahāyāna texts would dispel such a notion. Early Buddhism is not atheistic in the sense in which Materialism or Maxism is atheistic. Early Buddhism recognizes the validity of moral and spiritual experiences and values and asserts that *Nirvāna* is a transcendent reality beyond space, time, and causation. Consistent with this conception, it holds that it is incorrect to say that "one exists" or "does not exist" in *Nirvāna*, since such noumenal being is not a kind of personal existence in time nor is it annihilation. When the question was asked of the Buddha, "The person who has attained the goal—does he not exist or does he exist eternally without defect?", his reply was as follows: "The person who has attained the goal is without measure; he does not have that whereby one may speak of him." (*Sutta Nipāta,* 1076) It is said that the Buddha, when freed from the conceptions of bodily form, sensations, impressions, and ideas, purposive activities, and consciousness, is "deep, immeasurable, and unfathomable, like the great ocean." (*Majjhima Nikāya,* I, 487). When he was asked whether he was a human being, the Buddha's reply was that he was not a human being, but a Buddha, although any human being could aspire to attain such a state. Unlike a human being, the Buddha is not reborn and does not survive in time. So it is false to say that the Buddha becomes extinct in *Nirvāna*. The *Brahmajāla Sutta* (*Dīgha Nikāya,* I) says, "So long as his body shall last, so long do gods and men behold him. On the dissolution of the body beyond the end of his life, neither gods nor men shall see him." In the *Kevaddha Sutta* (*Dīgha Nikāya,* XI) the Buddha, answering the question, "Where is it that the four great material elements—earth, water, fire, and wind—cease leaving any trace behind?", says that the question should be reformulated in the form, "Where do earth, water, fire, and wind...no footing find? Where is it that both matter and mind cease to be without leaving a trace?" The necessity for the reformulation was to preserve the integrity of the material world. The answer given is as follows: "Consciousness, without distinguishing mark, infinite, shining in every direction there it is that earth, water, fire, and wind... no footing find." In the *Brahmanimantanika Sutta* (*Majjhima Nikāya,* I, XLIX), the Buddha claims that being one with the transcendent infinite consciousness beyond the reach of the material world and the empirical mind, he cannot be seen even by Brahmà (God), the highest being in, and the regent of, the cosmos.

When we consider the historical origins of the Mahāyāna, we find that they can be traced to certain ideas in early Buddhism, which received a special emphasis and development at the hands of a certain section of the disciples of the Buddha. In the very first Council held shortly after the death of the Buddha, there was a discussion about a statement of the Buddha to the effect that the minor rules of the Order be abrogated, presumably to suit changing social and historical contexts in which Buddhism was likely to spread. However, there was a serious difference of opinion as to what the minor rules were, and, as a result, the orthodox conservative Elders (Thera-s) decided to keep all the rules. Although no schism took place in the first Council, it is likely that there would have been others who would have welcomed such changes. When the second Council was convened a hundred years later to discuss such changes, which had already taken place in the Order, a clear schism took place between the orthodox conservative Elders and the liberals, who seemed to have outnumbered the former. Ten thousand of them are said to have held a separate convocation called the "Great Convocation" (*Dīpavaṃsa,* 5, 33).

These liberals, who were not so concerned about the letter of the Dhamma as the spirit, seemed to have adapted the original teachings in order to bring Buddhism to the masses in language intelligible to them. This seems to have been the *raison d'être* for the emergence of Mahāyāna. One of these early schools of the above *Mahāsanghikas* was the first to adopt a docetic theory about the birth of the Buddha, holding that "the Buddha's body was immaculately conceived" (na ca maithuna-sambhūtaṃ Sugatasya samucchritaṃ, *Mahāvastu,* III), although the early scriptures had merely stated that the mother of the Buddha had no thoughts of sex after the Buddha-child was conceived.

One can see, therefore, how the early Buddhist notion about the transcendent existence of the Buddha in *Nirvāna* was picturesquely portrayed by the conception of the cosmic Buddha. The Mahāyāna scriptures were merely representing, in simple symbolic terms, the more precise descriptions of early Buddhism. The early conception of the Buddha as the embodiment of the Dhamma (Truth, Righteousness), and of those who acquire a spiritual awakening after hearing and following the Dhamma as the "sons of the Dhamma" (Dhammajā), and therefore of the Buddha, is picturesquely presented in the *Saddharmapuṇḍarīka,* where the Buddha is the spiritual father of mankind, and the beings in the cosmos, who are going to profit by the three vehicles, are his prodigal sons who are eventually saved by means of them.

The concept of the Amitābha (Infinite Splendor) Buddha in the late Pure Land schools of Jodo and Shinshu seem to emerge from the earlier concepts of Buddha in *Nirvāna,* as being in a state of "Infinite Splendor" (*ananta sabbatopabha*). In the early scriptures there is also a conception of gods of the "Pure Lands" (*suddhāvāsadevā*) from where there is no rebirth back to earth (*Dīgha Nikāya,* II, 50). One of the denizens of this world comes to the Buddha on one occasion and says that "all those who have faith in the Buddha do not go into states of downfall but fill the divine abodes after leaving their human bodies." (*Dīgha Nikāya,* II, 225).

The smaller *Sukhāvatī-vyūha Sūtra,* the text of which went from India to China and thence to Japan, speaks of the heaven it describes as a place where Bodhisattvas are born "never to return again and bound by one birth only" (10). And it is said that there are also those born here in the company of the above, not as a reward of good works, but owing to their faith in the blessed Amitāyus (Infinite Life), whose name "they shall keep in mind with thoughts undisturbed for one to seven nights." The *Amitāyur-dhyāna Sūtra* describes various grades of beings born in the happy land as a result of their good works and faith. But it goes a step further in extending this possibility even to those sinners "who commit evil deeds and even complete the ten wicked actions, the five deadly sins, and the like" (30), provided on the eve of death on the advice of a good friend they repeat at least ten times with serenity and with the voice uninterrupted the formula "Obeisance to Buddha Amitāyus," continually thinking of the Buddha.

It is this latter "concession" which is not strictly in accordance with the teachings of early Buddhism, where the "five deadly sins" are considered to bear fruit in the successive life, despite the fact that one can understand the psychological need for holding out hope even to the worst sinners, regardless of the demands of justice and order in a causal universe. Except for this, the above Mahāyāna teaching is quite consonant with early Buddhism, which also taught that "those who had mere faith and affection for the Buddha are destined to heaven" (*Majjhima Nikāya,* I, 142), though it was a condition that could lapse (*ibid,* I, 444).

The apparent contrast between an original atheistic Buddhism, in which the Buddha was a mere human being, and the developed theistic

Buddhism of Mahāyāna, where Buddha is a cosmic being, has no basis in fact. Both original Buddhism and Mahāyāna Buddhism are atheistic in denying a Personal Creator God (Īśvara). The Mahāyāna holds that the universe has no beginning in time (*anavarāgra*), while early Buddhism has adduced two arguments against belief in a Personal Creator. One is that such a universe created in time by an omniscient and omnipotent deity will be a rigged universe in which everything will happen in accordance with the will of God resulting in even human beings being puppets (*Jātaka,* V, 238). The other is that in such a world the existence of certain evils cannot be explained (*Jātaka,* VI, 208). In this sense "the world is without refuge and without a God" (attāṇoloko anabhissaro, *Majjhima Nikāya,* II, 68). But neither form of Buddhism is atheistic in asserting the validity and worth of moral and spiritual experiences and values and admitting an impersonal transcendent reality beyond time, space, and causation, of which it is considered legitimate to use the term GOD (*Brahma*-bhūta). This is a conception of God going beyond the God of theism.

The conception of a transcendent Buddha working for the salvation of all beings appears at first sight to be a radical departure from early Buddhism. But a careful analysis would again show that, apart from the recognition of a transcendent reality, this is a representation in symbolic language of certain features about the universe itself referred to in the early Buddhist texts. The universe is said to be so constituted that the moral and spiritual life is both possible and desirable in it. It is also said that in a dynamic world we cannot remain static. If we do not progress we fall back, and progress has to be in the direction of the transcendent. In other words, we have to seek *Nirvāna* and this is pictured as quest for a passage from bondage to freedom, from imperfection to perfection, from unhappiness to perfect happiness, from ignorance to knowledge, from fear and anxiety to perfect security, from a state of mental conflict to a state of perfect mental health, from darkness to light. It is said that it is because man is mortal that he seeks immortality. It is also said that it is because of the desire for self-centered pursuits that we entertain the false view that there is a felicitous state of personal immortality. In Freudian language, the belief in personal immortality would be an illusion or a belief we cling to in an attempt to gratify a deep-seated wish. But. to quote Freud, "illusions need not necessarily be false—that is to say, unrealizable or in contradiction to reality." [1] In this particular instance, the Buddhist view is that the illusion of the belief in immortality has a certain factual basis in that there is, in fact, a realizable timeless state of immortality (*amata*), which is impersonal. And it is our very mortality and the suffering and insecurity of cosmic existence, whatever the forms of escapism we may indulge in, that makes us seek this. Thus, there is both a realistic as well as a quasi-teleological concept of suffering in early Buddhism. In fact it is expressly stated that "suffering is instrumental in arousing faith in moral and spiritual values, that such faith results in gladness and composure of mind, giving rise to insight regarding reality and eventual salvation" (dukkhūpanisā saddhā..., *Samyutta Nikāya,* II, 31). So the impermanence and insecurity of cosmic existence is a pointer to the goal which we should all seek. So suffering and the awareness of the truth about suffering is, as it were, a built-in "device" (upāya) employed by the "nature of things" (*Dhammatā*) to ensure our moral and spiritual progress and eventual salvation. These are the facts, for example, which the Mahāyāna tries to symbolize in graphic language, readily intelligible to the masses.

The transition from the standpoint of early Buddhism to that of Mahāyāna Buddhism is only a matter of degree, and there is no unbridgeable gap between the two. The furthest development away from early Buddhism would appear to be the way of faith in the grace of Amitābha (Infinite Light) or Akṣobhya (Calm), who are personifications of the infinite wisdom and compassion of the transcendent reality, of which the historical Buddha became the embodiment.

Such a development approaches the concept of God in Judaism, Christianity, and Islam, but differs from the latter in that such a Buddha is an infinitely wise and compassionate savior though not a creator of the universe or a judge of the beings in it. As such he is not responsible for pain and suffering. The universe itself is not created in time, and the operations of non-deterministic *karma* take the place of "judgement."

The emphasis on self-effort in Theravāda, as opposed to the emphasis on grace in certain forms of Mahāyāna, is again a contrast which is too heavily drawn. Theravāda certainly underlines the importance of self-effort:

---

[1] *The Complete Psychological Works of Sigmund Freud,* (The Hogarth Press, London, 1961), Vol. XXI, p. 31.

"Purity and impurity depend on oneself. No one can purify another"
—Dhammapada, 12, 165.

So do Tendai, Shingon, and Zen underline the importance of earnest effort in moral training and meditation. On the other hand, the Pure Land sects stress the value of grace or the "other-power" (*tariki*) as opposed to "self-power" (*jiriki*), but let us not forget even in them, according to the texts, the superior value of moral training and meditation is not denied. They merely hold out the possibility of relatively quick regeneration to the worst sinner. Yet, a genuine effort on the part of such a sinner is required to set in motion a process of regeneration, which shall eventually culminate in salvation. Although early and later Theravāda Buddhism denies the possibility for a person, who has for instance deliberately committed matricide, to be reborn in a "pure land" in his very next life, at least as a general rule, it does not deny the value of the slightest effort on the part of such a person to repent for his action and turn his thoughts to something good. On the other hand even as regards self-effort, the teachings of early Buddhism is quite emphatically that self-effort is a necessary condition, but not a sufficient condition, for salvation. Other factors such as time and nature have to play their part in making the latter a reality.

It will be seen that in general all schools agree with regard to the goal, the non-deterministic but causal conception of the universe in which everything, including all beings, is impermanent and lacking in essence, the limited freedom of the will, survival, moral recompense, and responsibility of the individual, whose path to salvation consists in following the message of all the Buddhas. This is summed up as "refraining from all evil, cultivating the good, and cleansing the mind" by growth in virtue, meditation and wisdom. In addition, the Pure Land schools held out the possibility of quick regeneration to the worst sinners without having to undergo the deserts of their deeds.

As we have observed, while the goal and the fruits of the spiritual life are the same, the "means" (*upāya*) adopted in imparting instructions have differed according to the position, needs, and capabilities of the individual, or the community to whom Buddhism was preached. The recognition of this fact by almost all schools of Buddhism has helped Buddhism to survive without friction or persecution and with the greatest degree of tolerance combined with mutual criticism of each other's views. Every Bodhisattva who dedicates himself for the salvation of others is expected to realize the value and practice the wisdom of "skillful means" (*upāya*) in imparting instruction. This is considered to be his seventh stage, called *dūraṅgama* (lit., going far), of his ten stages of spiritual development. It is, therefore, the similarity of the goal and the fruits resulting from the practice of Buddhism, which makes Buddhism one religion despite the apparent diversity in the forms of its teachings. It is a conception that could be extended to comprehend other religions so long as there is a similarity in the final or relative goals and the fruits of the religious life. In this connection it is worth recalling the words of St. Paul, who said that "the fruit of the Spirit is love, joy, peace, patience, kindness, goodness, faithfulness, gentleness, self-control" (Gal. 5: 22, 23). A Buddhist would state the fruit of the Buddhist way of life in identical words. I am in sympathy with many of the reasons proffered by Professor Wilfred Cantwell Smith for dropping our exclusivist labels, [1] but I think it is the exclusivist attitude that must go rather than the labels.

This doctrine of "means" (*upāya*) has a parallel in and reflects the universalism of Hinduism, which recognizes several paths to salvation, such as the way of ritual and social action (*karma-mārga*), the way of intellectual and intuitive realization (*jnāna-mārga*), and the way of faith and devotion (*bhakti-mārga*). Buddhism, while recognizing the value of these several paths for people of different capacities and interests, arranges them in a hierarchy recognizing the limitations and weaknesses of each one of them.

IV

Another fact we note in the history and expansion of Buddhism is its attitude to the religions and cults it came across in the lands to which it spread. The general principle adopted by Buddhism has consistently been that of adapting their potentialities for the promotion of good and eliminating their propensities for evil, without exterminating them altogether. This is in fact a concrete expression of the use of "skillful means" on the part of those who propagated the Dhamma of wisdom and love. The weakness of this method, however, is that many of these superstitious cults later came to be identified and confused with Buddhism. This resulted in the danger of the baby being thrown out with the bath-water in the desire for modernity on

---

[1] See Wilfred Cantwell Smith, *The Meaning and End of Religion*, (Mentor Book, 1964).

the part of youth, who are impatient of myth, superstition, and meaningless cults, especially if these are associated with an outmoded social and political order. The solution, of course, would be to replace the out-grown myths and cults with the essential beliefs and values of Buddhism, especially when they are seen to fit in with modern knowledge and are needed in the solution of some of the basic problems of modern living.

Both the doctrine of "skillful means" and the adaptation of cults to suit the ethos of Buddhism are by no means innovations of Mahāyāna or later Buddhism. It was merely the continuation of what was done by the historical Buddha in his own lifetime. For example, we find that in the early Buddhist texts the vengeful war god, Indra of Ṛgveda, is transformed into the benevolent and just God, Śakra.[1] The word, *upāya-kosallaṃ,* or "the skill in (devising) means (to instruct people)" occurs in the Canon (*Dīghā Nikāya,* I, 220) and, as regards the method of preaching adopted by the Buddha, it is held that he taught people according to their capacity and temperament, making use of his own "ability to comprehend the predilections of various beings" (*Majjhima Nikāya,* I, 70).

We can see concrete instances of this in several sermons which are of relevance to modern times. For example, when the Buddha addressed the intellectual élite of his time who were skeptical open-minded rationalists and who did not subscribe to any particular theory of survival in an age in which there were several thriving schools of Skeptics and Materialists, he used a "wager argument" (reminiscent of Pascal) to show that it was better even for a Skeptic to act on the basis that there was survival, free will, and moral recompense, rather than on their opposites.

On the other hand, addressing some personal theists among the Brahmins, the Buddha describes the path to fellowship (*sahavyata-,* lit., companionship) with God (Brahmā) and speaks of the necessity of cultivating selflessness, compassion, freedom from malice, purity of mind, and self-mastery for this purpose:

> "Then you say, too, Vāseṭṭha, that the Brahmins bear anger and malice in hteir hearts, and are tarnished in heart and uncontrolled, whilst God is free from anger and malice, pure in heart and has self-

---

[1] See Charles Godage, "The Place of Indra in Early Buddhism", *University of Ceylon Review,* Vol. III, No. 1, pp. 41-72.

mastery. Now can there be concord and harmony between the Brahmins and God?

"Certainly not, Gotama!

"Very good, Vāseṭṭha. That these Brahmins versed in the Vedas and yet bearing anger and malice in their hearts, sinful and uncontrolled, should after death, when the body is dissolved, attain fellowship with God, who is free from anger and malice, pure in heart and self-mastery—such a state of things can in no wise be."

—*Tevijja-Sutta (Dīgha Nikāya,* XIII, 35, 36)

Whatever the basis of the theistic myth they believed in, so long as these Brahmins could be persuaded to cultivate these virtues grounded on their faith in God, it was a step in the right direction. Thus on pragmatic grounds the belief in a Personal God is not discouraged so long as it is not a hindrance and could be utilized for the purpose of moral and spiritual betterment. At the same time we must not forget that, even according to the Buddhist conception of the cosmos, such a heaven had a place in the scheme of things, though the God who ruled in it, worshipped as the Almighty, was only very wise, powerful, and morally perfect, but not omniscient and omnipotent.

The above are two typical but radically different approaches in encouraging man to tread the path of moral and spiritual progress. Even in teaching the basic doctrines of Buddhism to laymen, the Buddha is often careful in giving a "seriated discourse" (*ānupubbī-kathā*) in which the subject is gradually introduced. It is said that the central truths of Buddhism pertaining to "suffering, its cause, its cessation and the way to it" are taught only if and when the mind is receptive, since the normal reaction to being reminded of the fact that we are all subject to decay, disease, and death is one of repugnance.

This relativist approach of Buddhism does not, of course, mean that Buddhism recognizes all religions as teaching the same thing and as being of equal value. When the Buddha was asked whether the main religions and philosophies taught during his time, among which were Materialism, Theism, Skepticism, etc. were all true or whether some or none were true, his reply was to the effect that they were true only to the extent that they contained and enjoined the noble eightfold path consisting of the right view of life, right aspirations, right speech, right action, right livelihood, right endeavor, right mindfulness, and right meditation. The metaphysical, theological, or mythical dressing in which the essential teaching was presented seemed to matter only as much as the sugar-coating in the pill.

One of the sermons preached by the Buddha's disciple Ananda, describing the views of the Buddha, gives the relative valuation that Buddhism makes of religions or philosophies of life different from it. Here it is said that there are four false religious philosophies in the world and four more which are unsatisfactory (*anassāsikaṃ*, lit., unconsoling) but not necessarily false. The false ones are (1) Materialism, which asserts the reality of the material world alone and denies survival; (2) a religious philosophy which recommends an amoral ethic; (3) one which denies free will and moral causation and asserts that beings are either miraculously saved or doomed; and (4) deterministic evolutionism, which asserts the inevitability of eventual salvation for all (*Sandaka Sutta, Majjhima Nikāya*, II).

The four unsatisfactory but not necessarily false religions are presumably those which in some sense recognize the necessity for a concept of survival, moral values, freedom and responsibility, and the non-inevitability of salvation. They are described as follows: The first is one in which omniscience is claimed for its founder. The second is a religion based on revelation or tradition. The third is a religion founded on logical and metaphysical speculation, and the fourth is one which is merely pragmatic and is based on skeptical or agnostic foundations.

We note here that the relativist valuation of religion in early Buddhism does not presuppose or imply the truth of all religions. Some types of religion are clearly condemned as false and undesirable, while others are satisfactory to the extent to which they contain the essential core of beliefs and values central to religion, whatever their epistemic foundations may be. Those based on claims to omniscience on the part of the founder, revelation, or tradition, metaphysical speculation, or pragmatic skepticism are unsatisfactory in so far as they are based on uncertain foundations. These essential beliefs and values may be presented in symbolic form, but such presentations must find their final justification in literal truths.

V

The religious philosophy of early Buddhism as found in the earliest portions of the Theravāda Canon presents "the right view of life" (*sammā-diṭṭhi*) in the form of verifiable propositions pertaining to the nature and destiny of man in the universe. They are supposedly verifiable in the light of personal experience, which includes both sense-experience as well as extra-sensory experience. This view and way of life has been partially veiled by later accretions and conventionalizations in the Theravāda tradition itself. But it contains the literal truths or the basis on which the symbolic or figurative statements of Mahāyāna can find their ultimate justification. Some of these symbolic forms, in trying to present certain aspects of truth in a manner intelligible to the masses, are errant if taken literally. Thus the docetic conception of the Buddha in certain schools of the Mahāyāna embodied the literal historical truth that the Buddha after his enlightenment portrayed transcendent truth and love in his life and teachings. But to have said that "the Buddha's body was not a product of sexual intercourse" was historically baseless.

The account of this right view of life as defined in early Buddhism is such that it comprehends the basic beliefs and values of the higher religions, viz. "There is (value in) alms, sacrifice (yiṭṭhaṃ), and prayer (hutaṃ); there is survival and recompense for good and evil deeds; there are moral obligations and there are religious teachers (plural) who have led a good life and who have proclaimed with their superior insight and personal understanding the nature of this world and the world beyond." (*Majjhima Nikāya*, III, 72). This summary of the right view of life, it may be observed, is comprehensive enough to contain, recognize, and respect the basic truths of all the higher religions. All these religions believe in a Transcendent conceived of as a Personal God in the theistic religions and as an Impersonal Brahman, Tao, or *Nirvāna* in the others. They all assert survival, moral recompense, and responsibility. They all preach "a good life," which has much in common and whose culmination is communion or union with, or the attainment of, this Transcendent.

The early Buddhist conception of the nature and destiny of man in the universe is, therefore, not in basic conflict with the beliefs and values of the founders of the great religions. Much of the apparent conflict is attributable to the undue emphasis on unessentials and partly to the literal interpretation given to the different symbolic presentations. The problem of the great religions today is not so much whether this or that religion is true or false, but that the religious conception of man and the universe has been greatly undermined, directly or indirectly, by the advances of science and technology. In such a context, men of good will in all religious traditions can do no better than to try and discover where they went wrong by applying the "fruit test" to the history of their respective traditions, and there is much that we can do to learn from, and perhaps even help, each other.

One of the great attractions of the early Buddhist theory of the nature of man and his destiny in the universe is that, long before the advent of modern science, it presented a picture of man and the universe which is consonant with the basic findings of science, and it encouraged an outlook, even with regard to matters moral and religious, which closely approximates what we today call the "scientific outlook." The main difference is that the outlook it recommends, while accepting the material reality of the external world, does not make a dogma of materialism. Buddhism recommends the "fruit test" for those who are unable to decide in the face of the apparent conflict of religions but goes further in encouraging a critical outlook. The following passage, which embodies an extract from a sermon of the Buddha and states the context in which it was preached, illustrates this:

> "There are certain religious teachers, who come to Kesaputta. They speak very highly of their own theories but oppose, condemn, and ridicule the theories of others. At the same time there are yet other religious teachers who come to Kesaputta and in turn speak highly of their own theories, opposing, condemning, and ridiculing the theories of those others. We are now in a state of doubt and perplexity as to who out of these venerable recluses spoke the truth and who spoke falsehood.
>
> "O Kālāmas, you have a right to doubt or feel uncertain for you have raised a doubt in a situation in which you ought to suspend your judgement. Come now, Kālāmas, do not accept anything on the grounds of revelation, tradition, or report, or because it is in conformity with the scriptures, or because it is a product of mere reasoning, or because of a superficial assessment of facts, or because it is true from a standpoint, or because it conforms with one's preconceived notions, or because it is authoritative, or because of the prestige of your teacher. When you, O Kālāmas, realize for yourselves that these doctrines are evil and unjustified, that they are condemned by the wise and that when they are accepted and lived by, they conduce to ill and sorrow, then you should reject them..."
>
> —*Aṅguttara Nikāya*, I, 189.

This critical attitude may also be focused on Buddhism itself:

> "If anyone were to speak ill of me, my doctrine, or my Order, do not bear any ill will towards him, be upset or perturbed at heart, for

if you were to be so, it would only cause you harm. If, on the other hand, anyone were to speak well of me, my doctrine, or my Order, do not be overjoyed, thrilled, or elated at heart, for if so it will only be an obstacle in your way of forming a correct judgement as to whether the qualities praised in us are real and actually found in us."

—*Dīgha Nikāya*, I, 2, 3.

The later tradition often underlines this attitude:

"Just as the experts test gold by burning it, cutting it, and applying it on a touchstone, my statements should be accepted only after critical examination and not out of respect for me." (Buddha)

—*Tattvasaṃgraha* (Sanskrit)
—*Jñānasamuccayasāra* (Tibetan)

A Buddhist's faith in Buddhism is, therefore, characterized as a "rational faith" (*ākāravatī saddhā*) as opposed to "blind faith" (*amūlikā saddhā*). One accepts the Buddhist point of view as being the probable truth about the nature of man and his destiny in the universe and makes it the basis of one's life, personally verifying the propositions of Buddhism pertaining to the moral and spiritual life. Going along with this outlook is the causal conception of the universe, which is a causal system in which there operate physical laws (*ṛtu-niyāma*), biological laws (*bīja-niyāma*), and psychological laws (*citta-niyāma*), as well as moral and spiritual laws (*kamma-, dhamma-niyāma*).

While this critical and analytical outlook is thus not alien to the religious outlook on life, the Buddhist conception of man and his place in the universe is on the whole compatible with the general picture of things accepted today on the basis of the findings of science.

Buddhism, for instance, does not have any cosmological problems. The early Buddhist description of the cosmos, as far as the observable universe goes, is claimed to be based on extra-sensory clairvoyant perception. It is remarkably close to the modern conception of the universe:

"As far as these suns and moons revolve, shedding their light in space, so far extends the thousand-fold universe. In it there are thousands of suns *(sahassam suriyānam)*, thousands of moons, thousands of inhabited worlds of varying sorts, ...thousands of heavenly worlds of varying grades. This is the thousands-fold Minor World System

(cūlanikā lokadhātu). Thousands of times the size of the thousands-fold Minor World System is the twice-a-thousand Middling World System *(majjhimikā lokadhātu)*. Thousands of times the size of the Middling World System is the thrice-a-thousand Great Cosmos *(mahālokadhātu)*."
—*Aṅguttara Nikāya*, I, 227, 228.

This conception of the universe as consisting of hundreds of thousands of clusters of galactic systems, each one containing thousands of suns, moons, and inhabited worlds, is not to be found in the Hindu or Jain scriptures and was much in advance of the age in which it appears. In the later Theravāda, it gets embedded in and confused with mythical notions about the universe. In the Mahāyāna the conception is magnified and there are references to the "unlimited and infinite number of galactic systems (*lokadhātu*) in the ten quarters" (*Sukhāvatī-vyūha*, I), but the original conception of a "sphere of million millions of galactic systems" (*Vajracchedikā*, XXX) survives. It may be noted that, despite such a conception of the universe, early Buddhism discouraged speculations about questions pertaining to the origin and extent of the universe as intellectually stultifying and morally fruitless.

A concept of biological evolution is not found in early Buddhism, but its picture of life as a struggle for existence in which one species of life feeds on another, "the stronger overpowering the weak", is compatible with the theory of evolution. The Vaiṣṇavite theory of Avatars (Incarnations), who seem to be representatives of the epochs of evolution, is also interesting in this respect, since the list mentions the Fish, Tortoise, Bear, Man-Lion, Pygmy Man, Rama with axe, Rama who rules a civilized community in accordance with laws, Kṛṣna who gives a spiritual guidance, and Buddha who is the enlightened man. [1]

Buddhist psychology is empirical and discards the concept of the soul. The mind is not a permanent unchanging substance located within the body but is a product of conditioned experiences which go to form "the stream of consciousness" (*vinnāna-sota*), which is said to be "divided into two parts" (*ubhayato abbhocchinnaṃ*), the conscious mind and the dynamic unconsciousness, the continuous impact of which, even after the death of the body, brings about survival.

---

[1] Professor C. D. Broad says, "Now I do not think that there need be any great difficulty in fitting religion in general, or certain of the great historical religions, such as Buddhism, into this changed biological framework." (*Religion, Philosophy, and Psychical Research*, Routledge and Kegan Paul, Ltd., London, 1953, p. 241, chapter entitled "Relations of Science and Religion").

Rebirth (lit., re-becoming) and karma are two of the basic doctrines of Buddhism which make the moral responsibility for our acts meaningful. They are not taught as dogmas to be accepted on faith but as eventually verifiable truths. Their significance for modern thought lies in the fact that there is some empirical evidence of a verifiable character in their favor. Age regression experiments have revealed that the unconscious minds of individuals contain traces of historical knowledge of a detailed, specific, and personal sort, which cannot easily be explained on the basis of knowledge acquired in this life. [1] The concept of rebirth cannot also be dismissed on logical grounds. A contemporary positivist philosopher, A. J. Ayer, grants the meaningfulness and "the logical possibility of reincarnation." [2] A psychiatrist who has examined several authentic spontaneous cases of recall of alleged prior lives mainly on the part of children from different parts of the world states his conclusion as follows, after trying to account for the evidence in terms of several alternative normal and paranormal hypotheses: "I will say, therefore, that I think reincarnation the most plausible hypothesis for understanding cases of this series." [3]

The Buddhist doctrines of rebirth and karma were put forward by the Buddha after examining several alternative theories regarding the question of survival, such as those of the Skeptics, Materialists, single afterlife theories, and other rebirth theories, when he was convinced of them on the basis of his alleged clairvoyant capacity to see his own past lives as well as the past lives of others. In this respect one may compare and examine the historically attested case of Mr. Edgar Cayce of the United States, who just over two decades back claimed the exercise of both these extra-sensory faculties and whose records are still available for inspection and study. [4]

I state this because, as I said earlier, myths which cannot be established on evidence acceptable to the modern mind have little chance in the modern world of being made the basis of a moral and spiritual life. The evidence and the experiments of Psychical Research on the question of survival, therefore, deserve to be studied with greater zeal wherever they may lead us, although in certain parts of the world

---
[1] See C. J. Ducasse, *The Belief in a Life after Death,* Illinois, 1961, pp. 241-299. 299.
[2] See *The Concept of a Person,* (Macmillan and Co., Ltd., London, 1963), p. 127.
[3] See Ian Stevenson, M. D., *The Evidence from Survival for Claimed Memories of Former Incarnations,* (Essex, 1961), p. 34.
[4] See Gina Cerminara, M. A., Ph. D., *Many Mansions,* (William Sloan Associates, Inc., New York, 12th Ed., 1960).

such a quest for truth would be taboo and even forbidden by the state.

The psychiatrist and the psychoanalyst are today playing an increasing part in society in helping individuals to maintain or recover their sanity of mind, and many argue that much of the anxiety and unrest in the modern world stems from the tensions of modern living, which cause such mental imbalance. The task of Buddhism too is to help individuals acquire a relative or complete sanity of mind as a prerequisite of personal happiness and social harmony. The Buddha was one of the first to point out that men suffer from bodily as well as mental disease, and he goes on to say that, while we are subject to bodily disease from time to time, we are almost continually subject to mental disease until we attain perfection. According to Buddhism the ultimate cause of this "mental disease" is the lack of a realistic understanding of the nature of man and his place in the universe (ignorance), the continual onrush of unsatisfied cravings (greed), and the aggressive tendencies (hate), which we continually try to satisfy and appease. The Buddhist analysis of our springs of action is as follows:

1. Greed *(lobha)*
    a. Desire for sensuous gratification *(kāma-taṇhā)*
    b. Desire for self-centered pursuits, such as power, fame, etc. *(bhava-taṇhā)*
2. Hate *(dosa)*; desire for destruction *(vibhava-taṇhā)*
3. Ignorance *(moha)*; i.e., erroneous beliefs regarding man and his place in the universe.
4. Selflessness, Charity *(cāga)*
5. Compassion *(mettā)*
6. Wisdom *(vijjā)*

The pleasures we get from satisfying our desires for sensuous gratification, self-centered pursuits, and aggression, or by entertaining illusions or rationalizations which go hand in hand with or promote the above, constitute much of the enjoyment of modern man. Buddhism contends that there is a greater happiness of a more serene and stable sort, which wells from selflessness, compassion, and a realistic view of life. We go "with the current" in acting out of greed, hate, and ignorance, but our endeavor should be "to go against the current" *(paṭisota-gāmi)* and replace greed with selfless service, hatred with compassion, and ignorance with wisdom, as our springs of action. This should be done by a process of sublimation whereby we develop a longing for (chanda) selflessness, compassion, and wisdom and a hatred of, or an attempt to eliminate, greed, hate, and ignorance. The commitment to or faith in the right philosophy of life, the discipline of a meaningful non-authoritarian moral code of behavior, and the practice of mindfulness or watchfulness regarding one's own thoughts and behavior, which results in increased self-awareness and control of one's actions, is the path to sanity as well as to personal happiness and social harmony.

The talk about man's freedom is of no avail if this freedom is not going to be utilized by each one of us for the purpose of transforming our human nature (the old Adam) in order to act with greater freedom, control, creativity, stability, and happiness. Our greater understanding through science of the nature of disease and death, as well as of our physical, social, and economic environment, would be to no purpose if, with increasing controls over our environment for our greater happiness, we lose control over ourselves and become slaves or automatons within the very organizations we set up.

VI

Thus we have in Buddhism a religion which is compatible with the spirit and findings of science but justifying the religious picture of the universe. Its concept of man and society is also very relevant to the modern age when man is within reach of attaining the ideal of a world community, if he can but outlive the storm which is gathering about him. This social philosophy of Buddhism is yet another aspect of the relativity of Buddhist philosophy.

Much of early Buddhism is addressed to spiritually hungry men bent on salvation, for whom the meditative development of the mind was a full-time job. But this does not mean that early Buddhism neglected the common man or taught the same things to him. One of the things the Buddha did, unlike the pre-Buddhistic Upaniṣadic teachers, was to take the message of Buddhism to the masses "for the good and happiness of the multitude" (*bahujana-hitāya bahujana-sukhāya*). Buddhism was also taught to all classes of people including rulers. As a result we find in early Buddhism a social and political philosophy about which not much is still known in the western world.

Buddhism stood for the oneness of the human species, the equality of man, and the spiritual unity of mankind.[1] The Buddha argued

---

[1] For an exposition of the source material, see G. P. Malalasekera and K. N. Jayatilleke, *Buddhism and the Race Question*, (UNESCO Race Series, UNESCO, Paris, 1958).

that, while there were different species among plants and animals, men belonged to a single species and that the differences in color, the form of the hair, nose, etc., did not constitute differences in species. Caste or racial purity was a baseless myth. There was no chosen race or caste, and men of all races and castes were capable of moral and spiritul growth and should be afforded an opportunity for such development. All men without distinction were subject to the laws of karma and ought to be treated equally before the secular law. It was one's economic power that determined one's status in society and not considerations of birth. When religious arguments were used to defend the institution of caste, as they are sometimes used even to defend *apartheid* today, the Buddhists countered the arguments of the Theists by showing that the fatherhood of God ought to imply the brotherhood of man. The *Vajrasūci,* a Buddhist polemic against caste, says: "Wonderful! You affirm that all men proceeded from One, namely God, then how can there be a fourfold insuperable diversity among them? If I have four sons by one wife, the four sons having one father and mother must be all essentially alike."

For the Buddhist, society, like every other institution or process, was a changing complex, changing in accordance with certain causal factors. The static conception of society, which prevailed at the time, was based on the idea that there was an eternal fourfold caste-order in society divinely ordained. The Buddha opposed this by presenting a dynamic evolutionary conception of society. A Buddhist myth of genesis gives such an account of society and shows how what later became caste divisions arose from a division of functions in settled society in a certain stage of social evolution, which necessitated such occupational divisions, the recognition of property rights, the law, and the guardians of the law. The Buddha also points out that the four social classes of Indian society were not universal since among the Yona-Kāmbojas (i.e., certain Persian states on the northwest border of India) there were only "two social classes" (*dve'va vaṇṇā*) and that not too rigid.

"The world," it is said, "is ruled by ideas" (*cittena loko nīyate*), but among the causes which bring about social change an important place is given to the economic factor. In a prophetic myth about the future of society the causal factors affecting social change are well illustrated. In it, it is stated that, with the maldistribution of goods, there would be economic inequality resulting in a division of the world into the rich and the poor or the haves and the have-nots. The have-nots or the poor will then make demands on the haves, and the latter will give ear and give in to their demands. But the demands merely increase as a result, and there is lack of initiative on the part of the have-nots. This results in a stiffening of attitude on the part of the rich rulers who now withdraw help and adopt stern measures. This has its repercussion in a corresponding stiffening of attitude on the part of the have-nots, and there is tension and organized violence between the two factions, resulting in a gradual loss of values in human society. This reaches a climax in catastrophic war in which the greater part of humanity will be destroyed. The remnant who manage to survive learn a bitter lesson from history and proceed to build the Just Society on firm moral and economic foundations:

> "...Thus from goods not accruing to the destitute, poverty becomes rampant. From poverty being rampant, stealing becomes rampant... violence... killing... lying... slander... sexual misconduct... abusive and idle talk... covetousness and ill-will... false view of life... wanton greed and perverted lust... till finally lack of filial and religious piety and lack of regard for authority... Among such humans the ten moral courses of conduct will altogether disappear, and the ten immoral courses of conduct will flourish excessively; there will be no word for 'moral' among such humans—far less any moral agent. Among such humans, it is to them who lack filial and religious piety and show no respect for authority that homage and praise will be given. The world will fall into promiscuity... keen mutual enmity will become the rule, keen ill-will, keen animosity, passionate thoughts even of killing... in a father towards his child and a child towards his father... Among such humans there will arise a war of seven days, during which they will look on each other as wild beasts. Dangerous weapons will come into their hands and they, regarding each other as beasts, will deprive each other of life... But to those to whom it would have occurred, 'Let us not slay each other'—they would betake themselves to dens of grass, or dens in the jungle, or holes in trees, or river fastnesses, or mountain clefts and subsist on roots and fruits of the jungle. And at the end of those seven days, coming forth from dens and fastnesses and mountain clefts, they will embrace each other, and be of one accord comforting one another and saying: Hail, O mortal, that thou livest still! Then it will occur to those beings that it was only because they had gotten into evil ways that they had this heavy loss of kin. They will then decide, 'Let us, therefore, now do good...' So they will practice these virtues... and they increase in length of life, in comeliness and prosperity... Among such humans there will be only three kinds of disease—unfilled wishes, natural

hunger, and decay. Among such humans, this India (v.l. this world) will be mighty and prosperous, populous, and with plenty of food, and having numerous villages, towns, and cities."

—Cakkavatti-sīhanāda-sutta,
Dīgha Nikāya, III, 70-75.

The above passage is a literal translation of the text, leaving out certain mythical elements, such as references to enormous decreases and increases in the human span of life, and, although Buddhism is non-deterministic in outlook and would not hold that such things will necessarily come to pass, it is certainly not without its moral for contemporary man. It may also be seen that while Buddhism was pessimistic about the immediate future of humanity it is optimistic about the not so immediate future.

We see that, from the Buddhist point of view, one of the basic factors determining changes in society is its economic foundations. Ultimately, it was the maldistribution of goods which precipitated the loss of values and eventually brought about a catastrophic war. Tracing the cause of this poverty, which led to dire consequences, it is said that the mistake that the kings made was to consider that their task was merely to preserve law and order without developing the economy. The king, it is said "provided for the righteous protection and security of his subjects but neglected the economy" (*dhammikaṃ rakkhāvaraṇaguttiṃ saṃvidahi, no ca kho adhanānaṃ dhanaṃ anuppadāsi,* Dīgha Nikāya, III, 65). Elsewhere, the Buddha in advising a king states that the best way to ensure peace and prosperity is not by wasting the country's resources in performing religious sacrifices but by ensuring full employment and thereby developing the economy:

> " 'So I would,' says the king, 'offer a great sacrifice—let the venerable one instruct me how—for my weal and welfare for many days.'
> "Thereupon the Brahmin, who was chaplain (the Buddha in a prior life), said to the king: 'The king's country, Sir, is harassed and harried. There are dacoits abroad who pillage the villages and townships and who make the roads unsafe. Were the king, so long as that is so, to levy a fresh tax, verily his majesty would be acting wrongly. But perchance his majesty might think: I'll soon put a stop to these scoundrels' game by degradation and banishment and fines and bonds and death!' But their license cannot be satisfactorily put to a stop so. The remnant left unpunished would still go on harassing the realm. Now there is one method to adopt to put a thorough end to this disorder. Whoever there be in the king's realm who devote themselves

to keeping cattle and the farm, to them let his majesty he king give food and seed-corn. Whoever there be in the king's realm who devote themselves to trade, to them let his majesty the king give capital. Whoever there be in king's realm who devote themselves to government service, to them let his majesty the king give wages and food. Then those men, following each his own business, will no longer harass the realm; the king's revenue will go up; the country will be quiet and at peace; and the populace, pleased with one another and happy, dancing their children in their arms, will dwell with open doors."

—Kūṭadanta Sutta, Dīgha Nikāya, I, 135.

While it is the duty of the state to provide opportunities for education and employment, it is the duty of the individual to try and discover his talents and to develop them so as to be socially useful and also at the same time to learn to live in a manner which makes for moral growth, working for the good of himself as well as of the community. The following relative valuation of persons would illustrate this fact:

"What sort of man is blind? Here a certain person does not possess that sight whereby he can discover and attain that wealth which has not been attained, or can augment it, he has not even that insight whereby he can distinguish good and bad, the blameworthy and the blameless... Such a person is said to be blind.

"What sort of person is 'purblind?' Here a certain person who has the eye of knowledge whereby he can attain that wealth which he could not attain before and can moreover augment it, but does not possess that mental vision whereby he can distinguish between the good and the bad... Such a person is said to be 'purblind.'

"What sort of person is two-eyed? Here a person possesses that eye which can help him to bring that wealth which he could not attain before and also to increase it, as well that insight which makes it possible for him to know the good and the bad... Such a person is said to be two-eyed."

—Puggala-Paññatti, III

The pursuit of one's material as well as spiritual well-being is what is required of man in society, such a quest being practicable where the wealth is righteously earned and righteously spent for one's good as well as that of others, without squandering or hoarding it. The Buddha speaks of the happiness of the average man as deriving from economic security (*atthi-sukha*), the enjoyment of one's wealth (*bho-*

ga-sukha), freedom from debt (*anaṇa-sukha*), and a blameless moral and spiritual life (*anavajja-sukha*).

It is said in the Buddhist scriptures that if Gotama did not become a Buddha he would have become the Ideal Ruler (*cakkavattirājā*), who would have established an ideal government, which like the spiritual message of Buddhism was also considered necessary "for the weal and welfare of the multitude." The primary task of such an Ideal Ruler or State was twofold, viz., (1) to respect the Dhamma and afford righteous protection and security for all subjects under the guidance of the Dhamma. The use of the word "righteous" (*dhammikaṃ*) and "under the guidance of the Dhamma" (*dhammā-dhipateyyo*) would imply that such security was to be provided so as to ensure that all subjects would enjoy what we today call "human rights." There is also specific mention of such protection of all "religious teachers" (*samana-brāhmanesu*) and even for "birds and beasts" (*migapakkhīsu*); (2) to see to it that there was no poverty and unemployment among his subjects (*ye ca te vijite adhanā assu, tesañca dhanaṃ anupadajjeyyāsi*) and ensure that there was a plentiful supply of goods that everyone could enjoy (*yathābhuttañca bhuñjatha*). We see here how Buddhism underlines the importance of two things necessary in the ideal state, namely Freedom and Economic Security. The problem today is the same, except for the fact that the question now is how to have sufficient controls so as to ensure economic security and prosperity for all and to combine this with a maximum of freedom for the individual to choose his way of life and to permit the propagation of whatever religious or political philosophy he may think is true.

There is little doubt that the great emperor Asoka, whom H. G. Wells called "the greatest of kings" [1] and of whom he said that "his reign of eight-and-twenty years was one of the brightest interludes in the troubled history of mankind," [2] was guided by these ideals in respecting the Dharma, treating all religions with respect and tolerance and adopting "welfare-state" policies. Max Weber [3] has pointed out that "for the first time in the Hindu culture area there appeared the idea of a 'welfare state,' of the 'general good' (the promotion of which Asoka regarded as the duty of the king). 'Welfare' was, however, partially understood to mean spiritual welfare (the furtherance of sal-

---

[1] See *A Short History of the World,* (Pelican Books, Revised Ed., 1964), p. 95.
[2] *Ibid,* p. 94.
[3] *The Religion of India,* (Illinois, 1958), p. 242.

vation chances), and partially to mean charities, but also rational and economic action."

In Ceylon, some of the ancient Sinhalese kings were also inspired by such ideals in setting up "tremendous irrigation works" [1] for the welfare of their subjects, transforming nature for the benefit of man. The ancient chronicles record a speech made by one of these Sinhalese kings, which reads as follows:

> "In the realm that is subject to me there are, apart from many strips of country where the harvest flourishes mainly by rain water, few fields which are dependent on rivers with permanent flow or on great reservoirs. Also by many mountains, by thick jungle, and by widespread swamps, my kingdom is much straitened. Truly in such a country not even a little water that comes from the rain must flow into the ocean without being made useful to man... For a life of enjoyment of what one possesses, without having cared for the welfare of the people, in no wise befits one like myself." (Eleventh century, A.D.) [2]

While Buddhism distinguishes between good monarchs and bad monarchs, it is interesting to note that the Buddha has spoken appreciatively of and showed a distinct preference for the form of government prevailing in the self-governing republics such as that of the Vajjis in his time. It is not surprising that a non-authoritarian doctrine teaching the equality of man, the importance of human rights, and respect for the individual should value democracy. In the Mahāparinibbāna Sutta, the Buddha urges that so long as the Vajjis keep to their democratic traditions, their continued prosperity was to be expected. Among the practices lauded were: assembling for their meetings regularly and in large numbers, holding meetings, conducting business, and dispersing in concord and harmony, respect for the Vajjian law and the constitution and not making any revolutionary changes in it, respect for elders or duly constituted authority, respect for women, respect for religious shrines, institutions, and holy men. The assemblies of the Buddhist Sangha have preserved the form in which the affairs of these democratic institutions have been conducted. [3]

---

[1] *Ibid*, p. 242. Weber is not correct in saying that the irrigation works of the Ceylonese kings were merely intended to augment the number of taxpayers and not to implement welfare politics.

[2] See Wilhelm Geiger, *The Cūlavaṃsa*, Colombo, 1953), p. 277.

[3] See *The Legacy of India*, Ed. G. T. Garratt, with an Introduction by the Marquess of Zetland, (Oxford, 1937), p. xi. "It is, indeed, to the Buddhist books that we have to turn for an account of the manner in which the affairs of these early exam-

It has been said that "parliamentary democracy really was the Russian and the Chinese peoples' first choice," [1] and as a Buddhist I would expect that when the masses of these countries have tasted the fruits of education (however secular this may be) and the prosperity of a planned economy, the desire for genuine freedom on their part, despite all efforts at indoctrination, will culminate in a return to democracy.

ples of representative self-governing institutions were conducted. And it may come as a surprise to many to learn that in the Assemblies of the Buddhists in India two thousand years and more ago are be found the rudiments of our own parliamentary practice of the present day. The dignity of the Assembly was preserved by the appointment of a special officer—the embryo of 'Mr. Speaker' in our House of Commons. A second officer was appointed whose duty it was so see that when necessary a quorum was secured—the prototype of the Parliamentary Chief Whip in our own system. A member initiating business did so in the form of a motion which was then put open to discussion. In some cases this was done once only, in others three times, thus anticipating the practice of Parliament in requiring that a Bill be read a third time before it becomes law. If discussion disclosed a difference of opinion the matter was decided by the vote of the majority, the voting being by ballot.'

[1] See Arnold J. Toynbee, *America and the World Revolution,* (Oxford University Press, 1962), p. 54.

THE JEWISH VISION OF HUMAN BROTHERHOOD

BY

LOUIS FINKELSTEIN
The Jewish Theological Seminary of America

Judaism, being a normative religion with precise regulations determining human conduct, had to face forthrightly the dilemmas and paradoxes involved in the idea of human brotherhood.

Without imputing to the ancients knowledge of modern psychology and psychiatry, some of the observations underlying today's theories were perhaps dimly recognized by the teachers of Judaism, although, of course, not formulated in scientific or philosophical propositions. The basic dilemma involved in the concept of universal human brotherhood is the logical one, arising from the inevitable conflict between duty to a natural brother and to an adopted brother.

Does the fascinating notion of universal brotherhood mean that I may love my brother no more than someone else at the end of the world? Does universal brotherhood, the idea so dear to the foremost prophets of mankind, imply dissolution of family and kindred ties? Obviously not. But how then resolve the problems arising from conflicting claims of kindred and mankind?

Beyond this logical difficulty lies the psychological dilemma that where there is love there is also hostility. Sibling rivalry is as much a fact as fraternal affection. One may be indifferent to people at the end of the world or may have mild liking or disliking for them, but relationship with a neighbor involves deeper emotions. When there is even a tendency to affection and love, there is a conscious or unconscious tendency to hate. Whether concealed or not, they are always mingled.

In a world become a neighborhood love may increase, but similarly there will be increased hostility. We now see more mutual concern of peoples for one another. Inevitably there is also much more fear, suspicion, and rivalry.

In addition to the problem of sibling hostility, involved in the concept of human brotherhood, there is also a biological problem.

Man as a vertebrate animal is afflicted with profound territorial possessiveness. Indeed this, perhaps stimulated by fear of the stranger—no less than the hunger for power, has stimulated the continuous expansion of human societies throughout the history of civilization.

Direction of hostility toward a common target unites the "in" group members who may have been hostile before. The twelve tribes of Israel waged war against one another but united under a common king when threatened by the Philistines. The thirteen American colonies united against the colonial empire of Great Britain. A long list of nations united against Napoleon and against Hitler.

But how can all humanity really be united if that requires one archenemy feared and hated by all? In modern times philosophers have tried to personify poverty, ignorance, disease, crime, and mutual hostility itself as such a common enemy. But these abstract targets have generally been powerless to unite the various nations. The medievalists hoped to bind men together in a common war against Satan, perhaps also too nebulous a figure to unite mankind in resistance to him.

I

To deal with each of these various paradoxes and dilemmas, Judaism evolved in its theology and norms not merely one system but two, in the usual Jewish pattern. The Shammaitic and Hillelite wings of Pharisaism each had a set of solutions to these problems. Professor Louis Ginzberg showed in his famous essay on "The Significance of the Halachah for Jewish History" (published originally in Hebrew, but translated into English, in *On Jewish Law and Lore*, pp. 77-124), and others have indicated that many of the differences between these schools originated long before their establishment as separate groups within Pharisaism. The differences may go back to the days of the Prophets or even to the origin of the Jewish religion.

The Shammaitic solutions in this regard, and others, were directed to the provincials and the villagers, for whom the idea of human brotherhood was particularly difficult because they were unaccustomed to meeting strangers, and who tended to be chauvinistic in their outlook on life. The Hillelite solutions were directed to the more sophisticated traders and artisans of Jerusalem who, accustomed to Gentiles in the metropolis, felt at home with them and could readily view them as friends and sometimes as brothers. By easy extension, Jews in the commercial center, Judaea's capital, could envisage brotherhood with the Edomites, the Egyptians, and the Assyrians.

The Hillelites readily resolved the logical paradox in the notion of universal brotherhood of mankind. This was done through the development of a system of priorities. In a family not all brothers are equally close to one another. In the greater family of mankind, universal love is reconcilable with varying degrees of love. Thus, when one has to choose between help for the poor of one's own city and the poor of another city, the poor who are one's actual neighbors have prior claim (*Mekilta Mishpatim*, chap. 19, p. 315).

Similarly, if one must make a choice between help for the poor of one's country and the poor of another country, one's fellow citizens have priority (*ibid*).

But there are occasions when the system of priorities could not justly be applied. Although the Israelite might rightly consider himself more responsible for the welfare of a fellow-Israelite than for that of a heathen, the Talmud declares that "One provides for the poor of the heathen together (i.e., on the same scale as) with the poor of the Israelites in order to promote harmonious relations" (*Yer. Gittin*, 5.9, 47c). "In a city, where the population is partly Israelite, partly heathen, the heads of charity funds should include both heathens and Israelites, and they should collect from both heathens and Israelites, for the sake of harmonious relations" (*ibid*).

Harmonization of these opposing norms and consideration of how and when each should be applied, required considerable discussion which left room for difference of judgement.

While differing in their approach to the psychological and biological dilemmas involved in the concept of universal brotherhood, the Shammaites and the Hillelites both held that to achieve a true feeling of human brotherhood, without undue concomitant hostility, it was necessary (in this instance and in many others) "to take account of the human impulse" (cf. *Sifre* Deut. 222, p. 225). The task of the moralist was therefore to turn the psychological and biological drives making for hostility into channels where they would become creative rather than destructive.

To discuss the whole problem in historical perspective, the clearest enunciation of this effort is manifested in the concept of the Chosen People, as defined in the Pentateuch mainly in the Book of Deuteronomy, and by the Second Isaiah, as well as in the Jewish Prayer Book—the most significant tract of Jewish theology.

In all these works the selection of Israel was translated into a command. Israel had been chosen for specific tasks and for particular responsibilities. At the very beginning of literary prophecy, Amos informed Israel that it is no different before the Lord than the Ethiopians, the Philistines, or the Aramaeans (Amos 9.7). But at the same time he insisted, "You, only, have I known among all the families of the earth. Therefore I will visit on you all your iniquities" (*ibid*, 3.2).

"And ye shall be unto Me a kingdom of priests and holy people" (Exodus 19.6) according to the Rabbinic interpretation implies simply "the holiness of the commandments" (*Mekilta* of R. Simeon, *ad loc.*, ed. Epstein-Melammed, p. 139). "For," continued the ancient Rabbi, "the more commandments God gives Israel, the greater is its holiness." Man's hunger for primacy is given satisfaction, but the primacy to be achieved is in service, not power.

Long before the Talmudic authorities, this doctrine had been formulated in great detail and with the utmost clarity by the great Prophet of the Exile, Deutero-Isaiah. Nowhere in Judaism are the problems raised by impulses of men more clearly recognized than in its delicate balance between universalism and particularism. And perhaps nowhere is this delicate balance more clearly discernible than in the teachings of Deutero-Isaiah.

Like Isaiah long before him, Deutero-Isaiah foresaw a world of peace, justice, and mercy among men. Early in his career, he apparently associated this vision with the rise of Cyrus, whom he called the Divine anointed (Is. 45.1), expecting him to unite the world under a beneficent rule, which recognized the king as servant of God. That earlier Prophets had foreseen this role for an Israelite King, scion of the House of David, did not seem to disturb the Prophet of the Exile. For him restoration of the deported Judaites to their country was the first step in a hoped-for world-wide revolution making for the unity of mankind.

When the Empire of Cyrus, no matter how benevolent—particularly to the Judaites, proved a tyrannical despotism, the Prophet sought the reform of mankind not through power, but through endless persistence and righteousness of the "worm of Jacob," the selfless "servant of the Lord," who would demand nothing for itself, but would seek to bring justice and righteousness into the world.

In later Prophecies, Deutero-Isaiah found another way to reconcile his universalism with his particularism which required some channel of expression, a way which became basic to much of later Jewish thought. He developed a particularistic eschatology but insisted on normative universalism. He welcomed the stranger who accepted belief in God and promised him an eternal place in the future of Israel. To Israel Deutero-Isaiah promised glorious fulfillment when its righteousness would be recognized by the nations of the world.

The holiness of Israel did not even mean that it was the only people to whom Divinely-inspired Prophets were sent. On the contrary, the assertion of Deuteronomy, "And there hath not arisen a Prophet *in Israel* like unto Moses" (Deut. 34.10), is interpreted to imply that "But such did arise among the nations of the world. And who was he? Balaam" (*Sifre*, ad loc., 357, p. 430).

Having had Prophets sent to them, the nations of the world are obliged to observe a number of commandments given them. These Noachic laws include the prohibitions against idolatry, murder, the infringement of chastity, robbery, blasphemy, and cruelty to animals, as well as the injunction to establish a system of civil law (*Tosefta Aboda Zara* 8 [9], p. 473).

But, according to Rabbi Meir Simhah of Dvinsk, one of the most erudite and ingenious interpreters of Judaism of the second half of the nineteenth century, the Gentile world is responsible only for the observance of these commandments, taught them by the Prophets sent to all mankind (see his commentary *Or Sameah*, on the Code of Maimonides, *Hilkot Melakim*, chap. 10). These commandments were repeated by Moses in the Pentateuch and declared binding on all men, because they had been revealed to all men through Prophets sent to them.

A Gentile who observes these laws because he accepts them as Divinely revealed to Moses is considered, according to Maimonides (as interpreted by Rabbi Meir Simhah), a "half-proselyte." Such a Gentile is under no obligation to observe the other commandments in the Torah, not being an Israelite. But his belief in the Torah of Moses gives him a special status in relation to Jews.

The School of Hillel considered the study of Torah the highest privilege which can come to man, and maintained that this study is of even greater importance than the actual execution of the commandments. This doctrine followed from the belief of the School of Hillel that the study of Torah is the most important factor in the development of character and personality; and that the development of character and personality is more significant in human life than the observance of any specific detail of the Law.

Hence, Rabbi Akiba, a great spokesman of the School of Hillel, held that "Study is greater than the execution of the commandments" (*Sifre* Deut. 41, p. 85). The issue became a practical one during the persecutions of Hadrian, when it became virtually impossible for Jews to observe the commandments. Many were tempted to leave the Land of Israel, emigrating to other countries where the Romans did not object to Jewish observances. But to leave the Land of Israel also meant to leave the great academies of Jewish learning and to abandon study of the Torah. Rabbi Akiba and his followers, putting into normative form the ancient teachings of their school, held that it was better to remain in the Land of Israel, where one could study even though one could not observe the commandments, than to emigrate in order to observe the commandments but sacrifice the opportunity to develop the study of Torah (*Sifre, ibid*).

Holding these views, the School of Hillel discovered sufficient satisfaction from the drive to primacy, in study and development of the Torah. Therefore they insisted that the "saints of the peoples of the world," who observed the commandments enumerated above, would be granted immortality, precisely as would pious Israelites. This view was articulated by Rabbi Joshua B. Hananya (*B. Sanhedrin*, 104a).

Moreover, a Gentile who devotes himself to study of Torah, i.e., presumably the seven commandments enumerated, the norms flowing from them and the philosophical premises justifying them, was held equal to the Jewish high priest (*Mekilta d'Arayot*, published with *Sifra, Ahare* perek 13. 13, 86b).

The pious of the Gentiles, said the Hillelites, would be resurrected together with those of Israel at the time of the Messiah. Witnessing the vindication of hte Prophetic vision of the coming of the Messiah, it may be presumed that many of the half-proselytes and pious Gentiles will then wish to become Jews, although conversion to Judaism will confer no benefits. But, in general, the Talmud held, proselytes will not be accepted in Messianic times (*B. Yebamot* 24b). An exception will be made for those resurrected Gentiles who have indicated their love and respect for Judaism in the present world. Hence, the Talmud remarked (in a passage whose meaning was first explained recently by Professor Saul Lieberman in *Greek in Jewish Palestine*, p. 78), "If proselytes will be accepted in the Messianic era, Antonius will lead them all" (*Yer. Megillah* 3.2, 74a).

The authors of the statement obviously assumed that in the Messianic Age the saints of the people of the world will be resurrected together with the saints of Israel.

Which Roman Emperor of all those who bore the title Antonius is indicated in this passage in not clear. The Rabbis may have meant Antonius Pius himself or Marcus Aurelius, or one of the later Emperors, who befriended the Jews. However, the theological principle underlying this remarkable vision of the future is unmistakable. The Rabbis expected the nations of the world to continue as separate entities in the Resurrected World of the Messianic Age. Judaism would have only two advantages over other traditions. The coming of the Messiah will vindicate the prediction of its teachers, and some of the pious of the nations of the world may consequently desire to join the future Jewish people.

In the theology of the School of Hillel thus no distinction whatever exists between Israel and the other peoples of the world. The distinctions are rather between the saints and the wicked, the pious and the impious, the students of Torah and those who spurn that study. For the Hillelites, psychological and biological drives to primacy, the need for particularism, were therefore to be satisfied—not by any special distinction granted an ethnic group—but by the special distinction achieved through study and righteousness.

II

Addressed to the peasantry, especially that of Galilee, Shammaitic theology could not stress the duty of study as did the Hillelites, for such sophistication was beyond the powers of the peasant. The Shammaites held that "Not interpretation is the root (of Judaism); but action" (Mishna *Abot* 1.17). Shammai himself used to say, "Talk little and do much" (*ibid.*, 1.15). (For a full discussion of the difference between the Schools in regard to the relative importance of study and action, see *Akiba,* pp. 49ff., 259ff. The problem is further discussed in my *Introduction to the Treatises Abot and Abot of Rabbi Nathan,* pp. 59 ff.).

Therefore the Hillelite view which based distinction on learning could not be accepted by the Shammaites. If the human impulse to primacy was to be given any satisfaction at all, it had to be in the eschatological future and in the doctrine that the pious of Israel who performed good deeds would be resurrected regardless of their degree of learning. This is the doctrine enunciated by Rabbi Eliezer, the leading Shammaitic figure of his day (*B. Sanhedrin,* 104a).

III

In a further effort to satisfy the spiritual and intellectual craving for universal human brotherhood and at the same time to leave some room for the human impulse to maintain one's national and traditional identity even in a world fully united, ancient liturgists resorted to the combination in prayer of a petition for the establishment of a Society of All Mankind dedicated to the Divine worship, with further petition that in such a world Israel may be given an honorable place, those who fear God (presumably whether Jewish or Gentile) be objects of praise, the Land of Israel and particularly the Holy City be granted joy, and the dynasty of David be restored to its ancient dignity. Such a world could come about only, however, if the "Kingdom of Arrogance" disappeared from the earth.

But what is the Kingdom of Arrogance? Like wickedness and evil, it is an abstraction. It is not that the population of the Kingdom of Arrogance will disappear or be punished; but the kingdom will disappear. Whether this prayer (recited on the High Holy Days) was composed during the Hellenistic period and was directed against the Hellenistic Empires, or under Roman dominion, directed against it, is not yet definitely known. But the ancient liturgist and theologian recognized the need to direct man's hostility toward some entelechy to bring about a sense of unity, and sought to find this target in he personification of wickedness—absolutist evil in the monarchical or imperial form of government.

Recognition of the need to deal with men's psychological drives if the doctrine of universal brotherhood is to be effective in this world, is reflected in one of the most interesting exegetical debates recorded in the Talmud. The controversy divided Rabbi Akiba and his son-in-law, Ben Azzai. It concerned the interpretation of the Biblical injunction, "And thou shalt love thy neighbor as thyself, I am the Lord" (Lev. 19.18).

According to Rabbi Akiba this verse is "the most comprehensive principle of the Torah," meaning that all the detailed norms of Jewish law, as well as all the principles of Jewish theology, flow from it. Hence, when asked by a young Jew to summarize the whole Torah in one sentence, Rabbi Akiba unhesitatingly replied: "What thou dost not like, do not to thy neighbor," which is the Aramaic translation of the command, "Thou shalt love thy neighbor as thyself" (*Abot of R. Nathan,* II, chap. 26, 27a). In the Babylonian Talmud, *Shabbat*

31a, the questioner was described as a pagan who wished to become a proselyte and the person questioned was identified with Hillel. But the account in *Abot of R. Nathan* II is probably the original.

But who is one's neighbor? Rabbi Akiba maintained (in *Abot of R. Nathan* I, chap. 16, 32b) that the final phrase of the verse, "I am the Lord," was intended for commentary on the word, "neighbor." "I the Lord have created him," explained Rabbi Akiba. The context suggested to Rabbi Akiba that anyone created by God must be granted love, the expression, "thy neighbor," there included all humanity.

Accepting this interpretation of the verse, Rabbi Akiba was compelled to explain it negatively rather than positively. He could not demand that one should offer all mankind the utmost positive love. That degree of devotion must be reserved for those nearest one, wife, children, parents, brothers. But one could refrain from doing injury to another, such as one would like to avoid for himself. This principle, according to Rabbi Akiba, underlies the whole normative system of Judaism, and following the interpretation of the Babylonian Talmud, in its version of the story, also the whole of Jewish theology.

But this interpretation of the term, "thy neighbor," rejected by most modern commentators on Leviticus, was opposed also by many of Rabbi Akiba's colleagues and teachers. They usually limited the meaning of the word *re^{c}a* (the Hebrew term rendered "thy neighbor" in this verse) to Israelites (cf. *e.g. Mekilta Mishpatim*, chap. 12, p. 290; chap. 15, p. 302; *et al.*). They held that the Jewish civil law outlined in Exodus and other parts of the Pentateuch applied only to Israelites, and need not be enforced on the pagan population, even when Judaea was a sovereign state. Rabbi Akiba's interpretation of the world *re^{c}a* would suggest that, while a Gentile could not be compelled to submit to Pentateuchal civil law, he was subject to both its penalties and its protection if he voluntarily accepted this Law (*Baba Qdmma* 113a). Rabbi Akiba's opponents held that a pagan could, if he so desired, accept the responsibilities of Jewish law, as opposed to the Hellenistic or Roman system; but he could not demand the protection of Jewish law when that happened to be more lenient (see *Sifre* Deut., *loc. cit.*; and cf. Yer. *Baba Kamma* 4.3, 4b).

Interpreting the word *re^{c}a*, in this narrow sense, Ben Azzai could not agree that Leviticus 19.18 was the all-embracing norm of the Torah. He found this underlying principle in the thrice repeated assertion of Genesis, "In the image of God, hath He made man" (Gen. 9.6; cf. *ibid.*, 1.27, 5.1).

Ben Azzai's doctrine maintained while it is not possible, and may not even be right for one to try to love all mankind as one's nearest kin, one could and should offer every fellow human being supreme respect, as being made in the Image of God. This Image was given Adam, inherited according to Genesis 5.2 by Seth, and from him descended to all human beings.

However, Rabbi Akiba, in his turn, could not accept the description of man being made in the Divine Image for a comprehensive premise from which to deduce the whole Pentateuchal law, because Rabbi Akiba denied that there was a Divine Image. He considered that anthropomorphic conception of God primitive and incorrect. That is why he stated, "Beloved is Man in that he was created in an Image. Special love was shown him, in that he has been told that he has been created in an Image" (Mishna *Abot* 3.14).

Rabbi Akiba thus rendered Genesis 1.27, "And God created man in his image; in an image, did God create him." Genesis 5.1 is to be translated according to this view, "In the day that God created man, in the likeness, He created him." The analogous passage in Genesis 9.6, is to be translated, "for in an image, did God create man." Rabbi Akiba's point is that all men have the same distinctive image given them by God, and different from that of every other living being. He found nothing in the verses quoted to suggest that God himself shares that image.

And, indeed, it may be argued that each verse cited is deliberately ambiguous, leaving room for a primitive anthropomorphic conception of God, yet also for the sophisticated interpretation given by Rabbi Akiba.

Both Ben Azzai and Rabbi Akiba agreed in demanding supreme respect for each individual Man. They disagreed only in regard to whether this supreme dignity of Man derives from his bearing a Divine Image or in his having been given the distinctive Image, which is his glory.

On another occasion Rabbi Akiba expressed his views somewhat differently. Apparently he bore in mind an ancient concept which interrelates the first five commandments and the second five, so that each of the first five corresponded in some way to each of the second five. Thus the First Commandment, stating, "I am the Lord thy God," corresponded to "Thou shalt not kill" (*Mekilta, Behodesh,* chap. 8, p. 233). Hence, continues the *Mekilta,* "we learn that anyone who sheds blood is considered as though he were diminishing the likeness of the King, as it is said, 'Whosoever sheddeth man's blood, by man shall his blood be shed, for in the Image, did God make man.'" (I take it that the Hillelite authors of the original homily in the *Mekilta,* like Rabbi Akiba, interpreted the verse non-anthropomorphically. Therefore use of the expression, *"is considered as though he were diminishing the likeness of the King."* The comment is elaborated in the *Mekilta* through the obvious contemporary parable that anyone who destroyed a statue of the Emperor was treated as having insulted the Emperor himself. But this parable may be an editorial addition to the original comment, which possibly derives from the oldest teachers of the Hillelite school or even their predecessors.)

But Rabbi Akiba, holding that the "likeness" to which Scripture refers was not the likeness of God, but "a likeness" or "an image," stated categorically (in *Tosefta Yebamot* 8.4, p. 250), "He who sheds blood *destroys* the Image, for it is said, 'Whosoever sheddeth man's blood, by man shall his blood be shed, for in the Image, did God make man.'" Rabbi Akiba would not use so strong an expression as "*destroys* the likeness," if he were thinking of the Divine Image. He would rather have employed a circumlocution, such as "is considered as though he diminished the Divine Image." The assertion that the murderer actually *destroys the likeness* points clearly to Rabbi Akiba's doctrine that "the Image" and "the likeness" mentioned in Genesis were the distinctive features of man, and not of the Deity.

In fact, the editors of *Bereshit Rabbah* (chap. 34.14, p. 326), no longer distinguishing Rabbi Akiba's theological doctrine from that of his colleagues, emended his statement, so that it read: "Whosoever sheds blood *is considered by Scripture as though* he had diminished the Likeness."

That the statement of Rabbi Akiba, as cited in *Tosefta Yebamot,* was formulated with deliberate intent to emphasize his theological anti-anthropomorphism, is clear from the contrast between his language and that of Rabbi Eleazar Ben Azariah and Ben Azzai, who took issue with him.

They and Rabbi Eliezer—whose views, omitted in *Tosefta,* are cited elsewhere (*B. Yebamot* 63b)—addressed themselves to a problem which threatened the very survival of the Jewish people after the destruction of Jerusalem by Titus. Discouraged by their defeat and, even worse, disillusioned in their faith that the Divine Temple would prove inviolable, many Jews (notably, it seems, influenced by the pro-Shammaitic priestly attitudes) decided that the time had come for the Jews to disappear as a people. A number chose the path of assimilation with the Gentile world (cf. *Yer. Yebamot* 9a). But some, unable to bear the thought of assimilation, refrained from marriage and refused to found families (*B. Baba Batra* 60b).

IV

Probably talking to them, Rabbi Eliezer maintained that "One who refrained from the duty of procreation (and perpetuation of the species) may be likened to one who sheds blood." Rabbi Eleazar Ben Azariah, his much younger colleague, also of Shammaitic bent of mind and doubtless with a considerable Shammaitic following, said that such a person, "acts like one who diminishes the Likeness." The point made by Rabbi Eleazar Ben Azariah was apparently that every human being is an Image of God, and might be compared (as in the *Mekilta* passage cited above) to a royal statue. Hence, one who has children multiplies Divine Images and likenesses. However, man's Divine likeness consists not in his physical features, but in his mind and spirit. Therefore one who refrains from begetting children, limiting the possible emergence of a human mind and spirit, is comparable to the person who fails to set up a royal likeness. Combining the views of Rabbi Eliezer and Rabbi Eleazar Ben Azariah, Ben Azzai maintained that one refraining from procreation may be considered both as though he had shed blood and as though he had limited the number of Divine likenesses.

It is clear that Rabbi Eleazar Ben Azariah interpreted the anthropomorphic verses in Scripture to mean that man is actually made in the Divine likeness, *viz.* in the sense that he shares Divine power of the right. Rabbi Eliezer did not wish to commit himself on the theological question of such anthropomorphism, but held that failure to procreate, leading to death of the species, could be compared to murder. Ben Azzai combined the two views, holding that the anthropomorphically minded should be impressed with the statement of Rabbi Eleazar Ben Azariah and the non-anthropomorphically minded with that of Rabbi Eliezer.

Both Ben Azzai and Rabbi Eleazar Ben Azariah employed the expression "acts as if," in drawing the analogy between the childless person and the one who fails to set up an Image fo the King. Rabbi Akiba, as we have noticed, used a much stronger expression in regard to the murderer. The murdered, he held, "destroys the Image."

Ben Azzai and Rabbi Eleazar could not accept Rabbi Akiba's view because they thought even a murder cannot destroy the likeness of God. If that were possible the Image would be destroyed by death—which is inconceivable. Identifying the "Likeness" with man's intellect and spirit, which are indestructible by death, they held that failure to procreate is, in effect, only to limit the number of Divine likenesses.

V

Seeking to find a system in this welter of opposing views, Maimonides in his Code necessarily accepted the view of Rabbi Joshua and the Hillelites that the "saints of the nations of the world will have immortality." In this decision, he simply followed the general Talmudic principle which in a controversy between the Schools of Hillel and Shammai, accepts the Hillelite view. In a controversy between Shammaite Rabbi Eliezer and Hillelite Rabbi Joshua, the view of Rabbi Joshua should prevail.

But Maimonides rejected the doctrine that a Gentile who studies the Torah is like a high priest, or that he is even required to study the Torah. He ought to devote himself only to the study and analysis of the seven Noachic commandments (*Hilkot Melakim* 10.9). Indeed, for a Gentile to study the Torah might be to court Divine punishment, according to Rabbi Johanan (*B. Sanhedrin* 59), presumably because, in the study of the Torah, he will become aware of the Divine will, as revealed to the Prophets of Israel, yet continue to violate it. Nor could Maimonides accept the view that in Israel immortality will be granted only to those engaged in study of Torah. On the contrary, practice of the Divine commandments was, for him, a symbolic assertion of belief in the reality of God, in the process of Creation, and in the fundamental doctrines to which (in his opinion) Judaism held all men should adhere.

Therefore he had to maintain that just as a Jew, who observed the commandments merely because he considered them wise, although of human origin and not Divinely revealed, would not obtain immortality; so also a Gentile, who followed the Noachic commandments only from philosophical conviction, did not really enter into their spirit, did not really understand them, and therefore could not achieve immortality. Such a person might be considered one of the Sages of the Gentiles (this is the correct reading of Maimonides' text, as shown by the comments of some interpreters), but was not one of "the saints of the peoples of the world."

In this respect, Maimonides appears to have added to the concept of the earlier Talmudists. In their enumeration of the Noachic laws, they failed to include belief in the God of Israel or worship of Him. On the contrary, the Noachic laws simply prohibited idol-worship and blasphemy which, in the Prophetic conception, were the equivalent of immortality, for the Cananite idol-worship involved many degraded practices, indicated in Leviticus 18.23 ff.

According to the Talmud, the Gentiles need not maintain the unity of God in order to achieve immortality. Jews are forbidden to associate the Deity with any other being, such as is postulated for example in Zoroastrian dualism, but the descendants of Noah are subject to no such prohibition.

In the Messianic Age, having witnessed the miracle of the Resurrection, the abolition of drives to aggression and competition, and hence the disappearance of war, (according to the Rabbinic sages, like the Prophets before them) all the nations of the world will worship the One God, but each will maintain its culture, its identity, its traditions and its way of life. The long struggle of Man to overcome divisive impulses will at last have come to an end. Freed from hunger for power and priority and from sibling rivalry, mankind will be filled with knowledge of the Lord, even as the waters cover the sea.

REFERENCES

FINKELSTEIN, Louis, *Akiba: Scholar, Saint and Martyr*, World Publishing Company, Cleveland, and the Jewish Publication Society, Philadelphia, 1962.

——, *Introduction to the Treatises Abot and Abot of Rabbi Nathan*, The Stroock Publication Fund, New York, 1950.

GINZBERG, Louis, *On Jewish Law and Lore*, The Jewish Publication Society, Philadelphia, 1955.

LIEBERMAN, Saul, *Greek in Jewish Palestine*, The Jewish Theological Seminary of America, New York, 1942.

THE ISLAMIC INVOLVEMENT IN THE PROCESS OF HISTORY

BY

A. H. ABDEL KADER

The Islamic Center, Washington, D.C.

Unlike its predecessors, Islam entered into history as both a religion and a state whose personality had transpired during the life of Muhammad over a span of twenty-three years. Islam as a religion injected into the nascent state new ideas and institutions, and nourished it with free thinking, discipline, and equality. Such ideas were destined to transform the whole structure of the social strata.

As such, Islam did not emerge in history only as a purely spiritual discipline inspired by God. On the contrary, Islam combined, from its very inception, the sacred and the mundane. This unique emergence of Islam made it possible for it to face up to the realities of life around it, and enabled Islam to confront the inhabitants of Arabia and radically transform their state of affairs. Not only did Islam change the old and anachronistic beliefs of the pagan Arabs, but it also ushered in a new era which gave rise to a new civilization which was destined to flower and attain the pinnacle of advancement in the Middle Ages.

The main assumption on which this present paper is based, then, is that Islam has a comprehensive nature which is intrinsically capable of setting forth guidelines to the society, and is equally capable of guiding the individual Muslim vis-à-vis his God, his fellow Muslims, and the human society at large.

Such unique nature of Islam has continued to affect the thinking and attitudes of Muslims throughout their long and variegated history, albeit such history waxed and waned and suffered moments of eclipse.

The comprehensive nature of Islam was a complete reversal of the old Arabian paganism, and an antithesis of their inherited provinciality and ignorance. It heralded the coming into focus of a new role of individual freedom since such individual freedom was not confined to any special stratum in the social hierarchy, but was equally shared by all.

Islam thus dealt a mortal blow to the idea that people were divided into commoners and nobles, and, at the same time, gave a vivid impetus to the idea of equality among all people. In other words, Muslims were supposed to be *one nation,* unified and indivisible.

> They were no longer the common people, the object of history, but the nation, the subject of history, chosen to do great things in which everyone, equally and individually, was called to participate. [1]

In his sense, Islam has founded a nation, for the first time in history, simultaneously predicated upon religio-socio and political underpinnings in which the individual was directly subject to the law of Islam. If this idea is carried further to its logical conclusions, and if we may consider the law of Islam as a sort of regional international law, according to the modern usage of the term, then the position of the individual in regard to Islamic law is a very revolutionary one indeed.

Transferred from the seventh century to the twentieth century, this means that Islam has made the individual a subject of international law, a position which modern publicists are desperately trying to gain for modern individuals.

One can easily construe from the idea of this notion that Islam permitted its adherents to maintain their different nationalities as long as they believed in one God and abided by the code of conduct set forth by Islam.

Again, this comprehensive nature of Islam manifests itself more readily when one deals with Islam as a religion in the technical sense of the word. In this regard, Islam projects its message as a universal call to all mankind conceived as a single human fraternity. It must be emphasized, once again, that the objective of Islam, though universal, was not meant in any way to obliterate all the national attachments of the people who had succumbed to its call and amalgamate them forcibly into a single national entity. This is why Islam can be adequately defined as the universal religion from which peoples, societies, and social and political movements derive their motivation, their rationale, their meaningful forms, and their influence. It is not only a commonplace word or a loose expression. It is a concrete word with a concrete and definable content, which encompasses both centrifugal and centripetal force which makes their influences felt both on the individual and the society.

---

[1] Hans Kohn, cited in *Religion and Progress in Modern Asia*, Robert Bellah, ed., (New York, The Free Press, 1965), p. 197.

This is why it can be broadly maintained that whatever happened in history since the beginning of Islam can be readily understood within the framework of Islam. Indeed, Islam never meant to melt away national entities and mold them anew into a single Islamic grouping. It has constantly adhered to and maintained the principle of human diversity. This is only a practical and realistic outlook on the part of Islam, since it is humanly impossible, though logically probable that different and often divergent groups can be made into a single nation under one central authority. In fact, this idea derives directly from the Holy Quran as the following verses indicate:

> "O Mankind! We created you from a single (pair) of a male and a female, and made you into nations and tribes, that ye may know each other (not that ye may despise each other)."
>
> (Chapter 49, verse 13)

The Quran also says:

> "If your Lord has so willed, he could have made mankind one people; but they will not cease to be diversified."
>
> (Chapter 11, verse 118)

Thus, while Islam recognizes the division of the world into different national groupings, it alludes at the same time to the idea of interdependence which is easily discernible from Islam's emphasis on understanding.

In light of these terms, it becomes easy to explain why so many national entities accepted Islam so readily and so willingly since they were assured, right from the beginning, that their acceptance of Islam was not to impinge upon their national heritage.

From the foregoing, one can reason why it is not unusual or strange, under the present circumstances, that the idea of pan-Islamism is not too powerful a force as might have been anticipated. Moreover, it is the national interest, and not the common religious heritage, which motivates, directs, and guides foreign policies of any given Muslim national state, as is the case in the west. This notion shall be explained further when we talk about the Muslim state and its external relations.

In order to understand the Islamic state, it is essential to bear in mind the premise which we have established at the very beginning of this paper, namely, that Islam is a state and religion or a way of life. The Islamic state is not a "theocracy" in the medieval sense of the word. Although God is the supreme ruler of the Islamic state and the originator of its fundamental law, the Islamic state nevertheless is distinctly characterized by the absence of a professional clergy. Moreover, the Muslim ruler is not the one to initiate law, but he supervises the execution of and abides by the law.

The head of the Islamic state is chosen by the Muslim community. His mandate and authority derive from his observance of the Holy Quran and its interpretation.

It is essential to know the manner in which the Muslim state communicates with non-Muslim nations. Although Muslim jurists agree, as we have indicated earlier, that Islam is a universal religion which ties its followers all over the world by the religious bonds, they nevertheless disagree on the manner in which the Muslim state should conduct its relations with other non-Muslim states. This disagreement has given rise to two diametrically opposed schools of thought.

The first school of thought can be understood in the following propositions: Since the message of Islam is universal, the experts of this school argue that the call to acceptance of Islam is compulsory. The mechanics by which Islam is conveyed to non-Muslims is twofold, peaceful and belligerent. At first, Muslims must invite unbelievers to Islam verbally, and when the latter refuse to accept Islam, then it becomes incumbent upon the former to fight them until they accept Islam.

This school of thought predicates its thesis on these premises:

1. The Jihad, or holy warfare, is compulsory and cannot be renounced or abandoned save for tactical reasons or military unpreparedness.
2. The basis of the relationship between the Muslims and non-Muslims is war unless the unbelievers have accepted Islam or there is temporary peace between the believers and the non-believers.
3. The world, as such, is divided into *Darul Islam* (the abode of Islam), and *Darul Harb* (the abode of war).

Such premises and assumptions are too fragile to stand any criticism. This school of thought is opposed by the very text of the Holy Quran, the main document of the religion of Islam. Yet it seems that, though weak and unauthoritative as it is, this school of thought has been magnified out of proportion. It is being held and expounded by some writers in the west as representative of Islamic legal theory.

To cite some examples of the proponents of this theory, such writers as Gibb, Bowen, and Khadduri readily come to mind. Professors Gibb and Bowen are of the opinion that the world is divided into two parts, "...the domain of Islam, and the domain of war. It is the duty of the true believers, where they can, to extend the first at the expense of the second." [1] At first glance, this quotation would immediately mean that Islam had to expand at the very edge of the sword. War, according to both writers, is motivated by religious faith and not by external dangers. One can easily construe from the theme of both writers that Islam is a very militant religion indeed.

Again, the same theory is brought into focus in the following manner: "The impossibility of universalizing Islam and the failure to set up a world state divided the world into the *world of Islam* and *the world of war*." [2] And, in another instance, writes Khadduri, "The Pax Islamica (or the abode of Islam) was in theory in a state of war with the *Darul Harb* because the ultimate objective of Islam was the world." [3]

Once more the same contention is brought into focus in another fashion:

"Islamic law recognizes no other nation than its own since the aim of Islam was the subordination of the whole world to one system of law and religion to be enforced by the supreme authority of the caliph." [4]

In other words, Islam has to go on fighting until the whole world is conquered and converted! One can go on citing numerous statements, especially from the last quoted writers, that leave no doubt in the mind of the reader about the bellicose nature of Islam.

It is our duty here in this august gathering to know the facts about the various religious systems of the world. It is not my duty to propagate Islam in this academic society or to any other society for that matter. This is why I am going to address myself to the refutation of the aforementioned theory which has prevailed for so long in the west.

The genuine Islamic theory in regard to how a Muslim state discharges its activities and conducts its relations with other non-Muslim states can be summed up as follows:

---

[1] H. A. R. Gibb and Harold Bowen, *Islamic Society and the West*, Vol. 1 (London, Oxford University Press, 1951), p. 20.
[2] Majid Khadduri, and H. J. Liebesny (eds.), *Law in the Middle East*, Vol. 1, *The Middle East*, Institute, Washington, D.C. (Richmond, William Byrd Press, 1955), p. 359.
[3] J. Harriss Proctor (ed.), *Islam and International Relations*, (Praeger, New York, 1965), p. 26.
[4] Khadduri, *op. cit.*, p. 350.

1. The first assumption is that the basis of a Muslim's relationship with non-Muslims is peace, not war. Islam only legalizes war against non-Muslims if and when they attack Muslims. This is a simple doctrine of self-defense which has been enshired in the fabric of modern international law, and this is the exact teaching of the Holy Quran as illustrated in chapter 60 as follows:

> "God forbids you not, with regard to those who fight you not for (your) faith nor drive you out of your homes from dealing kindly and justly with them for God loves those who are just. God only forbids you, with regard to those who fight you for your faith and drive you out of your homes, and support (others) in driving you out from turning to them (for friendship and protection)." [1]

Moreover, the Islamic verses dealing with war determine the causes of fighting as one of two things, to terminate injustice, or to protect the call. This is supported by the Holy Quran as follows:

> "Fight in the cause of God those who fight you, but do not transgress limits. For God loves not transgressors. And slay them wherever you catch them, and turn them out from where they have turned you out, for tumult and oppression are worse than slaughter. But fight them not at the sacred mosque, unless they (first) fight you there. But if they fight you, slay them. Such is the reward of those who suppress faith. But if they cease, God is oft-forgiving, most merciful. And fight them until there is no more tumult or oppression, and there prevail justice and faith in God. But if they cease let there be no hostility except to those who practice oppression." [2]

Again, the Holy Quran says:

> "Tho those against whom war is made, permission is given (to fight), because they are wronged:—and verily, God is most powerful for their aid:—they are those who have been expelled from their homes in defense of right—(for no cause) except they say, 'Our Lord is God.'" [3]

Once again, the Quran affirms the establishment of peace as follows:

> "Invite (all) to the way of your Lord with wisdom and beautiful preaching, and argue with them in ways that are best and most gracious...." [4]

---

[1] *Quran*, Chapter 60: 8-9.
[2] *Ibid.*, Chapter 2: 190-193.
[3] *Ibid.*, Chapter 22: 39-40.
[4] *Ibid.*, Chapter 6: 125.

2. The consensus of Muslim jurists forbids the killing of non-Muslim women, boys, monks, old men, the blind, the invalid, and the like, because they are not warriors. Had fighting been for the dissemination of Islam by force, such would have never been the case. The fact that they have been excepted is evidence that fighting is only invoked against those who start it.

3. It is a well-attested fact that Islam does not force non-Muslims to accept it. This is simply because to accept a religion is to commit its creed to one's heart, and this is only attainable through good reasoning and rationalization and not through the use of the sword. This is crystal clear in the Quran as it says:

"Let there be no compulsion in religion..." [1]

and

"If it had been your Lord's will, they would all have believed,—all who are on earth! Will you then compel mankind against their will to believe!" [2]

Thus, the proponents of this theory establish the relationship of the Muslim state with the non-Muslim world on two basic principles: The first is that the call to Islam is required only of *some,* not *all,* Muslims. The second is that *Darul Islam,* or the abode of Islam, is the territory in which Muslim law prevails, and in which Muslims enjoy complete protection, whereas *Darul Harb,* or the abode of war, is the territory or country whose relations with the Muslim country have undergone drastic and dramatic changes as a result of an act of aggression against the Muslim state or its interests. It is only under a state of war that we may apply such terminology as the abode of Islam and the abode of war. As for the non-Muslim nation that has not attacked the Muslim nation, but rather has maintained friendly relations with it, it is not permissible for Muslims to attack or terminate the friendly relations. It is incumbent upon Muslims to maintain peace with each nation, and it must be known that peace in this case is not the result of a treaty or an agreement, but it is the basis and rule of relationship.

From the preceding, it becomes evident that the contention of some writers that war is the basis for Muslims' relationship with non-Muslims is completely unfounded and has no support from the most

---

[1] *Ibid.,* Chapter 2: 256.
[2] *Ibid.,* Chapter 10: 99.

important document of Islam, namely, the Quran. It seems to me that their departure from the mainstream of Islamic legal theory came from their approach to, and emphasis on, the secondary sources they have utilized. They seem to have emphasized the opinion of some later jurists, without going back to the Quran, the origin of Islamic law.

At this point, it is fitting to examine how Islam got involved in the process of history. An understanding and appreciation of such an involvement cannot be adequately scrutinized without a rather thorough examination of Islam's primary source of legislation, the Quran. In the following analysis, the Quran is considered the postulate that cannot be disputed, since it has been held by all Muslim jurists that the Quran is the fundamental source of Islamic legislation.

It was the Quran, as the infallible word of God, which gave rise to the first Muslim state within the confines of the Arabian peninsula. It was on the principles of the Quran that the ever-expanding structure of the Muslim empire had been predicated. It was within the framework of the Quran that Muslim jurists, thinkers, and philosophers derived their reasoning and had given meaningful and authoritative expressions to their theories.

It was the principles of the Quran and its respect for science and learning that gave impetus to the spirit of research, translation, and academic endeavors that constituted the underpinnings of Islamic civilization and Islamic culture during the Middle Ages. In all their intellectual discourses, their scientific achievements, and their legal and theological theories, Muslims had always the Quran as their guide and the *raison d'être* of their thinking. All in all, the Quran had influenced and inspired the early Muslim intellectual community and made them dynamic in their various approaches and forward-looking in their rationalization.

Not only did the Quran influence the orthodox intellectual community, but it did also condition the attitudes and intellectual orientation of non-conformists or those who might be considered heterodox, such as the extreme Sufi sects. At this point, Goldziher observes that:

> "Every conspicuous intellectual current throughout the history of Islam had to measure its validity through the yardstick of the Divine text, and to use such text as evidence of its conformity to Islam. Only through such justification could any intellectual current claim and maintain a respectable place within the religious system of Islam." [1]

---

[1] Ignaz Goldziher, *Die Richtungen Der Islamischen Koranauslegung*, (Leiden, E. J. Brill, 1920), p. 180.

It could be said, then, that the whole fabric of Islamic culture in its glorious past and its present condition is no more than the product of the Quran and its various interpretations. Indeed, the Quran had provided early Muslim writers and thinkers with a living material from which they built up their theories and according to which they molded their thinking. Most legal, juridical, and ideological theories were only attempts at explaining the Quran and interpreting its general principles. This is what is referred to in the theological technical nomenclature as *hermeneutics,* whereby jurist-theologians would make interpretive explanations of the scriptures, resulting in the *exegesis,* or the critical evaluation, of the text itself. Although the meaning of these two words may overlap, both explain the same process. While hermeneutics refers to the method, exegesis refers to the by-product of the process.

The Quran and its interpretation, or exegesis, therefore, provided the framework within which Islamic doctrines and theories developed, beginning with the second century of the history of Islam through the tenth century, A.H.

The method by which the Quran was interpreted is twofold: The first is the apparent or immediate meaning of the text at hand which corresponds more or less with the linguistic definition of any given word. The second is the method by which explanation goes beyond the immediate meaning of the text and makes use of such logical devices as analogy and deduction. Islamic jurisprudence, therefore, is based on textual principles laid down in the Quran, on the one hand, and deductive and analogous ideas, developed by Muslim jurists, on the other. The latter includes a host of customs, mores, and usage long enshrined in old civilizations and bequeathed to Muslims, and which needed justification and sanction by the Quran. Ever since Muslims began to look into and examine such old customs and traditions, Muslim jurists directed their efforts to ground their existence and validity in the Quran and within its boundaries. And since the first method of interpretation, that which takes the text at face value, seemed rather inadequate, it was therefore necessary to utilize a more technical and elaborate method whereby the text could be interpreted in such a manner as to endow all legal and juridical theories with its aura of sanction, and at the same time to expand the text so as to meet the newly-arising needs under newly-arising circumstances in the ever-dynamic Muslim society. Islamic jurisprudence, accordingly, developed and expanded and evolved into novel ideas which met the requirements of the Muslim nation.

Such a technical and elaborate method was bound to produce new ideas with rather strained or unfamiliar constructions which had to be accepted or reconciled through the mechanism of *ijmā^c* (or the consensus of the Muslim society) which constitutes the third source of Islamic legislation. This third source was the primary factor of giving legal as well as juridical competence to the various theories developed by Muslim jurists, and still is the most dynamic and capable device to cope with the new problems and needs of the present time.

From the interpretation of the Quranic texts did emerge also what might be called *opinions,* or specific schools of thought that would have a limited applicability. Such schools of thought largely utilized such logical devices as the minor and the major, generalization, deduction, and analogy.

The evolution of Islamic jurisprudence in this fashion is generally credited to Shafei (150-204 A.H.) in his *Treatise* (*Risalah*), who used the Quran as the primary valid criterion by which the validity of his conclusions could be tested. Shafei also utilized the second major source of Islamic legislation, that is, the traditions of the Prophet. The Shafei *Risalah* was a significant point of departure in the history of Islamic legislation, since it distinguished the traditions of the Prophet Muhammad from other practices, designated such practices as one of the sources of Islamic law, and was a prelude to more intensive and rigorous studies of the traditions. Indeed, the authentic and verifiable traditions of Muhammad reflect the refinement and sophistication of Islamic social and cultural life, a fact often disputed by many orientalists, whose full exposition certainly requires more time, and which falls beyond the scope of the present paper.

From the foregoing, one could see that the Quran has been the prime mover which united Muslims throughout their history, defined their personality, and dyed Islamic culture with its unique hues from the very inception of this culture up to the present time.

Here, two points need to be emphasized. The first is that the evolution of the religious society to a legal order simply means the transformation of the Divinely-inspired ideas and ideals, which are embodied in natural law, from their pure abstraction to the realm of concrete practice and effective applicability. By the same taken, the evolution of the secular society into a legal system only means a continuing process of adaptation of certain old and, often, primitive and inadequate ideas to the mounting needs of the society. This is why we find that only in a secular society do juridical devices prevail, while in a religious society, their prevalence is not the rule, but rather, the exception.

The second point to be emphasized here is the idea of *maṣlaḥa*, i.e., public interest, which had been utilized by Malik and others, and which is considered an important element in the development of the religious society.

The concept of *maṣlaḥa* covers certain important and essential realms such as the preservation of self, property, mind, procreation, and religion. Such preservation requires the continuous and dynamic interpretation of the Quran to meet new needs in the Muslim society. The concept of *maṣlaḥa* and the idea of *ijmāᶜ* can adequately serve as the cornerstone which would provide the present Muslim society with adequate answers to its modern needs, and which would serve, at the same time, as a bulwark against all the encroachments of modern positive and secular law.

Societies, therefore, differ in the ways of their evolution and development. On the one hand, the religious society follows a vertical way in its extension and evolution descending from above downward. It evolves through the dynamic interaction of the Divine ideals with the realities of life. Such a process of interaction is meant to inject into the human existence a tempering and moderating spirit well-disposed to Divine guidance and laws.

On the other hand, secular societies follow a horizontal pattern in their development, in the sense that they are mainly concerned with everyday problems without necessarily aspiring for sublime ideals. Moreover, there is the realm of philosophy which, like the religious realm, follows a vertical approach from the higher to the lower. The philosopher, through his intellectual endeavor, tries to reach the high ideals and sublime values through humanism. Furthermore, there is the ecclesiastical community which serves as intermediary and which did not actually represent the religious society until the coming into existence of feudalism in the eleventh century.

Therefore, it can be said, in light of the preceding analysis, that Islam is the example *par excellence* of the religious society which codifies and legislates laws for its adherents within the framework of the Divine principles and natural law which are meant to be conducive to the attainment of public well-being in the Muslim society.

Indeed, the emergence of Islam in history ushered in a new era in the annals of civilizations. Different and divergent nations with conflicting interests were awakened by Islam from their long and dogmatic slumber and were united under Islam. The interaction of Islam with the various groups which came under its sway gave rise to a unique civilization based on the brotherhood of man, on the worship of one God, and on a genuine interest in world peace.

It is really amazing how Islam expanded far and wide in such a short span of time. It is even doubly striking how Islam resisted strain and stress when its adherents grew weak and defenseless. What is the secret then of Islam's ability to maintain its appeal and withstand overwhelming odds? In my judgement, this secret lies in Islam's unqualified tolerance; one of the conspicuous manifestations of such tolerance is Islam's espousal of such sublime ideas as peace, cooperation, and the freedom of worship. The expansion of Islam was bound to bring under its banner a host of diverse cultures and civilizations. The intrinsic quality of tolerance in Islam made it possible for it to assimilate such diverse cultures and "Islamize" them, i.e., make them Islamic. Islam was able to digest most of the indigenous customs of such peoples as the Persians, the Egyptians, and the Syrians, and adapt them to its flexible nature. Not only did Islam assimilate, digest, and adapt such customs, but it did contribute its own share in "developing" those peoples as it brought them new ideas and novel conceptions which became the solid premises upon which a new cultural edifice was established. In all its actions, reactions, and interactions with the various cultural systems, Islam never lost any of its basic characteristics or distinguishing features.

I think all of us here are aware of the Mongol invasions of the lands of Islam and their aftermath, of the Crusaders, and of the Spanish Inquisition and its inhuman treatment of Muslims. In all such unhappy episodes, Islam never withered away, but it withstood all these encroachments and even opened to its adversaires new vistas of knowledge and enlightenment and, in one instance, it attracted the very Mongol conquerors who were themselves conquered by its appeal.

The relative backwardness of the Muslim countries at the present time is not in any sense attributable to Islam, but to the Muslims themselves who, following the episodes of the Crusades in the eleventh to the thirteenth centuries, became overconfident of themselves, and who, during the last three cenutries of the Ottoman rule, plunged into an era of intellectual stagnation. Even then, and up until now.

Muslims have been trying to find a way out of their present impasse through the guidance of their own religion.

Students of present-day Islam all but agree on one thing, namely, that the Muslim world today is undergoing a process of transformation. Muslim societies today are being transformed from agricultural societies into industrial societies, from the traditional rural communities into the complex urban centers.

In this process of transformation, Muslim societies are in many ways analogous to European societies when the latter embarked upon an era of industrialization at the beginning of the last century. This process of transformation is bound to elicit inimitable social change which must be met with corresponding social and legal institutions capable of harnessing the potentials of such social change.

Muslim societies of the present are experiencing new innovations, inventions, discoveries, and even new behavioral patterns. The discovery of oil, industrialization, and migration of workers from their rural communities into urban centers are but a few examples of such new experiences. A concomitant result of all this is the erosion of the traditional role of the family in the Muslim societies. The family being replaced by such corporate bodies as unions, syndicates, and the like. This social change requires prompt and adequate measures for its regulation and institutionalization in order to preclude any inclination toward social anarchy.

Here we come to the crux of the problem which is facing the Muslim world today. How can Islam cope with this social change, and to what extent can it regulate it within its own framework, without losing its identity? In my judgement, the answer to this question can be readily obtained from a new outlook on Islamic legislation. Such new Islamic legislation must fully utilize the Quran and its liberal interpretation in the manner described above. The new customs and innovations are not unIslamic in spirit, but they only need Islamic justification. As such, Islam shall dominate such new inventions and discoveries and "Islamize" them, as it did in the past, while retaining its basic characteristics.

Indeed, the study of the Islamic legal system requires study of the economic basis which brought about this legal system. Even today we do not have sufficient knowledge of this economic basis nor of its juridical super-structure, nor anything precise regarding the evolution of his basis and its juridical superstructure during the last hundred years. We only see that in the different parts of the Islamic world, this economic and law phenomenon shows strong, differing movements, but we cannot recognize the exact connections about such differences.

There are four great law systems which practically put the stamp on the social and economic structure of the world. They are, to begin with, the system and mentality of the "common law" of the Anglo-Saxon version of the "general law", which also dominated the European continent until the great continental codifications of the eighteenth and nineteenth centuries.

These codifications became the starting point of a new form of sense of justice, of a new juridical system and technique which, especially under the influence of the Code Napoleon, attracted the countries of the Mediterranean sea and spread over to South America. People speak of the system of codified law when these forms of legal thought are referred to.

The third great law system is that of the Islamic law; the fourth is the Marxist system.

Theoretically, there is still a fifth system, namely the Catholic law system, explained in the *corpus juris canonici,* respectively in the *codex juris canonici*; but this system has, at the present time, no legal power in any part of the world, apart from the sovereign Vatican City.

The system of the "common law" and the European codified systems are of a liberalistic character. Until now, the much older Islamic law system has, in contrast hereto, a collective character.

The twentieth century, aparently, demands a new functionalistic, i.e., a collectivistic style, for which the Muslims have better preconditioning from their tradition than do the western Europeans. But for about a century, this collectivistic Islamic economic and legal system has been tussling with the liberalistic ideas of the other two legal systems, which will enforce their liberalistic thoughts by way of their industry and traffic economy on the Islamic world. The Islamic world has yielded in different ways to this pressure from the outside which caused, of course, a big confusion in the Islamic economic and legal system.

From this factor alone ensues a very decisive feature, the problematic development of the Islamic law. This is sharply accentuated because Islamic civilization is interwoven with a precisely calculated legal system which shows that binding power is still there, where it is only in fractures with an enforcible public law, or is merely surviving as a customary law. The dynamics of liberalistic industry and economy penetrating from the outside into the domain of the Islamic legal order superimpose a very dense social structure and stationary economic life.

In the opinion of western lawyers, the jurisprudence of the Islamic civilization is faced with the question of how far the legal order, administration, and jurisdiction must go in the technical and economic field to render the liberalistic industry and economy functionable in the countries concerned, without the apparently unavoidable decomposition process of the social structure standing in catastrophical social situations. It is obvious that such problems and their economic solutions demand a cooperation with the Islamic jurisprudence, especially in the Quran and its interpretation which widely brought Islamic law into existence.

How, for instance, is the collective factor seen in the Islamic legal and social structure? The concept of family, *"usra"*, includes, in Islamic law, the husband, wife, their children, the ascendants of the couple, their brothers, sisters, and their collaterals. The uncles, aunts, and their children belong likewise to the family. Within this big family, financial relations exist, forming the family into a kind of unionist economic and social unity. The essential feature of this unity is the mutual duty of maintenance. Still today any member of a clan is an integral member of this group. The Islamic society has no proletariat in the eastern European sense, but neither does it have a liberalistic freedom in the western European sense. There is only the collective, in the Islamic sense. There, where the liberalistic industrial-technical society planning has not yet appeared, the ancient rules are valid today: Water and agricultural implements are the property of the group. The soil is common property. The products are divided among all members. The individual is protected in the solidarity of the big family.

It is my conviction, therefore, that Islamic legislation is capable at the present time of guiding the Muslim societies in this crucial period of transformation. The Quran, therefore, must be understood in terms of a process meant to bring into focus the economic foundations of modern society. Islamic jurisprudence was never alienated or separated from the main current of Muslim life. It was always the living expression of this life, and only when Muslims abandoned the liberal outlook to the Quran, i.e., *ijtihad,* did Islamic jurisprudence lose its effectiveness and dynamism. In my judgement, therefore, the point of departure in the Muslim society today is this new outlook to the Quran and its interpretation.

Here, I find it necessary to say a word or two about some countries which, because of certain frustrations, illusions, and bewilderment, have resorted to secularism as the panacea to their social and political maladies. Had such countries interpreted the Quran in the manner discussed above, and had they considered Islam as one of the major legal systems in the world, they would probably never have thought of introducing secularism to their societies, and they would most certainly have saved themselves inevitable frustrations. This is because the collectivistic nature of Islamic jurisprudence is indeed a unique expression of the modern trends developing in the new international systems which is primarily based on interdependence and collectivism.

To sum up, one could enumerate the following conclusions:

1. Unlike other religions, Islam is both a religion and a state, a unique peculiarity that brought about its dissemination.

2. The illusory, and often misleading, idea of *Darul Harb* (Abode of War) and *Darul Islam* (Abode of Islam) is the invention of the later Muslim jurists, and has nothing to do with the genuine Islamic theory of international relations upon which we touched earlier. The idea was that Islam conceived of the old world as uncivilized, since its criterion of civilization was measured by the worship of one God. This old Islamic idea has striking similarities at the present time with the western conceptions of "developed" and "underdeveloped". Unfortunately, the idea of *Darul Harb* and *Darul Islam* has been taken seriously, though wrongly, by many orientalists and some writers here in this country.

Such overemphasis on erroneous concepts and unsubstantiated theories reveals the obvious and shocking unfamiliarity of such writers with the genuine Islamic doctrines, and, at the same time, beclouds the atmosphere of understanding between the Muslim world and the west. This is why it is high time for American scholars to open their hearts and minds for a new understanding of Islamic culture and principles which share a great deal with western civilization. If such an understanding is attainable, and I believe it could be attained, then western and Islamic cultures shall contribute immensely to world peace and world order.

3. The Quran was the rich and undefined source of legislation which gave support and meaning to all the Islamic intellectual activities in the past.

4. Islamic jurisprudence, which derives from the Quran and which reflects the needs of the Muslim societies, is the most valid legislation for Muslims in the twentieth century.

5. The introduction of secularism into the Muslim world is a sign of intellectual incompetence to portray a new Muslim personality in the context of modern times.

II

INVOLVEMENT OF THE RELIGIONS IN MODERN SOCIETY

THE HISTORIC CHINESE CONTRIBUTION TO RELIGIOUS PLURALISM AND WORLD COMMUNITY

BY

WING-TSIT CHAN

Dartmouth

A burning question for all of us is when and how Mainland China will again be a fully-accepted member of the world community. At the time when Mainland China is ruled by a monolithic system based on a single ideology requiring absolute conformity, it seems out of tune to speak of pluralism in China. Rulers in Mainland China proudly declare that they have the only system of belief that will bring happiness and freedom to all. It seems that China is destined to be under monolithic domination for a long time to come, permitting neither difference nor coexistence.

Yet if we look at the situation from a broader perspective, pluralism is by no means dead; in fact, it has been more alive than most people believe. After all, the Chinese Communists came to power through a way different from the orthodox one, that is, through revolution by the peasant rather than the proletariat. For many years the Chinese Communists promoted a third block of neutral countries, thus definitely showing a pluralistic tendency. The present controversy with Russia may be considered as a concrete attempt to overthrow the monolithic leadership of Russia. At any rate, the Fundamental Principle of the People's Republic formulated in 1949 is based on the both-and principle, equally emphasizing the worker and the peasant, industry and agriculture, urban and rural developments, national and international programs, etc. The "Let One Hundred Flowers Bloom and Let One Hundred Schools Contend" movement of 1957 was a clear admission of the existence of a pluralistic element in Chinese thought. The subsequent indoctrination and coerced confessions seemed to have reduced this element to the minimum. Nevertheless, in the debates on Lao Tzu and Confucius since 1959, the attempt of a number of writers and speakers to identify Lao Tzu as a materialist and Confucius as a feudalist has failed to obtain a majority support.

The two sages have been characterized by many others in a great variety of ways. The one hundred flowers may not be blooming at present but the one hundred schools are still contending.

I

On the religious scene, a similar picture can be seen. Of course, like other institutions, all religions have to support the state. Many Buddhist monks and nuns and Taoist priests have been forced back to lay life and to join agricultural production teams. Activities of noncooperative churches and temples, especially those of the Catholics, have been suppressed, but politically loyal institutions have been subsidized and encouraged. The Communists frankly say that religion is opium for the people and will be discarded by them as soon as they regain intellectual health and no longer need the narcotic. In the meantime—and the mean time may turn out to be a long time—the different religions in China are carrying on. The fact that government leaders have established a Chinese national organization of Catholicism should not be understood merely as a matter of politics. Underlying it is the refusal of the Chinese to accept a singular, universal religious authority.

The foregoing suggests that there has been in the Chinese tradition a strong sense of pluralism which persists even in a strongly monolithic situation. And this pluralistic spirit has been the most prominent and most enduring in the sphere of religion. It has often been said that in the last 1800 years the three religions of Confucianism, Buddhism, and Taoism have been going on in parallel, harmonized, or synthesized. (Confucianism is here understood not in the sense of an organized religion, for it is not an established cult but a system of doctrines that contains essentially religious features, and a movement that has promoted the traditional worship of Heaven and sacrifice to ancestors. It is not uncommon to find in a Chinese family a Buddhist father, a Taoist mother, and a Confucian son. In fact, it is incorrect to call a typical Chinese a Confucianist, a Taoist, or a Buddhist, so far as religious beliefs are concerned.) There are still thousands, or perhaps hundreds of thousands, of Buddhist monks and nuns who have renounced family life, shaved their heads, wear a religious robe opening to the left instead of the right as in the old tradition, become vegetarians, and live on alms. There are still Taoist priests who may or may not be vegetarians and live a celibate life—though their number is much smaller than that of the Buddhist priests. There are probably hundreds of thousands, if not millions, of Buddhists-at-home who are vegetarians and perform special rites at home on certain occasions. And there are millions of Catholics and Protestants and probably tens of millions of Muslims. Still all these constitute only a small minority of the Chinese population. Of course, Muslims and Christians follow one religion exclusively. The rest of the Chinese, the great majority, however, cannot be described as exclusive followers of Confucianism, Buddhism, or Taoism either in the broad sense of systems of thought or in the narrow sense of an organized religion.

In the realm of religion, many of them follow the three religions at the same time, visiting Buddhist or Taoist temples as the need arises and also perform Confucian rites before their ancestors. Temples dedicated to the Three Sages are found in all parts of China, and some of them even include representations of Islam, Christianity, and Judaism. In funeral and other religious ceremonies and in community festivals, Buddhist and Taoist priests and laymen of various beliefs perform the rites together. Religious doctrines, symbols, ceremonies, and even deities have been so intermingled that scholars cannot tell if they are of Confucian, Buddhist, or Taoist origin. It is often said that the average Chinese is one who wears a Confucian crown, so to speak, a Taoist robe, and Buddhist sandals. When Chang Jung (444-497) died, he held in his left hand a copy of the Confucian *Classic of Filial Piety* and the Taoist classic, the *Tao-te ching,* and in his right hand the Buddhist *Lotus Scripture*. He has been hailed as an exemplary Chinese.

II

This coexistence, harmony, or even synthesis of the three religions throughout Chinese history has been a shining example of the amiable relationship among religions. Lest I am drawing too rosy a picture, let me quickly add that Chinese history has by no means been completely devoid of religious controversy or persecution. Buddhists and Taoists quarreled off and on for three hundred years from the fourth through the sixth centuries. The controversy began with the Taoist Wang Fu (265-317) who, perhaps on the basis of a tradition a century or so earlier, spread the story that when Lao Tzu went beyond the pass to the west in the sixth century B.C., he was really going there to convert the barbarians. There he became a Buddha, Wang said. [1] It was claimed that Lao Tzu was Gotama's senior and that Gotama was Lao Tzu's disciple. The Buddhists rejected such a claim and maintained that the Buddha was Lao Tzu's senior and therefore Buddhism was superior. The controversy became as bitter as it was long lasting. In North China, the struggle was mostly for power and often resulted in actual hostility. In the south, the dispute chiefly centered on doctrines. The Taoists, who were joined by some Confucianists, denounced Buddhism on three grounds: that it was unsuitable to Chinese conditions and life, that Taoism was more basic whereas Buddhism was secondary, and that the fact that the spirit is destructible disproved the Buddhist doctrine of transmigration, the very foundation of the Buddhist faith at that time. The Buddhist countered with the assertion that Buddhism was more fundamental than either Taoism or Confucianism because, they said, while the two native religions offered a good way of life, Buddhism alone penetrated the very nature of existence. Both sides forged scriptures to prove their claims and invented more silly and more silly stories. The controversy became so intolerable that in 574 Emperor Wu (r. 561-578) ordered more than 20,000 Buddhist monks and Taoist priests back to lay life. Buddhists and Taoists have called this even a "catastrophe".

Fortunately for China, long before this catastrophe took place, the Buddhists, Taoists, and Confucianists began to resolve their conflicts. It is significant that even at the height of their quarrel, they did not condemn other religions as untrue or wicked. They conceded a degree of truth in them and granted that the others were also a good way of life, though not quite as good as their own. The bone of contention was priority or superiority but not absolute authority or exclusive domain. There was no attempt on the part of any to wipe out, swallow, or dominate the rest. Their approach was essentially a pluralistic and a comparative one. Once they started along this direction, they inevitably ended up in the coexistence, harmony, or synthesis of the three religions.

Two developments, quite unusual if not unique in human history, added impetus in this direction. One was that of "matching ideas." When Buddhist thought developed in China in the fourth century, many Buddhist works were brought into China and needed translation.

---

[1] In his *Hua-hu ching* (Scripture on the conversion of the barbarians). For the earliest mention of this story, see the *Hou-Han shu* (History of the Later Han dynasty), ch. 60, pt. 2.

A number of new ideas had to be explained. Monk Fa-ya invented the method of "matching ideas" whereby a Buddhist term or idea was explained by one in Taoism. For example, *tathatā* (thusness, ultimate reality) was equated with the Taoist term "original non-being" (*pen-wu*, pure being). The Buddha was called a sage. Perhaps the original intention was purely to resort to Taoist terms as an expediency in translation or perhaps as a convenient means to teach students, but it paved the way for close contacts between Buddhist and Taoist thinkers. This activity reached a high level especially in the south. When the capital of Lo-yang in the north fell in 316, the government moved to the south and many of the literati as well as Buddhist monks fled with it. Both groups being refugees, they became intimate and, as a result free and frequent interchange of ideas took place. The upshot was a new development in Buddhist thought essentially along Taoist, or rather, Neo-Taoist, lines. As the fundamental problem of Neo-Taoism was that of being and non-being, and since the Neo-Taoists conceived fundamental reality to be original non-being, the Buddhists similarly developed their own thought along these lines. The seven early Buddhist schools, six of which flourished in the south, regarded ultimate reality, as did the Neo-Taoists, as transcending all being, names, and form, and as empty and quiet in nature. This affinity in basic thought in the two systems not only brought themselves together but also had a liberalizing effect on Confucianism.

As to persecution, the most notorious were the so-called "three Wus and one Tsung," namely, the persecution of Buddhism in 446 under Emperor T'ai-wu (r. 424-452) of the Northern Wei dynasty, in 574 under Emperor Wu of Northern Chou, in 845 under Emperor Wu-tsung (r. 841-846) of T'ang, and in 955 under Emperor Shih tsung (r. 945-959) of Later Chou. Three of these were limited in extent of severity and in geographical scope. We have already referred to the painful event of 574. The persecution of 845, however, was far more vigorous and had a lasting effect. More than 4,600 large temples and monasteries and 40,000 smaller ones were demolished. About 260,500 monks and nuns were forced to return to lay life. Some 150,000 slaves were taken over. And tens of millions of acres of land was confiscated.[1] Buddhism itself did not die out, but Manichaeanism, Zoroastrianism, and Nestorian Christianity, innocent bystanders all, virtually ceased to exist. There can be no denial that the black mark of intolerance has marred the pages of Chinese history.

[1] According to the *T'ang-shu* (History of the T'ang dynasty), ch. 18, pt. 1.

However, two things can be said about the persecutions that will help us to see them in a proper perspective. One is that the persecutions lasted for only a short time in China's long history and have never attained the degree of bloodshed as in other countries. The other is that the persecutions were at bottom political and economic in nature rather than religious. In the case of 845, for example, no religious issue was involved. There was no intention to destroy the religion itself or to suppress its beliefs. Many temples were allowed to remain and priests permitted to stay to look after them. In the central capital and in the eastern capital, for instance, two temples were allowed to remain in each street and thirty monks permitted to stay in each of them. [1] The issues were basically political and economic, for too many able-bodied men had joined the monasteries and thus became unavailable for agricultural production and army or labor conscription, and too much land belonged to the Buddhist church and had thus become tax exempt. In these ways Buddhism not only deserted society but actually presented a threat to national defense and national economy. Significantly, confiscated images of bronze were made into currency, those of iron made into agricultural implements, and those of gold and silver turned over to the Treasury, while images of wood, clay, or stone were left untouched. The despotic measures are of course not to be excused, but the nature of the action, however undemocratic, was not anti-religious in the real meaning of the term.

III

Note that the controversies and persecutions we have been talking about took place more than a thousand years ago. In the last millennium or more, the three religions have been going on in harmony, at many points interlocked and syncretized. What is more remarkable is that at the very height of the anti-religious movement in the twentieth century, to which we shall return later, not only did new religious societies arise, but they were also all syncretic in character. We need not go into the details of this extremely meaningful development. Suffice it to identify them in rapid succession: The Society of World Religions was organized in Szechuan by T'ang Huan-chang in 1915, the International Society of Holy Religions was founded in Peking about the same time, the Society for Heart Washing was established in 1917 or 1920, the Universal Ethical Society was founded in 1921,

---

[1] See the Hsin-T'ang-shu (New History of the T'ang dynasty), ch. 52.

the Ethical Study Society was established in 1924, the Wu-shan She or the Society for Understanding of the Good in about 1915, the T'ung-shan She or Fellowship of Goodness in about 1918, the Tao Yuan or Society of the Way (also known as the Tao-te She or Society of the Way and Its Virtue) came into being probably in 1921, and the Ikuan Tao or the Way of Pervading Unity, founded much earlier, flourished around 1928.

The last four were quite extensive and influential. The Society of the Way spread over North China and the Yangtze area. It worshiped the Ultimate Sage and the Primeval Old Ancestor as the Great Unity. Below its altar were the names of Confucius, Lao Tzu, and the Buddha and also symbols representing Christianity and Islam. The Fellowship of Goodness claimed more than a thousand branches in all parts of China and Manchuria in 1923. It followed all the three religions and attracted mostly the educated. The arrangement of its halls resembled closely that of the Society of the Way, but it worshiped the three images of Confucius, Lao Tzu, and the Buddha. The Society of the Understanding of the Good was also called the Society of the Six Holy Religions. From Szechuan where it was founded it extended to Peking, Shantung, Nanking, and Shanghai and attracted mostly the uneducated. It followed Confucianism, Taoism, Buddhism, Islam, Christianity, and Judaism. In its beliefs the society traced everything to the First Cause, or Primeval Ancestor. This being was equated with the True Lord of Christianity and Islam. The Way of Pervading Unity believed that the One is the root of all things and, as the One Principle, penetrates through and pervades in all existence. Through the realization of the One Principle, all will be saved, and all systems—Confucianism, Toaism, Buddhism, Christianity, Judaism, and Islam—with all their sages, Gods, and Buddhas—are vehicles for salvation.

Many of these new societies have disappeared, have been absorbed into others, or have gone underground, but from fragmentary reports, the Way of Pervading Unity is still in existence in Mainland China, much to the concern of the Chinese Communists. [1]

IV

From the foregoing, it is clear that religious pluralism has been a continuing tradition in Chinese history. It is now necessary to explain how and why this pluralistic approach has developed. It was

[1] For further details of these societies, see Wing-tsit Chan, *Religious Trends in Modern China*, (New York, Columbia University Press, 1953), pp. 162-168.

not a matter of accident but the result of various forces at work.

When Chinese cultural patterns were being formed in the sixth to the fourth centuries B.C., China was under a feudal system in which a large number of states coexisted, loosely related to one another and pledging only nominal allegiance to the king of Chou. These states had different dialects, and different systems of thought. A large number of thinkers—philosophers, religionists, economists, diplomats, military strategists, astrologists, priest-magicians, agriculturalists— traveled freely from one state to another, offering service and selling ideas. Many formulae were presented to solve the same problems. Irrigation competed with prayer for rain, for example. Thus the One Hundred Schools of Thought contended and the One Hundred Flowers bloomed. Pluralism became a way of life. Practically every ancient philosophical school taught the doctrine of Tao. Each interpreted it differently and yet none deviated from the central meaning of "the way". At the same time, the yin yang doctrine cut across all schools of thought. According to this system, all things, whether concrete objects, ideas, situations, relationships, or what not, are results of the interaction of yin, the weak, passive, and negative cosmic principle or force, and yang, the strong, active, and positive cosmic principle or force. Anything conceivable can be so categorized.

One would expect that the two would result in opposite poles, incompatible and irreconcilabe. If so, Chinese thought would have been dominated by dualism and the either-or point of view. Instead, such an interpretation of yin and yang was rejected almost from the very beginning. In its place were the theories of succession, harmony, and synthesis. Day and night, and life and death, for example succeed each other. Man and woman, activity and tranquility, mountain and water in landscape paintings, etc. are to be balanced and harmonized. But the ultimate solution of the apparent conflict between yin and yang was synthesis. The son, for example, is both yin, because he is inferior to the father, and also yang, because being a male, he is superior to the female, Thus everything contains in it a multiplicity of elements and relationships, some conflicting and others harmonious. The pluralistic spirit in such a system of thought is obvious. Since no aspect of Chinese culture has escaped the influence of yin yang, be it cosmology, social organization, interpretation of history, principles of art, or even cooking, the pluralistic spirit may be said to have penetrated the entire fabric of Chinese life.

No wonder expressions of this sentiment can be found in virtually every Chinese classic—Confucian, Taoist, or Buddhist. Chuang Tzu said that we should "follow two courses at the same time." [1] In the *Book of Changes,* we are told that "In the world there are many different roads but the destination is the same. There are a hundred deliberations but the result is one." [2] The Confucian classic, the *Doctrine of the Mean* says that "the superior man honors the moral nature and follows the path of study and inquiry. He achieves breadth and the greatest height and brilliancy and follows the path of the Mean. He goes over the old so as to find what is new." [3] In other words, his choice is neither breadth nor depth, or the old versus the new, but both. The classic also says, "There are nine standards by which to govern the empire, its states, and the families, but the way by which they are followed is one." [4] With reference to knowledge and conduct, the classic says, "Some are born with knowledge, some learn it through study, and some learn it through hard work, but when the knowledge is acquired, it comes to the same thing. Some practice it naturally and easily, some practice it for its advantage, and some practice it with effort and difficulty, but when the achievement is made, it comes to the same thing." [5]

These sayings are quoted here because they are very often quoted in Chinese writings and even conversations. Another classical saying is that "There are hundreds of roads and thousands of paths to the capital and any one of them can take you there." In Buddhist philosophical treatises, one of the most common propositions is that "the One is the many and the many is the One." When a person of the either- or tradition hears a Chinese in the street say, "One is two and two is one," he will probably give up trying to understand the inscrutable Chinese. But if he scrutinizes a bit more, he will find there is a strong and persistent pluralistic tradition behind it.

Out of these convictions, the Chinese very early concluded that the three religions were three in one. This harmony has been understood in at least six ways. One is that each religion is but a system of education. The Chinese term for religion is *chiao,* meaning "to teach."

---

[1] *Chuang Tzu,* ch. 2. See Fung Yu-lan, trans., *Chuang Tzu,* (Shanghai, Commercial Press, 1943), p. 52.
[2] *The Book of Changes,* "Appended Remarks," pt. 2, ch. 5, See James Legge, trans., *Yi King,* p. 389.
[3] *Doctrine of the Mean,* ch. 27, See Wing-tsit Chan, *A Source Book in Chinese Philosophy,* (Princeton, N.J., Princeton University Press, 1963), p. 110.
[4] *Ibid.,* ch. 20, See Chan, p. 105.
[5] *Ibid.,* See Chan, p. 105.

We have already mentioned the fact that ancient Chinese thinkers offered various solutions to problems. In other words, they taught different ways of life; they were teachers first of all. Confucius and Lao Tzu were the greatest of them, but they were no more than teachers, claiming neither divine character nor miraculous power, and neither infallible authority nor monopoly of truth. When Chang Ling "founded" the Taoist religion in A.D. 142, he very sensibly assumed the title of a teacher, although the "celestial teacher." Since religion was understood as education, it could not have become a closed system and could not have taken on the element of exclusiveness or finality.

The harmony of religions is also understood in the sense of equality, that all religions are equal. As Ku Huan (392-453?) the Taoist put it, "Taoism and Buddhism are equal in illuminating and in transforming people." [1] It was agreed that different religions developed under different conditions and met different needs, but they are all "convenient means" to the same end. "Confucius sought order and peace in society," remarked Sun Ch'o of the Chin dynasty (265-420), and "the Buddha sought enligtenment in the fundamental nature of existence, but their goals are the same." [2] Hence the general feeling that while Confucianism is worldly and Buddhism other-worldly, they lead to the same results. By the same token, it is often maintained that "Confucianism and Taoism are equal."

Religious harmony is also understood in the sense of one complementing the others. We have already indicated ideas pointing to this direction. In actual operation, Confucianism has been chiefly concerned with the social order, Taoism with the individual, particularly his peace of mind and tranquility of spirit, and Buddhism with previous and future lives. It also happens that when the Taoist religion was founded, Confucianism had already developed ethics to a very high degree. It was only natural that Taoism drew heavily from Confucian ethics. Also, when Buddhism entered China, Taoism had already carried on a search for everlasting life for centuries but had neither organization nor creed. It was only natural for Buddhism to emphasize the Taoist tendency toward immortality and for Taoism to copy the structural and operational aspect of Buddhism. This explains why traditional and modern religious societies have followed

---

[1] *I-hsia lun* (On foreign and Chinese religions). See Seng-yu (445-518), ed., *Hung-ming chi* (Essays spreading and elucidating the doctrine), chs. 6-7.

[2] *Yü-tao p'ien* (Explaining the way), in Seng-yu, ch. 3.

Confucian ethical standards, Buddhist methods of meditation and discipline, and Taoist doctrines of long life.

Religious harmony is also understood in the sense of mutual identification. "The enlightenment that transforms a person into a Buddha." said Sun Ch'o, "is none other than the awakening which Mencius said the sage achieves for himself and helps others to achieve." [1] The Taoist desire for no death, it was thought, is in effect the same as the Buddhist search for freedom from birth. We have seen how philosophically the Taoist doctrine of non-being was identified with the Bullhist doctrine of the Void.

Still another sense in which the three religions are understood to be harmonious is that of One Source. "Traced to the source, the three sages are no different," said Emperor Wu (r. 502-549) of Liang. [2] To K'an Tse (third century), "All these religions have their source in Heaven which they obey." [3] As Chang Jung said, "Both Taoism and Buddhism, in their tranquil origin, are one. Only when they responded to external conditions have they become different." [4] "In their transcendental nature," said Chou Yu (d. 485), "they are no different. Differences appear only in the empirical sphere." [5] The consensus of opinion was that both the Tao and the Buddhist Dharma are derived from *li* or Principle, and Principle is one. Also, this Principle is intelligible because there is the Universal Mind, and the Universal Mind is one. Principle, let it be noted, became the Ultimate Reality and Truth in Neo-Confucianism from the eleventh century on.

The above conclusions of equality, complementarity, mutual identification, and One Source were reached, strangely enough, during the period of controversy and persecution. They were arrived at perhaps through sentiment more than through philosophical deliberation. In one area, however, and the most important, the three systems, from the very early days to the present, after much deliberation and reflection, looked to the same objective, namely the realization of one's nature. The word *hsing* meaning the nature of man and things, is not mentioned in the *Tao-te ching* but it runs through the *Chuang Tzu*. In both of them the ultimate goal is to preserve the essence and

---

[1] *Ibid.*
[2] See his poem on the three religions, in the Tao-hsüan (596-667), ed. *Kuang hung-ming chi* (Enlarged collection of essays spreading and elucidating the doctrine), ch. 39.
[3] *Ibid.*, ch. 1, seventh essay.
[4] *Hung-ming chi*, his first essay in ch. 6.
[5] *Ibid.*, his first essay in ch.6.

vitality of man. Consequently, in the Taoist religion the aim is to realize the Three Original Principles—Essence, Vital Force, and Spirit. From the third through the seventh centuries, both its development of ideas and its practice of alchemy were directed to this goal. In the Southern School of the Taoist religion, the emphasis is on the cultivation of one's nature, while in the Northern School it is on the cultivation and development of one's vital power. This is one reason why the Taoist religion has paid special attention to the human body. It has promoted exercise, refined Chinese cooking, and developed medicine, all dedicated to the fulfilment of human nature.

In early Buddhism, the idea of the realization of one's nature was not prominent. In the quest for rebirth in Paradise, the chief methods were to repeat the name of the Buddha, to express faith by making offerings, reciting scriptures, etc., and to take refuge in the Buddha. In the seventh century a revolt arose and demanded a shift to self-effort, and that was the realization of one's nature. The movement was led by Hui-neng (638-713), generally regarded as the founder of the Southern School of Meditation Buddhism (Ch'an or Zen). In his *Platform Scripture*, he emphatically urged his followers to take refuge in the nature within oneself instead of taking refuge in the Buddha outside, for, he said, what is called the great wisdom by which to reach the Pure Land is nothing but this self-nature, and all Buddhists, all dharmas, and all scriptures are immanent in it. If one sees his own nature, he will become a Buddha. [1]

The first to propagate the doctrine of fulfillment of human nature in China, however, were the Confucianists. Mencius said, "He who exerts his mind to the utmost knows his nature. He who knows his nature knows heaven." [2] This doctrine reached its zenith in the Neo-Confucianists of the eleventh and twelfth centuries, especially in the Ch'eng brothers and Chu Hsi, and has remained central in the Confucian tradition ever since. Ch'eng I (1033-1107) said, "The investigation of principle to the utmost, the full development of nature, and the fulfillment of destiny are only one thing. As principle is investigated to the utmost, one's nature is fully developed. And as one's nature is fully developed, destiny is fulfilled." [3] His brother Ch'eng

---

[1] *The Platform Scripture*, trans. by Wing-tsit Chan (New York, St. John's University Press, 1963), sec. 31.
[2] *The Book of Mencius,* bk. 7, pt. 2, ch. 1.
[3] *I-shu* (Surviving works), *Ssu-pu ts'ung-k'an* (The four Libraries series) edition, ch. 18, p. 9a.

Hao (1032-1085) said, "The investigation of principle to the utmost, the development of nature, and the fulfillment of destiny—these three things are to be accomplished simultaneously. There is basically no time sequence among them. The investigation of principle to the utmost should not be regarded as a matter of knowledge. If one really investigates principle to the utmost, even one's nature and destiny can be fulfilled." [1] And Chu Hsi (1130-1200) considered preserving the mind and nourishing the nature, and cultivating and controlling them, to be "the fundamental task." [2]

This trend of thought finds its modern expression in the contemporary Neo-Confucianism of Fung Yu-lan (1890-   ) and Hsiung Shih-li (1885-   ), undoubtedly the two most prominent Chinese philosophers in the last several decades. Fung said, "People in the moral sphere fulfill human relations and human duties. In doing so, they investigate human principles to the utmost and fulfill human nature. People in the transcendental sphere serve Heaven and assist in the natural transformation of things. In doing so, they investigate the principle of the universe and fulfill the nature of the universe... To penetrate the mysteries and know he transformation of the universe is to complete the work of the universe... and this is to serve Heaven." [3] Hsiung has expressed the same idea succinctly, saying, "One's self-nature is true and real. There is no need to search for a Heavenly Lord outside of oneself. One can develop one's own nature to the fullest extent. One need not desire Nirvāna." [4]

The last remark points up a radical difference among the Taoists, Buddhists, and Confucianists. For both the Taoist and Buddhists, the desire is to break the cycle of life and death. The Taoist religionists (but not the Taoist philosophers) try to live on earth forever and the Buddhists want to enjoy eternal life in Paradise. The Confucianists, on the other hand, accept life and death as natural. In this they are actually more naturalistic than the Taoist religionists. Immortality for them is not eternal life, either here or beyond, but what they call the "three immortalities," namely, the immortality of virtue, the immortality of accomplishment, and the immortality of wisdom. The Ch'eng brothers and Chu Hsi severely criticized the Taoists and Buddhists as

---

[1] *Ibid.*, ch. 2, pt. 1, p. 2b.

[2] *Chu Tzu ch'üan-shu* (Complete works of Master Chu), ch. 1, pp. 18a-19a.

[3] *Hsin yüan-jen* (New inquiry on man), (Shanghai, Commercial Press, 1943), p. 94.

[4] *Tu-ching shih-yao* (Important points in reading the classics), (Shanghai, Cheng-chung Bookstore, 1949), pk. 2, p. 53b.

selfish in wanting to live forever. Nevertheless they and their opponents were personal friends. They did not let their differences overshadow their common objective, the realization of one's nature.

V

Enough has been said about religious pluralism in China. But how is it related to the world community? Was China not anti-foreign in her attack on Buddhism? Didn't China give Catholicism a great deal of trouble? And was not the modern anti-Christian movement strong? In a certain sense the answer to these questions is "yes", but again we must put the matter in a proper perspective.

It is interesting to review, even briefly, how China imported and exported religion. Buddhism was known in China shortly before the Christian era, but the traditional account is that it was officially introduced as a result of a dream. According to the story, Emperor Ming (r. 58-75) had a dream of a golden image in the west and sent envoys to search for it. They returned in A.D. 67 or thereabout with two Buddhist priests and the *Scripture in Forty-two Chapters.* Leaving the matter of historical accuracy aside, the significant point to note is that in the memory of the Chinese, Buddhism came in at their invitation. For many centuries the Chinese overcame insurmountable hazards to go to the west to "seek the Law," as the movement has been called.

There have been many incidents expressive of this spirit of invitation. Perhaps the most dramatic was that concerning the half Indian and half Kuchean monk Kumārajīva (344-413) who opened up new studies of Buddhism in China, inaugurated a new era of translation, and trained as his pupils the famous Ten Philosophers of early Chinese Buddhism. Kumārajīva had such a great reputation in the western region that a Chinese king sent a general to bring him back to China. After the general had kept him in the northwest for seventeen years, another Chinese king sent an army of 70,000 men to bring him to the capital in 401.

But the most persistent and most unusual effort to welcome Buddhism was the Law-seeking movement from the third century through the seventh. During this period no less than 1,100 Chinese monks left China for India to visit holy places, to study, to search for scriptures, or to invite learned priests. They climbed snow-capped mountains and crossed deserts. Many never arrived at their destination. Others did but never returned. But a great number did come home to

China to enrich her religious tradition. Some made tremendous contributions to cultural history.

One of the most famous seekers of Law was Fa-hsien who left China in 399. He visited 130 countries in India, Ceylon, and other regions, and on his way back spent more than two hundred days on the seas, once drifting for thirteen days. He returned to China in 412 and recorded his travels in his *A Record of Buddhist Kingdoms*, translated by James Legge, which is the only source of information on those regions in the fourth century.

Another famous traveler was Hsüan-tsang (596-664). Defying the prohibition of the emperor, he secretly left in 596 for India. While there he visited many Indian centers of learning, debated with Indian philosophers, stayed for sixteen years, and returned with 617 works in 520 cases. For nineteen years he devoted his time to translation, finishing in all 73 works in 1330 chapters. He not only brought Buddhist thought in China to new heights; he also founded the Consciousness-only School. He was perhaps the most outstanding monk in Chinese history.

A similar Law-seeking movement ran in the opposite direction. For centuries Japanese Buddhists came to China by the thousands to import Buddhism. Almost all founders of Japanese Buddhist sects were students in China. Like the Chinese, they invited Buddhism into their country. More interestingly, it was the Japanese Buddhists who brought Confucianism into Japan. True, Confucianism went to Korea and Vietnam as part of the spread of Chinese political power, but in no case did any Chinese religion serve as an instrument of military invasion or political control. Nor has any Chinese religion replaced or dominated a native religion. More often than not, they have coexisted and did so without serious difficulty. In Japan, Buddhism has been synthesized with both Confucianism and Shinto in many respects. Of course there were many factors involved, including political necessity. But the fundamental factor that made possible the generally amiable religious situation was the basic conviction that religion is not to conquer or even to convert but to teach a good way of life.

As to the trouble with the Catholics in the seventeenth century, we cannot go into details here. For our purpose suffice it to say that the central issue was whether Chinese Christians were to be allowed to perform ancestral rites. In the Chinese view, these had a basic value that no foreign visitor should try to destroy. In the view of the Popes, some of them at least, they were evidence of idolatry. Ignorance and ill will on both sides finally led to the Pope's prohibition of Chinese Christians to participate in ancestral sacrifices and to the Chinese emperor expelling all missionaries. To the Catholics the basic issue was a religious one, but to the Chinese it was simply one of authority, whether the Chinese emperor or the Pope had the right to tell the Chinese what to do. This is not to excuse the destruction of some three hundred churches. Still the root of the quarrel was essentially political. It was not repression of a particular belief in favor of others.

In the case of the anti-Christian movement in the twentieth century, it was more of the nature of anti-imperialism than anything else. To be sure, there was an element of anti-foreignism. It was a factor in the persecution of 845. When the greatest Confucian scholar of the ninth century, Han Yü (768-824), petitioned the emperor in 819 not to welcome a relic bone of the Buddha into the capital, his chief argument against it was that Buddhism was a foreign religion. [1] It is probable that his argument contributed to the persecution of 845. However, a more important work of Han Yü's is his *Yün-tao* (An inquiry on the Way). In this famous essay, his main insistence is that the Buddhists perform their social and political functions as scholars, farmers, artisans, and merchants, and engage in the business of nourishing and sustaining one another. [2] At any rate, when Judaism, Manichaeanism, and other early Western religions came in, there was no effort to exclude them. They were given land to build places of worship and to practice their faith but were prohibited from proselyting the Chinese. There was a sense of cultural superiority and isolationism, but the idea of religious pluralism was unmistakable. When the Jesuits first came, there was even a degree of receptivity, for, after all, Father Matteo Ricci (1552-1610) converted the prime minister, Hsü Kuang-ch'i (1562-1633). The subsequent anti-foreign measures were not born of religious exclusiveness, but, as was pointed out before, an assertion of political authority.

There surely was anti-religious spirit in the twentieth century also. China was then obsessed with scientism, and intellectuals were almost in unison in denouncing religion as superstition and a conservative force. What was under attack, however, was not religion as such but superstition and conservatism. As modern Buddhists began to carry

---

[1] *Han Ch'ang ch'üan-chi* (Complete works of Han Yü), *Ssu-pu pei yao* (Essentials of the Four Libraries) edition, ch. 39, pp. 3b-5n.

[2] *Ibid.*, ch. 11, pp. 3b-4a. See English translation of the essay in Chan, *A Source Book in Chinese Philosophy*, ch. 28.

out reforms and introduce measures such as libraries, schools, and hospitals, intellectuals applauded them and rendered help. The so-called anti-religionists and Buddhist reformers became close associates. In the early years of the New Culture Movement that started in 1917, the popular belief was that the age of science had superseded the age of speculative philosophy and religion, but from the early 1920's, prominent intellectuals like Liang Ch'i-ch'ao (1873-1929) and Liang Sou-ming (1893-   ) argued that religion, if rational and progressive, had an important role in life to play. Throughout the anti-Christian movement, the Chinese attacked it chiefly as an instrument of Western imperialistic encroachment on Chinese sovereignty and as a beneficiary of "unequal treaties" that bound China in a semi-colonial status. At any rate, the attack was not on any particular religion. There was no attempt to play one religion against another, and no leader of any influence entertained the idea of one religion overcoming the rest. The multiplicity of religions was assumed all right along, although in the thinking of the intellectuals, they could survive only if they were baptized by science. In other words, religious pluralism was taken for granted. In fact, the whole New Culture Movement was characterized by pluralism. Atheism, mysticism, nihilism, anarchism, Marxism, pragmatism, Ibsenism, and all the rest had their respective advocates and followers. In the twentieth century, no less than in ancient times, One Hundred Schools contended and One Hundred Flowers Bloomed.

VI

What has China contributed to religious pluralism and the world community? Simply the fact that religions can flourish together and that one can follow them at the same time. As we have seen, this was made possible by the emphasis on the similarities of religions rather than their differences. It was made possible by the stress on religion as a way of life rather than structure, authority, clergy, or similar institutional elements. And it was made possible by attraction and influence rather than by active conversion. When China becomes once more a regular member of the world community, the pluralistic character of China will once more come to grips with Western religions. Past experience has taught us that trouble can be avoided if religions do not serve political and economical interests or have political and economic ambitions of their own. Difficulties about doctrinal differences, however, are not as easy to avoid. Specific issues like whether

God is personal, whether sin or goodness are original, whether there is personal immortality or not, and whether there are cycles of life and death, can perhaps be resolved, for about such matters there is ample room for discussion. But one basic conflict remains, namely, the claim of a religion as all-inclusive and supreme, on one hand, and Chinese traditional pluralism, on the other. Logically, one cannot be two and two cannot be one. Fortunately, logic has seldom led to solutions of religious problems. Perhaps the very desire to live together in a world community, a desire supported with sincerity, humility, and good will, will show us the way.

THE INDIAN AND BUDDHIST CONCEPT OF LAW

BY

HAJIME NAKAMURA
University of Tokyo

I. The Concept of Law

The concept of "law" in the juridical sense of the word was not so important as in the west, as has been noticed often by scholars. However, laws or norms of human existence were extremely important in eastern religions, especially Hinduism and Buddhism. In the following the writer would like to point out some features pertaining to the concept of "law" in Hinduism and Buddhism.

In this case we take the term "law," not in the meaning of "positive law," but in the wider sense which underlies such terms as the divine law, the moral law, the laws of nature, and other laws so called by way of analogy. Ancient India had no term exactly equivalent to the western word "law," in the same way that it had no word for "religion" or "philosophy." The fact is that Indians categorized the areas of human culture differently from westerners. What westerners call law falls into two of these categories without filling either one. The first category with which westerners are concerned is *dharma,* a word which means the correct traditional order of things—pure customs, correct sacrifices, the proper relation between the different classes of society. The literature of *dharma* contains a substantial part of Indian law. The second aim of human effort...is called *artha,* which means material advantage, social preferment, wealth, power... The culmination of this literature which serves this aim is the *arthaśāstra* or Book of Artha par excellence, which is a textbook on how to manage an empire. Accordingly, this category also contains a part of Indian law... It is profane as opposed to religious, materialistic as opposed to idealistic. Its purpose is avowedly nothing more than *artha,* material advantage, or as we would phrase it these days, efficiency and power of the state. In this article we would like to discuss the former term of law. [1]

---

[1] Daniel H. H. Ingalls, "Authority and Law in Ancient India," in Supplement to the *Journal of the American Oriental Society,* July September, 1954, p. 34.

The concept of "law" has been expressed by Indians up to the present chiefly through the term "dharma." This word comes from the root dhṛ, which means "to hold," "to sustain," or "to bear." [1] *Dharma* means "what serves as the norm to support human behavior," or in short, "the norm of action" or "the rule of conduct." The basic meaning of dharma is the moral law, which sustains the world, human society, and the individual. They affirm that the *Dharmas* differ from other things found in the natural world. Further, *Dharma* means "usage," "customary observance," "the thing to be done," or "duty." As a derived meaning from the basic one, dharma refers to the religio-ethical ideal, which we may translate as "virtue." Though dharma generally refers to religiously ordained duty, in other passages it may just mean morality, right conduct, or the rules of conduct (mores, customs, codes, or laws) of a group.

Furthermore, dharma refers not only to the whole context of law and custom (religion, usage, statute, caste or sect observance, manner, mode of behavior, duty, ethics, good works, virtue, religious or moral merit, justice, piety, impartiality) but also to the essential nature, character, or quality of the individual, as a result of which his duty, social function, vocation, or moral standard is what it is. [2]

To sum up: From the original meanings of the word various meanings derive; lexicographers mention the meanings of the word *dharma* as follows: [3]

1. religion; the customary observances of a caste, sect. etc.
2. law, usage, practice, custom, ordinance, statute.
3. religious moral merit, virtue, righteousness, good works (regarded as one of the four ends of human existence).
4. duty, prescribed course of conduct.
5. right, justice, equity, impartiality.
6. piety, propriety, decorum.
7. morality, ethics.
8. nature, disposition, character.

---

[1] The Sanskrit noun *dharma*, from the root *dhṛ*, "to hold, to bear, to carry" (Latin *fero*; cf. Anglo-Saxon *faran*, "to travel, to fare"; cf. also, "ferry"), means "that which holds together, supports, upholds." (Heinrich Zimmer, *Philosophies of India*. New York, Panthean Books, 1951, p. 163).

[2] H. Zimmer, *op. cit.*, p. 163.

[3] Prin. Vaman Shivaram Apte's, *The Practical Sanskrit-English Dictionary*, part II, Prasad Prakashan, Poona, 1957, p. 855, ed. P. K. Gode and C. C. Karve.

9. an essential quality, peculiarity, characteristic property (peculiar attribute).
10. manner, resemblance, likeness.
11. a sacrifice.
12. good company, associating with the virtuous.
13. devotion, religious abstraction.
14. manner, mode.

The readers might be surprised with the ambiguity of the word. However, these various meanings can easily derive from the original one, as will be explained below.

Most of the meanings of *dharma* used by Brahmins were inherited by Buddhists also. Usually dharma or dhamma is translated as "truth," "law." It involves the following meanings:

1. the principle of righteousness.
2. the consequence of action, of karma; the result of previous action which must work itself out.
3. the Doctrine of the Buddha (in this case capitalized).
4. the universal norms or laws which govern human existence.

Buddhist philosophy has developed a peculiar use of the word *dharma*,[1] the discussion of which will be out of scope for our thesis now.

Throughout all Indian religions dharma was regarded as that from which good results occur in the future. "Dharma, when violated, verily, destroys; dharma, when preserved, preserves; therefore, dharma should not be violated, lest the violated dharma destroys us." (Manu, VIII, 15).

The ancient Aryans held the concept of "cosmic law" already in early days. It was expressed by the term "*ṛta.*" The term was not irrelevant to westerners in antiquity, for we notice a remnant of the term in the names of Persian kings known to the Greeks, such as Artaxerxes. However, the Vedic word *ṛta* was replaced by the word *dharma*, representing the principle of cosmic ethical interdependence. "Rich in ghee (i.e., clarified butter considered as fertilizing rain), exceedingly glorious among beings, wide, broad, honey-dispensing, with beautiful forms, Heaven and Earth are, in accordance with Varuna's cosmic law (dharma), held asunder, both ageless and rich in seed." (*Ṛg-veda,* VI, 70, 1).

---

[1] Magdalene and Wilhelm Geiger, *Pali Dhamma,* Munich, 1921, Th. Stcherbatsky, *The Central Conception of Buddhism and the Meaning of the Word "Dharma",* The Royal Asiatic Society, London, 1923.

Throughout later Indian literature, righteousness, duty, or virtue (*dharma*) was mentioned as one of the four ends of man (*caturvarga*), together with pleasure (*kāma*), material gain (*artha*), and spiritual liberation (*mokṣa*). Some people came to think that among the four ends of man *dharma* is the best or the most fundamental. "From dharma issue profit and pleasure; one attains everything by dharma, it is dharma which is the essence and strength of the world." (*Rāmāyaṇa,* III, 9, 30). [1] "The science of dharma is of greater authority than the science of material gain." (Yājñavalkyasmṛti, 2. 2. 21.).

Dharma has been in fact a key word of Hindu culture, and Hinduism itself is sometimes designated as Sanātana Dharma, the Eternal Dharma. The concept of the eternal and universal law prevailed in Indian thought and took root among the people. King Aśoka believed in the eternal law which should be observed by all, regardless of race, religion, nationality, time, or place. This law is the norm of human behavior, and he called it *"dharma"* or "the time-honored rule." He stated in one of his Edicts that many kings preceding him had intended in vain to rule the people on the basis of the *Dharma,* and that the reign of the *Dharma* was first realized by him. [2] King Khāravela who ruled over South India in the second century B.C. was called "the universal monarch (Cakravartin)." [3] After Khāravela, the kings of this country sometimes claimed the title of "the king faithful to the law." [4]

II. The change of the content of Dharma

With Vedic Aryans dharma consisted in the practice of religious rites and rituals. The Vedas, the oldest records in India, are collections of ritual recitations and commentaries on the rites. They are compiled chiefly for the purpose of ritualistic practices. Actual sacrifices are officiated after the pattern of the first norms (dharma) of sacrifice. (ṚV. X, 90, 16).

The Vedas preserve many legends and myths in their original forms. But for the Indo-Aryans, myths concerning the origin of their race or the legendary histories of their expansion and the lineage of their dynasties were not matters of importance. What was crucially important for them was the measure of *their direct relationship with the*

---

[1] *Sources of Indian Tradition,* compiled by Wm. Theodore de Bary, *et al.,* (Columbia University Press, 1958), p. 215.

[2] The Pillar Edict, VII.

[3] The Inscription of King Khāravela.

[4] It can be learned from the words inscribed on the coins issued by those kings.

gods. They were religious people occupied in the consideration of gods, or more properly speaking, of a world governed by cosmic law. On the other hand, they had a rather dim sense of national or racial consciousness. Indeed, in ancient India the aristocrats and the intellectual class took pride in their Aryan descent, which accounted for the sense of unity among them. But this unity was the result of the conviction they held in common, their faith in one superior religion, and not from their awareness of any racial oneness. This idea of dharma was inherited and developed especially by the Mīmāṃsā school in later days.

With the development of ideas the Hindus replaced the practice of sacrifices with that of virtues. Dharma came to mean moral virtues. Rāma, the hero of the *Rāmāyaṇa,* was dharma in flesh and blood. Rāma's noble example of devotion to duty, to his father, and to his people, as well as Sita's long-suffering fidelity to Rāma, have been looked to as religious and ethical ideals down through the ages. Up to the present Rāma has been regarded as the embodiment of dharma, and his triumph over wicked Rāvaṇa as the overcoming of vice (*adharma*) in order that virtue and the moral law might prevail in personal and public life. Rāma, the embodiment of dharma, is also adored as the incarnation of the Supreme Lord Viṣṇu who has come into the world to restore the moral order.

And in the course of time, this norm of behavior for the realization of morals was raised to the position of the Absolute. Indians came to think that the *Dharma* is the basis of the whole universe and that all things in the universe rest on the *Dharma.* "This whole universe is in the *Dharma.* Nothing is more difficult to do than the *Dharma.* On this account, they hold the *Dharma* in high esteem." [1] "The *Dharma* is the basis of the whole universe. In the world, people wish to emulate a man who keeps the *Dharma* best. They eliminate all evils by force of the *Dharma.* All beings rest in peace in the *Dharma.* On this account, they say that the *Dharma* is the highest being." [2] "Dharma is the foundation of the whole universe. In this world people go unto a person who is best versed in dharma for guidance. By means of dharma one drives away evil. Upon dharma everything is founded. Therefore, dharma is called the highest good." [3] Dharma is to be extinct just before the end of the world, but will endure as long as the

---

[1] *Mahānārāyaṇa-Upaniṣad*, XXI, 2.
[2] *Ibid.,* XXII, 1.
[3] *Taittirīya-Āraṇyaka,* X, 79; De Bary, *op. cit.,* p. 220-221.

universe endures; and each participates in its power as long as he plays his role. Furthermore, it is maintained that the *Dharma* has a form superior even to that of the creator of the universe (the Brahman). [1] In the Vaiseṣika, it is assumed that the rise and the deliverance of the soul is attained only on the strength of the *Dharma*. [2]

Sacrifice was abolished and religious rites of traditional Brahmanism were denounced by Buddhists, but the feature of thought that the true religion consists in the practice of dharma was inherited by Jains and Buddhists also. According to them, the true Doctrine reflects the fundamental moral law of the universe. The religion which was the true one in the eyes of its believers was called "dharma." All the teachings of the Buddha can be summed up in one word: Dhamma. It means originally law, the law which exists in a man's own heart and mind. It is the principle of righteousness. It means truth. Therefore the Buddha appeals to man to be noble, pure, and charitable not in order to please any Supreme Being, but in order to be true to the highest in himself.

The Buddha is said to have been silent on metaphysical problems, and to have asserted partial veracity of all philosophical thoughts. This does not mean that he refrained from philosophical thinking as such, but he admitted the validity of universal norms concerning human existence.

Buddhism presupposes the universal law of human existence. However skeptical a man may be about everything, the phenomenon of skeptical thinking itself argues the existence of some kind of universal law, although it may be very difficult to grasp it. Without admitting it, men cannot engage in consecutive thinking. Buddhists thought that in our human existence there work many universal and consecutive norms, which they named dharmas (or *dhammas*). Gotama was called *dhamma-vādin*, one who reasons according to the truth (that is, not on the basis of the authority of the Vedas, or of tradition). In this sense we can call his standpoint extremely rationalistic, or normalistic. He did not claim any sanctity of his own or any traditional authority. His greatness lies in that he has seen the truth and nothing more. The Buddha said, "He who sees not the dharma (truth or doctrine) sees not me. He who sees dharma sees me." [3]

In the Bible also we can find a similar teaching. Jesus said, "I am

---

[1] *Bṛhad. Up.* I, 4, 14.
[2] *Vaiseṣika-sūtra*, I, 2.
[3] *Itivuttaka*, 92.

not speaking of you all; I know whom I have chosen: it is that the scripture may be fulfilled. 'He who ate my bread has lifted his heel against me.' I tell you this now before it takes place, that when it does take place you may believe that I am he. Truly, truly, I say to you, he who receives anyone whom I send receives me; and he who receives me receives him who sent me." [1]

But here Christ stressed personal relationship to him, while the Buddha stressed rather the universal validity of the truth. The saying of Christ here is somewhat irrational and personal, while that of the Buddha is rather rationalistic. Man is accountable to Law and not to a more or less arbitrary and capricious divine will.

According to the Buddha, personal relations should be brought into harmony with the universal norms. When the Buddha was going to die, he admonished his attendant Ānanda, saying that it is the norms (*dharma*) that the brethren should rely upon. "It may be, Ānanda, that in some of you the thought may arise, 'The word of the master is ended, we have no teacher anymore!' But it is not thus, that you should regard it. The Truths (Dhamma), and the Rules of the Order (Vinaya), which I have set forth and laid down for you all, let them, after I am gone, be the Teacher to you." [2] It is the norms (*dhamma*) that the brethren should rely upon. "In whatever doctrine and discipline the Noble Eightfold Path is not found, neither in it is there found a man of true saintliness." [3]

All schools of Buddhism have presupposed universal laws, called dharmas, which govern human existence, and may be known by reason. The universal laws apply to all existence, in conformity to the nature of the universe. The concept of dhamma governing the natural world has been inherited by contemporary Southern Buddhists also. One of their leaders says: "Dhamma, this law of righteousness, exists in the universe also. All the universe is an embodiment and revelation of Dhamma. When the moon rises and sets, the rains come, the crops grow, the seasons change, it is because of Dhamma, for Dhamma is the law residing in the universe which makes matter act in the ways revealed by the studies of modern science in physics, chemistry, zoology, botany, and astronomy. Dhamma is the true nature of every existing thing, animate and inanimate." [4]

---

[1] John 13: 18-20, Revised Standard Version.
[2] *Mahāparinibbāna-suttanta*, 6, 1.
[3] *Ibid.*, 5.27.
[4] U Thittila in Kenneth W. Morgan (ed.), *The Path of the Buddha*, (New York, The Ronald Press, 1956), p. 67.

The word dharma is often used as meaning the doctrine of the Buddha. In this sense, the Dharma is not really a dogma, but it is rather a path, which was regarded as the universal norm for mankind. "If a man will live by Dhamma, he will escape misery and come to Nibbana, the final release from all suffering. It is not by any kind of prayer, nor by any ceremonies, nor by any appeal to a deity or a God that a man will discover the Dhamma which will lead him to his goal. He will discover it in only one way—by developing his own character. This development comes only through control of the mind and purification of the emotions. Until a man stills the storm in his heart, until he extends his loving-kindness to all beings, he will not be able to take even the first step toward his goal." [1]

The Buddhist takes refuge in the Dhamma, because it enables one who follows it to bring an end to all troubles and suffering through the attainment of Enlightenment, perfect wisdom, and perfect equanimity. The best way to follow the Dhamma is to practice it in one's daily life. As we are all subject to birth, old age, sickness, dissatisfaction, sorrow, and death, we are all sick people. The Buddha is compared to an experienced and skillful physician, and the Dhamma is compared to the proper medicine. However efficient the physician may be, and however wonderful the medicine may be, we cannot be cured unless and until we take the medicine ourselves. Realization is possible only through practice. It was only in later days that the way in which one can truly express one's gratitude and veneration for the Buddha with infinite compassion was encouraged.

On this point we find extreme similarity to the assertion of Confucius and Mencius. "The master said Heaven begat the power (tê) that is in me. What have I to fear from such a one as Huan T'ui?" [2, 3] "Constantly strive to be in harmony with the (divine) will and thereby get for yourself much happiness." [4] The Buddha affirms that dharma or righteousness is the only way to welfare on earth as in heaven. On this point we find extreme similarity to the assertions of Chinese thinkers also. Confucius proclaims that the will of Heaven shall prevail; Lao Tzu declares that there is no getting past the Tao. They all mean that against the rock of moral law the world's exploiters hurl themselves eventually to their own destruction.

---

[1] *Ibid.*, p. 67-68.
[2] Minister of War in Sung.
[3] Analects VII, 22. Translated by Waley.
[4] *Mencius*, II, 1; IV, 5, 6.

The western counterpart of the concept of *dharma* can be said to be logos, although in the sense of "word" it occasionally corresponds with Indian *śabda* or *vāc*. The rhythm of events of the universe or the uniformity of Nature under law, which alone is permanent, was termed by Heraclitus the destiny (*heimarmene*), the order (*dike*), the reason (*logos*) of the world. [1]

In the philosophy of Plato, the idea of the Good, which is the source of all the ideas, is supreme. The truly real and the truly good are identical; the idea of the Good is the *logos,* the cosmic purpose. The universe is conceived by him as a logical system of ideas, an organic unity, governed by a universal purpose, the idea of the Good. It is the function of philosophy, by the exercise of reason, to understand the inner order and connections of the universe, and to conceive its essence by logical thought. [2]

The *logos* doctrine of Heraclitus seemed to present itself as the central point of Stoic metaphysics. The Stoics said: all life and movement have their source in the logos: it is god; it contains the germ or seeds (*spermata*) of life; in it the whole cosmos lies potential as the plant in the seed. The entire universe forms a single, unitary, living, connected whole, and that all particular things are the determinate forms assumed by a divine primitive power which is in a state of eternal activity. As actively productive and formative power, the deity is the *logos spermatikos,* the *vital principle* or creative reason, which unfolds itself in the multitude of phenomena as their peculiar, particular *logoi spermatikoi* or formative forces. [3]

The sum-total of the divine activity in the world, Philo designates by the Stoic conception of the Logos. The Logos is, on the one hand, the divine wisdom, resting within itself, and the producing rational power of the Supreme Being; it is, on the other hand, Reason as coming forth from the deity, the self-subsistent image, the first-born son, who is not, as is God, without origin, nor yet has he arisen, as have we men; he is the *second God.* [4]

The concept of logos was early introduced into Christianity, as is noticed in the Gospel of St. John. Christian Neoplatonism tended by

---

[1] W. Windelband, *A History of Philosophy,* translated by James H. Tufts, (New York, Macmillan, 1914), p. 36.

[2] Frank Thilly, *A History of Philosophy,* revised by Ledger Wood, (New York, Henry Holt and Company, 1952), p. 81.

[3] W. Windelband, *op. cit.*, pp. 180-181; 186.

[4] *Ibid.*, pp. 241-242.

its principle of emanation to make the *Logos,* identified with Christ, a kind of secondary deity, intermediate between a transcendent God and the world of sensible things. Origen thought of Christ as the Logos, or the hypostatized Divine Wisdom of the transcendent deity. [1] Justin said: God has indeed revealed himself internally through the rational nature (*sperma logon emphyton*) of man who is created in his image, as he has revealed himself externally through the perfection of his creation. [2]

In spite of so many similarities which we find between the concept of *dharma* and that of *logos,* we are inclined to think that the former concept of the East tended to be subjective, controlling human behavior, whereas the latter concept of the west tended to be rather objective, controlling the world or natural surroundings in which human beings live. In this connection we should not fail to mention the historical fact that some Hellenistic Greeks translated the Indian term *dharma* with the Greek *dīkē*. [3]

On the other hand, the Buddhist canon law was codified in what is called *Vinaya,* i.e., "Guidance" or "Book of Discipline." The Pali Vinaya consists of 227 rules to regulate the conduct of the members of the Order in outward affairs, and some supplementary chapters on special subjects. They are concerned with monks alone. For nuns there exists another *Vinaya*. Each order had a Vinaya of its own. Customs as to marriage and divorce, the inheritance and division of real or personal estate, the law of contract and criminal law, were all purely secular matters to be determined by the sense of the lay community.

The expression "Buddhist law" as used of law administered in English courts in Ceylon and Burma had a very different meaning. In Ceylon, the British, in their early days, incorporated into the law of the Island the customs prevalent there among the majority, the Buddhists, on some points. In Burma the gradual growth of the cusomary law among Buddhists can be traced. [4]

Things being so, all the followers of the religious sects in India

---

[1] Thilly, *op. cit.,* pp. 162, 176.
[2] W. Windelband, *op. cit.,* p. 223.
[3] Sten Konow, *Kharoshṭhī Inscriptions,* (Government of India, Calcutta, 1929), Introduction; p. xxviii.
[4] T. W. Rhys Davids, *Encyclopaedia of Religion and Ethics,* (Edinburgh, T. and T. Clark, 1940), vol. 7, p. 828a.

were taught that to observe the law was the most precious of the virtues. [1]

The *Dharma,* as the norm that *guides* a man to establish and to perform moral acts, is the power that realizes "Truth" in this world. Thus, the ancient Indians understood the D*harma* to be truth that works as a creative power, and identified the two. "Thus the Law is what is called the true. And if a man declares what is true, they say he declares the Law; and if he declares the Law, they say he declares what is true. Thus both are the same." [2]

The idea of dharma as the source was taken over by Buddhists. "The blessed Buddhas of virtues endless and limitless, are born of the Law of Righteousness; they dwell in the Law, are fashioned by the Law; they have the Law as their master, the Law as their light, the Law as their field of action, the Law as their refuge. They are produced by the Law... and all the joys in this world and the next are born of the Law and produced by the Law." [3]

III. Some features

a) *Law is the Principle on Which Social Welfare is Secured*

Indians recognized the fact that social welfare and peaceful life can be secured, based on the principle of law. It is the law that can protect people. By means of law the life of the weak is vouched and the strong cannot persecute the weak by force. Indians were conscious of the fact that even the weak can control the strong by means of law. "There is nothing higher than justice (dharma). So a weak man hopes (to defeat) a strong man by means of justice as one does through a king." (Bṛhad. Up. I. 4, 14.) Without the protection of law the weak would be overrun immediately by the powerful. Indian imagination sets forth the fear with the metaphor of rain water: "Verily, justice (dharma) is water. Therefore, when rain water pours on the earthly world, all the world follows justice. However, when it does not rain, the strong will plunder the weak, for justice is water." [4] "Dharma (from a root dhṛ, "to sustain") is so called on account of

---

[1] *Praśnottara ratna mālikā,* 4.
[2] *Bṛhad. Up.* I, 4, 14. *Sacred Books of the East,* vol. XV, p. 89. There are many cases of the identification of *satya* and *dharma.* Cf. *Chānd. Up.,* VII, 2, 1; VII, 7, 1; *Tait. Up.* I, 11, 1.
[3] *Dharma-saṃgīti-sūtra,* De Bary, *op. cit.,* p. 182.
[4] *Mahābhārata,* 10, 110. 11. De Bary, *op. cit.,* p. 221.

its capacity for the sustenance of the world. On account of dharma, people are sustained separately in their respective stations." [1]

This thought was inherited by Buddhists, although in a fairly different connotation. "The Law is not guarded by beings. Beings are protected by the Law." [2]

However, kingly law did not interfere with the daily life of common people as in other countries. "The great virtue of the religious legal tradition of India was that it caused the state to interfere as little as possible with the individual. In most of his affairs the individual was guided and judged by his neighbors, his caste brotherhood, his village council or headman. Only in his dealings with the outside world was he subject to the king's laws as interpreted by the king's pundits." Modern Indian village men said: "We observe our own rules. Where there is no rule we ask the pundits." "And the kings were so anxious not to interfere as the subjects were to preserve their own customs." [3] In Indian religions occasionally the highest dharma was regarded as nonviolence (*ahiṃsā*) or loving-kindness (*maitrī, karuṇā*). "For the sake of the promotion of strength and efficacy among beings the declaration of dharma is made. Whatever is attended by non-violence (*ahiṃsā*) that is dharma. Such is the fixed opinion." [4]

b) *The Perennial Character of Law*

In Indian and Buddhist thought law was regarded as perennially valid, regardless of the change of times. Indians considered that the *Dharma* exists *eternally*. Already in an old Vedic text, a wife is required to lie down on the pyre beside her dead spouse at the cremation of her husband on the grounds that it is the "time-honored rule" (*dharmaḥ purāṇaḥ*): [5] As the following quotation tells us, the *Dharma* is allegorically identified with eternal absolute being: "He from whom the sun rises, and into whom it sets ... Him the *Devas* (gods) made the law, he only is today, and he tomorrow also." [6] At the end of the Mahabharata it is stated: "Neither for the sake of pleasure, nor out of fear or avarice, no, not even for the sake of one's life should one give up dharma; dharma stands alone *for all time*." [7]

---

[1] Śatapatha-Brāhmaṇa XI, 1, 6, 24.
[2] *Dharmasaṃgīti-sūtra*, De Bary, *op. cit.*, p. 182.
[3] Daniel H. H. Ingalls, *op. cit.*, p. 43.
[4] *Mahābhārata* XII, 110, 10. De Bary, *op. cit.*, p. 221.
[5] *Atharva-Veda*, XVIII, 3, 1.
[6] Bṛhad-Up., I, 5, 23. Sacred Books of the East, Vol. XV, p. 98.
[7] De Bary, *op. cit.*, p. 212.

This idea of the eternal universal law was inherited by the Jains and the Buddhists also. The Jains, from their very rationalistic standpoint, assert that there exist universal laws (*dharma*) which all mankind should observe at all times and all places. For instance, one of their sacred books teaches:

> "They say all the perfect souls and blessed ones, whether past, present, or to come—thus they speak, thus they declare, thus they proclaim: All things breathing, all things existing, all things living, all beings whatever, should not be slain or treated with violence, or insulted, or tortured, or driven away.
>
> "This is the pure unchanging eternal law, which the wise ones who know the world have proclaimed, among the earnest and the not-earnest, among the loyal and the not-loyal, among those who have given up punishing others and those who have not done so, among those who are weak and those who are not, among those who delight in worldly ties and those who do not. This is the truth. So it is. Thus it is declared in this religion.
>
> "When he adopts this law a man should never conceal or reject it. When he understands the Law he should grow indifferent to what he sees, and not act for worldly motives." [1]

The founder of Jainism, Mahāvīra, set forth the philosophy and the practical morality of this religion in accord with what he believed to be the true principle or law.

Buddhists hold a similar view of the law. "The law is not dependent upon time. Timeless is the Law." [2] Buddhists consider that the law of causal origination is the unchangable truth. "Whether there is an appearance or non-appearance of a Perfect One (Tāthagata), this causal law of nature, this orderly fixing of things prevails ..." [3] A Perfect One is one who, having realized this law of nature, endeavors to reveal it to all sentient beings. The enlightened one is not to be considered as a mystic, inspired by a revelation, but only as a man who has fully perceived the true law of nature that exists eternally. Buddhism, or at least Buddhism in its early stage, pays special reverence to the law that is eternally valid, and assumes that the authority of the law precedes that of the Buddha. All beings, including even the gods, adore the law that the Buddha has revealed and accept it. [4] Even the gods are bound

---

[1] *Āyāraṅga-sutta* I, 4, 1. De Bary, *op. cit.*, pp. 61-62.
[2] *Dharmasaṅgīti-sūtra*, De Bary, *op. cit.*, p. 182.
[3] *Aṅguttara-Nikāya*, ed. by Pali Text Society, I, p. 286.
[4] e.g. *Saṃyutta-Nikāya*, Mahapadana-sutta.

to worldly sufferings, and they have to follow the law to free themselves from the sufferings of rebirth.

Here one may find an analogue of this Buddhist idea of the law in Hugo Grotius' *jus naturale* or "natural law." His natural law is supposed to be impartial to any person or nation and unchangeable under any circumstances. Even God cannot alter this product of his reason. But it should be remembered that natural law regulates human existence. The law is valid without necessarily referring to God's authority so long as it is clear to reason as a universal principle necessary in governing the relations of human beings in this world. The Buddhist law of nature, on the other hand, is not the law regulating the relations of individual human beings, but it is the law controlling the relations between the state of ignorance (which is inevitably attached to individual human existence and behavior) and the way of deliverance from it. Though Grotius' natural law and the Buddhist law of nature are similar in form, they are quite different in essence.

Another important point is that law should be applied impartially and equally. The view was expressly admitted by Buddhists. "The Law is equal, equal for all beings. For low or middle or high the Law cares for nothing." "The Law has no preferences. Without preference is the Law." [1] However, among Hindus this principle was interpreted as law applicable among persons belonging to a specific class. This is to say, they admitted equal application of law within a limited caste. This point will be discussed in the next section.

c) *Dharmas as Specific Laws*

The central concept which was elaborated and emphasized by Law Texts (Smṛti) was that of dharma. The Sacred Law is the codification of dharma, denoting different ideas, such as, Vedic ritual, ethical conduct, caste rules, and civil and criminal law. Actually, the concept of dharma is all-comprehensive and may be, broadly speaking, said to comprise precepts which aim at securing the material and spiritual sustenance and growth of the individual and society, from the viewpoint of Brahmanism. The word *dharma* implies not only a universal law by which the cosmos is governed and sustained, but also particular laws, or inflections of "the law", which were regarded as natural to each special species or modification of existence. Hierarchy, specializa-

---

[1] *Dharmasaṅgīti-sūtra*. De Bary, *op. cit.*, pp. 182-183.

tion, one-sidedness, and traditional obligations are thus of the essence of the system. [1]

The law institutionalized in the Sacred Law was a specific one, the validity of which was limited to a particular body of men. Specific laws which are valid with specific groups of men were admitted by the Hindus. "The laws of specific countries, the laws of specific castes, the eternal laws of individual families, the laws of heretics and (tribal) communities—all these topics Manu has expounded in this treatise." [2] One belongs to a species of men—a family, guild and craft, a group, a denomination, etc. The correct manner of dealing with every life problem that arises is indicated by the laws (*dharma*) of the caste (*varṇa*) to which one belongs, and of the particular stage-of-life (*āśrama*) that is proper to one's age. The Law Texts prescribe "the dharmas of the four classes, the four stages of life and others." [3] Already before the compilation of the Law Texts an old book of rites in Brahmanism prescribed the four *Dharmas* of the Brahman: to be a man of a Brahman family; to do what becomes the dignity of the Brahman; to maintain honor; and to lead the people. As to the duties that a layman should observe toward the Brahman, it mentions the four different *Dharmas*: to pay respect to the Brahman; to make offerings to the Brahman; to protect the Brahman from harm and injury; and to refrain from condemning the Brahman to death. [4] These dharmas were elaborated and developed in later Law Texts.

"In spite of the comprehensive character of dharma, in its most common connotation it was limited to two principal ideals, namely the organization of social life through well-defined and well-regulated classes (*varṇas*) and the organization of an individual's life within those classes into definite stages (*āśramas*). Thus, in popular parlance, dharma almost came to mean just varna-ashrama-dharma, that is the dharmas (ordained duties) of the four classes and the four stages of life." [5] Elaborate discussions occurred in minute details in the texts of the Sacred Law concerning their respective duties, and social and legal privileges and disabilities.

Each class had its own set of duties and obligations (*svadharma*)

---

[1] H. Zimmer, *op. cit.*, p. 163
[2] *Manu* I, 118. De Bary, *op. cit.*, p. 223.
[3] *Yājnavalkya-smṛti* I, 1, 1.
[4] *Śatapatha-Brāhmaṇa* XI, 5, 7, 1.
[5] De Bary, *op. cit.*, pp. 219-220.

definitely prescribed and, for the sake of the solidarity and welfare of society as a whole, each class or social unit was expected to act up to the following teaching of the Bhagavad-gītā (3.35):

> "Better one's own duty, (though) imperfect,
> Than another's duty well performed;
> Better death in (doing) one's own duty;
> Another's duty brings danger." [1]

d) *The Source of Law*

In ancient times the Vedic scriptures were regarded as the main source of dharma, but, as they were limited and the environment always changed, the Hindus had to admit other sources of dharma, especially with regard to legal affairs. "Four persons versed in the Vedas and dharma, or a group of those who are adept only in the three Vedas, constitute a court. Whatever that court declares would be dharma; or that, which even one person who is the best among the knowers of the lore of the Self declares, would be dharma." [2] The four Vedas, together with auxiliary literature, are confined to the consideration of religious rites, and contain very little of secular law. So, *Dharmaśāstras* or *Smṛtis* were the real sources of law from a legal point of view. But Hindus went still further. Beyond positive laws there lies the ultimate source based upon which one can pass judgements, and that was the Self.

Then, where had they located the foundation of dharma, based on which all actual dharmas were to be ruled? That must have been some principle which was beyond the Vedic scriptures and traditions.

"Over and above such acts as sacrifice, traditional practices, self-control, non-violence, charity, and study of the Veda, this, verily, is the highest dharma, namely, the realization of the Self by means of yoga." [3]

In Buddhism the source of Teachings was thought to be the law of human existence. The Teachings of the Buddha were called Dhamma because they enable one to realize the truth of human existence. The doctrinal aspect of the Buddha's Teachings has been preserved in the Pali scriptures.

---

[1] Franklin Edgerton, *The Bhagavad Gītā,* part I, (Cambridge, Harvard University Press, 1946), p. 39.
[2] *Manu* II, 6; 12.
[3] *Yājñavalkya,* I, 8.

As Indians put great emphasis on the universal law that stands above individuals the significance of the individual personality is in many cases thoroughly ignored by them. And even Gotama the Buddha, the man of greatest character, is considered to be only one of many men who realized the universal law in this world. Buddhists espouse the idea of the multiplicity of Buddhas. The Jains, in a similar manner, assume the existence of twenty-three founders preceding the historical founder, Mahāvīra.

In the thought of the Indians, Buddhas or the founders of religion, however deified they are as the object of worship, are human beings who are not different from ordinary people. A man can be a Buddha or a founder of religion if he has accomplished the works necessary for enlightenment. We are all in essence one and the same with the absolute Being. This assertion is correct also in the case of Bhaktic Buddhism. The man saved by the grace of Amitābha-Buddha becomes a Buddha equal in all respects to his savior.

e) *The Absolute beyond "Lawful" and "Unlawful"*

It is admitted that in Mahāyāna and Advaitic philosophies the absolute was regarded as lying beyond the opposition of "lawful" and "unlawful," "virtue" and "vice." This thought was expressly set forth by Gauḍapāda, a forerunner of the Advaita Vedanta philosophy. [1] Sankara placed the study of brahman higher than that of dharma which was practised by the Mīmamsakas. [2]

Although it is not clear in the philosophy of the Advaitic Vedānta, in which way moral behavior is justified, the philosophy of Voidness solved the problem in a unique way of its own. According to the teaching of the void (emptiness, *śūnyatā*) of Mahāyāna Buddhism, there is no real existence; all things are but appearance and are in truth empty. Even non-existence is not reality; everything occurs conditioned by everything else. Voidness or emptiness is not nothingness, nor annihilation, but that which stands right in the middle between affirmation and negation, existence and non-existence, eternity and annihilation.

The doctrine of the void (*śūnyatā*) is not nihilism. On the contrary, Mahāyāna Buddhism asserts that it is the true basis for ethical values. The void is all-inclusive; having no opposite, there is nothing which

---

[1] *Gauḍapādiya-Kārikā* II, 25.
[2] *Brahmasūtrabhāṣya* I, 1, 1.

it excludes or opposes. It is living void, because all forms come out of it. The Void is compared to a mirror. As it has no image of its own, it can reflect all images. If it is filled with something, it cannot reflect any image. All virtues are established in the Void, and whoever realizes the Void is filled with life and power and the Bodhisattvas love of all beings.

Loving kindness is the moral equivalent of all-inclusiveness, which is nothing but the Void. If you do anything good to somebody else with the consciousness, "I have done something good to him," it is not completely good. You are then obsessed by the three notions, "I", "he", and "something good." Anything good should be done in the state of the Void, without attachment, without selfishness. This teaching is called "The Purification of the Three Things." This should be the basis for all ethical values.

f) *Universality of Law or "Tao" (The Way) Conceived by the Chinese and Japanese Thinkers*

Chinese Buddhists disapproved the authority of the religious organization or church as the medium between the Absolute and the individual, and they exclusively followed the *dharma* (the norm or principle) or the *tao* [1] (the way) which was considered the Absolute itself. Indian people made use of the term *dharma* in many cases but the Chinese preferred the term *tao*. The word *tao* possesses a more concrete connotation than the word *dharma*. Otherwise, the meaning of these two words was essentially the same in the eyes of the Buddhists at that time. The practice of Taoists is similar to the Indian practice of Yoga with respect to seeking tranquillity of mind, longevity, miraculous powers, etc. [2]

In this sense the Chinese have been fully conscious of the universality of *tao*. They assume that even though countries differ, the same moral principles are observed and followed all over the world, [3] and that a certain thought system transcends time and possesses a universal validity true for all ages. [4] They believe that the idea of *tao*, which can be found in all religions in various forms, is also universal

---

[1] Cf. Huston Smith, *The Religions of Man* (Mentor Books, the New American Library, 1961), pp. 184 ff.
[2] Arthur Waley, *Three Ways of Thought in Ancient China* (New York, Doubleday Anchor Book, 1962), pp. 48 ff.
[3] *Mo-ho-chih-kuan*, X, part. 1. Taisho, XLVI, 134b.
[4] Cf. Waley, *op. cit.*, pp. 62 ff.

truth. Therefore, it is said that *"tao* is not able to realize itself, but can be realized by man. Even though there are various ways to realize it, the *tao* itself, however, does not change through the ages. That which changes in time and place is not *tao,* but men and the world. The theory of *one principle covers all* (Confucius), the idea of *non-creation* (Lao-tzu), and the goal of *nirvāṇa* (Śākyamuni), all point up the fact that different men taught the same truth." [1]

For some thinkers, the idea of *dharma* in Chinese Buddhism was a higher principle than that of the Buddha. The authority of the Buddha is established only insofar as it is based upon the authority of the *dharma.*

"Those who realized the *dharma* are called Buddha." [2] It is said that Tan-hsia, a priest of the Zen sect, burnt a wooden image of the Buddha to admonish people who idolized the Buddha but ignored the significance of the *dharma* embodied in it. The Pure Land teachings state that one should meditate on Amitābha Buddha with all one's heart and soul. Modern Chinese interpreted this teaching as none other than to meditate on *Tathatā* (thusness). Chinese Buddhists also esteemed the authority of the *dharma* more highly than filial piety, as is shown in the statement: "The obligation to ancestors covers only seven generations, while the obligation of the Buddhist teacher is so great that it covers a great many *Kalpas."* [3]

To respect a Buddhist teacher does not mean to respect the teacher himself as an individual, but it means to respect the person who realized the truth of Buddhism by himself. [4] Tsung-mi (780-841) taught that only those who were inferior in their spiritual capacities had to depend upon a teacher. [5] To keep the precepts does not merely mean to follow ascetic practices or continue a life of mortification.

In Japan, law-giving was not lacking even in the genuinely Shintoist, pre-Buddhist age. To illustrate, it is said that Emperor Seimu determined the frontiers and civilized the country, and that he issued laws. He held sway, reforming the surnames and selecting the gentle names. The laws of the primitive Japanese, as of all ancient peoples, were those of custom. Though their details have been lost, it is likely that the two fundamental principles—Imperial sovereignty and the

---

[1] Wu-wai's preface to reprint of *Chan-yüan-chu-chüan-Chi-tu-hsü.*
[2] *Ch'uan-hsin-fa-yao.*
[3] Tao-hsüan asserted this. (Taishō, XLV, p. 833b.)
[4] Ch'an-yüan-chu-chuan-Chi-tu-hsü, 11.
[5] *Ibid.,* 35.

family system—were firmly established even in those days. But no positive law of those days is now known to us. It is with Prince Shōtoku that we first come to know something of laws in the modern sense.

Prince Shōtoku, the real founder of the centralized State of Japan, proclaimed the Seventeen-Article Constitution in A.D. 604. This was the first legislation in Japan—the characteristic expression of the original and creative development of the Japanese in those days—adopting the civilizations and thoughts of China and India sufficiently for their purposes, based chiefly upon the spirit of Buddhism. This is, so to speak, the *Magna Charta* of Japan. The Constitution prescribed the rules of conduct which the officials of the Imperial government should obey, thereby, perchance, revealing how badly needed such rules were. It has been confirmed by scholars that there is a close connection between the spirit of Shōtoku's Constitution and the political regime established at the Taika Innovation, which brought about the unified State of Japan.

In contrast to Prince Shōtoku and his Seventeen-Article Constitution, King Songtsan-Gampo, the founder of the centralized State of Tibet, proclaimed his Sixteen-Article Law of similar purport at nearly the same time, and, looking back to antiquity, we find that King Aśoka published many Rock and Pillar Edicts which proclaimed various precepts whose number was not fixed. The characteristic common to all of these is that they approximate moral precepts in the form of representation, and that they were different from positive laws in practice.

The move to conceptualize human affairs in terms of laws and concepts which are universals has been effected by the Japanese to some extent. The concept of universal law came into existence very early in the time of Prince Shōtoku, when he said: "Sincerely revere the Three Treasures. The three Treasures, viz., the Buddha, the Law (*Dharma*), and the Congregation (*Saṅgha*), constitute the final ideal of all living beings and the ultimate foundation of all countries. Should any age or any people fail to esteem this truth? There are few men who are really vicious. They will all follow it if adequately instructed. How can the crooked ways of men be made straight unless we take refuge in the Three Treasures?" [1] Here we find the concept of a universal law which is something beyond laws based on the inductively

---

[1] Prince Shōtoku's Constitution, Article 2.

given status of the individual in the joint family and of the family in its respective tribe or caste. According to the Prince, the "Law" is the "norm" of all the living creatures. The "Buddha" is in fact "the Law embodied," which, "being united with reason," becomes the *Saṅgha*. So, according to his teaching, everything converges in the one fundamental principle called the "Law."

It is likely that other Asian kings who adopted Buddhism thought in the same way. Aśoka, however, resorted to *dharma*, which is valid for various religions, and not necessarily Buddhism alone. Things being so, it may seem that there was a fundamental difference between Aśoka and other Asian monarchs, including Prince Shōtoku. Investigating the fundamental ideas which brought these historical facts to reality, however, we find there was not much difference. In the case of Prince Shōtoku, there was only one philosophical system which taught universal laws, Buddhism. It was natural that he termed Buddhism "the final ideal of all living beings and the ultimate foundation of all countries." In the case of Aśoka, however, many religious systems had already become highly developed, and there were many other religions which claimed to be universal philosophical systems. So, he had to consider many religions. When we examine the situation more deeply, we find that the quintessence of Buddhism consists in acknowledging the universal laws taught by all religions and philosophies, as is evidenced in both early and Mahāyāna Buddhism. So, we are led to the conclusion that there is no fundamental difference in ideology between King Aśoka and Prince Shōtoku.

g) *The Origin of Law by Means of a Social Contract*

Concerning the origin of law, most Indian religions expressed the view which might be classified as that of the natural law school, as grew out of the Stoic philosophy and Roman jurisprudence, to the effect that law is the expression of right reason inhering in the nature of man and society which is ethically binding as a rule of civil conduct. This feature has already been discussed. However, Indian religions were not lacking in the view of the analytical school, as was definitely formulated by Thomas Hobbes in his Leviathan (1651), but became dominant among English-speaking peoples through the writings of John Austin (1790-1859). According to the view, law is the command of the sovereign to his subjects to perform or abstain from performing definite acts, to the breach of which a definite penalty is attached.

Exactly the Indian counterpart of the theory can be found in

Buddhist and Jain literature. Concerning the problem of the origin of law, early Buddhists held a theory which reminds us of that of social contract. According to it, the authority of sovereignty was not conferred upon kings by gods, but was given them by people through the process of election.

According to a legend, in ancient times human beings began to feed on hoarded rice. They divided off the rice fields and set up boundaries round them. Now someone being of greedy disposition, watching over his own plot, stole another plot and made use of it. They took him and holding him fast, said: "Truly, good being, you have done evil in that, while watching your own plot, you have stolen another plot and made use of it. See to it that you do not such a thing again!" "Aye, sirs," he replied. And a second time he did so. And yet a third. And again they took him and admonished him. Some smote him with the hand, some with clods, some with sticks. With such a beginning stealing appeared, and censure and lying and punishment became known. Now those beings gathered themselves together, and bewailed these things, saying: "From our evil deeds, sirs, becoming manifest, inasmuch as stealing, censure, lying, punishment, have become known, what if we were to select a certain being, who should be wrathful when indignation is right (*sammā*), who should censure that which should rightly be censured and should banish him who deserves to be banished. And we will contribute to thee a proportion of our rice." And he consented, and did so, and they gave him a proportion of their rice. "So Mahāsammmata (literally, 'chosen by the whole people') was the first standing phrase to be applied to such a king. Buddhists thought that the king was originally elected by the whole people." In this connection the scripture repeatedly says: "Law is the supreme one among people." (*dhammo hi seṭṭho jane*) [1]. The rights of a king were not considered to be sacred.

h) *Flexibility of Law*

There is an important question, i.e., whether this universal law was ever conceived in *specific determinate terms* as the western notion of abstract, universal, determinate law is. A distinction should be drawn about the universality of law in the Hindu view and that of the west. Also the Hindu's distrust of any *specifically formulable* law applicable to *all* cases should be considered. Hindu laws were more

---

[1] *Dīgha-Nikāya*, XXVII, 17 ff.

flexible, and commentators on established laws allowed modifications of them in applying them to each new case.

A significant characteristic of dharma which deserves to be specially noted is that it was regarded as not being static. The content of dharma often changed in the changing contexts of time, place, and social environment. In this connection, Northrop's discussion, [1] giving specific examples to substantiate his view that the Indian is distrustful of the abstract formulation of the law and wants to consider each individual case on its own merits, should be considered relevant. However, there remain various problems for critical reflection.

In the eyes of the Hindus, dharma is not static. The concept and content of dharma change in accordance with the changing circumstances. Ancient tradition speaks of four ages (*yugas*)—Krita, Tretā, Dvāpara, and Kali—their duration, respectively, 1,728,000; 1,296,000; 864,000; and 432,000 human years. It is believed that each of these four succeeding ages is characterized by an increasing physical and spiritual deterioration. No one uniform set of dharmas can, therefore, be made applicable to all the four ages.

"Austerities (*tapas*) constitute the highest dharma in the Krita age; in the Tretā, sacred knowledge is declared to be the highest dharma; in the Dvāpara they speak of the performance of sacrifice as the highest dharma; giving alone is the highest dharma in the Kali age." (Manu, I. 86.)

Already in early Buddhism it was admitted that the Buddhist canon law should be changed according to the change of environments in which monks lived. "The Buddha said: 'I tell you, O monks! Even what I have prescribed should not be practised, if it has come out not to be pure in other districts. Even what I have not prescribed should not fail to be practiced, if it has come out to be practiced necessarily in other districts.' " [2] "One should be in accord with the secular laws of each country in which one lives. One should not consent to it, nor should one blame it." [3]

This characteristic of early Buddhism was preserved by later Buddhists in other countries. The Tibetan Buddhist is not required to toe the line of any accepted creed—he has perfect freedom to establish

---

[1] F. S. C. Northrop, *The Taming of the Nations,* (New York, Macmillan, 1953).

[2] The Chinese translation of the *Mahisasaka-vinya,* vol. 22. *Taisho Tripiṭaka,* vol. 22, p. 153a. Cf. *Taisho Tripiṭaka,* vol. 40, p. 2a. The Sanskrit text of the original is lost.

[3] The Chinese translation of the *Madhyamakāgama-sūtra,* vol. 43, *Janapadaniruttiṃ nābhiniveseyya.* (*Majjhima-nikāya,* ed. by the Pali Text Society, London, vol. III, p. 234.)

his own philosophy or doctrine provided only that he can demonstrate in his own life the results of whatever methods of spiritual training and understanding he advocates. Tibetans think that it is because of this tolerant attitude that Buddhism has been able to develop its vast and varied doctrines which are not just differences of opinion but are the different outcomes of a variety of successful experiments. [1]

A prominent characteristic of Chinese Buddhism in contrast to Indian religions appears in the fact that the idea of precepts for virtue or *dharma* was highly esteemed in both countries but was accepted in different ways. The Chinese emphasized only the concrete worldly aspect of this idea of *dharma,* so that for them the universal principle of virtue appears in different forms according to the time and place. The principle can be universal only by changing its form in different contexts. The idea of *dharma* set forth in Buddhism is not a stagnant one, and therefore, ethical principles or *dharma* naturally change and develop with the lapse of time. A characteristic of Chinese Buddhism in the later period can be seen in the greater attention given to the individual concrete form of the principle of *dharma* as interpreted by the Chinese Buddhists when compared with the attitude of most Indian Buddhists earlier.

In Japan the Buddhist concept of law was considerably affected by the traditional way of thinking of the Japanese. As has often been pointed out, the inclination to regard as absolute a limited specific human nexus naturally brings about a tendency to disregard any allegedly universal law of humanity that every man ought to observe at any place or time. Instead, the standard of the evaluation of good and evil is identified here with the consideration of the appropriateness or inappropriateness of conduct, judged solely by reference to the particular human nexus to which one happens to belong.

The ambivalence and conflict of universalism and nationalism appeared in the pattern of the acceptance of Buddhism. At first Buddhism was accepted, by Prince Shōtoku and a group of bureaucrats under his control, as a universal teaching that everyone should follow. Buddhism was estimated thereby as "the terminating end of four lives (four kinds of all living creatures) and the ultimate religion of all nations," and among the Three Treasures of the Buddha, the Law, and the Brotherhood (*saṅgha*), the Law or the religious doctrine was especially esteemed. They preached in consequence, "Why should any period or

---

[1] Lhalungpa in K. W. Margan's *The Path of the Buddha*, op. cit., p. 272.

any man not reverence this law?" [1] According to Prince Shōtoku, "The Law" is "the norm" of all living creatures, "the Buddha" is in fact "the Law embodied," which "being united with Reason" becomes *saṅgha*. So, according to this way of teaching, everything converges on the one fundamental principle called "the Law." [2]

Even among the various sects of Buddhism during that characteristically Japanese period of Kamakura (1185-1333), the sense of the universality of "the Law," as preached in Buddhism, was not lost. Dōgen (1200-1253), the Zen master, says: "Because there is the Way, Buddhas and their forerunners are comprehended. Without the Way there is no comprehension. Because there is the Law, things are originated. Without the Law nothing is originated." Here too the Law and the Way are used interchangeably. Shinran (1173-1262) himself quotes a sentence by Nāgārjuna: "See, enter and acquire the Law, and live in the solid Law, and don't vacillate." [3] Nichiren also esteems the Hokke Sūtra as the Truth more highly than he does the Buddha. "I am asked why I should make the prayer of the Hokke Sūtra, instead of the Buddha (Shākyamuni), the principal object of worship. I answer that...while the Buddha is the body, the Hokke Sūtra is the spirit." [4] "The Hokke Sūtra is just as superior to a Buddha as the moon to a star and as the sun to artificial light." [5]

Among the Japanese, however, there is a strong tendency to understand such a universal law only in reference to some particular or specific phase of things. Moreover, the Japanese sought a standard for the evaluation of different thoughts by laying emphasis upon historical and topographical specificity or particularity.

In Japan, the Tendai doctrine, which laid the foundation for the doctrines of other sects of Buddhism in Japan, puts emphasis upon "Things," while in China the doctrine of the same sect regards "Reason" as most important. "Things" here mean observable *specificities or particularities* limited in time and space. Shimei (Ssuming, 1060-1128), a Chinese Tendai scholar, preached that the first half (Shakumon) of the Hokke Sūtra explains the perfect Truth in conformity with the Law of Reason (the perfect Reason), while the second half (Honmon) of the Sūtra exposes "the perfect Truth" in accordance

---

[1] Prince Shōtoku's Seventeen-Article Constitution I.
[2] His Commentary on the *Shōman-gyō*.
[3] *Kyōgyōkhinshō*, chapter 2.
[4] *Honzon-Modō-shō* (Questions and Answers on the Main Buddha).
[5] In his Letter to the Nun Kubo.

with phenomena (perfect Things). Even this latter truth expresses for him the eternal Buddha. In contrast, Eshin (942-1017), a Japanese Tendai scholar, while accepting this twofold interpretation, interpreted "the perfect Reason" to mean the comprehension of the multiplicity of the phenomenal world through the indiscriminatory Truth (Sessō Kishō), and "the perfect Thing" to mean the revelation of the Truth through the multiplicity of phenomena. [1]

The tendency to attach more importance to things than to reason is one of the characteristics of the Japanese Zen sect, in contrast to that of China, and the teachings of the Japanese priests like Dōgen (1200-1253) and Hakuin (1685-1768) prove it.

Based upon this pluralistic way of thinking, most of the Buddhist sects in Japan teach that doctrines should always be made "apropos of the time." Especially the idea of the age of degeneration penetrated deep into the core of the doctrines of various sects, which admitted that they were in the age of degeneration and religious doctrines ought to be made suitable to it. Each of the sects ended up claiming the superiority of their respective sūtras or doctrines, as most suited to the age of corruption. This fundamental tendency is most manifest in the teachings of Nichiren, based upon the Japanese Tendai doctrine. He lays special emphasis upon the particularity and specificity of the truth of humanity. "The learning of just one word or one phrase of the Right Law, only if it should accord with the time and the propensity of the learner, would lead him to the attainment of the Way. The mastery even of a thousand scriptures and ten thousand theories, if they should not accord with the time and the propensity of the one who masters them, would lead him nowhere." [2] Nichiren's evaluation of sectarian doctrines is called "The Five Standards of Religion." It sets five standards from which to evaluate the depth or shallowness and the superiority or inferiority of all the Buddhist doctrines originated from the Buddha, these five standards being the teaching (of the sūtra), the propensity (the spiritual endowments of the learner), the time (the demands of the age), the country (where the doctrine is practiced), and the order (before and after the propagation of the doctrine, or the preceding circumstances under which the doctrines were practiced). Nichiren concluded, judging from those five standards, that the Hokke (Lotus) Sūtra was the superior one. Saichō regarded the time and the country as important factors, but he did not

---

[1] Daitō Shimaji, *Tendai Kyōgaku-shi* (History of Tendai Theology), p. 492.
[2] *Sado-gosho*.

go so far as to establish them as basic principles. It was Nichiren (1222-1282) who presented them in a clear and distinct form, and it was Nichiren who first put forth "the circumstances" before and after the propagation of the doctrine. The tendency of the Japanese Tendai sect to lay emphasis upon actuality was brought to its extremity by Nichiren, and such a method of evaluation has hardly been found either in India or in China. Herein lies a reason why Nichirenism in the past was so easily tied up with nationalism.

Such a particularistic way of thinking as discussed above seems to be a general trend during the medieval period. The *Gukanshō*, for instance, often uses the word "reason," which by no means signifies the universal reason that applies to any country of the world, but which means each of the historical manifestations of reason peculiar to Japan. The historical manifestations, where political and religious factors are closely entangled, are not analyzed from a universal standpoint, but are classified according to the particular periods of development.

This characteristic which can be found in the process of the introduction of Buddhism also applies to the influence of Chinese thought. Discussions on its details will be skipped. Anyhow, the tendency of Japanese Buddhism to put "Things" before "Reason," as already discussed, also appears in the formation of late Japanese Confucianism.

If both Buddhists and Confucianists emphasize that in Japan there ought to be a way appropriate to Japan, and if they push that theory to its logical conclusion, will it not become meaningless for them to remain Buddhists or Confucianists? It amounts to believing that for the Japanese it is enough to observe the *Way of Japan,* even when the equally valid claims of both Confucianism and Buddhism for guiding man to the right conduct are to be taken for granted. Such a logic was presented by some staunch Shintoist leaders.

Those scholars who claimed to be independent of Buddhism, Confucianism, or Shintoism also followed suit. For instance, Nakamoto Tominaga (1715-1746), an Ōsaka merchant, scholar, and freethinker, advocated "the true Way" or "the Way of Ways" which he defined as "the Way that should be practiced in present-day Japan." In order for the "true Way" to be realized, it should be limited both in time, i.e., "the present day," and in space, i.e., "Japan." Thus his theory evidently claims that "the Way" as the principle of human existence manifests itself in the form inevitably determined historically and geographically. He denounces as "the ways against the true Way" the

Shintoism advocated by his contemporary scholars of Japanese classical literature, the Confucianism taught by the Confucianists, and the Buddhism preached by the Buddhists, because, he says, all of them took no notice of the historical and topographical pecularities of human existence.

We are now led to conclude that it was a distinctive characteristic of many Japanese scholars to use the idea of "historically determined present-day Japan" as the measuring rod for evaluating all systems of thought.

When such a way of thinking is pushed to its extreme, it ends up with its emphasis on the limited human nexus, in ethno-centricism or supernationalism, and with its emphasis upon the specificity of the time, in opportunism, which leads to compromise in a given particular situation. It is easily turned into a tendency to neglect the universal law that ought to be observed by mankind everywhere. Any system of thought inclined to disregard the universal cannot attain a permanent place among the systems of thought of mankind.

The Japanese inclination to lay too much emphasis upon particular facts or specific phases amounts to the anti-intellectual standpoint of no theory or anti-theory. It ends up with the contempt of rational thinking and the worship of uncontrolled intuitionism and activism. Herein lies the intellectual cause of the failure of Japan in the past, and the danger still lies in this direction today. In order not to repeat the same failure, we ought from now on to learn to seek universal "reason" through specific "facts." [1]

i) *Less Control by Legislative Body*

Among Indians the attitude of reverence for universal standards in behavior was very conspicuous. As a result of their inclination to submit themselves to a universal Being, Indians harbor an ardent desire to have direct relations with the Absolute and refuse to have any intermediate agent. They assert that the salvation of one's soul should be attained only by one's own efforts without relying upon others. In the philosophy of Brahmanism, regarding the emancipation of the soul, it is taught that a man who has realized the truth of the universe "gets into his own Self by dint only of his Self." [2] And Buddhists, though they do not engage in any metaphysical consider-

---

[1] *Okina-no Fumi*, Chapter 2.
[2] *Vājasaneyi-saṃhitā*, XXXII, 11. Cf. Māṇḍūkya-Up. 12.

ation of "the Self" (*Ātman*), acknowledge its moral significance as the subject of action saying that only the Self can save the Self. A passage from the *Dhammapada* reads as follows: "Sons are no help, nor a father, nor relations; there is no help from kinfolk for one whom death has seized." [1] Jains, too, admit that all things other than one's self are useless for one's salvation saying: "They cannot help thee or protect thee." They say again: "Man! Thou art thine own friend; why wishest thou for a friend beyond thyself?" [2]

In later periods the Mahāyāna Buddhists had faith in salvation through the power of the great compassion of the Buddhas and the Bodhisattvas, and the schools of Hinduism emphasize salvation by the grace of Viṣṇu or Śiva. But, it should be noted, even in such cases one confronts the absolute by pleading directly to these gods for the salvation of one's soul. And here little significance is attached to any intermediate agents between the absolute and the individual beings.

It is natural that from such views of the Indians on salvation no religious order, which is itself a limited social organization, would take active leadership as the absolute source of authority. In Europe, the monks sometimes had political power equal to that of the king. In India, on the other hand, the political influence of the religious bodies was very weak. Brahmanists maintained a consanguineous cultural unity among themselves. This unity, however, served only to form their own particular exclusive class, and this body of Brahmanists did not function as a political unit. What is more, they had no leader to rule over the body, and an individual Brahmanist could behave at his own will without any check by a supervising authority. It is natural that such a loose organization had no solid financial basis like the Roman Catholic Church.

It is true that Buddhists established the Sangha (monastic order). The Sangha is the point at which the Dhamma makes direct contact with humanity; it is the bridge between living man and absolute truth. The Buddha strongly emphasized the importance of the Sangha as a necessary institution for the good of mankind. If there had not been the Sangha, the Dhamma would not have been conveyed to posterity. It is the Sangha which has preserved not only the Word of the Master, but also the unique spirit of the Noble teaching since the Master's passing away. However, since the time of its establishment the Bud-

[1] *Dhammapada*, 288.
[2] *Āyāraṅga*, I, 2, 1, 2.

dhist Saṁgha was also without political or economic unity. Even while the Buddha was still alive, his followers lived apart from him, and no regulation was made binding all of these followers. After the death of the Buddha, they were intent only on the faithful observance of the doctrines and the disciplines set forth by their late teacher, and did not choose to have a political leader of their Saṁgha.

Moreover, the Buddhist Saṁgha *did not claim to be a legislative authority* or *an authority on the interpretation of the doctrine.* This assertion can be safely made at least in respect to its attitude toward important issues. Buddhists attributed the authority of legislation exclusively to the Buddha. They considered that all the rules of the Saṁgha are authorized by claiming that they all came under the title "the Buddha's own discourse." Even the new rules established after the Buddha's death to meet the changing social situations were also attributed to the Buddha's authority. One of their books of precepts states as follows: "If a new situation arises at some time to confront the Saṁgha, not ordaining what has not been ordained, and not revoking what has been ordained, one should take it upon himself to direct himself always according to the precepts laid down. This is the resolution." [1] Interpreting the vague statements in the old texts, Buddhists attributed their own interpretation to the Buddha, and for authority they referred not to the Saṁgha but to the Buddha. This is the attitude of the Buddhists, at least the Buddhists of the early days, in their interpretation of the texts.

The same features of thought discernible in the early Buddhist Saṁgha are found among the Jains. The Mahāyāna Buddhists who appeared later in history assumed the same attitude, as did the schools of Hinduism. Although some of the Indian sects—the most distinct example being the Sikhs—kept a systematic unity in their body, they were exceptional cases. Indians, in contrast to their indifferent attitude toward social organizations like the Saṁgha, attach the greatest importance to the authority of the universal law—the law that all individuals and all social organizations should follow.

Chinese Buddhists did not form religious organizations which governed priests and temples. Nevertheless, they did greatly esteem the observance of the precept and believed that it was the essential basis of all good actions to keep the precepts, because they were fully conscious of the importance and sacredness of the *dharma* as the Ab-

---

[1] *Vinaya*, Cullavagga XI, 1, 9.

solute. Even at present, Chinese priests observe and practice the precepts. It is said that priests who violate the precepts cannot be respected by the people. The laymen, as well as priests, observe the precepts very strictly in China. There is no governing religious organization in China. Therefore, Buddhist followers are not punished or expelled even if they do not observe the Buddhist precepts. Nevertheless, they follow them closely. On the other hand, in the Japanese Buddhist societies where the precepts are not necessarily observed by the followers, these followers are strictly controlled, politically and economically, by the sectarian organization.

j) *Rationalism and the Concept of "Law"*

Both Buddhism and Jainism belonged to the movement of heterodoxy (nāstika): both were originated not by the Brahmin priests but by members of the warrior and merchant classes, in a reaction against sacerdotal ceremonialism and theology; they aimed at establishing their religions by means of free thinking independent of the Brahmanistic tradition.

The attitude to esteem universal norms was the heart and essence of the Buddhist reformation in the religion and philosophy of India. Its central tenets are all drawn up so as to exclude any reference to gods or souls in their strictest application. Buddhists asserted that even the existence of Brahma, the greatest god esteemed in those days, could not be proved. Buddhists assumed no Creator.

In a Buddhist scripture there is a dialogue to the effect that the Buddha pointed out the fact that not one of the Brahmins, even up to the seventh generation, has ever seen Brahma face to face, and that even they did not pretend to know, or to have seen where or whence or whither Brahma is. Then, the talk of these Brahmins, versed in their three Vedas, turned out to be ridiculous, mere words, a vain and empty thing.

Just in the same way, Brahma, the highest god, cannot be seen. Therefore he must not be believed in. [1]

Magical power in the command of the Brahmins also was refuted by the Buddha in the same way. "If a great river were full of water, and overflowing and a man with business for the other side, bound for the other side, should come up and want to cross over, and he, standing on this bank, were to invoke the further bank, and say, 'Come

---

[1] Tevijja-sutta. T. W. Rhys Davids, *Indian Buddhism*, pp. 56-60.

hither, further bank! Come over to this side!' Now what do you think of him? Would the further bank of the river, by means of that man's invoking, and praying, come over to this side?"

"Certainly not, Gotama!"

"In just the same way, Vasettha, the Brahmins versed in the Vedas say thus: 'Indra we call upon, Soma we call upon, Varuna we call upon, and so on.' By reason of their invoking and praying such a condition of things will never happen!" So invocation is of no use.

The Buddha introduced another parable: "Suppose a man should say so, 'How I long for, how I love, the most beautiful woman in this land!' And people should ask him, 'Well, good friend, this beautiful woman in the land, whom you thus love and long for, do you know whether that beautiful woman is a noble lady, or a Brahmin woman, or of the trader class, or slave?'

"And when so asked, he should answer, 'No!'

"And when people should ask him, 'Well, good friend, this most beautiful woman in all the land, whom you so love and long for, do you know what her name is, or her family name; whether she be tall or short, dark or of medium complexion, black or fair; or in what village or town or city she dwells?'

"But when so asked, he should answer, 'No!'

"Now what do you think of him? Would it not turn out that the talk of that man was foolish talk?"

His conception of religion was purely ethical; he cared everything about conduct, nothing about ritual or worship, metaphysics or theology. When a Brahmin proposed to purify himself of his sins by bathing at Gaya, the holy place, the Buddha said to him: "Have your bath here, even here, O Brahmin. Be kind to all beings. If you don't speak false, if you don't kill life, if you don't take what is not given to you, secure in self-denial, what would you gain by going to Gaya? Any water is Gaya to you:" [1]

The Buddha rejects outward signs of asceticism as they do not purify our personal existence. "Not nakedness, not matted hair, not dirt, not fasting, not lying on the ground, not rubbing with ashes, not sitting motionless purify a mortal who is not free from doubt." [2] (We hear the same echo in the west also. "For I desire steadfast love and not sacrifice, the knowledge of God, rather than burnt offerings.") [3]

---

[1] S. Radhakrishnan, *Indian Philosophy*, Vol. I, *op. cit.*, p. 421.
[2] *Dhammapada*, 141.
[3] Hosea, VI. 6.

"If a man month after month for a hundred years should sacrifice with a thousand sacrifices, and if he but for one moment pay homage to a man whose self is grounded in knowledge, better is that homage than what is sacrificed for a hundred years." [1] In the west also, "Behold, to obey is better than sacrifice." [2]

The Buddha repudiated all religious customs that were observed only conventionally. "What is the use of matted hair, O fool, what of the raiment of goat skins? Your inward nature is full of wickedness; the outside you make clean." [3] Jesus also cried to the same effect: "Woe to you, scribes and Pharisees, hypocrites! For you are like whitewashed tombs, which outwardly appear beautiful, but within they are full of dead men's bones and all uncleanness. So you also outwardly appear righteous to men, but within you are full of hypocrisy and iniquity." [4]

(In Greece Theodorus taught that all ethical and legal prescriptions were ultimately merely institutions that were valid for the mass of men; he bore the surname "the atheist," and put aside all religious scruples which are opposed to devotion to sensuous enjoyment. Epicurus, whose ethics had so many features in common with the Buddhist, also was exceptionally hostile to traditional religion.)

Considering these assertions we may say that the attitude of Early Buddhists was highly positivistic. But it does not mean that the scriptures of Early Buddhism do not contain anything miraculous or supernatural. In order to edify the common people they resorted very often to various forms of popular faith. Miracle stories and legends of the Buddha and the saints are very often mentioned, but they are not essential to Buddhism.

What Southern Buddhist leaders assert nowadays is as follows:

> "Because the Bhudda's way is the way of rationality, he did not ask for absolute faith in himself or his teaching. Rather, he said that we must not believe anything merely because it was handed down by tradition, or said by a great person, or commonly accepted, or even because the Buddha said it. The Buddha taught that we should believe only that which is true in the light of our known experience, that which conforms to reason and is conducive to the highest good and welfare of all beings. The follower of the Buddha is invited to doubt

---

[1] *Dhammapada*, 106.
[2] I Samuel XV, 22.
[3] *Dhammapada*, 394.
[4] Matthew XXIII, 27-28. Cf. Luke XI, 39.

until he has examined all the evidence for the basic facts of the teaching and has himself experimented with them to see if they are true. Having proved by these means that they are true he is able to accept them. One of the qualities of the Dhamma, the path of the Buddha, is that it is 'Ehi Passiko'—that which invites everyone to come and see for himself." [1]

For the first time in the history of the world, it proclaimed a salvation which each man could gain for himself, and by himself, in this world, during this life, without the least reference to God, or to gods, either great or small, although this feature greatly changed in later days. Concerning this feature, Nietzsche said: "Buddhism is a hundred times more realistic than Christianity: posing problems objectively and coolly is part of its inheritance, for Buddhism comes after a philosophic movement which spanned centuries. The concept of 'God' had long been disposed of when it arrived. Buddhism is the only genuinely positivistic religion in history." [2] Nietzsche's comment is still liable to objection. But we have to admit that it has brought to light some features of Buddhist thinking.

According to Buddhism, faith becomes superstition when it is not examined by reason. Gotama, the founder of Buddhism, was described as one who reasons according to the truth rather than on the basis of the authority of the Vedas or tradition. It was on the basis of reasoning that Buddha refuted the personal God (Brahma). He claimed "enlightenment," but not inspiration. How much less of revelation! Southern and Northern Buddhism have accepted two standards for the truth of a statement: first it must be in accord with the scriptures and, second, it must be proved true by reasoning. No Buddhist is expected to believe anything which does not meet these two tests.

Buddhism, from the outset, has presupposed universal laws called *dharmas,* which govern human existence, and may be known by reason. This notion has been inherited by all schools of Buddhism. According to the Buddha, personal relation or personal conduct should be brought into harmony with the universal norms, the universal laws which apply to all existence. The word *dharma* is often used as meaning the teachings of the Buddha; in this sense *dharma* is not dogma, but is rather the Path which is regarded as the universal norm for all mankind, comformity to the nature of the universe.

---

[1] U Thittila in K. W. Morgan's *The Path of the Buddha*, p. 72.

[2] Friedrich Nietzsche, *The Antichrist, The Portable Nietzsche*, Selected and translated by Walter Kaufman, (New York, the Viking Press, 1954), pp. 586-587.

This acceptance of rational analysis of the nature of human existence has been a continuing characteristic of Buddhism, but it should be noted that metaphysical speculation concerning problems not related to human activities and to the attainment of Enlightenment has not been considered to be a proper part of Buddhist rationalism. Thus, the teaching of the Buddha is not a system of philosophy in the western sense, but is rather a Path. A Buddha is simply one who has trodden this Path and can report to others on what he has found. This path is called "Law."

All metaphysical views are only partial apprehensions of the whole truth which lies beyond rational analysis.

Only a Buddha can apprehend the whole truth. Rational analysis is useful in making clear the limitations of rationality. The teaching of the Buddha transcends comparison; it is neither inferior, nor equal, nor superior to other doctrines. It is by detaching oneself from philosophical oppositions that one is able to grasp the truth. Thus in Buddhism there is no dogma which opposes other dogmas. Of course, Buddhism as a cultural and historical product developed many different systems of thought in the course of time, but it has always sought to avoid obscurantism or coercion to believe what seems to be irrational.

The Buddha set forth many teachings which later scholars elaborated. Sometimes the scholars contradict each other. However, all Buddhists, whether Theravada or Mahāyāna, agree that they aim to teach the way to realize an ideal life. In Buddhism the entire stress lies on the mode of living, on the purification of life, on the removal of vices. A merely theoretical proposition, such as "there is no ego," would be regarded as utterly sterile and useless.

All Buddhists follow the Buddha in wanting to teach how to lead a selfless life. Rational analysis is no more than a tool which is justified in its products. That is why there are so many teachings even on one subject, such as dependent origination, the Four Noble Truths, etc.

The Buddha's doctrine is called a vehicle in the sense that it is like a ferryboat. One enters the Buddhist vehicle to cross the river of life from the shore of worldly experience, the shore of spiritual ignorance, desire, and suffering to the other shore of transcendental wisdom which is liberation from bondage and suffering. Suppose a man builds a raft and by this means succeeds in attaining the other shore. "What would be your opinion of this man," asks the Buddha, "would he be a clever man if, out of gratitude for the raft that carried him across the stream to safety, he, having reached the other shore, should cling to it, take it on his back, and walk about with the weight of it?" The monks replied, "No." The Buddha then concludes, "In the same way the vehicle of the doctrine is to be cast away and forsaken, once the other shore of Enlightenment (nirvāṇa) has been attained." [1] Just as the diference in shape, weight, and materials among rafts does not matter, difference in teachings does not matter. This point of view is set forth both in Southern and Northern Buddhism. In Zen Buddhism the famous comparison to fingers pointing to the moon is very often set forth. The truth is compared to the moon, whereas fingers of different persons pointing to the same moon are compared to the different doctrines of the Buddha, or occasionally to various religions.

While such an attitude toward the teachings of Buddhism seems quite contradictory, this attitude can be justified. If one says something, it is justified only by what is called "skill in means." Words like "enlightenment," "ignorance," "freedom," and "attachment" are preliminary helps, referring to no ultimate reality, mere hints or signposts for the traveler on the Path, serving only to point out the goal.

The wisdom which is sought in Buddhism is not the wisdom of conflicting metaphysical systems, it is the wisdom of Enlightenment as the true nature of human exitence.

We shall be able to illustrate this in the case of Zen Buddhism and Pure Realm Buddhism. These two types of Buddhism differ from each other, but they are not exclusive to each other. A Catholic should not be a Protestant at the same time, and vice versa. But a Zen Buddhist can be a Pure Realm Buddhist at the same time, and vice versa, when necessary.

Due to the above-mentioned fundamental character of Buddhism, there is no case of conflict between science and religion throughout Buddhist countries, although the development of technology in modern civilization has caused so many troubles there.

Rationalistic attitude can be noticed in the philosophers of other religions of India also. Haribhadra, the Jain philosopher, went to the length of saying that Lord Mahāvīra is not his friend and the others are not his foes; that he is not biased in favor of Mahāvīra and feels no hatred for Kapila and the other philosophers, but that he is desirous of accepting whosoever's doctrine is the true one. [1]

---

[1] *Majjhima-Nikāya*, I, 3, 2. No. 22.
[2] M. Winternitz, *A History of Indian Literature*, vol. 2, (University of Calcutta, 1933), p. 583.

Even Hindus said as follows:

> A śāstra, though it was made by men, deserves to be accepted, if it is reasonable. One must follow reason. A speech, if reasonable, must be accepted even from a child, but that which is not reasonable should be rejected like a piece of straw though it might be uttered even by Brahman, the creator. That man is not certainly wise who, rejecting the beautiful water of the Ganges flowing before him, drinks from a well thinking only that it belongs to his father. [1]

The Indian religion which acknowledges the authority of the eternal universal law is very rationalistic in its character and it offers a striking contrast to some less logical, personal religions of the west. Schopenhauer once said that the Indian religion which has developed from rational speculation about the world is superior to Christianity. [2] Setting aside the question of whether he is right or wrong, his remark indicates the essential difference between the Indian and Christian religions.

For Indians, it is a matter of the greatest moral and religious importance to know the Universal Law and to submit themselves to it. This feature of Indian thought can be observed also in their concept of "faith." *Śraddhā* is the Sanskrit word that is usually translated into western languages as *"fides," "Glaube,"* or *"faith."* But what Indians mean by the word is not exactly the same as the faith of western religions. *Śraddhā* means to believe in and rely upon a man of superior wisdom and at the same time, it indicates wholehearted acceptance of the doctrines that the man professes. Ancient Indians, refusing to place faith in a particular person or saint, hoped to submit themselves to the Universal Law that stands above all individuals.

In early Buddhist texts, faith in the Buddha is expressed, but this should not be understood as being a worship of a particular saint, Gotama and the Buddha. Gotama is one of the Buddhas—the Enlightened Ones. Buddhist faith in the Buddha means faith in the law that makes the Enlightened One as he is. Jains hold a similar view of faith. Jains in the early stage of their history taught "not to have faith in the illusory power of god." [3] They express true faith by the word *samyagdarśana* or "right-seeing," and thus true faith in

---

[1] Vidhushekhara Bhattacharyya, *The Āgamaśāstra of Guaḍapāda*, (University of Calcutta, 1943), p. 303.
[2] Quoted in Albert Schweitzer, *Das Christentum und die Weltreligionen*, (1924), p. 29.
[3] *Āyāraṅga* I, 8, 8, 24.

their sense in none other than to see the truth in the right way.[1]

For Indians, faith is not the worship of particular individuals, and this nature of their faith can be more clearly observed in the statements of Brahmanists. Psychologically Śaṁkara defines *śraddhā* as "a particular kind of mental state (*pratyayaviśeṣa*),"[2] the nature of which is "delicate (*tanu*)."[3] As the active and practical significance of *śraddhā*, two views are given by the Brahmanists: (1) According to the Vedānta, *śraddhā* is not to put faith in a teacher, but "to accept as true the words in the *Upaniṣads* that the teacher introduces to us."[4] All other schools of Brahmanism agree with the Vedānta in the view that *śraddhā* means the acceptance of the sacred doctrine. (2) As a logical consequence of the first view, *śraddhā* is applied to mean the ideology that urges people to do the things generally approved as good in the Hindu community, especially to perform religious works in a broad sense of the word.[5] It is "the factor which makes all living being do good deeds,"[6] and it is in essence "the idea of traditionalism."[7]

Since the oldest days of their history, Buddhists use the word *prasāda* to mean faith in their sense. As the Chinese translate this word by "*ch'eng ching*" (purity) or "*hsi*" (bliss), it means the calm and pure state of mind in which one feels the bliss of serenity. Buddhist faith is far from fanatic worship. The enthusiastic and fanatic form of reverence, which urges ardent devotion (*bhakti*) to the gods, was advocated by some Buddhist sects of later development and by the schools of Hinduism, but this kind of fanatic devotion to an individual Guru or God failed to win the heart of most Indian intellectuals of antiquity. However, we should not minimize the tremendous vogue of *Bhakti* cults among the common people of India, especially in the second millenium A.D. The most conspicuous starting point of this trend seems to be in the *Bhagavadgītā,* where Vishnu says, "If you surrender everything to Me, you will undoubtedly gain salvation." This trend still lingers in contemporary India, so that we should recognize the existence of various trends in the history of thought in India.

---

[1] *Tattvādhigama-sūtra*, I, 2. Cf. Yogaśastra, I, 17. *Sarvadarsanasaṃgraha*, III, line 155f.

[2] *Brahmasūtrabhaṣya*, vol. II, p. 143, line 9 (*Ān. SS.*).

[3] *Brahmasūtrabhaṣya* II, 144, line 8.

[4] *Vedāntasāra*, 23.

[5] Śaṅkara on the *Brahma-sūtra* II, p. 144, line 10.

[6] Śaṅkara on *Praśna-Up.*, VI, 4.

[7] āstiKyabuddhi, *Ibid.*, I, 2.

For Indians, the essence of faith is *to see* the truth or law through any means possible. Whether Buddhists, Jains, or Brahmanists, religious adherents in India all agree in their assertion that right wisdom (*samyagjñāna*) is the way to liberation. [1] They say that liberation means the awakening of mind attained by dint of right wisdom. [2] And they all pay great respect to a man of wisdom (*vivekin*) [3] They call such a man "the man who climbed the terraced heights of wisdom." [4] Thus, in India, *faith and knowledge are understood to be compatible*; consequently, the Indian religion bears a strong *tinge of philosophy*. That is why in India, such ideas as "I believe it because it is absurd (*credo quia absurdum*)," are rarely, if ever, held, and there is no conflict between religion and philosophy.

In fact, the Indian religion is based on philosophical contemplation and its philosophy is indistinguishable from religion. As Masson-Oursel has ponted out, in India and China, religion is not antagonistic to philosophy or to science. [5] Indians are traditionally a religious and, at the same time, a philosophical people.

Some Buddhists and Hindus, relying upon a unique universalistic way of thinking, have seen what they think to be truth codified as scriptures. (*sic*) In India there are many forged manuscripts, though there are, of course, many such also in China and in western countries. But far exceeding anything like it in other countries, there exist in India a great many books claiming to be the works of ancient saints. Almost all the religious scriptures which mention the names of the authors are spurious documents. This sort of forgery is understandable in the light of the tendency of most Indians toward self-effacement and philosophical minimization of the importance of unique individuals. All the Mahāyāna texts claim unduly to be "the Buddha's discourse." They are forgeries in the sense that they were not expounded directly from the Buddha's own mouth. Even the texts of the Buddhists of earlier days, nearly all of them, were in reality completed after the Buddha's death by his followers. But all of them claim to be "the Buddha's discourse." Then, the question arises, how could the ancient Buddhists make such claims without damaging their moral conscience?

It is natural for the Buddhist devotees to assume that the Buddha's

---

[1] Cf. *Praśnottara-ratnamālikā*, 3.
[2] Cf. *Ibid.*, 10.
[3] Cf. *Ibid.*, 4.
[4] *Dhammapada* 28. Cf. Mahā-bhārata, 12, 151, 11.
[5] Masson-Oursel, *La Philosophie Comparée*, 40.

teachings are absolutely authentic. King Aśoka stated in one of his Edicts that "whatever the Buddha taught is a good teaching." [1] The Buddhists after the death of the Buddha went further and asserted that *any* idea insofar as it is good and correct is the Buddha's teaching. The *Aṅguttara-Nikāya* reads as follows:

> "Imagine, O King, a great heap of grain near some village or market-town, from which country folk carry corn on poles or in baskets, in lap or hand. And if one should approach the folk and question them saying: 'Whence bring you this corn?', how would those folk, in explaining, best explain?"
>
> "They would best explain the matter, sir, by saying, 'We bring it from that great heap of grain.'"
>
> "Even so, O King, *whatsoever be well spoken, all that is the word of the Exalted One, Arahant, the Fully Awakened One*, wholly based thereon is both what we and others say." [2]

The ancient Buddhists thought that *whatever is true should and must have been taught by the Buddha.* Thus, it is not surprising that most Indians were not concerned with the identity of the authors; their only concern was whether or not a certain work expounds the truth. Because the Buddha is any man who realizes the truth perfectly, any book containing the truth is rightly assumed to be the Buddha's teaching. Thus, we see why the ancient Indian Buddhists had no feelings of guilt in claiming the title of "the Buddha's discourse" for their own works.

k) *The Spirit of Harmony or Concord in Contrast to Legal Assertion*

The unanimous moral solidarity of a community has been sought as the social ideal in various countries of Eastern and Southern Asia.

In early Buddhism the ideal of "non-dispute" (*avivāda*) was declared, and this ideal was inherited literally by Advaitic Vedāntins. Concord (*sāmaggī*) among people was especially esteemed. Emperor Aśoka said: "Concourse (*samavāya*) is commendable." [3]

Nearly the same ideal was aimed at intuitively in the spiritual atmosphere of the primitive society of Japan. Later, when the centralized State was established after the conflicts among various tribes

---

[1] Calcutta-Bairāt Edict.
[2] *Aṅguttara-Nikāya,* (ed. by Pali Text Society), IV, p. 163.
[3] Rock Edict XII, D. R. Bhandarkar. *Aśoka.* Third edition, (University of Calcutta, 1955), p. 289.

had ended, "concord" was stressed as the most important principle in the community. Prince Shōtoku emphasized "harmony" or "concord" in human relations. With deep self-reflection, he advocated such concord in the first Article of his Constitution: "Above all else esteem concord; make it your first duty to avoid discord. People are prone to form partisanships, for few persons are really enlightened. Hence, there are those who do not obey their lords and parents, and who come in conflict with their neighbors. But when those above are harmonious, and those below are friendly, there is concord in the discussion of affairs, and right views of things spontaneously gain acceptance. Then what would there be that could not be accomplished?" Some scholars say that this conception of concord (*wa*) was adopted from Confucianism, for the word "*wa*" was used in the *Analects* of Confucius. [1] But the term "*wa*" was used in connection with propriety or decorum in that work, [2] and concord was not the subject being discussed. Prince Shōtoku, on the other hand, advocated concord as the principle of human behavior. [3] His attitude seems to have been derived from the Buddhist concept of benevolence, or compassion, which should be distinguished from the Confucian concept. Men are apt to be bigoted and partial. Within a community or between communities conflicts are sure to occur. One should overcome such conflicts, and concord should be realized, so that a harmonious community may be formed in an ideal way. The spirit of concord was stressed throughout all the Articles of the Constitution. Concord between lord and subject, between superior and inferior, among people in general, and among individuals was taught repeatedly. Prince Shōtoku did not teach that the people shall merely follow or obey but that discussion should be carried on in the atmosphere of concord or harmony, so that one might attain right views. Earnest discussion was not desirable. If we discuss affairs with the feeling of harmony, desisting from anger, difficult problems will be settled spontaneously in the right way. In this way alone is it possible that decisions may be reached at conferences.

The democratic way of managing a conference was achieved in the remote past. In the Rigvedic India people got together in assemblies

---

[1] Confucius, *Analects* I, 12: "In practising the rules of propriety a natural ease is to be prized." Here "a natural ease" is the translation of the Chinese word "*wa*". In James Legge's version, edited with notes by Yoshio Ogaeri, (Tokyo, Bunki Shoten, 1950), p. 4.

[2] In the Chinese versions of Buddhist texts such words as *wakyō* and *wagō* are frequently used.

[3] Prince Shōtoku's Constitution, Article 10.

(*samiti* and *sabhā*) to discuss various things, and this practice lasted for many generations of posterity. In later India the institution of pancayat was implemental in managing things in a democratic way. The Buddha extolled the regime of republic by the Vajjians, saying, "So long as Vajjians meet together in concord, ... so long may the Vajjians be expected not to decline, but to prosper." [1] In the Buddhist order of India things were decided by voting.

In the mythology which reflects the primitive society of Japan, deities gathered in a divine assembly in the bed of a river. This tradition was followed and developed by later monarchs. Prince Shōtoku denounced dictatorship and stressed the necessity of discussing things with others: "Decisions on important matters should generally not be made by one person alone. They should be discussed with many others. But small matters are of less importance, and it is unnecessary to consult many persons concerning them. In the case of weighty matters, you must be fearful lest there be faults. You should arrange matters in consultation with many persons, so as to arrive at the right conclusion." [2]

This trend developed into the edict after the Taika Innovation (A.D. 645), which denounced the distatorship of a sovereign by saying that things should not be instituted by a single ruler. The ancient way of ruling represented in Japanese mythology is not dictatorship by a monarch or by the Lord of All, but a conference of gods in the bed of a river. Where public opinion was not esteemed, a conference could not have been held successfully. So, the spirit of primitive Shintoism must have been inherited and developed by later rulers. This idea was preserved in the days when the emperors were in power. Japanese monarchy or the Emperor Institution developed as something different from dictatorship.

Professor Northrop holds that when a dispute arises among Asians one does not settle it by recourse to determinate legal principles, but pursues the "middle way" or mediation between the determinate theses of the disputants, by fostering the all-embracing intuitively felt formlessness common to all men and things. [3] Chiang Monlin writes, "Modern legal sense as the west understands it is not developed in

---

[1] *Mahaparinibbana-suttanta*, I, 4. T. W. and C. A. F. Davids, *Dialogues of the Buddha*, (London, Luzac and Co., 1951), p. 80.

[2] Prince Shōtoku's Constitution, Article 17.

[3] F. S. C. Northrop, *The Taming of the Nations*, (New York, The Macmillan Co., 1953), p. 62.

China. Avoid the courts if you can. Let us settle our disputes without going to law. Let's compromise. Let's have a cup of tea and sip together with friends and talk things over." [1] This is exactly the situation we find among the Japanese also. There is a well-known Japanese proverb which is understood by everybody in practice: "In a quarrel both parties are to blame."

In India also we find a similar situation. One frequently has the impression that the administrators regarded lawsuits as a nuisance. Witnesses are fined for wasting time. In the Mahratta Confederacy, the last great Hindu state and, accordingly, the one of which our knowledge is most detailed, we know just how lawsuits were treated. Where a village dispute came before the king's officer his regular procedure was simply to refer the case to the council of a neighboring village. In this way he washed his hands of it. [2]

But this is not due to lack of esteem for law on the part of the Indian or Japanese people, but due to financial, social, and other considerations. If they should go to court, they would lose much time; sometimes it would take several years to settle even one case. They would have to employ lawyers and spend much money. Even if they should win at court, they would get very little. So, to resort to legal measures very often impairs, taking everything into account, the happiness and welfare of the people concerned and others around them. Barristers-at-law are not always respected, but very often abhorred, by the common people of Japan and Korea, who fear that they may take advantage of the people's lack of legal knowledge in order to make money for themselves. The writer personally knows some Japanese intellectuals who claim to be businessmen at home, but to be lawyers when they go abroad. They want to conceal their status as lawyer while they work with the Japanese.

But this does not mean that Japanese or Indian laws are applied partially. The Japanese meanings for the expressions of definite laws or codes are the same for all men and occasions. There is no difference at all. Yet, they do not always want to resort to legal measures.

As the objective causes which brought about such a tendency in Asians, we may cite the social life peculiar to their land and climate. The primitive Indo-Europeans, being nomadic and living chiefly by hunting, were in contact with alien peoples. Here human relations were marked by fierce rivalry. Peoples were in great migration; one

---

[1] Cited by Northrop, *ibid.*, p. 126.
[2] D. H. H. Ingalls, *op. cit.*, p. 44.

race conquered another only to be conquered by still another. In such a situation struggles for existence were based, not on mutual trust, but on rational plan and strategem. This mental feature seems to have been preserved even in modern times in the west.

The societies of Eastern and Southern Asia, on the other hand, developed from small localized farming communities. Asians did away with nomadic life early, and settled down to cultivate rice fields. People living on rice must inevitably settle permanently in one place. In such a society *families* continue generation after generation. Genealogies and kinships of families through long years become so well-known by their members that the society as a whole takes on the appearance of a single family. In such a society, individuals are closely bound to each other, and they form an exclusive human nexus. Here, an individual who asserts himself will hurt the feelings of others and thereby do harm to himself. Asians learned to adjust themselves to this type of familial society, and created forms of expression suitable to life in such a society. This tendency is deeply rooted in people, and it has led to their stressing of human relations, especially the spirit of harmony or concord in society.

IV. Conclusion

In the above we have pointed out some features of the Indian and Buddhist concept of law, and we have found that to all these some western counterpart can be found. It is rather difficult to demarcate between East and West distinctively with regard to the concept of law also. Humanity is one. But we can locate some features which are predominant in Hindu and Buddhist culture. To make them clear will be useful for the mutual understanding between East and West.

ISLAM IN THE MODERN WORLD

BY

ANNEMARIE SCHIMMEL

University of Bonn

Since Lord Cromer expressed, about ninety years back, the view that "Islam reformed is Islam no longer," the situation in the Islamic world has considerably changed, and the Muslims have striven to find different solutions for their problems: be it a complete secularization as in Ataturk's Turkey (where, however, middle-class people and peasants still continue living in unbroken loyalty to the values of Islam), or be it by the emegerence in the name of Islam of a nation like Pakistan. Is it thus true to say that Islam is fossilized, or, in the words of a prominent Muslim scholar like A. A. A. Fyzee, that Muslims are often economically poor, educationally backward, spiritually bankrupt? Still, the same critical observer is proud of belonging to the Muslim community; and there can be no doubt that a religion which is being professed by approximately 13% of the human race is bound to frame for its adherents a way of life that meets the exigencies of the present and, even more, of the future.

We need not enter here into a discussion of the history of Islam, its birth, and its rapid spread over three continents, its marvelous contributions to human culture and civilization, nor the dangerous process of its fossilization under the pressure of legal hairsplitting when its original dynamism was often forgotten.

Not only European orientalists, but also far-sighted Muslims themselves, have recognized, rather early, that two dangers especially threaten the vital issues of Muslim life, hampering the free development of thought. They are pantheistic mysticism in the form of what Iqbal called Pirism, and the role of the religious-juristical leaders, the mullas.

Mysticism, which contributed to the development of personal religious life in Islam by laying stress upon the eternal values of the personal relationship between man and God, turned from about the thirteenth century onwards, towards a kind of monistic view. The ideas of ibn-Arabi, popularized by numberless mystical poets in all countries of Islam, together with the political and social stagnation after the fall of Bagdad in 1258, led to a certain quietism. By overstressing the concept of *tawhīd*, the confession of God's unity, into the idea that there *exists* nothing but God the Creator and Judge, Allah was converted into the Eternal source of things. By overstressing the noble feeling of *tawakkul*, trust in God, one reached a mere passive acceptance of whatever afflictions were showered down on individuals and nations. On the other hand the influence of the religious leaders, the *shaykhs* or *pirs*, grew to a hitherto unknown extent, and they held under their sway millions of uneducated followers who venerated them during their lives and after their deaths.

The fact that great parts of the Muslim masses, especially in the non-Arab countries, were teeming with believers who had accepted Islam after having belonged to more primitive forms of religions, the relics of which they brought with them, was considered to constitute a great obstacle for a modern development—all the more since here the influence of certain mystical fraternities and even heterodox groups was visible. On the other side there are the jurisconsults, the theologians of orthodox bias who advocate a conservative following of the letter of the revealed law, watching over the smallest detail lest the faithful leave the path once prescribed by the Prophet. "Nomocracy," as the Islamic way of life once has been called, for centuries ruled the Muslims in their daily life, prescribing their duties in this world, and thus preparing them for the Hereafter with arguments derived from medieval sources. Without taking more than a negative interest in the modern development of the world, the mullas often condemned it on the whole as anti-Islamic and dangerous, seemingly incompatible with their traditionals ideals.

It is well known that the outspoken antithesis, Islam versus west, was launched first, to a greater extent, by Jamaladdin al-Afghani, the first roaming propagandist of Islamic revival and Pan-Islamism in the nineteenth century. That is quite natural since the Muslim community at that very time realized a strong reaction against the Christian west, not only because of its colonial attitude and its material superiority, but perhaps even more because of an increasing awareness of what had been written in the west since the middle ages about Islam and its founder. We can discern this feeling of bitterness in the Indian Muslims who saw the west admiring the Hindu scriptures and the mysticism of the Upanishads as high revelation, whereas the role of Muslim culture was never described adequately. Islam always remained a stumbling-block for historians and theologians. Cultural tension of this kind, as well as the occupation of great parts of formerly Muslim areas which had fallen under the rule of non-Muslims (*dār-ul-Islam* thus being converted into *dār-ul-harb*), forced the Muslims to create a defensive theology and historiography. From this point of view we may understand the role apologetics have played, and are still playing, in modern Islam. The wish, quite natural, to show the world the great past of Muslim culture, to prove the superiority of the heritage, is reflected in poems which compare the present state of the oppressed Muslim with that "of the lofty heights of Umar's time" (Cragg). This urge to demonstrate a superior heritage led to the composition of innumerable books on the glorious past which, as the Pakistani magazine *Islamic Literature* in Lahore writes in 1965, aim at the goal:

> To reflect in a worthy manner Islam's ambition to reconquer its lost field of cultural glory, present the new interpretations of Islam that would fit in with the changed conditions of the world, analyze baldly and critically the present situation, unearthing the hidden treasures of Islam's actual past, ignorance of which has had Muslims feel so doubtful about their future.

Thus, thinkers and theologians, poets and writers have tried to prove anew the eternal truth which has once been revealed to the Prophet in the Divine word of the Qur'an, striving to find out its meaning for life in our time which is so different from the days of the Prophet, different also from the days of the Abbassid caliphate when the Islamic world was confronted with Greek science and adapted it with remarkable skill.

It goes without saying that the attempts of today's theologians are not as much concerned with metaphysical questions as they are with the social and political injunctions of the Qur'an and the prophetic traditions. A glance at Baljon's study about *Modern Qur'an Interpretation* shows that most of the interpreters have laid stress on the practical side of Islam, and almost every modern Muslim will praise the perfect unity of *dīn* and *dawla*, of religious and socio-political orders in the Qur'an which form, as Iqbal says, only two aspects of the one reality. Yet, there are also some attempts at understanding the concept of the Deity in a new way. We find theologians who see in Allah in the first line an ethical principle, the great Law-Giver who has revealed himself in the *sharīʿa* which must, therefore, be obeyed unto the iota.

Others carefully avoid the concept of Allah as he is often shown in western literature—the tremendous transcendent Being beside whom man is simply annihilated, and who, consequently, acts according to his whim like an omnipotent tyrant without being held responsible for any of his actions, as a Lord who can throw even the righteous into Hell if He so wills. Theologians in this second group have, in a kind of neo-Mu͑tazilite strain, underlined that God is the God of Justice who acts perfectly justly, and who treats man only according to his merits and his transgressions. Still others, and perhaps they are in the majority, have gone back to the Qur'anic conception of God as the creator. This view has inspired the most beautiful passages not only of the Qur'an but also of the works of the mystics. It seems to give a perfect explanation of the marvelous findings of modern science and the faithful can, without difficulty, accept whatever atomic physics or astronomy, biology or any other science discovers because he sees here again the work of the One creator whose grandeur is proved by every scientific discovery.

The concept of God as the *prima causa*, the *motor immobilis*, the eternal essence from which everything emanates and into which it returns (an idea so dear to philosophers and mystics) has been challenged and branded as un-Islamic by some of the modernists, headed by Iqbal who has again and again repeated that God is a personality, and that exactly his infinity is proof for the person-being which is attested in the Qur'an by giving Him the name of Allah. The combination of infinity with personality, which seems contradictory in itself, has been maintained, by the way, also by western Christian thinkers, like Friedrich von Hügel; and the importance of the personal aspect of God, whom man can call and who answers his prayers, has been stressed in contemporary Christianity by Scholz, Tillich, and many others, and seems to be a typical reaction of modern religion against the fathomless abyss of the Nothing which threatens modern man.

This concept of a personal God leads us to the problem of prayer as faced in modern Islam. The importance of prayer, prescribed in its details and timings, has never been seriously questioned. But the minutiae have to be discussed. Can, ask the rigorous modernists (e.g., many modern educated Turks), work in a factory where every movement is organized be combined with five daily prayers? Is prayer not an unnecessary interruption, even a danger for the mechanical work, and is not the modern narrow dress in itself unpractical for the genuflexions in prayer? Orthodox and even moderate circles would answer the first question by stating that there is no difficulty of combining two prayers into one, thus interrupting the work only once, and that this could be done even during the break for lunch or so; a worker who could spare five minutes for smoking a cigarette could as easily spare them for performing his religious duty. There remains, then, the question of ritual purity—it is strange to see how here the smallest, and for an outsider most insignificant, details are being observed most carefully. Even in Turkey I know of middle-class people who would never use water from the tub directly for their ablutions but fill it, in the traditional way, into a small vessel—ablutions being considered not as much a material purification as a spiritual act which has to be performed exactly according to the example of the Prophet. On the other hand there is no lack of modernists who have called Islam, due to the rigid system of ablutions, "the religion of hygiene"—no doubt rightly when one compares the bathing facilities in medieval Europe with those in medieval Islamic countries.

Prayer can be performed in solitude, but it is preferable to pray in community. The importance of congregational prayer as a means to social equality has often been expressed, as in Iqbal's famous statement:

> What a tremendous spiritual revolution will take place, practically in no time, if the proud aristocratic Brahman of South India is daily made to stand shoulder to shoulder with the untouchable. From the unity of the all-inclusive Ego who creates and sustains all egos follows the essential unity of all mankind... The Islamic form of association in prayer, besides its cognitive value, is further indicative of the aspiration to realize this essential unity of mankind as a fact in life by demolishing all barriers which stand between man and man.

But another aspect of worship should not be neglected: that of preaching. In many Muslim countries the sermon during the Friday worship is still delivered in Arabic, though most of the people do not understand it. The education in the local languages of preachers who are equipped with a fair knowledge of modern life, technique, etc., is more important for a revitalization of Islamic values than articles on the social level during the high time of the Righteous Caliphs. The example of Turkey in setting up vocational schools for imams and preachers, where they are not only trained in Islamic traditional knowledge but also, as far as a secondary school can, in modern science, is in this respect of greatest importance.

As to the third pillar of Islam, *zakāh*, it is no longer anywhere the regular state tax as it used to be. But the *zakāh* regulations have been quoted more than once by Muslim modernists as the only effective remedy against both capitalism and communism, securing a sound distribution of wealth. The Muslim Brethren have stressed this point as well as Iqbal, who saw in the *zakāh* a counterweight against Nehru's atheistic socialism. From this point start the discussions about Islamic socialism which is differently explained; but even Liaqat Ali Khan, second President of Pakistan, had stated in 1949 at Lahore that the social and economic program given 1350 years back is still the best program possible. And a prominent scholar like M. Hamidullah sees in the *zakāh* the perfect model of a state-budget in which every working person in the country partakes, even the non-Muslim subjects.

Though the question of *zakāh* is being discussed more on a theoretical level, i.e., as a possible foundation for the different kinds of Islamic socialism, the problem of the fourth pillar of Islam, Fasting in Ramadan, is much more vital to millions of Muslims. The fact that fasting at daytime during a whole month is not easily feasible in a modern industrial society has been recognized by some of the reformers; but still Ramadan is being observed by a greater majority than those who perform their prayers regularly. That holds true even for secular Turkey. There are attempts at explaining fasting as a weapon for self-control, as a medical cure, etc.; others dwell upon the possibility of feeding a needy person instead of fasting, thus underlining the social implications of the fast. Others, again, have stated that the Divine Wisdom is visible in the institution of a pure lunar calendar which enables everybody to keep the fasting whereas it would be very difficult to obey the law if Ramadan were constantly in summer.

Even the problem of fasting in northern countries has been discussed, bearing in mind the conversion of people living far away from the centers of the Islamic world. For them the hours of their fasting are to be given according to the clock, not according to sunrise and sunset, which would compel them to fasting for weeks during a Scandinavian summer. But why, we may ask, do nearly all the Islamic countries still continue the old practice of ending Ramadan only after the new moon of Shawwal has been seen by trustworthy witnesses (according to Sura 2/181), with a few exceptions, like Turkey and Tunisia? Modern astronomical means could afford them easily with the exact dates of the beginning of the new moon. I remember the confusion in Pakistan in March, 1961, when the Government had announced ᶜId for Saterday, and the moon had not yet been seen.

The problem of how far fasting is compatible with hard work has been discussed during the last ten years in several countries, and again, Tunisia proved to be most modern, when we consider the *fatwās* issued in 1960 by different jurisconsults in defending President Bourgiba's view: since fasting is not obligatory during the Holy War, one declares, e.g., agricultural work, at harvest times, as a war against hunger and poverty, and argues in a similar strain that it is more important for the Muslim to fulfill his duties in factories and offices, thus securing a better life for his co-religionists than to fast at daytime, and to spend the nights indulging in unreligious pleasures, being, then, unable to work next morning. Whosoever is able to fast and to continue his work will gain twofold reward, but work and duty are more vital for society than fasting.

As to the pilgrimage, it is always considered as a means of understanding the Muslim brotherhood, as a glorious occasion for uniting the faithful from all countries. Due to the facilities introduced by the Saudi Arabian government, the performance of the pilgrimage is now comparatively easy. But strangely enough in the strictly puritan homeland of Islam, where just now a poignant booklet against the art of making pictures was issued claiming that every painter and photographer will go to Hell, very beautiful color postcards of the Kaᶜba and the holy places in Medina are sold.

We know that the *jihād*, the Holy War, was not far from being reckoned among the pillars of Islam; it is, therefore, small wonder that in modernist circles ideas on *jihād* are discussed sometimes, though in a different context. The opinion that aggression against one Islamic country is an aggression against all of them has been often repeated, thus leading people to dream of a *jihād* of the united Muslim forces against Israel. One of the arguments of the orthodox against the Qadiani-Ahmadiya movement is the denial of the duty of *jihād* by this group. In the same category lies the attack against mysticism which prefers death on the path of the Beloved to death for the sake of defending Islam, thus weakening the fabric of Islam. The attitude of many Muslims against the colonial powers, and that means against great parts of the west, can be envisaged under the headline of *jihād*, of winning back what was formerly *dār-ul-Islam*. For it is the duty of the Muslims to build God's kingdom in this world, making His word known and obeyed everywhere. However, no stringent formulations about the *jihā*d as such are existent in modern theology.

The tendency is, quite naturally, to go back to the words of the Qur'an and to cling to them as closely as possible. One agrees—both orthodox and liberal wing—that the ᶜibādāt, the injunctions for worship, are eternally valid. As to the legal prescriptions, there are different opinions: from the strict Wahhabi acceptance of every order of punishment up to those countries which have accepted legal principles and law codes of the west; from a Shiᶜa jurisconsult like A. A. A. Fyzee who thinks that a Muslim living in a secular or modern state must have freedom and independence to obey new laws, to Maulana Mawdudi who holds that the *sharīᶜa* remains inviolable and is applicable for all time. Since the *sharīᶜa* is the revealed Will of God, its suspension would be, according to fundamentalists like the Muslim Brethren, the suspension of Islam. The discussion about *taqlīd*, acceptance of the decisions and statements made by the jurisconsults of earlier generations, and *ijtihād*, the right to investigate into the sources of Islam for finding new solutions for the urgent problems, has gone on for decades, and even rather liberal theologians deny non-specialists the right of using thier own discretion for solving this or that problem. And there is always a tendency to wrap even the most modern and daring ideas and interpretations into a garment that looks quite like *sharīᶜa*.

This is visible in the confrontation of the Muslim with modern science. The wish to show that everything imaginable, including scientific results, was contained in the Divine word much earlier than the westerners dreamed of it, had led scholars to devote their lives to proving that the sputnik was alluded to in Sura 55/33 and the A-bomb in Sura 81/6, since God knows everything and reveals His signs for people who understand. One of the most curious books of this kind is the *Müspet Maneviyat etüdleri* by Sadettin Evrin, a retired General and for a certain period vice-president of the Office for Religious Affairs in Turkey. Though this kind of quasi-scientific exegesis, as started by the *Manār* movement, has been sometimes ridiculed by western scholars, one should not forget its real concern, the desperate wish to prove the superiority of the God-given revelation in the face of so many strange and overwhelming forces—and we have known similar Biblical exegesis too. As long as even educated Muslims— as I have witnessed in Turkey—express the view that the Qur'an is not Arabic and cannot be understood by means of Arabic grammar but has to be memorized just for the sake of its holiness, a change of this attitude will be difficult.

The numerous translations which have been made of the Holy Book into every Islamic language—not for ritual purposes but for explaining its contents—show the interest in its meaning; and perhaps the uncritical acceptance of the explanations given by the theologians to those who do not know Arabic will slowly be changed into a more understanding way of reading so that people may come to know the real importance of the Qur'an, instead of regarding it as something sacred or a kind of talisman which protects the house. Iqbal has, in his *Javidname*, given a vivid picture of the ideal world of the Qur'an when its innumerable possibilities—inexhaustible since they are one with the Divine Being—unfold in every time afresh. But, he adds in another verse, the book must be revealed to the human heart, otherwise no commentary could open its knots.

In modern Qur'an interpretation, very little weight is given to the purely religious contents. The important eschatological *sūras* of the early period are either not taken into consideration or are interpreted in a demythological way. That angels and *jinns* have been transformed, by various authors, into psychical powers or microbes, is well-known. Metaphysical hair-splitting seems unimportant for the burning issues of today. Religion being, in Iqbal's words, a *social* force of great value, the social side of the Qur'an is more interesting for the reformers than anything else. Only one religious or philosophical problem has been discussed several times, that of fatalism and free will, since the acceptance of free will leads to a higher responsibility which is necessary for facing successfully the new situation of the world. After centuries of patient acceptance of the destiny sent by God, it was high time that a man like Iqbal reminded the Muslims that man is called to be the vice-regent of God on earth, and that fatalism is not blind acceptance but rather a conformity of will with the Divine order—freedom in obedience, activity out of the spirit of continuous communication with God in prayer, and thus re-evaluation of man. But it is a problem whether this subtle interpretation of one of the greatest mysteries of religion, which was gladly accepted by many of the reformers, could reach the average believer who was still clinging to the letter not only of the Qur'an but of the interpretation offered to him by the theologians.

Another problem with which the modern Muslim is confronted is that of the person of Muhammad. When modern Islamic apologetics emerged, partly from the necessity of giving a truer picture of Islam than that presented by the western orientalists and missionaries, this necessity was even more urgently felt concerning the person of the Prophet. For the love of Muhammad is the strongest tie uniting Muslims all over the world, and the veneration of him, who did not claim to be more than a messenger bearing a revelation, the servant of God, had developed so many times in forms which seem scarcely compatible with orthodoxy. The legends around his birth, the miracles of his ascension and the splitting of the moon, the speaking gazelle and the rain-prayer have been told and retold by poets thousands of times in the different regional languages. Thus, millions of faithful would see in Muhammad a nearly supernatural being, the beloved of God, the bearer of the prophetic light, and, more than anything else, the intercessor at Doomsday, to whom they address their humble supplications.

But they did not know anything about his life here on earth. The reformers became conscious of the necessity of studying Muhammad's life from the sources, and since Ameer Ali's *Spirit of Islam* in 1892 a large number of biographies have been produced in all parts of the Islamic world (all of them, by the way, quoting with a certain predilection the praising words of Europeans like Carlyle about Muhammad). The last very interesting work in the long line is that by M. Hamidullah, well-trained in western scholarship, entitled *Le Prophète de l'Islam* (1955). In schoolbooks, Muhammad is being presented as a model of ethics, thus inspiring the children to lead a truly Islamic life. For the apologists, another side of his life was even more important: the Medina period, i.e., his role as statesman and social reformer. The twofold aspect of the founder of Islam, Prophet and Statesman, which has always puzzled Christian critics of Islam, appears to the Muslims exactly as his distinguishing feature. They see in him, therefore, a model not only for religious behavior but for every decision in the political and social field. Islam is proud of having here the cornerstone on which the whole system of modern politics, education, and social life can be built.

The fact that Muhammad is the last in the long chain of messengers is interpreted either in the classical way that this message is valid once for all times, or, as Iqbal has put it, that in Islam prophethood felt the necessity of abolishing itself, thus opening the way to a new kind of scientific Weltanschauung. If true, the second view would grant the Muslims a new approach toward the problems of today. The claim of the finality of prophethood, as accepted by every Muslim, has served in the last decades as a shibboleth against the Qadianis, whom some tried to place outside the frame of Islam. At any rate, the acceptance of the manifold revelation between Adam and Muhammad grants the Muslim the possibility of using the results of history of religion, of archeology, and research into past civilizations, and, so to say, of an Islamization of the prophetic personalities like Zoroaster or Lao tse, or statesmen like Hammurabi. Not everyone among them, however, will agree with Maulana Azad's view that "all religions are in their own sphere perfectly true; all teachers sent by God are true teachers"—since the last law always abrogates the previous laws.

The most crucial question in connection with the Prophet is how far the traditions related about him and from him can serve for the solution of the difficulties of modern life, "How far *ḥadīth* is still a valuable source for today's life" (Fazlur Rahman). The criticism of Goldziher and his followers against the authenticity of *ḥadīth* can no longer be accepted to the same extent since many traditions which go back far behind the canonical collections of Bukhari and Muslim have been discovered in the Near Eastern libraries, and the age of many a tradition has, thus, considerably increased. Yet not all of them can be considered genuine sources for a fresh interpretation of Islam. That is why e.g., Parwez, the leader of the *ṭulūᶜul-Islām* movement in Pakistan, rejects *ḥadīth* as a whole, relying only upon the text of the Qur'an without realizing that a complete denial of traditions breaks up the historical continuity of Islam, and that *ḥadīth* indeed enables today's theologians to understand how Muslims in the earliest times have acted and reacted in this or that matter so that by careful analogical deduction even now possibly solutions could be reached in congruence with the classical Islamic way of arguing. What is being carefully avoided even by those reformers who stress the informative value of *ḥadīth* is the clinging to later interpretations and commentaries which have led to a fossilization of the original issues.

The painstaking work of modernists, combining the explicit words of the Qur'an and the sentences related from the Prophet, with the problems of the twentieth century, is visible in every aspect of life, be it in the problem of lawful national laws on interest despite the usury laws or be it in the formation of an Islamic political community. The discussions about an Islamic state have been repeated, especially since Pakistan came into existence, from the very idea that Muslims need a state of their own where they could perform the prescribed duties without impediment. But what is the ruling principle of the Islamic State? Is it theocracy in the strictest sense of the word? Is it nomocracy, rule of the *sharīᶜa?* What will be the situation of non-

Muslim minorities? Is it bound to a certain form of government? There are views that the classical caliphate was not a monarchy in the strict sense of the word; the caliph was elected; and the state was more like a republic (though the word republic, *jumhuriya*, was first used for the Azerbaijanian state in 1918). The only *conditio sine qua non* is that the head of the Islamic state is a Muslim, since he—the imām in traditional definition—is the leader of the community in prayer and in war. It has often been claimed that democracy is the basic principle of an Islamic state—relying on the *shūrā* mentioned in Sura 42/36—but how is a true democracy realized in countries where majorities are still illiterate? Ayub Khan's Basic Democracies in Pakistan present a possibility for overcoming these difficulties.

And, more exciting even than the discussions about the political form of an Islamic state seems the problem: What is the relation between Islam and nationalism? Islam wants loyalty to God, not to thrones, says Iqbal—the same thinker who has denounced patriotism as a subtle form of idolatry, and has understood the Prophet's *hijra* as a gentle hint in fact that a Muslim does not cling to his birthplace or family but is at home wherever Islam is being practiced (an idea which became manifest in 1947 in the exodus of millions of Muslims from Bharat to the promised land of Pakistan, as it had been practiced by many Indian Muslims who left the country during British rule).

Pan-Islamism, as preached by Afghani and defended by a number of religious leaders like the Muslim Brethren and similar groups, is of the opinion that Islam has made the whole world a vast sanctuary in which God has to be worshiped in every action and every moment. The Islamic fatherland is one, and all Muslims belong to the same nationality—that is witnessed by their unity in front of the real center of the Islamic world, the Ka'ba in Mecca. The East had become self-conscious as East due to the western nationalist theories; and its leaders seem sometimes to attack this very nationalism as if they were attacking imperialism and colonialism. But no practical solutions are offered to realize the dream of a united Muslim world or a confederation of all Muslim countries, a realization which would become more and more difficult the more countries in Africa of a cultural level quite different of that of Egypt or Iran become Islamized.

Orthodoxy would like to see Islamic ideology absorb nationalism; but there are others who would admit at least for the Arabs a certain preference, since they are, as Bazzaz says, the backbone of Islam; and even Iqbal has centered his ideals around the homeland of Islam, the pure and unpolluted representatives of early Arabic Islam, thus creating a romantic picture of "Arabia" in contrast to countries like Turkey or Iran which, in the twenties, started glorifying their pre-Islamic past and non-Arabic heritage. However, conferences of Muslim theologians, of Muslim youth organizations, etc., show that the feeling of solidarity among the religious leaders is rather strong, in spite of political tensions.

Even greater than the importance of political discussions seems to be that of social questions. The social revolution which has changed the world more than sheer politics has, in many parts of the Islamic countries, started shattering the old family units, creating new types of working conditions, and, partly, of facilities. The introduction of broadcasting, movies, and television has produced a more impressive change in the mind of the Muslim population than anything else. Now, even the illiterate villager can look at the pictures and listen to the news which is spread from Eastern or western sources, and is willy-nilly dragged into the stream of events, the turmoil of clashing ideas which fill the world. Quite naturally the large masses, for the most part slightly-educated middle class people, are falling under the spell of western technique, seeing in it, rather materialistically, the only means for securing a higher standard of life which they equate with higher civilization.

Modern oriental novels often reflect the problem created by the introduction of electricity, etc., in simple families: the gap opening then between generations; the way which leads from the amazed admiration of the glittering surface of technical perfection to materialism and atheism, thus uprooting a society which is unable to find its way between the traditional religious values (which, of course, are often ridiculous to the younger generations) and what is offered them of western products. We cannot deny, however, that the image of the west with which these people are confronted in the movies is far from edifying. What is called in the East "Hollywoodism" constitutes not only a danger for the Muslim but also for the west itself. The average citizen will take this image according to these pictures at its face value, and in this case the theologian and the jurisconsult of orthodox bias will be justified in objecting to this kind of civilization as a devilish invention, produced only for leading the pious Muslim, and even more the pious Muslim woman, astray.

The discussions around the question of liberation of women has continued for a long time. Not only have Muslim apologists written dozens of books in order to prove that Islam is the only religion which has given women certain social and economic rights, and enumerating the names of numerous ladies who have excelled in learning and piety; novelists, too, have tried to make women aware of their long-forgotten rights. In 1892, seven years before Qāsim Amīn in Egypt wrote his *Tahrīr al-Marʾa* (Woman's Emancipation), Mirza Qalich Beg, a Sindhi writer, had taken the heroine of his novel out of purda and made her learn foreign languages, geography, etc., so that she could gain her living even during the absence of her husband. A study of novels of this kind would yield interesting results for the history of social and educational ideals in Muslim countries during the last hundred years.

Modernists like Zia Gökalp have voted for an equal distribution of heritage among the children, regardless of their sex, but Iqbal and Hamidullah, to mention only two prominent examples, held that the smaller shares in heritage are made up by the dowry and by the fact that women can keep their own capital for themselves—the Qurʾan cannot be unjust in such a fundamental question. But what of the unmarried girls?

No doubt in many Islamic countries a remarkable number of women held high posts in universities, diplomatic service, economy, etc. But orthodoxy still brands these unusual ladies, in the words of Maulana Mawdudi, as "storm centers of that satanic liberty which women seek and which is threatening to demolish the entire structure of human civilization." The idea that the emancipated woman is a manifestation of satanic powers, so aptly expressed in Iqbal's *Javidname* in the person of the European girl who intrudes upon the peaceful meadows of Mars, and featured already in the earliest Indo-Muslim novels on female education, is an idea still valid for many of the orthodox theologians who see in woman nothing but a being created for satisfying man, for bearing and rearing children. Is it perhaps a certain fear of their own unbridled desires which make members of orthodox circles defend the institution of seclusion or of complete veiling which cannot be deduced from the Qur'an? At the very moment when woman is being recognized as a thinking and responsible being, able to be the companion of man, not only the problem of seclusion—which is in any case gradually diminishing even in the most backward parts of the Middle East—but also that of polygamy is more easily solved.

The ideas of Muslim modernists about this last subject are sufficiently known—part of them see in the injunction of the Qur'an that the wives should be treated with equal justice in every respect an implicit order to monogamy. Others argue (and perhaps they are not completely wrong) that a legal possibility of polygamy in certain cases is sounder than the illegal relations for which the west is, unfortunately, known among the critics of its civilization.

The problems with which the Muslim world is faced today concern everybody, to whatever denomination he may belong. The fact that Islam is, as has been very well said, rather orthopraxis than orthodoxy, keeping everybody inside the Muslim community provided he acknowledges the binding and absolute character of Divine injunctions and practices a certain minimum, has led in our time to a less rigid attitude towards the different sects. In spite of the sharp Sunni-Shiᶜa controversies in India during the sixteenth and seventeenth centuries, to mention only one example, there exists now nearly no discrimination. On the contrary, of the leaders of Islamic modernism in the Subcontinent, Ameer Ali was an *ithna ᶜashariya* Shiᶜite, the Muslim-League leaders Nawwab Salimullah of Bengal and the Agha Khan belonged to Shiᶜa sects, and the same holds true for M. A. Jinnah, the founder of Pakistan. The community of the Ismailiya, once considered highly heterodox, has now gained increasing influence in East Africa to which it came from Indo-Pakistan. It had always played an important role in the Indus valley. Political reasons have led Turkey, Iran, and Pakistan to strengthen their political and cultural relations, thus forming a kind of unit which is historically and culturally justifiable although interrupted by the Sunni-Shiᶜa antagonism when Iran became Shiᶜa in 1501 and thus barricaded the big Islamic land bridge that stretched from the Bosporus to the Gangetic plains.

As we have seen, differences between the sects are more and more losing their importance. Still, the attitude of the average Muslim, and the Muslim modernist, towards mysticism is yet to be discussed. We have already mentioned that *tasavvuf*, in many cases, degenerated in the later middle ages, and is now held at least partly responsible for the stagnation of Islamic life. On the other hand the most decisive role which orders and fraternities have always played, and are still playing, in the missionary sector, cannot be denied. To read about the political achievements of the Tijani order in North and West Africa is as exciting as to follow the political activities of the Sanusiya in the nineteenth century, or the role of the Qadiriya in the Quit-India-movement in Sind, not to mention the attempts at social revolution made in earlier times by Sufi leaders. No doubt, the influence of the *pirs* and *shaykhs* was, in many a case, rather dangerous. One could witness that during the Menderes period in Turkey when the village *shaykhs* from

Eastern Anatolia again started meddling in politics—though Atatürk, wisely enough, had already abolished the orders in Turkey in 1925, fearing their unhealthy influence upon the reforms he was going to introduce. Nevertheless, not only did the villagers remain more or less faithful to the inherited, rather primitive, types of piety, but the ethical influence of mystical leaders was also palpable, especially in educated circles. At the same time that outward manifestations of religious life were nearly impossible, no religious education was given in Turkish schools and the whole system of Islamic law and traditions was being abolished, the inner values of Islam gained a new importance.

Certain mystics remarkably influenced a small but very enlightened group of followers, who succeeded in deepening their personal religious life exactly as it had been taught by the mystics of the classical period. Even Iqbal, who once said that one will scarcely find today any more ignorant Muslim than the mystical leaders, tried to get the help of the Nizamiya-leaders in Delhi in his attempt at reviving Islam, teaching his coreligionists the warmth of love, active trust in God, and humanitarian values. The foreign observer, who will find it easier to come in touch with such members of society as are imbued with mystical ideas—maintaining that Islam is the religion of eternal love and acknowledging that all religions are like beams of the same sun—this foreign observer will often be inclined to see the future of Islam in its re-evaluation of the spiritual side of life, the elaboration of purely ethical values, precisely that aspect of Islam which is closer to a westerner's understanding of religion.

He will, however, be told by many of the orthodox Muslims—as Jomier has rightly pointed out—that this picture of a kind of "Christianized Islam" is wrong, that Islam is a religion of force, of *al-fatḥ al mubīn, or jihād* against everything which contradicts the Divine word and will, a totalitarian way of life which embraces every act and thought. Indeed, the program of Islam in modern times has been formulated by an old style orthodoxy rather than by the liberals who lack a theoretically formulated program, or by the mystics who do not give any formal prescriptions save for individual spiritual development. No doubt Kenneth Cragg is right in writing that "If one is looking for a serious Islam making a sustained effort after loyalty of worship and the sense of God in the midst of bewilderment and shifting passions and much time-serving, one may find it in the discipleship of al-Bannā and Mawdudi."

But even these groups cannot answer every question, and the lack of an authoritative institution for formulating the duties of a Muslim gives room to a large number of independant attempts for a solution of the issues at stake. Some of the answers that rigid orthodoxy and liberal-minded reformers are formulating to meet the challenge of the most essential problems of our time are scarcely valid in the new fields discovered by Islam in Africa—Africa "the great opening occasion of Islamic decision" (Cragg). Here, social structure and the necessity of first introducing Islam and of catechizing poses a number of problems quite different from those faced by the reformers in the highly civilized "classical" countries of Islam. The influence that the Sufi orders with their partly rather primitive views and practices are exercising, or the role which the Ahmadiya is trying to play in this part of the world, will create in the future, unexpected difficulties for the interpreters of Islam in modern terms.

One of the most moving documents of the situation of some of the Muslim theologians in our day is the *Munir Report* which was issued after the Punjab riots in Pakistan in spring, 1953. The haziness of the answers given by many of the mullas who were questioned about the distinguishing feature of a Muslim is really saddening for anybody who knows the great intellectual achievement of the Islamic society of old; and it is somewhat frightening to see the gap between traditional orthodox ways of thinking and the mentality of liberally western-trained Muslim jurisconsults in one and the same country which has been created in the name of Islam and is considered a sort of melting pot for the different interpretations of Islam.

We need not agree with Fyzee, however, that Islam in its orthodox interpretation has lost the resilience needed for adaptation to modern thought and life—we have seen that just here at least an image, a *Leitbild*, of Islam is being produced. Nor need we agree with the word of my venerated teacher H. H. Schaeder, who thought that for a real renaissance of Muslim life there is only one way open, that very way which Europe found five centuries ago—the way back to Greek civilization as the source of humanitarian values and of real democracy. The spirit of the Qur'an is anti-classical, incompatible with the Greek ideals, though Islam has served as a transmitter of Greek culture to Europe. Yet it has in itself enough values to survive in its peculiar form.

Scholarly research, carried out by Muslim scholars with an unbiased mind, would be very helpful in this formation of a new Islamic way of life. The education of the future imams in modern institutions, acquainting them with the results of scientific research and leading them to the study of history, including the history of religions, in order to teach them the art of asking, not blindly accepting whatever is transmitted to them as inherited truth, would be likewise useful. The *naql*, the transmission of chains of information which is sanctified by tradition, and the absolute faith in the word of the teacher (which can be witnessed even in secular universities) has formed a lifeless crust on the spirit which once lived in the Muslim community. Not to recall over and again the Golden Age of Islam but to ask for what reasons Muslims have created these great works of art and science would help mold the future destiny of the community.

No outsider can judge, either from his own experience or from hundreds of books, what will be the best way the Muslims could choose in the bewilderment of our time which puzzles not only them but all of us. For all the great religions are confronted, in the age of science, with the same vital problems; i.e., the loss of the spiritual axis, growing materialism, overwhelming fear of the results of the glorious scientific research, and the loneliness of man in a world without faith We can only hope that the Muslims, by deepening their insight into the distinctive values of their religion, and that means, of their civilization, will find the right way—the straight path— for living their lives according to the Divine order, so that the praising word of Muhammad Abdallah Draz, former rector of the Azhar, may become true one day, namely that Islam is external peace and internal peace, peace with God and peace with all creatures.

RELIGION AND THE POPULATION EXPLOSION

BY

H. C. GANGULI
University of Delhi

Introduction

The term population explosion expresses very adequately and in a synoptic form the implications of rapid population growth in the world today. The term refers not only to the increase in world population and its various social implications, but to the more disconcerting fact of the ever-accelerating rate of this increase. The implications of such an accelerated increase in population can be seen at a glance by scanning the titles of popular books and scientific treatises on the population problem one finds in any modest library. Food, education, economic development, quality of the population, national power, international peace are all affected, one way or another, by this inexorable march of humanity towards larger numbers. All nations are worried—the comparatively affluent ones fear the lowering of their standards of affluence, while the "have nots" see the chance of actualization of their rising expectations recede into a distant future.

What is the role of religion and of religious leaders in such a contingency? To the extent that religion tries to give meaning to man's multifarious activities, to the extent that it provides guidelines for his conduct in this world, religion is concerned with this very fundamental problem that has repercussions on certain aspects of the individual's personal behavior (for example, as a parent) and in the larger context, on the structure and culture of the human society itself. Many religions have adopted characteristic positions over this issue, positions which have to some extent undergone modifications due to changing circumstances. Before discussing the postures of various religions on the question of population, it may be useful in the beginning to examine briefly certain implications of this rapid population growth and means of population control.

I. Population Explosion, a Factual Analysis

A historical analysis of the growth of the human species distinguishes three broad periods: Period I extends from about 600,000 B.C.

(approximately the time of man's beginning) to 6,000 B.C.; Period II from 6,000 B.C. to 1650 A.D.; and Period III from A.D. 1650 to the present day. During Period I it is estimated that the population grew to about five million, that man's birth rate was about fifty per thousand and that total number of births during this period was approximately twelve billion.[1] Period II which starts from the New Stone Age and extends right through the Reformation showed an increase from five million to half a billion and a total of about 42 billion births. It was during this period that man began to produce food whereas formerly he had simply consumed what nature had laid before him. In Period III, there has been a sixfold increase—from about a half-billion in 1650 to over three billion in 1962. Total number of births during this period has been 23 billion.

The U.N. Department of Economic and Social Affairs has attempted to project the population growth up to the year 2,000. It is estimated that at this rate, the world population will stand at six billion by the year 2,000. It will thus be seen that whereas it has taken more than 600,000 years for the human population to reach the three billion mark, in about another forty years, assuming that the current growth rate remains unchanged, humanity will add another three billion to its number and reach the staggering total of six billion. Thus:

	Year	World Population
I.	6,000 B.C.	5 million
II.	A.D. 1650	0.5 billion
III.	A.D. 1960	3 billion
IV.	A.D. 2000	6 billion

Figure I below indicates the growth of the world population from 1,000 to 1950 A.D. and its projected growth up to the year 2,000 A.D.[2,3]

Concentrating our attention on Asia, we see from Table I below that increase in population for the entire region was 33 per cent between 1920 and 1950 and is expected to be 72 per cent in the next

---

[1] Desmond, Annabelle, "How Many People Have Ever Lived on Earth?", in Mudd, Stuart (ed.), *The Population Crises and the Use of World Resources*, (W. Junk Publishers, The Hague, 1964), p. 29.

[2] Bennett, M. K., *The World's Food*, (New York, Harper and Bros, 1954).

[3] Carr, Saunders, A. M., *World Population, Past, Growth and Present Trends*, (Oxford, Clarendon Press, 1936).

thirty years, between 1950 and 1980. This is a glaring example not of growth only but of accelerated growth of population.

It must be mentioned that to add to the burden of some nations, the population growth is not uniform but varies from country to country. During the first two decades of the twentieth century, population

FIGURE I

Growth of World Population Between 1000 to 2000 A.D.

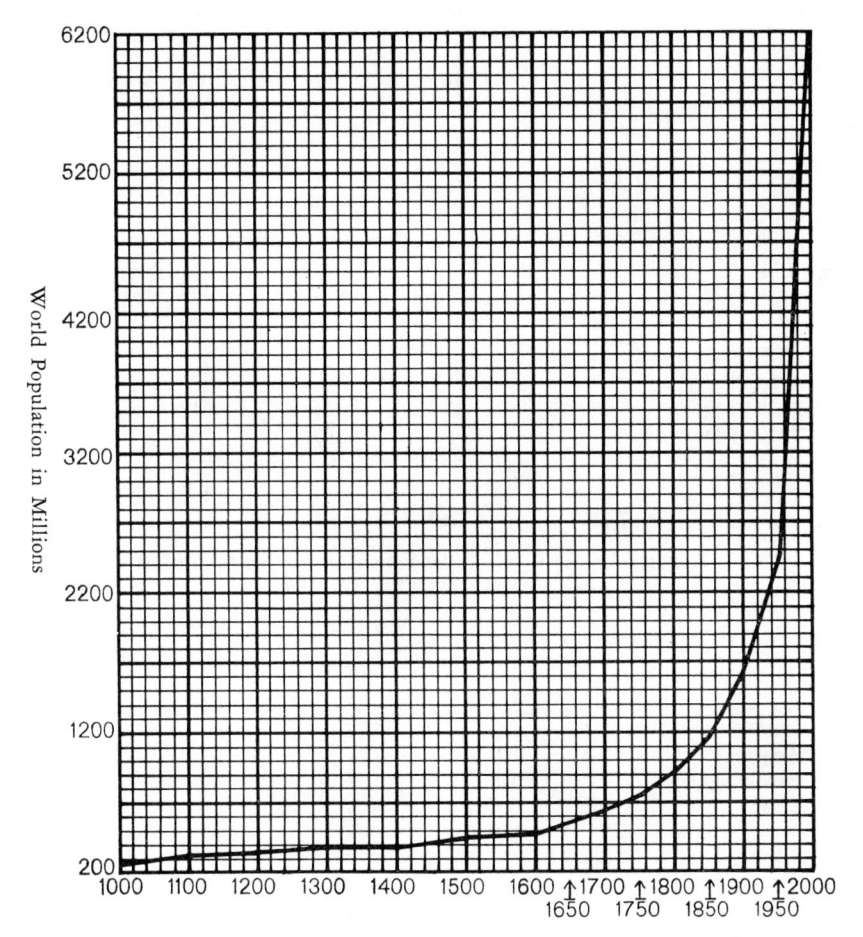

growth was nearly twice as rapid in the developed parts of the world (North America, Europe including Russia and Oceania) as in the less developed countries (Japan was an exception). However, since World War I the rate of increase in underdeveloped countries improved from 1.3 to 1.9 and thus was substantially higher than in developed countries (see Table II).

TABLE I

Population Trends in Asia and the Far East, 1920-50

(Populations in millions)
Regions *

Year	Total	Central-South	Southeast	Continental East	Maritime East
Estimated:					
1920	991	326	110	478	77
1950	1,317	466	172	559	120
Projected:					
1960	1,572	555	210	670	137
1980	2,268	833	348	906	181
Increase *amount:*					
1920-1950	326	140	62	81	43
1950-1980	696	278	138	236	44
Increase *per cent:*					
1920-1950	33	43	56	17	56
1950-1980	72	79	103	62	51

TABLE II

Average Annual Rates of Population Growth by Continents and Regions: 1900-57 (Percentage)

Regions	1900-20	1920-40	1940-50	1950-57
Underdeveloped Areas	0.4	1.3	1.5	1.9
Africa	0.7	1.0	1.5	1 8
Latin America	2.1	2.1	2.3	2.6
Asia	0.2	1.1	1.2	1.8
Excluding Japan	0.2	1.1	1.2	1.8
Japan	1.3	1.3	1.6	1.3
Developed Areas	0.9	0.9	0.3	1.2

* The regional groupings are as follows: Central-south Asia—Afghanistan, Bhutan, Ceylon, India, the Maldive Islands, Nepal, Portuguese India, and Pakistan; Southeast Asia—Cambodia, Burma, Indonesia, Laos, Malaya, the Philippines, Timor, Singapore, Thailand, and Vietnam; Continental east Asia—Peoples Republic of China, Hong Kong, Macau, and the Mongolian Peoples Republic; Maritime east Asia—Taiwan, Japan, Korea, and the Ryukyu Islands. Vietnam and Korea are the undivided countries.

Table III below also indicates the differential growth of population in four countries, India, Brazil, U.S.A., and Japan.

TABLE III
Annual Population Growth Rates of Four Selected Countries

Country	Average annual growth rate (1950-1955)
India	2.0
Brazil	2.4
Japan	1.4
U.S.A.	1.5

To conclude therefore: The rate of population growth tends to be higher in the less developed countries than in the developed countries —about seventy per cent higher on the average. In many less developed countries the rate of population growth exceeds three per cent a year.

II. IMPLICATIONS OF POPULATION GROWTH

One danger about population growth is that this takes places unobtrusively, insidiously. Consequently use of such terms as "population explosion" or „population bomb" attempts to arouse the public to this danger. No one would imagine, unless specifically pointed out, that the increase in population of Asia between 1950 and 2000 A.D. will be roughly equal to the population of the entire world in 1958 or that the two Americas will increase their population by a factor of two and one-fourth in the forty years between 1960 and 2000. The implications of such a rapid population growth, particularly for the countries in Asia, Africa, and Latin America for social and economic development programs have been spelled out by the U.N. Department of Economics and Social Affairs. [1] To quote:

First, it can increase the pressure of population on land that is already densely settled and so retard increases in the productivity of agricultural labor. This effect is seen not only in countries where nearly all the cultivable land is now occupied but also in many underdeveloped countries where the density of agricultural population in the cultivated areas is high, although large amounts of potentially productive land lie unused because of land ownership systems, lack of capital or techniques to exploit available land, or for other reasons.

---

[1] U.N. Dept. of Economics and Social Affairs, *Report on World Social Situation 24*, (ST/SOA/33), 1957, in Shimm, Malvin G. (ed.), Population Control, Oceana, 1961, pp. 10-11.

Accelerating population growth can aggravate the problem of capital shortage, which is one of the most important obstacles to economic development of nearly all underdeveloped countries. The faster the population grows, the larger the share of each year's income which must be invested in increasing the stock of productive equipment merely to maintain the existing level of equipment per worker. The larger the investments required for this purpose, the smaller the share of annual income that will be available either to raise the level of current consumption per capita or to make investments which would increase productivity and permit higher levels of consumption in the future.

While in a well-developed dynamic economy the demand for such capital investments may serve as a stimulus to continuing economic growth, the case of the underdeveloped countries, with their narrow margin of income over subsistence needs, is different. For most of them it is difficult to save and invest enough from their meager annual income to permit economic development to proceed at a satisfactory pace, even without rapid population growth. It is true that if these countries can industrialize and better utilize their human as well as their natural resources, some of them, at least, will undoubtedly benefit in the long run from a substantially larger population. But even where a larger population would be advantageous in the long run, economic progress will be hindered if numbers increase so rapidly as to put an excessive strain upon the economy.

Third, the high birth-rates of the underdeveloped countries create a heavy load of dependent children for the working population... the percentages of children under fifteen years of age in the less developed countries of Asia, Africa, and Latin America are generally in the order of forty per cent or more of the total population, while the range of this ratio in the European countries is from about twenty to thirty per cent. This difference is the consequence of the higher birth-rates in the former areas. The necessity of supporting so many children puts the workers of the underdeveloped countries at an added disadvantage in their efforts to save and invest for economic development. It also complicates the problem of providing the children with the education that is essential for social and economic advancement in the long run.

To illustrate the question of pressure on land, Table IV below gives the man-land ratios in seven selected countries in terms of crude density per square mile, *per capita* of arable land, and *per capita* of agricultural land. Arable land is used for field crops and orchards, and agricultural land includes arable land plus land for meadows and pastures, altogether about a quarter of the earth's land surface. The choice of the countries in Table IV has been deliberate. It will be seen that the three Asian countries, India, China, and Japan are in a very unfavorable position as compared to such countries as U.S.A., U.S.S.R., etc. The three Asian countries are considerably below the world average of 3.3 acres of agricultural land and one acre of arable land, both per capita. Any increase in the population is going to lower the land resources available to a dangerous level. Over the years, the area of cultivated land per capita in India, according to the 1951 Census Report, had declined from 1.09 acres in 1891 to 1.01 in 1921 to 0.84 in 1951. In fifty years, 1900 to 1950, the drop has been about twenty per cent.

For a country like India, with a poor man-land ratio, any substantial increase in population is likely to offset the advantages of industrialization and scientific methods of agriculture as the rate of capital formation is not very high.

TABLE IV
Man-Land Ratios in Representative Countries

Country	Crude density in number of inhabitants per sq. mile	Arable land in acres per capita	Agricultural land in acres per capita
U.S.A.	54.6	3.0	7.0
Mexico	39.0	1.7	11.3
Australia	2.6	5.5	117.3
U.S.S.R.	26.0	2.7	4.2
India	299.0	0.9	0.9
China	156.0	0.5	1.5
Japan	618.8	0.2	0.1

Source: U.N. Food and Agriculture Organization, Yearbook 1954. Vol. VIII, Part I; U.N. Demographic Yearbook, 1955.

To carry the argument further, Table V gives an idea of increase in food supply needed in the different regions that will be sufficient to meet the minimum adequate nutritional requirements of their population between the years 1958-1980. [1] The table shows that the supplies in the underdeveloped countries must be more than doubled between 1958 and 1980 if the increasing population is to be fed at a minimum adequate nutritional standard. This means an annual average rate of increase of nearly 3½ per cent in food supplies. This is a

---

[1] Cook, Robert C., "Population and Food Supply", in Mudd (ed.), 1964, p. 462.

higher rate than the average annual increase in food production over the past seven years in these countries. Food thus becomes a major problem for Asian countries in the context of its population growth.

TABLE V

Percentage Increase of Food Supply Needed During 1958-1980 to Meet Anticipated Requirements in Various Regions of the World

Regions	Total increase of food Supply, 1958-1980, required to meet nutritional target and population growth	Rate of annual increase needed, 1958-1980	Recent annual rate of increase in food supply
Underdeveloped countries	107	3.4	2.7
Latin America	94	3.1	2.5
Far East Asia	86	2.9	3.0*
Near East Asia	90	3.0	3.1
Africa	555	2.0	1.3
Developed countries	28	1.2	3.6
World	69	2.4	2.9

* Excluding Mainland China.

About capital shortage in a growing population, the argument goes something like this. Assuming that a country's wealth amounts to three or four times its national income, then to maintain the wealth per capita or the wealth-population ratio of a country growing in population at the rate of one per cent a year, there has to be a saving of three to four per cent of its income, convert this saving into wealth and thereby increase the wealth by one per cent.[1] For a country like India whose population is growing at the rate of nearly two per cent a year, the annual savings from income has to be of the order of six to eight per cent just to maintain the present wealth per capita value. To improve upon the existing situation, saving has to be over and above the eight per cent level. In fact, India's average domestic annual saving during the period 1961-66 has been between eleven and twelve per cent. A high rate of population growth diminishes per capita savings since these include family savings and large families save less than small families with similar income.

---

[1] Spengler, Joseph J., "The Economics of Population Growth", in Mudd, (ed.), 1964, p. 77.

Again, there may be a change in age composition due to a shift from low to high fertility. The age range of fifteen to fifty-nine years is known as the productive age, above and below this interval being dependents. Table VI below gives the number of dependents per thousand in the productive age group for five countries in 1960-63 and 1975-78. Table VII gives the number of children requiring elementary school education during this same period. [1]

TABLE VI

Number of Dependents Per 1000 in the Productive Age Group, 1960-1978

Country	1960-63	1975-78
India	816	897
Pakistan	903	967
Indonesia	812	900
Mainland China	945	1,018
Japan	623	463

TABLE VII

Children in Elementary School Age (5 to 14 years) in 1960 and 1975

Country	1960-63 (in thousands)	1975-78 (in thousands)	Per cent increase
India	100,000	150,300	50.1
Pakistan	24,323	38,752	59.3
Indonesia	21,363	34,666	62.3
Mainland China	182,800	292,700	60.1
Japan	20,242	13,300	—34.3

It is obvious from the above tables that for the four countries, with Japan excepted, the level of consumption, personal development, education for children, savings, etc., will be adversely affected due to the growth in population and change in age structure. The retardation in education effort due to difficulties in providing for more schools, more teachers, more maintenance cost, etc., at the lower level and more universities, technical institutes, etc., at the higher level, will tend to keep these societies traditional, illiterate, low productive, and simultaneously highly reproductive.

---

[1] Irene B. Taeuber, "Asian Populations: The Critical Decades", in Mudd (ed.). 1964, pp. 138, 139.

The consideration of overpopulation is closely related to the idea of a standard. This standard is expressed through the concept of optimum population. This concept signifies that under given conditions in a country, there is a population size that is preferable to any other smaller or larger size. The optimum size for any country will vary according to the criterion the country sets before itself. It is the "best" population for the country and obviously the "best" may be viewed from diverse points of view—standard of living of the people, defense of the country, international power game, and so on. In the first case, maximizing per capita income would be the major aim, and the appropriate population level may be called income-optimum population. In the last case populousness by itself becomes a major factor, and hence the optimum is likely to be much higher. From the economic point of view, which is practically the only point of view taken into consideration by deliberations of international agencies, the optimum population is that which makes possible the greatest production and greatest consumption of goods per person. This optimum is, of course, not stationary but moves according to means of production, material resources available, and other factors like the percentage of the productive part of the population tied up in non-productive work like military service. It depends also to some extent on the nature of people's wants and to what extent they are able to satisfy these through external trade relations. What is definite, however, is that the upper and lower limits within which the optimum population or optimum rate of growth for a particular country lie are measurable.

In discussing the optimum for India, Chandrasekhar,[1] a renowned Indian demographer, has this to say, "In general, it seems to be reasonable to assume that a population policy for India so far as gross numbers are concerned should be directed towards maintenance of population at a fairly constant level in preference to either rapid increase, as is happening today, or rapid decrease."

The discrepancy between the actual and optimum population existing today leads to the question as to the means of achieving the optimum. This requires a brief analysis of causes of accelerated growth of population and means of checking it.

---

[1] Chandrasekhar, S., *Population and Planned Parenthood in India*, (Allen and Unwin, Ltd., London, 1955).

III. Causes of Population Growth and Means of Population Control

Basically the factors governing the growth of a population in any country are the birth rate, the mortality rate, and immigration and emigration. In recent times, the last two have been major factors for the New World and a few other countries like Australia. Birth and mortality rates have played the dominant role for most countries and, of course, for the world population. The relative role of the two forces, however, have varied in importance through the long centuries of world history.

In the past centuries, increase in human population has been regulated by three major mortality factors—war, pestilence, and famine. Human survival was a touch and go affair. High fertility had to balance high mortality, and the human female had to reproduce at nearly her physiological limits to enable the family and the clan to survive. Till recently, at least half the babies born died before reaching maturity. Man took recourse to magic, prayers, and "mantras" to gain protection against the major killers. As late as A.D. 1500, the percentage of new-born females in Europe who would survive to age twenty was about thirty per cent and to age fifty about ten per cent. In 1950, the corresponding values are, for India, about 85 per cent and 45 per cent.

It is modern science, and particularly medical and public health breakthroughs like the discovery of vaccination, miracle-working chemicals, antibiotics, pesticides, etc., which have broken the mortality pattern of nearly a million years. The application of scientific methods to agriculture and development of agricultural technology together with the opening of new land masses to the plow increased the availability of food. This together with better transportation and communication have effectively reduced the dangers of famine. It is estimated that Europe used to have, on the average, two famines every century during the middle ages. Today, thanks to the high level of international cooperation, famine is unknown even in the poorest of countries in Asia and Africa. The only factor not yet controlled in the world is war. However, technology has made it almost an all-or-nothing affair—the alternatives are nuclear war and total devastation or peace. Small wars will continue, but their toll of human life will never be the same as in the great wars of history.

Thus the greatest single factor in the growth of human population has been man's increasing control over mortality factors. Death rates have been drastically lowered and although there has been some reduction in birth rates in a few countries, the principal factor in the accelerated increase in population during the last century has been this lowering of death rates. Death rates have dropped, very often without any relation to conditions of living or ways of living, as in Ceylon, and population has moved upward.

Today all national governments and international agencies like the World Health Organization are cooperating in improving public health services and thereby reducing the death rates. Prolongation of life is also looked upon with favor by most men. However, if population growth is to be controlled and kept within optimum limits, birth rates must be reduced simultaneously. This is the core of the problem. Science has freed death rates from their age old ties with food deficiencies and environmental hazards. The question is being asked increasingly: Can science free birth rates from their close line with traditional social structure and values and the sex life of the person? The present demographic crisis can only be averted if such a check on birth rates can be effectively achieved.

IV. Human Fertility and Family Planning—Techniques and Necessary Conditions

Control of human fertility can be effected by postponing marriage or through control within married life. Ireland is an example of the first method. Its average of early marriage was, according to the 1951 census, 31 for men and 27 for women. About 31 per cent of the men and 26 per cent of the women never married up to fifty years of age.

Fertility control within marriage is effected by adoption of contraceptive measures or through sterilization, abstinence, or abortion. The contraceptive measures are usually divided into two groups—appliance methods (mechanical devices and spermicides) and non-appliance methods (for example, the rhythm method). Status of oral contraceptives is not yet clear. The Roman Catholic church distinguishes between "natural birth control" (e.g., the rhythm method) and "artificial birth control" (other methods). Several studies [1,2,3] have

---

[1] Whelpton, P. K. and Kiser, C.V. (ed.), *Social and Psychological Factors Affecting Fertility*, Vols. I-V, (Milbank Memorial Fund, New York, 1946-1958).

[2] Westoff, Charles, et al., *Family Growth in Metropolitan America*, (Princeton University Press, Princeton, 1961).

[3] Tietze, Christopher, "The USE-Effectiveness of Contraceptive Methods", in Kiser (ed.), *Research in Family Planning*, (Princeton University Press, Princeton, 1962), pp. 357-369.

attempted to assess the failure rates for these different devices, this rate being the (accidental) pregnancy rate per hundred years of use, the so-called Pearl Formula. According to this formula, the failure rate is:

$$\frac{\text{number of accidental pregnancies}}{\text{number of months of use}} \times 1200$$

Whereas the actual failure rates noted from different studies vary, the relative effectiveness of these devices are fairly constant. Diaphragm and the condom are most effective (failure rates around ten) and the douche and the rhythm method least, their failure rates varying from twenty to forty. Coitus interruptus is of medium effectiveness, with a failure rate of about twelve, only slightly more than of the condom or the diaphragm but substantially lower, by half or more, than the rates for the safe period and the douche. Incidentally, it may be mentioned that the findings that the withdrawal method is only slightly less effective than the condom has come as a great surprise to many clinicians who had all along considered this as a most unreliable method. The effectiveness of the other methods like foam tablets, jelly, etc., is mostly the same or worse as for douche.

V. Attitude of Religions to Fertility Control

Most religious leaders maintain that the present rate of population growth is undesirable and also that increase in human longevity and fall in mortality rates are essentially desirable. Thus by the process of elimination fertility control remains to be the only method of checking population growth and it is precisely in the degree of support they give to practice of contraceptive techniques that religious leaders differ. Their attitude varies from outright opposition to the use of such techniques through acceptance of some techniques and rejction of others to no opposition or complete acceptance. Besides those religions which take up some position on this issue, there is at least one which has not made any issue of this.

It must be mentioned that influence of religious opinion on family planning is always through changing people's values in a characteristic manner and thereby affect their attitude and motivation towards the use of contraceptive techniques. Thus religion operates through creating a psychological and social climate. Therefore, before taking up the role of religion, it may be useful to have a brief discussion of those psychological conditions that facilitate effective fertility control programs. Religion helps or hinders family planning programs only through its influence on these psychological and social factors.

One investigator, [1] on the basis of his experience of family planning programs in the Caribbean region, mentions three necessary facilitating conditions:

1. Ends or values which explicitly favor a family size less than is normally achieved without control.
2. Awareness of the means of achieving family limitation.
3. Acceptability of the known means.

The following three facilitating conditions have been mentioned:

1. Accessibility of mechanical, chemical, and surgical techniques to different classes and groups within a given society.
2. Some characteristics of the social organization like the family structure and the extent to which this permits development and sharing of goals and knowledge regarding techniques, etc., the segregation of the sexes, the pattern of dominance in the household, norms regarding cross-sex discussions of intimate topics, etc.
3. Priority of limited family size in a hierarchy of values.

Put another way, the significant socio-psychological areas in family planning are:

a. The attitude of married couples and of society at large toward the undesirability of having large families.
b. The acceptability of the various techniques for curtailment of birth by married couples.
c. The nature of social organization in which the married couples are placed with regard to:
   i. acceptability of new values on population;
   ii. the extent to which the society is prepared to go in enforcing its convictions on the population boom, both by direct action like supporting family planning programs and indirectly by building this program within a larger social framework of welfare of the people;
   iii. at an action level, the extent to which social values are converted into hard action—in other words, the value-action discrepancy. Note that in Japan, for every five mothers who used contraceptive appliances, twelve took recourse to surgical abortion demon-

---

[1] Stycos, J. Mayone, "Experiments in Social Change: The Caribbean Fertility Studies", in Kiser ((ed.), 1962, p. 306.

strating thereby their reluctance to change over from normal carefree conjugal habits in spite of a desire to avoid unwanted pregnancies. [1]

A detailed analysis of the attitude of different religions shows that, barring the Roman Catholic religion, none of the other major religions have taken a hostile attitude toward family planning. Although certain aspects of the philosophy of some faiths do tend to encourage large families, it is generally agreed that, with the exception mentioned above, religious ideology does not engender a positive resistance on the part of common people in adopting population control techniques.

There are three sources of evidence on religious attitude. First is the writings in sacred texts like the Koran, etc. The other two sources are the pronouncements of religious leaders or the clergy, and pronouncements and perceptions of the common people for whom population control techniques are actually meant.

The religious texts were written at a time when population growth had not reached this frightening proportion; indeed in some places, there was need for a rapid increase in population to settle the country or for economic, social, religious, and military well-being. Quotations can therefore be found in most of the religious texts which directly or indirectly encourage people to propagate; the support for polygamy in Islam may be interpreted in this light.

Hinduism. To understand the position of Hinduism, one should know something of the religion. Hinduism is amorphous and complex. It has no church and clergy or a clearly-defined body of dogma in the Christian sense. Though it seems that the only way of becoming a Hindu is to be born one, it has absorbed many groups. It has a variety of religious ideas and practices, of gods and of means of salvation. However, underlying these are certain definable elements. One most prominent of these is its fundamental religious relativity, meaning, thereby, that many ways of life are religiously acceptable and that there is no exclusively single approach believed to be valid for approaching the divine. Talcott Parsons says that in this "religious sense India presents probably the most radically individualistic situation known to history." [2] Further, there are no beliefs or institutions common to all Hindus and which mark them off from others. "Every

---

[1] Gopalaswami, R. A., "Family Planning: Outlook for Governmental Action in India", in Kiser (ed.), 1962, p. 77.

[2] Parsons, Talcott, *The Structure of Social Action*, (Free Press, Glencoe, 1949), p. 558.

belief considered basic to Hindus has been rejected by one group or another." [1] However, it is not difficult to identify a person as a Hindu for ideas of Karma and Dharma, institutions like caste, and deities like Shiva and Vishnu are widespread among them. Dharma is the total body of moral and religious rules accepted both by common people and in great works like the Bhagavadgita.

The traditional Hindu way of life revolves around four supreme goals or purposes of life—Dharma or right conduct, Artha the economic goal, Kāma or the satisfaction of desires, and Moksha or salvation. The first three goals are external to man and should lead to the last one which is immanent in him. "In Hindu theory, therefore, the instinctive, moral, and spiritual aspects of man are all considered legitimate, and worthy of expression." The Hindu way of life is the ascetic way, but this is an otherworldly asceticism, and Max Weber contrasts it to the active worldly asceticism which is the essence of Protestant ethics.

Family and conjugal life was the subject of discourse in ancient Hindu texts—Vātsayan's Kāma Sūtras discusses the question of union between husband and wife, their timings, poses, and postures. It also discusses the chemical and occlusive methods of birth control. The Dharma Sutras of Manu and Brhadāranyak Upanisad discussed similar questions, particularly the rituals and mantras to be adopted for begetting intelligent and lovely children, something which the modern science of eugenics also aims at. Even the great Vedas, the Rg and Yajur have prayers addressed to the god Indra for granting to the new bride ten children. At least one son is essential for the Hindu to perform religious rites at his death and save him from the hell called Puth. Manu has called the first child as Dharmajā—born out of a sense of duty, and has called children born after the first as Kāmajā—born out of lust.

The ancient Hindus were thus aware of techniques of population control and were sufficiently broadminded to discuss these in important texts. There was emphasis in begetting sons, at least one, and this was tied to performance of important religious rituals. To this was added only subsequently the superstition of having large families as something desirable and auspicious in itself. However, in the entire Hindu sacred books, there is nothing to suggest any opposition to planned parenthood or against fertility control techniques. There is em-

---

[1] Srinivas, M. N., *Caste in Modern India*, (Asia Publishing House, 1962), p. 150.

phasis on marriage, for it is a necessary condition for physical and spiritual fulfillment. The marriageable age for men was put at twenty-five and for women at sixteen, and prolonged celibacy was deemed undesirable. However, life was regulated along the way of the four āshramas. The life of the householder, the "grhasta asrama," did not last throughout the normal reproductive period, and it is quite possible that if the Hindu injunctions governing our daily life were followed, there would be no population problem for India today.

To conclude, therefore, the ancient Hindus tried to bring some system in the family life by various injunctions and by emphasizing different ages for different types of activities. Some techniques for birth control were known, and there is nothing in the most sacred texts suggesting opposition to these. Sons were deemed desirable but not a large family. The latter became a vogue only much later.

In modern times also social reformers have consistently supported the idea of planned parenthood. Gandhi, for example, has this to say: "There can be no two opinions about the necessity of birth-control... The world depends for its existence on the act of generation and, as the world is the playground of God and a reflection of his glory, the act of generation should be controlled for the ordered growth of the world." [1] And above all, the relativity of Hindu rites, customs, and traditions to changing needs of the times is a paramount characteristic of this religion, and has been stated by Radhakrishnan thus: "The Hindu Dharma gives us a program of rules and regulations and permits their constant change. The rules of dharma are the mortal flesh of immortal ideas and so are mutable." Rightly has it been said that "no Hindu need run off out of his conscience by practicing contraceptions."

It has already been mentioned that Hinduism has no system of organized clergy. To some extent their place is taken by social reformers and intellectuals, and through their utterances and writings they mold public opinion. Nearly all of them support family planning, and only one, Mahatma Gandhi, insisted on family planning through abstinence only. To quote:

Rabindra Nath Tagore: "The birth control movement is a great movement... In a hunger-stricken country like India it is a crime thoughtlessly to bring more children to existence than could probably

---

[1] Radhakrishnan, S., *Religion and Society*, (Allen and Unwin, London, 1948), p. 108.

be taken care of... I believe that to wait till the moral sense of man becomes a great deal more powerful than it is now and till then to allow countless generations of children to suffer privations and untimely death for no fault of their own is a great social injustice which should not be tolerated." Mahatma Gandhi: "There can be no two opinions about the necessity of birth control..." [1] Radhakrishnan: "If, therefore, your main interest is to secure the health and happiness of both mothers and children, if your main interest is to bring down the infant and maternal mortality in this country which is so ruinous, it is essential for us to adopt a system of family planning... Now, when we have all these methods, when the teachers tell us that it is essential for us to control increase of population, it is open to us to find out, *each for himself*, what is best adapted to his own development." Jawaharlal Nehru: "whether it is from a political, economic, or social point of view, all these problems drive us to the conclusion that we must take up this question of family planning and press it forward and with vigor and intelligence."

Thus all the authorities of modern India favor family planning. Techniques are not a major point of controversy except for the Mahatma who is against all artificial techniques. This question of technique, which ties up with the Roman Catholic views also, will be discussed at a later stage.

The Indian people who are the referrent for all family planning programs in the country have, on the whole, no objection on religious ground to family planning. This has been brought out clearly in about thirty or more attitude surveys carried on in different parts of the country. It has been found from these surveys that "There is no organized religious or social opposition to family planning." [2] "While on the one hand, it shows that the actual practice of family planning, even in a city like Poona, is extremely limited in scope, it also reveals a general receptive attitude, extensive readiness to obtain useful and effective information, and considerable preparedness to adopt family planning in case the means are suitable and appropriate. It appears clear that there exists no important element in the ideological make-up

---

[1] Prabhu, R. K., and Rao, U. R., *The Mind of Mahatma Gandhi,* (Oxford University Press, 1945), p. 108.

[2] Aragwala, S. N., *Attitude Towards Family Planning in India,* (Asia Publishing House, Bombay, 1962), p. 34.

of the people which would make progress impossible if a movement towards family planning is launched properly." [1]

Islam. In countries where Islam is an important though not the only religion, there is a feeling among non-Muslims that Muslim population increases faster than non-Muslims. While perhaps the natural rivalry between the religions may be mostly responsible for this perception, facts do tend to support this fear to some extent. In Lebanon, for exemple, where the Christians and Muslims are finely balanced, a study of differential fertility of the two communities are summarized as follows: [2]

	Muslim	Christian
Rural uneducated	High	High
Urban uneducated	High	Low
Urban educated	Moderate	Low

The question, however, is if there is anything in Islam that favors large families and/or opposes family planning. In traditional Islam it is not difficult to quote such statements as "When a servant of Allah marries, he perfects half his religion"; "Marry and multiple so that I may be glorified in my community over other communities"; "The best man in our community is he who has most wives". Besides scriptural support like the above, other social and economic aspects of Muslim life like polygamy, divorce, relatively better status for women in personal law (at least in India) have encouraged large families.

The personal laws affecting birth, marriage, divorce, etc., of the Muslims are regulated by the Islamic Law (Shariat) and the Islamic jurisprudence. Interpretations or rulings on specific questions can be given by the Supreme Teacher, the Grand Mufti of Egypt. On the question of family planning, the Grand Mufti issued the following Fatwa on January 25, 1937: "It is permissible for either husband or wife by mutual consent to take any measures (both natural and artificial methods) in order to prevent conception." Later scholars of the Hanafi School consider that such consent is not even necessary if either husband or wife has reasonable ground for family planning. On abortion, the clarification was as follows: "Opinion on the subject

---

[1] Gadgil, D. R., Foreword to Dandekar and Dandekar's *Survey of Fertility and Morality in Poona District; Gokhale Institute of Politics and Economics*, Publication No. 27, 1953.

[2] Yankey, David, "Differential Fertility in Lebanon," in Kiser (ed.), 1962, p. 138.

has differed but the majority are inclined not to allow it, except for a reason such as the interruption of the mother's milk, when she has another baby and the father cannot afford a 'wet nurse' and the baby's life is therefore endangered. After the quickening of the embryo, abortion is absolutely prohibited."

The above Fatwa permitting birth control was obtained in 1937 on the initiative of the national forum for population control formed in Egypt at that time. Since then no serious objection has been raised against planning on religious grounds. Indeed, national leaders of Islamic countries support this movement. President Nasser announced in the National Chapter in 1962: "The population increase constitutes the most dangerous obstacle that faces the Egyptian people in their drive towards raising the standards of production ... attempts at family planning with the aim of facing the problem of increasing population deserve the most sincere efforts supported by modern scientific methods."

The mass of Muslim population very rarely reject family planning techniques on the ground of religion, as numerous studies in India have shown. For example, in rural West Bengal surveys showed that forty-six per cent Hindus and fifty per cent Muslims responded in favor of restricting family size, though only forty-four per cent and thirteen per cent of these communities respectively favored the use of contraceptives. There are occasional examples of refusing family planning advice on the ground that "It is against God", but this view is not widespread enough to justify regarding religious beliefs as the first of ten motives opposing family planning, as one another has done. [1]

Christianity. In New York in July 1958, Dr. Hillman, a Protestant physician employed in one of the city hospitals, announced that he was going to fit a Protestant patient with a contraceptive device and was forbidden to do so by the New York City Commissioner of Hospitals. "A public controversy followed, with Protestants and Jews demanding that the ban be lifted in the interest of accepting therapy and preventive medicine and with the Roman Catholic chancery office stating, 'It would be extremely unfortunate if our hospitals and medical facilities, aimed for the preservation of life, should be perverted to seek for the prevention of life.' " [1] This controversy

---

[1] Bogue, Donald J., "Some Tentative Recommendations for a Sociologically Correct Family Planning Communication and Motivation Program in India," in Kiser (ed.), 1962, p. 516.

typically represents the points of view of the two schools of Christianity and of the Jewish religion in the United States. It also shows that, unlike Eastern countries, religion plays an important role in opinion formation on family planning in the United States. Indeed, religion has been called "the social attribute of the greatest single importance" in the adoption of family planning programs in the U.S.A. and "exerts much more influence, for example, than does occupational class or, for that matter, any of the socio-economic variables." [2] Both the leaders of Protestant and Catholic faiths are active in this public opinion formation process, and they take very different views.

The Roman Catholic opposition to contraception is based on scriptural texts as well as its conception of the natural law. Contraception is regarded as sinful by the church fathers. For example, St. Augustine declared that "intercourse with one's legitimate wife is unlawful and wicked where the conception of the offspring is prevented." The Roman Catholics have based their opposition to contraception on their idea of the primary end of marriage. The natural law tradition accepts the view that the primary purpose of sexual activity is procreation, the continuation of the human race. Consequently any arrangement that blocks this end is against nature and should be condemned. This approach to the understanding of the goals of marriage is in terms of social and procreative purpose outside the life of the spouses and disregard the personal factors of friendship and love between the partners.

Contraception is looked upon as corrupting the individual as it reduces self-control and conjugal union takes place for selfish reasons. However, the rhythm method is approved by the authorities of the Roman Catholic church. We shall see later how the very ethical and logical position the Catholic church has taken regarding the use of contraceptives is seriously jeopardized by the sanction of deliberate use of the safe period as a means of family planning.

It may be mentioned that the Catholic church does not support indiscriminate breeding but enjoins family planning as a duty. Its only objection is to the mode of family planning, the rhythm method being

---

[1] St. John, Stevas Norman, "A Roman Catholic View of Population Control," in Shimm (ed.), 1961, p. 82.

[2] Westoff, Charles F., "The Family Growth in Metropolitan America Study, A Progress Report", in Kiser (ed.), 1962, p. 185.

regarded as the only acceptable technique besides abstinence. Regarding the world population problem the Roman Catholic attitude is very humanitarian though perhaps impracticable. The population problem is looked upon as a force that will lead to the development of a universal community. Pope Pius XII declared that the human race has a "true unity of nature, unity of purpose, and a unity of dwelling place on earth; of whose resources all men can by natural right avail themselves to sustain and develop life." This is a very noble position, worthy of the best traditions of the Catholic church. He enjoins the affluent countries to share their resources with other countries less well-developed on the principles of justice and charity. However, it is perhaps doubtful whether such sharing, even if possible, will actually continue to compensate for the continuous depredation caused by increase of sheer numbers of the human race.

The Protestant view is based on its slightly different concept of the ends of marriage. Firstly, marriage is regarded as good in itself and not as a means to some other end. Secondly, marriage is a spiritual reality and trnscends the law of nature which irrevocably ties the sexual function to procreation as in the lower species. As Archbishop Michael Ramsey said, "The purpose of matrimony is perfection of the married couple... a cooperation with Divine omnipotence." Companionship between the spouses is as much an end of marriage as procreation and such companionship is primarily social and spiritual rather than sexual, a sharing of mind, interest, and experience. Thus although procreation is certainly an end of marriage, children are to be regarded more as fruits of conjugal relation, divine gifts blessing the married condition, rather than its primary end. Marriage is a spiritual reality, a gift of God, the gift union or "henosis", which is a physical union but yet transcends it.

The Protestant view has thus detached procreation from the act of love. It has also developed the concept of responsible parenthood. The 1958 Lambeth conference states: "Children may be born within the supporting framework of parental love and family concern, with a right to an opportunity for a full and spiritually wholesome life." It is on these two arguments that family planning is justified. Thus medical, eugenic, economic, and social indications do justify limiting the number of children a couple can have, and such prevention of conception does not make the sex act against God so long as it fulfills and completes the desire for companionship and love on the part of the spouses.

If the motives for family planning are proper, the means or techniques are of not much importance. This rationale covers nearly all the means of contraception, though abstinence on the basis of mutual consent and the rhythm method are preferred. Voluntary sterilization is not always supported, mostly on ground of its irreversibility. Abortion as a means of family planning, of course, is condemned as it is not really prevention of conception.

If the behavior of individuals is analyzed, the religious factor is seen to play a role in the total number of children wanted as well as in the method of family planning adopted. It has been seen in an American study that Catholics want the largest families, and the Jews the smallest, with the Protestants coming in between. Similarly, the Jews begin contraception earlier, have the longest birth intervals and fewest unplanned pregnancies. The Catholics are at the opposite end of this pattern with Protestants occupying an intermediate position.

However, other factors also play a role, especially the educational system followed and the felt need for education of the offspring. A Catholic educated in a Catholic college or university has higher fertility and higher optimum family size as compared to Catholics educated in secular institutions. This is through reinforcement of the Catholic attitude and intensification of religiousness. Characteristically enough, high religiousness is negatively or insignificantly correlated with fertility in Protestants and Jews. Among other non-religious factors that are important is nationality. Irish Catholics have the highest fertility and Italian Catholics the lowest in the U.S.A. The Jews have a low fertility rate, largely motivated by their heavy emphasis on education of children. It may also be mentioned that the Catholic religion has little or no effect on fertility in other countries, like Puerto Rico, Argentina, etc. Catholic Argentina has about the lowest birth rate in Latin America although in the United Nations and elsewhere it has fought against any program for promoting the birth control movement. In Puerto Rico the Roman Catholics favor a smaller family size and in general have higher acceptance of contraception. In meetings on birth control, Roman Catholic women are more likely to attend than non-Catholics and churchgoers more than non-churchgoers. Quite possibly this paradoxical situation is due to the low influence of the church in these countries, though some experts believe that this low influence is partly due to the hostility of the people to the Catholic church's stand on fertility control. This latter point would imply, as has been found in other cases like that of prohibition, that the Church may not fare well where its tenets are against the perceived economic or other interest of its followers.

Concluding Remarks

We have examined very briefly the position of different religions on population control. The author is not a specialist in theology but nevertheless hopes that his summarizing of these positions has been adequate and objective. Of the major world religions, Hinduism has not taken up any formal posture regarding population control. Indeed, there being no organized clergy, Hinduism rarely gives an "official" opinion about matters of social importance, which is at once its strength and weakness. The social reformers and intellectual leaders of Indian society are all for population control with artificial devices, the sole exception being Mahatma Gandhi. Islam is supportive of the idea of fertility control both by natural and artificial devices. By and large it has been noted by many social scientists that religious belief is not a barrier to the adoption of birth control techniques in the Eastern world.

Judaism, or at least contemporary Jews, is very particular in limiting their families, and the major factor is their heavy emphasis on children's education. This has also been the official position of American Jewish Rabbis since 1930 when they lifted the ban on the use of contraceptives. It is with respect to the two churches of Christianity, the Roman Catholic and the Protestant churches, that formal positions have been adopted deliberately and consciously, and attempts are made to justify these positions from the theological point of view. Thus in contrast to the indifference or purely pragmatic approach of other religions, the two Christian schools have carried on the debate on birth control over so many decades.

There are two factors in the approach to this problem by religious and other leaders, one of some practical importance and the other of considerable theoretical weight. The practical consideration is the fear that extensive use of contraception by one's religious group will reduce its representation in the total population and through this lead to a fall in the particular church's influence and power. This fear is very rarely voiced openly although the careful examination of relative weights of different religious groups in the total population clearly indicates the existence of this fear. This is a real fear among Hindus in India, Christians in certain Middle Eastern countries like Lebanon, and perhaps in the U.S.A. also among Protestants and Catholics. The changing religious composition of national populations constitutes the basis for such fears. In the United States, for example, during the days of President Washington, the white Protestant group constituted about three quarters to four fifths of the population, while Catholics and Jews were confined to about one per cent only. In 1957, the U.S. Bureau of Census reported that in the age group fourteen and above, white Protestants were fifty-eight per cent, Catholics twenty-seven per cent and Jews three per cent. The fertility rates are highest for Catholics, and least for Jews.

The first practical point deserving attention from religious leaders should be to decide what to do about this very real fear of domination by a different religious group. In India, for example, this fear is not vocal now but is likely to be so as soon as the present family planning movement shows significant results. The social and political consequences of differential decline in birth rates in multi-religious countries will assume large proportions and deserve careful thinking on the part of leaders of religions.

The second point is a question of ethics, namely, the extent to which separation of procreation from the act of love is morally justified. The strictly rigid and logical view is that of Mahatma Gandhi; the Protestant church has tried to come out of the dilemma by postulating other equally important purposes of marrige besides racial survival. The Roman Catholic view appears to the present author as a very good compromise attempt between the two above positions but like most compromises has had to sacrifice intellectual rigor on the one hand and practicality on the other.

Gandhi's opinion, which is essentially the same as adopted by most religious leaders till recently, may best be given in his own words:

> "Man is, undoubtedly, an artist and creator. Undoubtedly, he must have beauty and, therefore, color. His artistic and creative nature at its best taught him to discriminate, and to know that conglomeration of colors was no mark of beauty, nor even sense of enjoyment good in itself. His eye for art taught man to seek enjoyment in usefulness. Thus, he learnt at an early stage of his evolution that he has to eat not for its own sake, as some of us still do, but he should eat to enable him to live. At a later stage, he learnt further that there was neither beauty nor joy in living for its own sake, but that he must live to serve his fellow creatures and through them his Maker. Similarly, when he pondered over the phenomenon of the pleasurableness of sexual union, he discovered that like every other organ of sense this one of

generation had its use and abuse. And he saw that its true function, its right use, was to restrict it to generation. Any other use he saw was ugly, and he saw further that it was fraught with very serious consequences, as well as to the individual as to the race... Sex urge is a fine and noble thing. There is nothing to be ashamed of it. But it is meant only for the act of creation. Any other use of it is a sin against God and humanity."

Gandhi's basic position of linking the sex act with procreation logically leads to his extreme position of propagating birth control only through complete abstinence and total condemnation of artificial devices. Thus:

"There can be no two opinions about the necessity of birth control. But the only method handed down from ages past (here Gandhi is wrong) is self-control or brahmacharya... Artificial methods are like putting a premium upon vice. It is wrong and immoral to seek to escape the consequences of one's act...

"This sex urge has been isolated from the desire for progeny and it is said by the protagonists of the use of contraceptives that conception is an accident to be prevented except when the parties desire to have children. I venture to suggest that this is a most dangerous doctrine to preach."

To sum up, therefore, it must be conceded that once Gandhi's basic assumption is accepted, namely that the only purpose of the sex act is procreation and that the emotional accompaniments are secondary and incidental, no logical contravention of his position that abstinence is the only method of birth control is possible. Logically and ethically brahmacharya is the only acceptable method of fertility control.

The Protestant church has controverted Gandhi's position by attacking his major premise, and holding that there are other equally important objectives of the act of love besides the desire for children. Such other objectives are companionship between the spouses and the emotional intimacy, love, and happiness which follow, or should follow, from love-making. While these objectives are different from the rigorous moral approach of Gandhi, it nevertheless reflects a genuinely new approach in the best of traditions of Protestant ethics, responsive to changing social and ethical values.

The Protestant church has very rightly not laid much emphasis on techniques of family planning, adopting a generally supportive posture except for condemning abortion and emphasizing the beauty and strength of abstinence mutually accepted. One does not know if the reason for putting less emphasis on methods than on motives is correctly stated by Fagley [1] when he says, "If the motives are wrong, no method will make them right. On the other hand, if the motives are responsible, there is considerable latitude as to means." Without going into the age-old ethical controversy of ends and means, it may be said that in practical life, means or methods are almost as important as the ends and behavior. The Protestant church should take up a position regarding means or methods, as indeed it has done. It is only hoped that the statement quoted that means are of no import does not represent the typical Protestant view.

The Roman Catholic view is based on its concept of the natural law according to which the conjugal act is destined primarily for the begetting of children. This position logically leads to the conclusion that if one does not want children, one should practice abstinence. The Catholic position is considerably jeopardized, however, when spouses are allowed love-making, deliberately choosing a time when conception is physiologically not possible. The author would submit that the difference between a deliberate choice of the "safe" period and adoption of so-called artificial techniques of contraception is one of degree only and not of quality. Motivationally both fall under the same category, namely, indulgence in the sex act for the sake of pleasure and avoiding consequences of that act. Since intention or motive is the criterion for judging the ethicality of an act, the "safe" method as well as artificial contraceptive techniques are equally unsupportable, so long as the assumption remains that procreation is the primary objective of the sex act. It would seem therefore that Gandhi's strict insistence on abstinence is the only ethical method of population control, when one argues from the point of view of natural law.

It must be pointed out that the concept of abstinence, however ethical and logically consistent it might be, is in practice possible only for a few. The general mass of humanity at its present stage of development cannot be expected to practice this. Religious leaders must therefore take this into account. The alternative to an unchecked growth of population is to sanction contraceptive techniques that are acceptable to people. Indeed people are using different methods of contraceptives more or less independently of their religious belief and what remains is to find ethical justification for something that is already

---

[1] Fagley, Richard M., "A Protestant View of Population Control", in Shimm (ed.), 1961, pp. 107-108.

happening. Although such *post facto* justification is always galling to the honest, this is exactly what is happening to the Roman Catholic Church—the Pope is even now thinking of setting up a commission of Bishops to examine the question afresh. The Protestant churches have been fortunate in that they changed their stand before the problem became highly controversial. Gandhi did not shift his position but then very few follow him, even in India. Traditional Hinduism has enjoined its followers to give up the way and life of the householder and become an ascetic after a certain age. Strictly followed, this means no children after that age; but even then the population problem would not be solved for a reproductive period of twenty years for women under modern hospital and public health conditions is long enough.

Having examined the position of different religions on population control and noting that there are certain inherent dificulties in the traditional viewpoints, the question comes up: Must religion continue to tolerate this ambiguous situation? Is there no way for religion to put its great moral weight behind the population control movement, take it out of the hands of the intellectuals and other élites and place it before the mass of humanity as a worthwhile aspect of human endeavor? The present author respectfully submits that this can be and indeed should be done.

Major religions have set the tone for civilization and shaped cultural values in different parts of the world. Hinduism in India, Confucianism in China, Judaism in Israel, and Christianity in Europe and America have molded the culture and lives of peoples. Max Weber has shown how the peculiar nature of Protestant ethics with its emphasis on personal asceticism and dedication to work provided the character background for the development of capitalistic economy (for a good summary of Weber, see Parsons. [1]) Whether Protestantism is a sufficient cause or not of this development may be questioned; it is certainly not a necessary cause, for non-Protestant nations can also be very advanced. However, the basic assumption of Weber that each major religion of the world gives its own distinctive orientation towards all the major phases of human activity and influences the development of major institutional systems of the society cannot be seriously doubted. Modern studies on the influence of the religious factor, for

---

[1] Parsons, Talcott, *The Structure of Social Action*, (Free Press, Glencoe, 1964).

example, the one by Gerhard Lenski, [1] have found empirical support for Weber's historical analysis.

In all its aspects, religion itself has been a product of the society, a social institution of a sort. Functions of religion differ for given times and places; they also change with the developmental phase of the religion or the denomination. Modern religions turn away from the supernatural to the social, from transcending the human to the serving of human needs. To a certain extent, therefore, religion must be responsive to social needs of the people. If religion is defined as a "system of beliefs about the nature of the force ultimately shaping man's destiny," there is no compulsion that such a system of belief should not change with increasing knowledge of the environment and of the self. Rightly has it been pointed out that religion is deeply rooted in the mores and must gradually change in harmony with the mores and other social institutions. [2] Indeed, it can and should be a vehicle of social change, while itself changing under the impact of new scientific and cultural forces.

Applying the same arguments to the problem of population control, cannot all religions take a point of view that fully recognizes the demographic danger and points a way out? There are indeed signs that this is happening. However religions must not only tolerate fertility control techniques in the interest of the future generations, but propagate it, and give it all the weight of their authority. The only restrictions to fertility control should be on medical grounds and not on any other. The danger is too great, and a radical shift in opinion is indicated. It is easier for some religions to take an active part in this movement because they possess the necessary clerical organizations; those religions which do not have the necessary organization can certainly sanction it, at least when the question comes before them. And the only way religion can do so is by widening our concept of the purpose of marriage, as Protestantism has already done. There seems to be no way out of this.

---

[1] Lenski, Gerhard, *The Religious Factor*, (Doubleday and Co., New York, 1961).
[2] Mordoskos, John Eric, *Social Change*, (McGraw-Hill, 1960), p. 287.

III

DESEGREGATION
OE RELIGIONS AND CULTURES:
GUIDELINES

A NEW AWARENESS OF TIME AND HISTORY

BY

S. G. F. BRANDON

University of Manchester

Many scholars, after devoting years of study to the history of religions, have felt moved to define the origin of religion—to isolate some entity which seems to supply the original motive or impetus to man's religious faith and practice. When we contemplate the amazing complexity and rich variety of the religions of mankind, such a quest would seem to be utterly hopeless; some would doubtless judge it as ill-conceived. We can recall the attempts of Tylor, Max Müller, Frazer, Freud, Rudolf Otto, and many others, to formulate a definition of either the origin or the essential nature of religion. Some of their definitions we may recognize as stimulating in their influence upon subsequent thought; but none has become established as the definitive formulation of what religion is in origin and essence.

All this should constitute a sufficient warning to any scholar to go quietly about his ways, devoting his efforts to more limited but more practicable tasks. However, the problem of the origin of religion is one of such basic and perennial interest that it will always tempt men to speculate about it and essay some solution. I have felt the temptation and have succumbed to it. The results were published last year in a book entitled *History, Time and Deity*.[1] The three nouns grouped together in this title denote the three concepts which I believe to be basic to this problem. It is their interrelations, i.e., the relationship between "History," "Time" and "Deity" that will be the theme of my paper now.

I

Of the three concepts, I regard Time as the most significant in terms of the origin of religion. By Time, in this connection, I mean human awareness or consciousness of Time—in other words, that every one of us is aware that the phenomena that constitute the world of our experience are ever changing and that we are implicated in this process of change, of coming into being and passing away.

---

[1] New York: Manchester University Press and Barnes and Noble, Inc., 1965.

So basic is this experience of temporal change that we may justly say that to be conscious of being alive is to be conscious of Time. But, here, we must note that this existential experience of Time is made up of three forms of awareness, which are related to the three temporal categories: Time Past, Time Present, and Future Time. At any given moment, if we analyze our consciousness, we realize that the "here-now" of present experience is conditioned by memory of past experience and by the anticipation of future experience. Indeed, it is impossible to be aware of what is purely "here-now"; for the present is a razor-edge line, between past and future, which is ever moving, so that what is "now" has become "past", as we contemplate it, and in the very act we have moved into the future.

Now, this awareness of Time, essentially elusive as it is when we try to analyze it, is a faculty or endowment which is characteristically human and from which has stemmed mankind's success in the struggle for existence. It has meant that man has been able, in the present, to draw upon past experience, to anticipate future needs. None of the other animals has so well-developed a Time-sense; hence, despite their possession often of greater physical strength or swiftness of movement, they have been defeated and dominated by man. Upon this Time-sense the whole complex structure of our cultural and technological civilization has been built—whether it be planning for next year's harvest, getting a rocket to the moon, or taking out an insurance policy, every activity or transaction involves the visualization of future needs in the light of past experience. When our remote ancestors began chipping flints to make them into tools, already they were using in the present their knowledge of the past, to prepare for the future—already, in other words, man was acting teleologically; for the very conception of purpose implies an effective awareness of the temporal categories of Past, Present, and Future.

How basic and how essential Time-consciousness is to human life and achievement needs no further emphasis; its fundamental character is obvious in whatever direction we turn our attention. But, now, it is important to notice that this endowment has an ambivalent nature. It is a kind of two-edged gift: on the one hand, it has given mankind its mastery in the struggle for existence; but, on the other, it has robbed *homo sapiens* of his ability to enjoy life as other species do. Whereas the healthy, well-fed animal, when it is not alerted to immediate danger, can apparently immerse itself wholly in present contentment, man, even when physically satisfied, cannot do this. His Time-sense prevents him. Unless he dulls his consciousness by drugs, he cannot shut out his memory of the past and anticipation of the future, so as to live wholly in the here-now of present experience.

In other words, man's consciousness of Time causes him always to be aware that he is immersed in an unceasing process of change—that he can never stay and rest in the present; that what seems to be here and now is inexorably moving into the past as he seeks to apprehend it, while a new situation is ever confronting him as it emerges to present reality from its state of non-being in the future. But this is not all. Man also knows that he is no mere spectator of an ever changing phenomenal world which the Time-process presents to him—for he is, himself, part of that process and is himself subject to that change of being through which Time manifests itself. He knows that he has been, that he now is, and that he will be—but for how long?

It is here that man's Time-consciousness makes its other aspects so disturbingly felt. As the individual looks out towards his own personal future, he knows that the passage of Time will bring to him, inevitably, the experience of ageing and, ultimately, of death. In other words, through his awareness of Time, man anticipates his own death—he knows that he is mortal. This fatal knowledge man alone possesses. The poet W. B. Yeats perceived this truth, and expressed it in lines of rare insight:

> Nor dread, nor hope attend
> A dying animal;
> A man awaits his end
> Dreading and hoping all.

This knowledge is indeed both fatal and fateful. Every human being discovers, some time in childhood, that people die, and an instinctive logic, inspired by his Time-sense, at once causes him to realize that he will die. Once this truth is grasped, it is never forgotten; indeed, it grows in significance and urgency. No sane human being can ever escape making this discovery, and becoming aware of its disturbing logic. Such has been the experience of every member of our race back into the past, to that unknown time when the human mind became effectively conscious of past, present, and future.

Now, it is obvious on reflection that the knowledge, that Time must bring old age, decay and death, is, and must always have been, profoundly disturbing to that "pleasing, anxious being," which constitutes the sense of self, and to which we give utterance every time we say

"I." Faced with the sense of our own impermanence and the prospect of our personal extinction, reaction is immediate—we instinctively seek to avoid this fate; to find some assurance of immunity from Time's awful logic, to be saved from its disintegrating and mortal process.

The urge to seek immunity or security is naturally universal, since it stems from a common human reaction to what is the inevitable destiny of every human being. And it must have been felt by mankind from the moment when the human mind attained to an effective consciousness of Time, which really means from the dawn of rationality. Now, it is in this common and abiding urge to seek for security from the effacing flux of Time that I see the origin of religion. I would define my conclusion as follows: religion is the expression of man's instinctive quest for security, which results from the sense of insecurity caused by his consciousness of Time.

If religion, thus, originates from the Time-sense common to all mankind, the security or immunity that is sought has, however, been conceived of in a variety of forms. The religions of mankind, both those that are now extinct and those still current in the world, reveal how various and often how strange have been the ways in which it is to be attained. Let us look briefly at some examples by way of illustration.

II

In the earliest known corpus of religious literature, the *Pyramid Texts*, which date from the Old Kingdom period of ancient Egypt, i.e., about the middle of the third millennium B.C., we find the dead pharaoh seeking safety from the disintegrating effect of Time, manifest in death, by flying up to heaven to join the sun-god Re on his perpetual journey across the sky and through the nether-world. To the Egyptian mind, association with such an unceasing process meant security from the change and decay that existence in Time involved.

Let us take another Egyptian concept, because it constitutes the earliest example of the quest for eternal salvation by ritual means. We also find evidence in the *Pyramid Texts* that immunity from the consequences of death was sought by assimilating the deceased king ritually with a divine being who was believed to have risen from death. The divinity concerned was Osiris, who, according to the well-known legend, had once been a good and wise king in Egypt, but had been foully murdered. By the efforts of his wife, Isis, aided by other deities, the decomposed body of Osiris had been reconstituted, and then resuscitated. The Egyptian mortuary ritual was modeled on this legend. By assimilating the dead person, by means of a complex ritual, with Osiris in his death, it was believed that participation in his resurrection would follow. That the deceased, in his resurrected state, would be secure from Time finds striking expression in the so-called *Book of the Dead*. In the passage concerned, the dead man is represented as claiming that he himself embodied Time in its threefold aspects: "I am Yesterday, Today and Tomorrow."

This mode of achieving eternal security, by ritual identification with a savior god, is of considerable phenomenological significance. It finds expression in the mystery religions, and it has been established in Christianity through Paul's doctrine of baptism, as set forth in the sixth chapter of his Epistle to the Romans. According to this Pauline conception, the neophyte is ritually identified, through immersion in the baptismal water, with Christ in his death, in order to participate in his resurrection. This new risen life, "in Christos," is conceived as a state of eternal well-being.

The fear of Time has led, in some other religions, to the deification of Time as the highest form of deity. Ancient Aryan religion, in both its Iranian and Indian forms, provides examples of this reaction. The mysterious god Zurvān was a personification of Time, which plays an important, though problematical, role in Iranian religion. In the later forms of Zoroastrianism, Zurvān appears to have been conceived under two forms. As Zurvān "dareghochvadhata," i.e., "Time of the Long Dominion," the deity was regarded as ruling over this world, bringing old age, decay, and death to all men. Under this guise, Zurvān appears to have been equated with Ahriman in Mithraism, being depicted in the "mithraea" as a lionheaded monster, entwined about by a serpent and bearing the signs of the zodiac on his body. In its other form of Zurvān "akarana,' Time was conceived as Infinite and was the highest form of deity. Aspects of these conceptions can be traced in Manichaeism.

The deification of Time in Vedic religion can be traced through Varuna and Rudra to Siva, who under his forms of "Mahā-Kāla" (Great Time), and ,,Kāla-Rudra" (all-devouring Time) is represented with a terrible symbolism—in his many hands, he holds, variously, a human figure, a sword or sacrificial axe, a basin of blood, and a sacrificial bell, while with two other hands, he extinguishes the sun. This deification of Time in the person of Siva has produced an even stranger imagery. By hypostatizing the activating energy of Siva (his "sakti") as the goddess Kālī ("kālī" being the feminine form of the

Sanskrit "kāla," Time), an awesome presentation of the destructive aspect of Time has been achieved in Hinduism. This goddess has a horrific mien: her color is black, she wears a chaplet of severed heads, and her many hands hold symbols of her nature—the exterminating sword, scissors that cut short the thread of life, and the lotus of eternal generation; for Time is an unceasing cycle of birth and death. She is often represented as trampling on the corpse-like body of Siva, great god from whom she has emanated.

Time also plays the supreme role in the other great theistic tradition of India, namely, that which centers on Vishnu. In that noble poem which has sometimes been called the New Testament of India, the *"Bhagavadgītā"*, Time is revealed as the highest form of deity in the famous theophany passage. After the prince Arjuna has realized that his charioteer is Vishnu, and when he beseeches him to reveal his divine being, Vishnu shows himself in all the multiplicity and complexity of his being as the Creator and Sustainer of the universe. Arjuna is suitably impressed; but he feels that he has not seen all that supreme deity embodies. His request for a complete revelation is granted, and the truth that is revealed is terrible. The terrified Arjuna sees all forms of life passing to their destruction through the horrible jaws of the god who now reveals his other aspect as the Destroyer. The prince cries out in fear, "Thy mouths with many dreadful fangs beholding, Like to Time's universal conflagration, I know the quarters not, I find no shelter, Be gracious, Lord of gods, the world's protection." And Vishnu speaks in explanation, "Know I am Time, that makes the worlds to perish, When ripe, and come to bring on them destruction."

The revelation is profoundly significant. Deity, in its highest form, is ambivalent, being both Creator and Destroyer. In its latter aspect it is revealed as Time. Salvation from it, in this popular form of Hinduism, is sought through "bhakti," an intense personal devotion to the deity, which, despite its essentially ambivalent nature, is regarded hopefully as the Savior.

In more sophisticated systems of religious belief and practice, reaction to the menace of Time has taken a more complicated form. In certain Indian systems, in Buddhism, and in ancient Gnosticism, security has been sought by denying the ultimate reality of Time. Time's empirical reality has been admitted, it being argued that it is the inherent process of the phenomenal world, and that all who take this world to be real become subject to it. Time, evaluated in this manner, is invariably regarded as cyclical in its process, and it involves for all forms of life an unceasing cycle of births and deaths. The prospect, despite its implied assumption of the survival and continuity of the self, is feared; for it also implies ceaseless pain and suffering. Salvation, in terms of such a conception of Time, takes the form of the acquisition of a "gnosis" or knowledge, which usually involves a discipline of living, which confers insight into the true nature of reality—that the phenomenal world is essentially an illusion, together with the Time-process that governs it. Emancipation from the illusion means cessation of existence in a space-time universe, and absorption into a state of being that is beyond Time and its inexorable logic.

III

The reactions of Time, which we have so far surveyed, have been inspired by fear of the destructive and effacing effect of the temporal process in human experience. Time is seen as the Destroyer, and it is associated with pain, decay, and death. Even when it has been personified, as in India or Iran, it remains essentially an irrational process, whose operations inevitably defeat man's natural aspiration for significance, both in terms of his own individual being and that of the species to which he belongs. This irrational aspect of Time finds appropriate expression when it is conceived as a cyclical process, whether in the Indian concept of "samsāra", or the Stoic idea of the Great Year, or the Chinese principle of the alternation of Yin and Yang. The conception is, of course, empirically justified; for natural phenomenon, so often used for the measurement of Time, appears to be cyclic in its process—the movements of the sun and moon, and of the stars, the alternation of day and night, and the procession of the seasons. It has, in turn, been natural to connect this cyclic, or alternating process, with the opposing phenomena of birth and death. Hence, Time has been conceived as the "sorrowful, weary wheel," that keeps aimlessly turning, dragging all forms of being through an unending process of birth and death.

There has, of course, been, and there still is, another conception of Time, which endeavors to see it as exemplifying reason, although regarding it also with profound fear. This view conceives Time as linear in its process not cyclic, and as the embodiment of purpose. In terms of this evaluation, Time is not regarded as a fundamental entity, "sui generis", and self-existent, so that it can reasonably be both personified and deified, as we have seen. Instead, it is seen as the creation of an omnipotent God, or, to be more precise, as the process of the gradual unfolding of the purpose of God. It is visualized as having a beginning, which is the moment of God's creation of the universe, and it will have an end, when the divine purpose will achieve its "telos" or goal.

This conception of Time as the progressive manifestation of the purpose of God is peculiarly the product of Hebrew religious thought. It finds superb literary expression in the Hebrew Bible, and it has been incorporated into the two world-religions which have stemmed from it, namely, Christianity and Islam. Through Christianity, it has profoundly affected the "Weltanschauung" of the western world.

Such an estimate of Time can only be built upon a basis of monotheism; for such a teleological interpretation of the temporal process presupposes that only one purpose is being unfolded in the universe, and the conception of that purpose and its ultimate achievement necessitates the concept of a single omnipotent Creator and Sustainer of the universe. This presupposition or postulate, however, inevitably contains within itself the seeds of a truly insoluable problem of evil, which profoundly affects the evaluation of human destiny. The increasing seriousness of this problem is very evident in Hebrew religion, and it finds its most poignant expression in the Book of Job.

The Hebrew idea of Time, as the gradual revelation and achievement of the purpose of God, was not in origin the product of philosophical reflection; nor was it conceived in response to the individual's quest for security from the effacing flux of Time. Because Yahwism was in essence an ethnic religion, the destiny of the individual was not the primary issue, but the relations of the Elect People and its God. As I have attempted to show elsewhere, the teleological conception of Time among the ancient Hebrews arose out of the tendency of the Yahwist prophets to appeal to the past experience of the nation as evidence of the power and providence of Yahweh. The Exodus and the Settlement in Canaan became the supreme events of a veritable "Heilsgeschichte"—the proof of what Yahweh had done in the past was proclaimed as the assurance of what he would do for his Chosen People in the future, if they would repent and serve him. In this ethnic pattern of salvation, it was the nation, Israel, as a whole, not the individual Israelite, that ultimately mattered. Indeed, the official Yahwist doctrine of Man offered to the individual, after death, only a dim shadowy existence in the gloomy realm of Sheol.

The profoundly unsatisfactory nature of this view of personal destiny caused an increasing tension in Hebrew religion, especially as the Yahwist prophets progressively emphasized both the omnipotence and justice of Yahweh. In the Book of Job we see that these tensions have reached a breaking point, as the individual seeks for the assurance of ultimate significance from a religion that offers only virtual extinction of the self at death.

The problem found solution only in the second century B.C., when Yahwism admitted belief in a post-mortem resurrection and judgement. But even then Jewish eschatology remained essentially ethnic, not personal. Individuals would be ressurrected and judged as members of the Holy Nation. Israel would be vindicated before the Gentiles, and so the purpose of the God of Israel would be finally achieved.

This "Heilsgeschichte" finds superb expression in Hebrew literature, particularly in the Hexateuch. Yahweh is depicted as guiding the history of mankind from the very Creation to the establishment of Israel in Canaan. Israel's later vicissitudes of fortune are accounted for in the prophetic writings, and its future deliverance is the supreme topic of the later apocalyptic literature. Hence, in the Hebrew Bible a most impressive philosophy of History is presented—History, or rather Salvation History, in terms of Israel's destiny, is the manifestation of Yahweh's purpose in Time.

IV

This Hebrew philosophy of History has had an incalculable influence upon the lives of a large part of the human race, owing to its adoption into Christianity. In its original form it was primarily concerned with accounting for the destiny of Israel, and of the individual Israelite by virtue of his membership of the Elect Nation. But Christianity, owing largely to the genius of the Apostle Paul and the ruin of the Jewish nation in A.D. 70, universalized this essentially ethnic interpretation of History, making it into the record of God's preparation for the incarnation of His Son, who was to be the Savior of mankind. Yaweh's dealings with Israel were consequently seen as the divine "Praeparatio Evangelica" or as the era of the "Old Testament", which became the accepted designation of the Hebrew scriptures.

But, although Christianity inherited the idea of an Elect People, styling itself the New Israel, it was, and is, essentially a religion of personal salvation. As we have already seen, in noting the phenomenological significance of Paul's doctrine of baptism, eternal salvation is obtained through ritual assimilation to Christ, the savior-god. However, owing to the peculiar origins of Christianity, and the fact that it stemmed from Judaism, the Christian religion embodies an historical element or factor that is basic to its validity and structure. It finds expression in this way.

The crucifixon of Jesus, which was an historical event, enacted by the Romans outside Jerusalem in about A.D. 30, is interpreted as a transaction planned by God, whereby the human race has been redeemed from a state of perdition, due either to its subjection to demonic powers or to the wrath of God. Accordingly, the incarnate life of Christ, culminating in his redemptive death, is seen as dividing the stream of Time into two parts—a belief which has been commemorated in our chronological system of the era B.C. (before Christ) and that designated A.D. (*anno Domini*).

The latter era, i.e., the period since the Incarnation of Christ, has been regarded as the era of mankind's salvation. It is believed that this era will be terminated, because Christian thought from the beginning has been molded by Jewish eschatology, which conceived of the "Day of Yahweh," when the present cosmic order would be catastrophically ended. Consequently, Christians have believed that, when God has completed the number of His Elect, the world will end with the Return of Christ, the Resurrection of the Dead, and the Last Judgement. "There will be Time no more," according to the Apocalypse of John.

Into this long-termed eschatology, which concerns the Purpose of God for the whole human race, the destiny of the individual person has been incorporated. The unexpected delay of the Parousia-hope caused some adjustment of the primitive view, particularly in the matter of post-baptismal sin, and the doctrine of Purgatory had to be introduced to account for the condition of the departed soul during the intervening period between death and the Resurrection and Final Judgment. However, a synthesis was gradually worked out which related the fate of the individual to the Purpose of God as manifest in Time and History. It reached its fullest expression in medieval Christianity. According to the doctrine of Man, in which it was embodied, the individual soul is specially created by God for one single incarnate life in this world. This life is a testing ground for eternity. Through the saving grace of Christ, mediated through the sacraments of the Church, it is hoped that the individual will come safely through the temptations of this world. Death is followed by a judgment, in which the destiny of the individual is assessed for the period remaining before the Last Judgment. Since most souls have been guilty of venial sins, they are purged of these in Purgatory. Then, at the Resurrection and Last Judgment, if they are deemed worthy, they will be admitted to the Beatific Vision, which they will enjoy for eternity.

Thus, complicated though Christian soteriology is in its concepts, ultimate salvation here, as in other religions, places the individual beyond Time, in a state of eternal beatitude. Even his body, which has been subject to the decay of Time, is renewed and rendered incorruptible—an end which the ancient Egyptians had sought through their ritual of embalmment.

This Christian scheme of salvation has implicated a philosophy of History of a thoroughly teleological kind. Nurtured upon the Hebrew "Heilsgeschichte", the Christian has been taught to see Time as the process of God's Purpose—indeed, in the words of the well-known hymn: "God is working His purpose out, as year succeeds to year." The original intent of God having been thwarted by man's original disobedience, the whole course of History, since that Fall, is interpreted as being divinely guided to achieve the ultimate salvation of mankind. As St. Augustine put it in his *City of God*, God guides events, to the end that the "Civitas Dei" will ultimately replace the "civitas terrena."

V

This Christian evaluation of History, which endowed Time with an essential significance in the economy of God's Purpose, has profoundly conditioned the "Weltanschauung" of western society. Even from the period of the Enlightenment, when its supernatural sanctions began to be rejected, it continued to be effective, and from it stemmed the secularized Idea of Progress, which reflected the optimism and confidence of the nineteenth century. But now its validity is no longer accepted, although its ghost still haunts western thought and culture. And here we come to what may aptly be described as the malaise of western society today.

The immense increase of our knowledge of the past of mankind during the last century—a knowledge, incidentally, which has pushed back the origins of *homo sapiens* far beyond that contemplated in the Bible—this knowledge has rendered wholly untenable that philosophy of History upon which the structure of Christian soteriology was erected. But that is not all. The daunting immensity and complexity of the data concerning the past, which archaeological and historical research has amassed, permits of no teleological interpretation, beyond that of the biological success of mankind as a species. In other words, we cannot today, despite our far greater knowledge, discern any purpose or pattern in History such as to inspire us with a sense of Time's significance for human values and aspirations.

That great philosopher, English-born, but who spent most of his working life at Harvard, A. N. Whitehead, once wrote, with deep insight, "I hazard the prophecy that that religion will conquer which can render clear to popular understanding some eternal greatness incarnate in the passage of temporal fact." In the light of that statement, and what I have endeavored to set forth in my paper, I accordingly submit that we have here an issue of immense significance and grave urgency, concerning the evaluation of human nature and destiny, which merits our careful consideration and discussion.

METHODOLOGY AND THE SCIENCE OF RELIGION

BY

C. J. BLEEKER
University of Amsterdam

Young people sometimes are under the delusion that world history starts with their birth. They think that nobody ever has been in love, has suffered, or has searched for truth as they have. It is dubious whether our generation realizes that it is entering a new epoch and that the decades of the middle of the twentieth century, which we are passing, may mean a decisive turn in the history of mankind. For the mood of a great many of our contemporaries has a pessimistic tinge, and that not without reason. Everyone, who daily reads his newspaper, must get the impression that we live in a world in which morality is rapidly vanishing. After the first World War, O. Spengler wrote, in German, a voluminous and stirring book predicting the decline and downfall of western civilization. The atrocities, committed during the second World War, gave new food to the pessimism of people who were convinced that humanity was on the decline. They looked at the future with uneasiness and distress. For in their fearful expectations they saw the sword of Damocles, of a third World War, fought out by atomic weapons, hanging on a silk thread above the heads of the present generation.

And yet hope has not left the earth. Everybody who is young in spirit should foster the hope that a new era will dawn. Fortunately he can do so not only on the strength of his confidence in mankind, but primarily because there are many signs indicating that the world is entering a new period of its existence. This will be the epoch in which the world community becomes a reality. This time is near at hand. We need the full power of our imagination to realize what this fact implies. In the past, courageous and adventurous men went out to discover unknown parts of the earth. The continents were far away from one another. Idealists dreamt of a future in which the nations of the earth would harmoniously live together. Today there is theoretically no longer any *terra incognita*. Thanks to faster and more modern means of communication the citizens of Russia, of Congo, of

South Vietnam, of China, and of many other distant countries have, so to say, become our neighbors, whom we know a bit better and with whose interests we have to reckon.

I

The earth has become smaller and, at the same time, wider. I may feel myself released from the duty of analyzing and describing the forces which inevitably transform the world into a unity, in different respects, economically, politically, and culturally. This work has been done ably by several experts in recent publications. Suffice it to state that, if at present the world community is not an established fact, it will be such a reality in the near future. And not only a reality, but even more, the sole condition of the well-being of humanity. There is an austere truth in the well-known slogan: One world or none.

However, this does not mean that the art of thinking of the nations will be streamlined. At the moment there are all kinds of misunderstandings among the peoples of the five continents. Some of them look at each other with suspicion and hatred. It would be unrealistic not to notice that in the hearts of many people there is a deep-seated resentment on account of what they suffered through the brutality of nations that dominated them. One has even to admit that there have been periods in history, i.e., the Middle Ages and in certain decades of the eighteenth and the nineteenth centuries, in which there prevailed a greater unanimity than is present today. It sometimes looks as if the differences and the antipathies between the ideals and the world conceptions of the nations have, of late, been heightened rather than reduced. However, one may expect that these forms of disharmony will die out, though it will take time before they have totally disappeared.

But even when the various reasons for distrust and resentment are removed, there will still remain a great multiplicity of persuasions, primarily in the field of religion. This means that within the growing world community we have to reckon with the existence of an extensive religious pluralism, not only at present, but also for the future. The reasons behind this paradoxical fact are twofold: In the first place, all believers are very keen on keeping their special type of faith as their dearest treasure by which they safeguard their personality, their spiritual identity, and their religious independence against all tendencies toward the merging of individual man into the masses. Secondly, the world religions are still fully alive. Each of them claims to possess absolute truth. They are propagating their ideas and show missionary zeal in a higher degree than in the last century. It is not to be expected that they are willing to give up their independence.

Thus the surmise is that, whether we like it or not, we have to reckon both at present and in the future with the existence of a religious pluralism. This statement implies that, within the framework of this lecture, two questions can be discarded, though they as such are important and of current interest. These are, first, the question of whether we have to look out for a coming world religion, and, secondly, the problem of the significance of religious pluralism. Let me restrict myself to a few remarks on both points.

There are people who expect that the world community in the making will be accompanied by the fading out of the differences between the religions and the gradual rise of a world religion. I earnestly doubt whether they are right. I cannot imagine how Buddhism, Judaism, Islam, and Christianity—to mention but four religions—could ever be forged into a unity. Secondly, as to the problem of the philosophical or theological significance of religious pluralism, I would advise that we leave this intricate question untouched. It is easy to state that there occur three well-known shades of opinion: All religions are false; all religions are true; or only one's own religion has the truth, and all others are in error. In discussing this issue, we would be in danger of differing in opinion so strongly that the problem at stake would fade out of the picture.

This problem is that, whereas religious pluralism is an undeniable fact in the growing world community, we have to ponder the means and methods to increase the mutual understanding between adherents of the different religions and forms of belief, and to accept their actual coexistence. Referring to the remark which I made at the beginning of this paper, namely that humanity now apparently enters a relatively new period, I can now proceed to say that we have never before been confronted so intensely with the problem of the relationship between the religions of the world as we are at this juncture. In my opinion this also implies that we have to seek for new and better methods of handling these difficult problems.

In the course of my life I have participated in many meetings dealing with this matter. Though papers were delivered by able and right-minded scholars, the results were at most meager. I must confess that I have little confidence in discussion even among brilliant and high-spirited people, when it is not conducted under strict scientific rules.

We are living in the age of science. Natural science has won dazzling victories, thanks to the fact that its students submit to a strict scientific discipline and apply a great accuracy in their terminology and in their research. In the field of humanistic studies, we should clearly realize that it is a requirement of the times that we introduce the right methodology into the science of religion.

II

This leads to the core and kernel of the subject of this paper: methodology and the science of religion. Mutual understanding within the range of the existing religious pluralism can only be brought about if we scientifically inquire into the conditions of such a religious harmony. These are twofold: first, the willingness to take an interest in forms of foreign religion and to make an attempt at understanding their value and essence; and, secondly, a clear insight into the necessity of availing oneself of all the knowledge which the science of religion puts at one's disposal.

The indispensable presupposition of mutual understanding among adherents of different religions is that they be prepared to listen to one another, to put aside their preconceptions about the religious standpoints of people belonging to other religions than their own, and to take their fellow believers of another type absolutely seriously when these earnestly testify to their faith, even when their behavior and their utterances look queer and unintelligible. Let us be aware of the fact that understanding foreign religions is a difficult art which some people have received by nature or by grace, while others learn it slowly and imperfectly. In the latter case not only might loving interest be lacking, but also the psychological capacity for broadening one's spiritual horizon to embrace all types of religion. In my opinion we should have a realistic look at man's nature. That means that, notwithstanding the fact that we are living in the age of psychology and that the knowledge of psychological notions is widespread, the range of interest of the average man is bafflingly narrow. Therefore, we should not too soon condemn the narrow-mindedness of other people, knowing that we ourselves often fail in this respect. We should have much patience, because we clearly realize that only an education during many generations can lift people up to a level that enables them by virtue of their spiritual outlook to embrace the whole world.

The second condition of creating mutual understanding is that one make use of the method and of the insights which the science of religion puts at the disposal of everyone who is desirous of penetrating into the hidden depth of foreign religions. Uncritical admiration of exotic religious life and well-meant, but unsystematic, deliberations about the topic in question are of no avail. Clarification can be reached only by applying the normative principle of the science of religion, i.e., the phenomenological method. This thesis requires explanation. This can best be done by presenting a short description of the nature and the aim of the phenomenology of religion.

III

It is to the credit of the Leyden historian of religion, P. D. Chantepie de la Saussaye, that he has presented the first sketch of a phenomenology of religion. It is part of his "Lehrbuch der Religionsgeschichte" in its edition of 1887. It is quite clear what Chantepie meant by introducing this new science. He must have realized that the study of religions leads with logical necessity to phenomenological investigations. For the history of religions not only studies the separate religions *in toto* or in parts, but also involuntarily compares the different religions of the world. Thus the so-called "Allgemeine, vergleichende Religionsgeschichte," or comparative religion, arose.

However, the penomenology of religion takes a further step, as its name indicates: the theory of the (religious) phenomena. In the process of research this science pays attention not so much to the historical surrounding of the phenomena, but rather to the ideological connections. This means that the facts are severed from their historical contexts and that they are combined in such a way that the meaning of certain phenomena such as sacrifice, magic, or prayer become transparent. In this sense Chantepie wrote a first draft of the phenomenology of religion.

Since 1887, the phenomenology of religion has successfully developed. Gradually it evolved into an independent branch of the science of religion. In order to avoid misunderstandings, it should be clearly realized that the term, phenomenology of religion, can be used in a double sense. It means both a scientific method and an independent science, creating monographs and more or less extensive handbooks. In this paper I should like to focus attention on the value and implications of the phenomenological method. Then one should know that many phenomenologists have been influenced by the philosophical phenomenology of which E. Husserl is the chief exponent. We can skip an exposition of this type of philosophy. Suffice it to know that several phenomenologists make use of two of the principles of Husserl, i.e., the epoché and the eidetic vision.

The first princple means the suspension of judgment. In using the epoché one puts oneself into the position of the listener, who does not judge according to preconceived notions. Applied to the science of religion, this means that it cannot concern itself with the question of the truth of religion, neither drawing a distinction between true and false religion, nor pronouncing a judgment on the question of whether religion has a metaphysical background. Phenomenology of religion must begin by accepting as proper objects of study all phenomena that are professed to be religious. Subsequently the attempt can come to distinguish what is genuinely religious from what is spurious. The second principle, that of the eidetic vision, can easily be understood. It has as its aim the search for the eidos, that is the essentials of religious phenomena.

For clarity's sake, it should be added that the phenomenology of religion uses the Husserlian principles in a figurative sense, without further philosophical implications. It is also good to know that there exist students of the science of religion—certainly not the less prominent scholars—who never use the Husserlian terminology, though they actually apply these principles. Be that as it may, it is essential that in studying foreign religions one tries to creep, so to say, out of the skin of one's own thought forms and to investigate the religious facts unbiasedly.

This attitude was admirably sketched by the late Professor W. B. Kristensen in Leyden when he wrote: "Let us not forget that there is no other religious reality than the faith of the believers. If we want to make the acquaintance of true religion, we are exclusively thrown on the pronouncements of the believers. What we think, from our standpoint, about the essence and value of foreign religions surely testifies to our own faith or to our own conception of religious belief. But if our opinion of a foreign religion differs from the meaning and the evaluation of the believers themselves, then we have no longer any contact with their religion. Not only our religion, but every religion is, according to the faith of the believers, an absolute entity and can only be understood under this aspect."

IV

Naturally the question arises as to the results to which the phenomenological method leads when applied to the problem at stake. It is evident that I have to limit myself to those phenomenological insights which are relevant to the problem of clarifying the present religious pluralism. Let me draw your attention to the following points:

1) Religion is a universal human phenomenon. Everywhere in the world and at all times since the evolution of homo sapiens, people both collectively and individually have worshiped superhuman force. No tribe or nation has ever been found that was wholly without a religious consciousness. Such a statement is only correct so long as it is realized that in certain cases the religious consciousness finds expression not so much in religious notions as in sacral actions. For the impartial investigator, religion, even appearing in queer, crude, and repelling forms, is recognizable, because the practiced eye can discern the fear for the Holy which is characteristic of true religion. Hence religious belief is inherent in human nature. Nevertheless disbelief has been widespread since the dawn of history and primarily in modern times. This is not the place and the time to investigate this crucial question. It might be enough to say that nobody can understand man's behavior, neither in the past nor in the present, without taking into account the religious motives prompting his religious attitudes. This holds especially true for the nations of the East, whose life is still permeated by religious notions.

2) As Professor Kristensen stated in the words which I quoted, every religion claims to possess absolute truth. In order to understand the believer, we must take his words seriously when he declares that he has encountered God, at least when he is sincere in his confession of faith. Unfortunately hypocrisy often corrupts religion and spoils its good reputation. Everywhere human passions, such as ambition, thirst for power, vanity and all kinds of sexual drives are allowed free rein under the guise of piety. No student of the science of religion should be blind to the flaws in all religions. Nevertheless religion is and remains the highest good of humanity because man in his religious belief faces Ultimate Reality and Eternity.

3) Religious pluralism is in itself an amorphous body of thousands of forms of beliefs and practices. In order to get a grip on this heterogeneous material one needs a definition of religion by the aid of which one is able to distinguish pure religion from non-religious elements. The formulation of a definition of religion is an extremely difficult task because it should neither be too narrow so that it excludes a part of the religious phenomena, nor too broad so that it includes some forms of pseudo-, or, as Tillich calls it, quasi-religion. One of the

best definitions is given by Tillich himself. It runs like this: "Religion is the state of being grasped by an ultimate concern, a concern which qualifies all other concerns as preliminary and which itself contains the answer to the question of the meaning of our life. Therefore this concern is unconditionally serious and shows a willingness to sacrifice any finite concern which is in conflict with it." It is evident that a definition like this can serve as an operative and heuristic principle.

4) One of the generally accepted results of phenomenological inquiry is the thesis that the formal structure of religion falls into three parts. In religion there are three recurring factors, namely God, man, and the relation between God and man, which is expressed in the cult and in the observance of God's laws in man's personal and social life. To put it differently, we may say that a religion is made up of a) a holy vision of the Supreme Being or of the being and the will of the Deity, b) a holy path that a man must pursue in order to be freed from his sin and suffering, and c) a holy action that the believer must carry out in the cult and in his personal religious life. Of these three factors the notion of God possesses a logical priority; for it is the nature of the holy vision that determines the character of the holy path and the holy action and makes them comprehensible. In this complex of ideas the inner logic of the religion is revealed.

5) In addition to these formal characteristics phenomenologists have also drawn attention to structural relations of a more substantial nature which reveal the logical construction of the religious phenomena. These factors underlying the ideological structure of religion would appear to be the following:

a) The number of ways in which religious belief expresses itself is relatively limited. The same religious symbols are found throughout the world. These parallels soon attracted the attention and have been the subject of many studies in the field of comparative religion. Their real significance consists in the fact that they represent the constant forms of religion, of which the number is limited. The relation between God and man is, for instance, expressed in four constantly recurring images, namely the relation between father and child, master and servant, friend and friend, and lover and beloved. Striking similarities between religions should not, however, blind the student to the fact that the resemblance is usually superficial and that the idea and the intention behind identical formulations may be completely different.

b) Religion is *sui generis* and cannot be explained by non-religious factors. Every religion possesses its own individuality and can only be comprehended and described after long study. It is, however, an illusion to believe that one can ever follow a religion which one does not personally profess. It must be remembered that the believer keeps a secret which he cannot and does not wish to reveal to non-believers or to believers in other faiths. Nevertheless it is possible to obtain by factual knowledge and by religious intuition insight into what is unique in the forms of the religion one is studying.

c) Every religion has its own distinguishing factors. This is an element of truth which also occurs in other religions, though in a subordinate position, but which especially characterizes one particular religion. When describing a religion great attention should be paid to its distinguishing feature. This structural element may be illustrated by a few examples. The distinguishing feature of the religion of Zarathustra is the notion of militant piety; Judaism is pervaded by a deep fear of God's holiness, while Islam is the religion of boundless surrender and obedience.

d) The surest method of becoming acquainted with the structure of a religion is to pose the question: How do its believers receive their knowledge of God? It soon becomes evident that there are various types of "revelation". On looking at this question from the viewpoint of the historian of religions, we may say that a higher necessity has obliged various types of believers to adopt different attitudes of belief and to orientate themselves religiously in different directions in order to meet the Holy. A few examples will illustrate the princple. The religions of antiquity are founded on a cosmic vision; the universe testifies to a divine order. Indian religious thinking wrestles with the problem of transitoriness and suffering, a problem which is solved when the liberating insight is attained that the finite is but a veil, and life itself is an illusion. The mystic strives to release himself from all institutionalized forms of worship and to achieve the mortification of the ego in order to behold in complete emptiness and to experience in bliss the fullness of God. Adherents of the historical religions which are based upon prophetic revelation receive their knowledge of God from sacred history in which divine messengers have appeared as testimony to the way in which God has intervened on behalf of his children throughout the ages.

e) Insight into the structural element previously mentioned leads to the conclusion that every religion is a meaningful combination of various lines of thought. This may be exemplified by applying the principle to Christianity. Obviously there are many traits of similarity between Christianity, on the one hand, and Judaism and also the Hellenistic religions, on the other. However, on closer observation one will descover that the spiritual climate behind these parallels is totally different. This means that Christianity in many respects shows a unique character. As to the way in which knowledge of God is obtained Christianity is based on the idea of God's revelation in history. The distinguishing feature in Christianity is the idea of love. In order to grasp the essence of Christianity, one should pay attention to the intertwining of those four structural lines.

6) In my opinion the present religious pluralism can be clarified when its different forms are studied with the aid of the principles which I developed. Then the fundamental pattern of the different religions will prove to be easily discovered. However, most religions possess a long history during which many changes in their structure have taken place. Moreover, all religions are today subjected to a number of factors which dissolve the fundamental pattern to such a degree that at times it can hardly be recognized. Religious pluralism undergoes a period of crisis. This paper does not offer sufficient room to picture the transformations which the different religions undergo, apart from the fact that nobody is able to give an adequate description of what is going on in the religious sphere in the different corners of the world. However, the main lines can be clearly distinguished. On the one hand the original character and the inner strength of the different religions are weakened by nihilistic, humanistic, and atheistic tendencies. On the other side this crisis works as a purification and often has the effect that religions pass through a renaissance. This development should be taken into account, when the components of religious pluralism are analyzed.

7) Religious people nowadays meet each other more frequently than ever before and talk with one another on religious topics more openly than they once did. To their surprise they discover that when they approach each other humanly the points on which they agree are more numerous than they had imagined. This experience may give rise to the conception that religious pluralism could easily be straightened out, when you look at it from the anthropological angle. To my

mind this is a fallacy. It should be realized that human life has different spiritual dimensions. In the first place man all over the world understands the typical human needs and reactions of his fellow creatures without any difficulty, whatever the color of the skin, the race, or the rank in society. Because men are capable of the same emotions and the same thoughts, there exists, in the second place, a human religiosity in which religious people all over the world take part. In the religious feelings of confidence, love, and peace, in the strife for religious truth and righteousness, people of different races and regions of the world can meet each other. However, there is a third and most important dimension. This is the level of the typical pattern of each individual religion, which ultimately determines the actions and evaluations of its adherents. This pattern is unique and exceptional. It cannot be explained anthropologically. It is the task of the phenomenology of religion to make religiously understandable what is not humanly understandable.

V

Lastly I should like to point out and to stress that knowledge of the method and the insights of the science of religion is no matter for amusement or some kind of spiritual luxury, but is a modern requirement. I am under the definite impression that all kinds of blunders, made on the fields of national and international politics and of economics and in cultural and religious affairs arise from a lack of knowledge of the religious emotions and ideas of the people who are affected by certain kinds of political, economic, or cultural measures. In my opinion, all people who are destined to play a leading role in the world, as politicians, economists, owners of big concerns, engineers, doctors, or churchmen, should be obliged to master the principal insights of the science of religion. I am convinced that this measure would dissipate many misunderstandings and would create more harmony among the nations.

THE IMPACT OF MODERNITY ON ISLAM

BY

FAZLUR RAHMAN

Islamic Research Institute, Islamabad, Pakistan

I. The Problem

Like all great religions, Islam has apparently felt the impact of, and responded to, the manifold forces of modern life—intellectual, scientific and socio-political—since the dawn of the impingement of modernity on Muslim society. There is hardly a facet of the life of Muslim society which has remained untouched, and the story of these impacts and the Muslim attempts to absorb, transform, reject, or adjust to these forces, is fascinating for the historian and instructive for a reformer. This paper, however, does not try to portray the details of this confrontation; nor does it essay to depict the historical development of the various stages of this impact in terms of movements, persons, or governmental actions. The problem that I shall address myself to is much more restricted and modest but one which is, at the same time, of the most immediate importance both to the Muslim world and to the world at large. I propose to talk about the difficulties of modernization or, rather, modernism and to try to give an overall assessment of how far modernity may be said to have had an impact on the Muslim world. This may help to indicate both for the Muslim world itself and for the world at large the nature and extent of changes that may reasonably be expected in the Muslim society in the near future. My intention is certainly not to make any kind of prophecy but simply to elucidate the possibilities for the future by attempting to identify what exactly has happened so far and what has *not* happened.

Whenever we speak of the impact of modernity on Islam, we should first of all clearly understand that not all reform in Islam in recent centuries dates from the dawn of modernity—if by "modernity" we mean those specific forces which were generated by and were also responsible for the intellectual and socio-economic expansion of the modern west. Reform movements and their offshoots had been a ubiquitous phenomenon in the Muslim world during the eighteenth and nineteenth centuries—beginning with the movement of Muhammad ibn-ʿAbdal Wahhāb in Central Arabia—displaying varying degrees of intensity of bellicosity to attain their ends. Some of these movements, like that of the Sanusis in the nineteenth century, were in some ways affected by the west or western penetration, but they can hardly be termed "modernist reform movements" since the frame of reference for their reformist activities lies entirely in the Muslim past.

It should be clearly admitted, then, that the impacts of modernity on Islam were preceded by reform movements which arose from the interior of Islam itself. This fact is so important that ignoring it would result in almost a colossal misunderstanding of both the nature and the extent of modernism that has taken place in the Muslim world. This is because one is otherwise led to think of Islam as a more or less inert mass upon which the modern influences started working as an external force of movement. But even a more fatal misconception than this and arising from the first one would be to grossly overrate the importance of modernity in present-day Islam. This mistake is liable to be still further aggravated by the fact that the world is at present divided into aid-giving countries and aid-receiving countries and the Muslim countries fall into the latter category. From the standpoint of the aid-giving countries, it is perhaps natural to think that since a great deal of *technological* development is taking place in the aid-receiving countries, the latter are experiencing an equal degree of *modernizing* processes at the intellectual and social level. We shall indicate the extent to which this is so but also the very serious limits to which such an expectation must necessarily be confined at the present.

Modernism made its first impact on the world of Islam through the military and political confrontations of the western powers with the Muslim states. In these confrontations, the Muslims were invariably vanquished sooner or later, directly or indirectly. The very first impression created upon the Muslim societies was that of the politico-military supremacy of the west. The next step in the Muslim analysis of western supremacy was the conviction that the west was vastly superior in scientific skills to which it owed not only its military power but its economic ascendancy. The Muslims—that is to say, the progressives among them—decided to import the scientific techniques of the modern west as quickly as possible. But as soon as this need was perceived, it was seen that the situation was much more complex than it appeared at first and that the inculcation of scientific techniques themselves required all kinds of changes at other levels which became the task of the modernist to formulate and effect. For example, without some kind of democratic or, at any rate, constitutional government, it was impossible to create a strong enough unity necessary both for modern developments and for a successful confrontation of the western powers. Hence, some kind of democracy or constitutional government must be introduced if the confidence of the people as a whole was to be won.

Again, the learning and application of modern scientific techniques systematically entailed the acceptance of the modern world-view and, above all, a radical change in the traditional habits of thought. The introduction of political reforms themselves entailed other changes in the classical Muslim political theory and, on the whole, quite a drastic adjustment to new norms. So far as the learning of scientific techniques and importation of technological progress were concerned, not much opposition was experienced and, although voices were raised from various traditionalist quarters even against these, these were silenced without much difficulty. Although a stray Imam of a mosque in an outlying district may still today be found objecting to the use of microphones in prayers, nobody takes this kind of opposition either as formidable or even as serious.

To the amenities of life which modern science brings, even the most reactionary person today not only does not object but in most cases even uses them without any question. When, however, it comes to questioning the traditional social complex as a whole and the norms upon which it was constructed, the result is very different indeed. It is here that modernism has made the least impact on Muslim society and, in so far as it is difficult to imagine how technological progress can be sustained without changing traditional habits of thought and certain set social norms, one must exercise due caution in categorically affirming that modern developments have taken root in the Muslim society.

The need for an intellectual re-orientation of the Muslim society, with a view to achieving modernist progressive ends, was first felt by several Muslim reformist thinkers in the latter half of the nineteenth century. Shaikh Muhammad ᶜAbdūh in Egypt (under the inspiration of Jamāl al-Dīn el-Afghānī) and Sir Sayyid Ahmad Khān in the Indo-Pakistan sub-continent are classic examples of the intellectual modernist direction. There is, no doubt, a difference of method and approach between these two men, but in the results of their teachings they are not very different. Not only were both zealous advocates of the modern scientific spirit and had a zest for inquiry, but even in the content of what they taught they are remarkably similar *in results*.

Sir Sayyid Ahmad Khān denies, for example, the validity of miracles by rejecting their very possibility in the interests of safeguarding the sanctity of natural law. Muhammad ᶜAbdūh, even though he does not formally deny the validity of miracles, nevertheless seems to reach the same result by saying that any given miracle, when claimed, may be safely denied, although the possibility of miracles in general may be retained. Muhammad ᶜAbdūh's teachings, however, when they percolated and resulted in the Salafi movement led by Muhammad Rashīd Ridā, became radically transformed in spirit; although his reformist impulse still remained to a considerable extent, the liberalism of Muhammad ᶜAbdūh was replaced by a controversialist type of attitude and in proportion its political content increased in contradistinction to the purely educational-intellectual content of ᶜAbdūh's teachings.

In the sub-continent of India and Pakistan, the "scientific" teachings of Sir Sayyid Ahmad Khān met with a much more disastrous fate. Whereas his efforts to introduce modern western lay education achieved a remarkable measure of success, the *content* of his religious thought was generally rejected *in toto*. This fact also underlines one major difference between the rhythm of modernism in the sub-continent and in the Middle East: whereas in the Middle East a lesser degree of radical modernism is exhibited, but a greater equilibrium seems to be maintained, in the sub-continent there is much less equilibrium. There may be two explanations for this peculiarity of the situation in the sub-continent, both of which seem to be true.

First, the Ulama of the sub-continent are by and large much more isolated from the currents of modern life and thought than are, say, the Ulama of Egypt. This is in turn due to the fact that, ever since the advent of the British in the sub-continent, and particularly since the introduction of the seats of western learning, the Ulama boycotted all modern learning and imposed a total isolation upon themselves. Secondly, also perhaps because of the direct British rule in the sub-continent, the modernist classes there are much more influenced by western ideas than are the corresponding classes in the Middle East, and therefore the gap between the modernist and the conservative is proportionately greater.

Be that as it may, the fact remains that, apart from stray individual examples, the *thought* of the early reformists particularly in the sub-continent can be said to have found little root. This phase was succeeded by another—more or less parallel to the Arab Middle East—wherein reform was mixed with controversialist and apologetic trends. The apologetic-controversialist probably hoped to succeed in his reform both by creating self-confidence among the Muslims and by obtaining the necessary *bona fide*. An example of this is Sayyid Amīr Alī, whose work, particularly *The Spirit of Islam,* is a superb example of the intermingling of a reformist impulse with an apologetic-controversialist attitude. It is this fateful turn which modern reformists took both in the sub-continent and in the Middle East that is to some extent responsible for whatever modernity has been accepted by the Muslim community in terms of ideas and values but which has largely proved calamitous for creating a formidable barrier against further modernist developments as the present analysis will try to show.

This phase was still further succeeded by another which may be called the phase of Muhammad Iqbal (preceded by several other relatively minor figures). During this phase, the paradoxes of the earlier phase came to the surface, probably accentuated by the virulent political struggles for freedom against western domination which reached a decisive stage during the 1920's and 30's. The general characteristics of this stage are a vehement political opposition of the west combined with a strong socio-ethical denunciation of it, but, at the same time, a certain vague openness and admiration for the intellectualism of the modern west, more particularly its scientific achievements.

In this phase the Muslim apologetic takes on the form of an attack upon the west and the defensive mood changes into an offensive one. This attitude towards the west, which is palpably ambivalent, drew the ranks of the conservative and the modernist very close—indeed, so close that it is sometimes difficult to differentiate between the two. In fact, one is not infrequently surprised to find a person from the traditionalist school sometimes to be more open-minded, liberal, and receptive of ideas than many of the so-called modern-educated classes. One wonders how far-reaching and profound the reception of purely lay modern intellectualism and scienticism can be if the traditional religious ideas and practices are kept strictly out of it. Experience shows that it cannot unless, of course, religion ultimately is allowed to lose its grip on life.

But so long as religion keeps its grip, it will effectively keep even lay ideas from penetrating deeply if the two are kept very strictly apart. This may seem paradoxical but it appears to be the case. The reason is that no new idea can take root in isolation but must be integrated into the structural mass of ideas which serve as a matrix for it, and these ideas—concerned as they are with life and one's world-view—are *par excellence* religious. Particularly in a religion like Islam where the "religious" has no boundaries but governs the entire field of life, this must be all the more true. It would be instructive at this stage to recall the fate of the intellectual movement in medieval Islam which could not grow—and without which, in turn, science could not grow either—because of this constitution of Islam.

The chance that the hold that Islam has on its followers will weaken may be written off because, not only are the Muslim masses intensely religious but, as we have pointed out just above, even the modernist has had to fall in line with the impulses of the masses during the recent decades. This tendency of Islam has been further invigorated by the liberation struggles everywhere in the Muslim world where Islam offered itself as one of the mainstays of these struggles. Nor can the Muslim world afford to keep modernism out for obvious reasons. Indeed, Muslim societies have introduced avenues of vast socio-economic changes in their midst which cannot fail to break the old order in the forseeable future. Yet it is more than doubtful whether the modern mind has made any real impact on the Muslim world. It is on this problem that we must now concentrate.

II. Search for an Adequate Method

It would seem surprising at first glance that forces of modernity should have existed in Muslim society for a century without resulting in modern Islamic intellectualism, i.e., in a systematic expression of Islam in effective modern terms. We have pointed to some factors viz. politico-economic subjection of the Muslim world resulting in pronounced apologetic-controversialist tendencies and the educational dichotomy. Largely because of these factors, Muslims have not yet found an adequate method for interpreting the Qur'ān and the Sunnah (or practice) of the Prophet to meet modern needs. Although almost all sections of the Muslim society are agreed in accepting at least the economically developmental forms of modernity and at the same time to preserve Islam, it has been difficult for them to devise a method whereby both are meaningfully integrated. So far as the Ulama are concerned, although they accept the technological benefits of modern life, they are not only not willing to accept the consequences of modern education but are even, by and large, quite unaware of these consequences and think that both the traditional beliefs of Islam, as they were formulated by medieval theologians, and the traditional law can be kept completely intact and immune from modern influences. They would, for instance, while welcoming modern industry, still think that the giving and taking of interest can be strictly forbidden. It is this attitude of the Ulama which is directly responsible for secularism in the Muslim world.

Let us give another illustration. The Qur'ān, in order to fulfill its fundamental objective of social and economic justice, has ordered the levying of a tax known as *zakāh*. From the uses, enumerated by the Qur'ān, of the expenditure of this tax, it is evident that it was a social welfare tax in the widest possible meaning of "welfare." Further, this was the only tax levied by the Qur'ān. Now, the Prophet had fixed a certain rate, which leads one to believe that, for the normal needs of that society, he must have judged this rate adequate. The needs of a modern society, however, have expanded immensely. Education, communications, and other developmental schemes are now considered to be among the necessities of modern social welfare. This would, therefore, argue for a re-adjustment of the rate of *zakāh* tax to modern needs.

The Ulama, however, forbid any change in the rate of *zakāh* and assert that if *zakāh* is inadequate to meet the larger welfare needs of the Muslim society, then Muslim governments can levy other taxes. It is at this critical juncture that the administrator tells the Ulama, "You say there is only one *Islamic* tax, which is *zakāh*. When this proves inadequate, you forbid any change in the *zakāh*-rate but you say that I can levy other taxes. You are, thereby, introducing a dualism which I find unworkable. If I can levy other taxes, I shall levy them and fulfill the needs of my society and your *zakāh* is superfluous." This is the essence of secularism. Indeed, all along the line of confrontation of modernity with traditional Islam, the majority of the Ulama exhibits an attitude which is directly conducive to secularism.

The second method, which has been followed by the vast majority of the Muslim modernists and which is calculated to save Islam and accept modernity, shows important shades of difference, but, by and large, this method involves some kind of mechanical or artificial manipulation. The most common form of this method is to interpret individual verses of the Qur'ān or the traditions, according to subjective and not infrequently arbitrary predilections arising out of the acceptance of various beliefs and practices from the modern west. This approach, which was practiced also by Sir Sayyid Ahmad Khān and, to some extent, Sayyid Amīr Ali, is still in dominant vogue in the Indo-Pakistan sub-continent.

This approach often violates history and sometimes imposes arbitrary meanings on words. An example of such an interpretation is the translation of the Qur'ānic word "*yatīm*", which means an "orphan", by the word "widow" in the verse pertaining to the permission for polygamy on the part of many modernists who assert, contrary to historical facts and philological justice, that polygamous marriages were allowed by Islam only in the particular circumstances when the number of widows had increased because of wars. In the same category are the forced interpretations of the Qur'ān to prove that slavery was abolished by Islam.

A second and allied form of this method of interpretation is to invoke some kind of traditional authority to support an interpretation reached on grounds of modernist thinking. This is particularly true of the method followed in Egypt in the field of Islamic law but is applied elsewhere also. This method, which consists of picking and choosing from the various schools of thought at one's own wish, has sometimes been described as *talfīa* or patchwork. An example of this approach is afforded by modernist legislations introduced in various parts of the Muslim world, with regard to the period of time which must expire, in case a husband absents himself from his family, for the wife to re-marry. According to the Hanafi school, a husband has to be absent for at least ninety years before his wife can re-marry, while according to the school of Mālik, the period is only four years. The modernists in most Muslim countries have chosen the Māliki view because the Hanafi stand seems too harsh on the wife. However, the grounds on which the Hanafis and the Mālikis reach their conclusions are totally different.

The Hanafi says that a woman should not re-marry so long as there is the slightest chance of her husband surviving somewhere in the world, and this is generally in tune with the spirit of the Hanafi *fiqh* on the subject, which seeks to make the marital bond as nearly permanent as possible even though the measures advocated often lead to opposite results. Hence, the Hanafis say that the woman should wait for 90 years, which is the "normal span" of human life. But the basis of Mālik for his decision is very different. He says that the term of four years is the maximum possible period of gestation and that, therefore, after this period there is little likelihood that the pregnancy of the wife from her former husband would remain.

But the modernist has simply opted for the more convenient view irrespective of the basis on which it rests, and the modernist himself has not dared to perform his own *ijtihād*. This second form has the merit of avoiding radicalism and ensuring traditional continuity. But it is unsatisfactory because it is often illogical and can never be welded into a system. The same holds true of the Egyptian solution of the problem of providing for the orphan grandchild from the inheritance of his grandfather by a putative will on the part of the latter without realizing that will pertains to the law of bequests and not to the law of inheritance strictly speaking.

The only acceptable method of interpretation which would do justice both to the demands of intellectual and moral integrity, is that which resorts first of all to historical criticism in the widest possible meaning of the term. It is only in this way that a genuine appreciation of the objectives of the Qur'ān and the Sunnah can be achieved. Take, for example, the question of polygamy. That the Qur'ān had generally improved the rights and status of women is beyond doubt. It is also true that the Qur'ān says that men should not marry more than one wife if they fear they cannot do justice among them, adding categorically that no matter how much men may try, they will not be able to do justice among several wives. However, it remains equally true that the Qur'ān had given permission to marry up to four wives.

The only way to understand the Qur'ānic pronouncements as a whole is to say that, whereas the Qur'ān desired to promote the maximal happiness of the family life and, for this purpose, stated that a monogamous marriage would normally be ideal, this declared *moral* purpose had nevertheless to be compromised with the actual seventh century Arabian society into which polygamy was deeply structured and, hence, could not be *legally* rooted out except on pain of utterly defeating the moral purpose itself. The Qur'ān, therefore, accepted polygamy at the *legal* level, restricted it, and put as many safeguards against it as possible, but at the same time the moral ideal was enunciated as that of a monogamous society towards which the Prophet may have hoped the Muslims would move.

History, however, proved otherwise and the vast conquests after the Prophet's death which brought a tremendous influx of women and slave girls into Muslim society helped to thwart the very purpose of the Qur'ān from this point of view. So is the case with slavery which was tolerated and accepted at a *legal* level but a moral process was sought to be set in motion whereby slavery might be abolished. This purpose was again defeated by Muslim history for historical reasons.

The illustrations we have chosen so far have been from the legal-social field; but the realm of belief is no less important. The world-view of the modern man, despite all the differences that it may exhibit, is essentially different from the medieval outlook and traditional habits of thought. Belief in authority and credulity are two sides of the same coin, a coin which has necessarily lost currency in the modern world. Belief in authority, in fact, both leads to and assumes credulity. And credulity is the father of all types of occultisms, miracle-mongering and crass forms of spiritual exploitation.

The story of Muhammad's Ascension (Mi'rāj) is an example of such superstitionism which finds little support in the Qur'ān. The Qur'ān, in several places, speaks of certain expansive experiences of the Prophet wherein his religious personality broke the normal limits and became identified with the entire expanse of reality. But the Qur'ān not only does not speak of a physical ascension of the Prophet but even describes it as an act of the heart; and in two places, far from speaking of the Prophet as ascending, it speaks of God as descending to him. It seems, however, that when the Muslims confronted the Christians outside the Arabian Peninsula and particularly in Iraq, they were forced to interpret this experience as that of an ascension in answer to the Christian dogma of the Assumption of Jesus.

Similarly, the doctrine of intercession (*shafā'a*) was the Muslim counterpart to the Christian redemption, even though intercession has been explicitly and recurrently rejected by the Qur'ān. On the whole, a plethora of miracles came to be attributed to the Prophet as part of a successful campaign to semi-deify him in direct opposition to the explicit teachings of the Qur'ān. This process of the mythologization of the Prophet, which had its source in more than one factor, was equally shared and adopted by the orthodoxy itself. This traditional picture, instead of being exposed to historical criticism, has been essentially accepted by the modernists generally, even though some of them reject miracles in a technical sense.

It is true that the modernist is mainly interested in attributing to the Prophet the virtues of a great leader of mankind; but he has not done so on the basis of historicity and of the assessment of the actual historical performance of the Prophet but has constructed the image of Muhammad on the pattern of his own hero. He has, therefore, been forced to accept an overlay of all kinds of superstitious elements in the traditional image of the Prophet. The least of it is that the modernist has thereby done a disservice to Islamic modernism. However, if the modernist claims—as he patently does—that the Prophet is the model for a Muslim to live by both at the individual and collective levels, then genuine guidance and inspiration cannot be obtained from a semi-mythical figure but only from the model of a truly historic personage.

III. Recent Developments

Since the political independence of the greater part of the Muslim world during the past two decades, the career of modernism has entered its most crucial test and with it so has the whole question of the future of Islam. The question has become most acute because, with the exception of the official attitude of Turkey (there is more than minimal evidence to believe that people in Turkey are not prepared to accept the formal official view that Turkey should be a secular state), everywhere in the Muslim world both the peoples and the governments have been saying that Islam is a "complete way of life" rather than being either merely a set of religious rites or pertaining exclusively to the private relationship between the individual and his God. This can be documented by the statements of leaders of government almost in every major Muslim country.

The curious paradox, however, is that in most Muslim countries Islam is not actually treated as basis of state policies—either socioeconomic or external policy or in any field directly touching public life except personal law; for all practical purposes, Islam is treated as a narrow religious sphere in official policies which either leave it to itself or, at best, have established "departments of religious affairs" —which in itself tends to show that officially these countries actually believe in a bifurcation of life into the religious and secular domains whether they admit, or dare to admit, it or not. Their claim that Islam is a "total way of life" is either an expression of their double-mindedness or a pure lip-service to the popular aspirations. The main reason for the official double-mindedness cannot but be the difficulty of working Islam in a modern state, particularly in face of the stark opposition of the Ulama to modernism and the intellectual failure of the official classes to represent or reformulate Islam in consequential modern terms.

It is only in Pakistan that this mental hiatus has been superseded through various factors. The most important of these factors are that the state of Pakistan was itself carved out in the name of Islam, which was the only force which inspired the masses. Secondly, Pakistan, like India, is composed of so many races, languages, and colors that it is extremely dificult to find any basis for national unity except Islam. Indeed, Pakistan is composed of two physically separate units which is not the case even with India. Unless secularism can be made into an effective force for positive progress, the only way for these countries seems to be to accept religion as the basis of state and to find within their religions not only adequate safeguards but formulas of genuine equality for minorities with the majority communities. Otherwise, sooner or later, but probably in the predictable future, these countries would break up into racial and/or linguistic units on the pattern of Europe.

Our most important problem just now, however, is to describe the fact of Islamic modernism in Pakistan and the intricate struggles in which it is involved today. As soon as Pakistan was created, it faced the problem of how to implement Islam in collective existence in a twentieth century polity. The question as to what safeguards or rights the minorities would have in an "Islamic State" has, I think, somewhat disproportionately vexed both some leaders of Pakistani minorities, whose reactions are visible in the debates of the National Assembly, and also many of the foreign observers.

The question as to how minorities are to be treated in an Islamic state of the twentieth century is one of the problems of Islamic modernism, and the fundamental question is how Islam is to be interpreted for modern life. For if an adequate method of such interpretation can be found, the question of the status of minorities will automatically be solved along with other acute problems. So far as the factual situation is concerned, minorities in Pakistan do not seem to have fared badly, particularly with the background of the throes of partition. But it is precisely this question viz. of finding a modern approach to Islam, whose solution by Pakistan official policies, at the intellectual level, has been disappointing.

It must be admitted, first, that it is much easier to find solutions of all such problems—like treatment of minorities and developmental programs with all the social consequences of industrial and technological change—in a secular state, because secularism is simply a desperate measure to get rid of traditional impediments and prejudices at a tremendous cost. The task of Pakistan is, therefore, immeasurably more difficult.

Secondly, unlike the majority of other Muslim countries, Pakistan at least got over the mental hurdle and *formally* declared herself to be an Islamic state. But the intellectual equipment of the Pakistani modernist was little better than that of his counterparts in other Muslim countries. In the actual operations, therefore, of official Islam on modern lines, Pakistan can hardly be said to have fared better than other Muslim countries in an overall assessment.

One of the chief difficulties of Pakistan in this field is the Civil Service inherited from British days (which is no doubt its great advantage in other ways). In the British times, when the primary aim of Civil Service was to keep law and order and collect revenues, it was hardly development-oriented and the question of socio-economic reforms on an Islamic basis was out of the question at the official level. After the creation of Pakistan, however, the Civil Service was, for the first time, called upon to carry out Islamic reform in various socio-economic and legal fields. But since every reform entails opposition—the degree of its intensity depending upon the gap between what exists and what is to be brought about—the majority of the civil servants is until today unable to face this situation. Although, therefore, the government is committed not only to a program of socio-economic development, but to carrying it out on Islamic lines, its machinery acts as a great conservative force. Indeed, besides feudalism, the Pirs and the Mullahs, the government machinery itself is the third formidable force of conservatism in the country even though it is the only organized force of progress as well.

But this is not the whole story, nor even the main part of it. The central fact about modernism in Pakistan since its creation has been a lack of intellectual adequacy in the country to formulate modernism and its approaches. So far as the record of the administrators before 1958 is concerned, the only thing it shows is a formal declaration that Pakistan is an Islamic state. But in order to introduce programs of development, the strategy resorted to was, on the one hand, to set up a Board of Ulama known as the *Taᶜlīmāt-i-Islāmīya* Board, and, on the other, to go ahead with all developmental programs irrespective of whether the Board approved these on Islamic grounds. But the creation of the *Taᶜlīmāt-i-Islāmīya* Board at least pacified the conservatives of various shades, including the *Jamāᶜat-i-Islāmī*, which demanded a pure and simple return to the seventh century Arabian state of the Prophet and his immediate successors.

This pacification was disturbed occasionally by events like the appointment of the *Muslim Marriage Law Commission* in 1955, the one traditionalist member of which violently opposed the recommendations of the rest of the Commission to bring about changes in the Muslim law of Marriage and Divorce. So far as the minorities' question was concerned, there was no solution of it at the intellectual level, but the constitution adopted in 1956 simply confirmed the equal rights of all citizens irrespective of race, color, or creed.

In the face of this inadequacy, the traditionalist groups charged that the government was behaving hypocritically and that, on the one hand, it paid lip-service to Islam through fear of mass disturbances and, on the other, was introducing policies which squarely contradicted the traditionalist view of Islam—coeducation resulting in increasing emancipation of women, films, changes proposed in the Family Laws of the Muslims, banking—to mention only a few. The modernist seemed to reach a deadlock, and there were some voices, although feeble, calling for a secular state.

The government of President Mohammad Ayub Khan established, in 1960, a Central Institute of Islamic Research to carry out research into, and interpretation of, Islam for modern needs. In 1962, this institution was given a constitutional status and, in addition, another body was created known as the Advisory Council of Islamic Ideology to take the place of the old *Ta῾līmāt-i-Islāmīya* Board. Whereas the Institute was the place of scholarly research, the Advisory Council was declared as the competent body to give advice to the government and the assemblies on the basis primarily of the research carried out by the Institute.

The very first test, however, which came in 1963 over the question of bank-interest, showed that the answer to the problem of Islamic modernism does not really lie in creating this institution but rather in the training of proper personnel for this purpose. To illustrate the inadequacy of the modernist approach in Pakistan, this controversy over the question of the Islamicity or otherwise of the banking institutions is illuminating. The Institute's research showed that the acual system of *Ribā*, or usury, prevalent in Arabia was a crass form of economic exploitation and was therefore banned by the Qur'ān after a series of warnings; that the Muslim *Fuqahā* in the succeeding generations extended this ban unnecessarily to all sorts of financial transactions in which any increment over capital was involved. The Institute, therefore, argued that, in order to apply Islam today, it is in the first place essential to understand the background of the Qur'ān in order to determine the kind of purposes in moral, spiritual, and socio-economic fields which the Qur'ān wanted to fulfill.

The implementation of the Qur'ān cannot be carried out literally in the context of today because this may result in thwarting the very purposes of the Qur'ān and, although the findings of the *Fuqahā,* or Ulama of Islam, during the past thirteen centuries or so should be seriously studied and given due weight, it may well be found that in many cases their findings were either mistaken or sufficed for the needs of that society but not for today. This approach is so revolutionary and so radically different from the approaches generally adopted so far in that it seems to bring under strictly historical study not only *Fiqh* and *Sunna* of the Prophet, but the Qur'ān as well, that not only the traditionalists, but even most of the modernists seriously hesitate to accept it.

But this would seem to be the only honest method of appraising the historic performance of the Muslims and of genuinely implementing the purposes of the Qur'ān and the Prophet. There would be naturally bitter opposition to this kind of approach and particularly to the results reached through it. But there is reason to believe that, in a span of a decade or so, the larger part of the liberals will come round to some such view. Failing that, this writer does not see any other alternative for Islam except, in the course of time, to be reduced to a set of rites which will claim emotional attachment for some time to come. For the pace at which five-year plans of development are being conceived and executed is likely to change the entire structure of these societies within a generation or so. It is also conceivable that in some countries such radical change may be preceded by a brief interval of the heyday of the rightest, although his chances are not strong. Should, however, the traditionalist come to the top in a country, his inevitable failure would only serve to hasten the process of modernization—but at the expense of Islam.

THE SITUATION OF THEOLOGY

BY

ROBLEY EDWARD WHITSON

Fordham University

The title of this exploration, "The Situation of Theology," was chosen because of the peculiar suggestiveness of the word "situation." Situation points towards the human condition, the historic reality of the life-situation of actual men which has given rise to whatever theology is and which remains the norm for judging what it can be. Emphasis on situation will demand that we explore the meaning of theology within the context of its actual occurrence as a phenomenon of human knowing and not as a mere abstraction. Real people have "theologized," and apparently still do. Our question, therefore, is not: What is theology; is it of any significance? We ask, rather: What are people doing when they "theologize"; what of themselves (at least in part) are they expressing?

If we take the orientation of human situation we will see immediately that theology today is striving to express something of profound significance in man's continuing expansion of his awareness. The entire spectrum of activity which we designate as theology is undergoing internal upheavals of maximum proportions. Some presume these are the death throes—and among them are what might be called apocalyptic theologians who interpret such developments as the "death-of-God-theology" as triumphalistic signs of the imminent end of the world (a periodic hope of some theologians!). Others see contemporary theological upheaval as in complete continuity with the general crisis in civilization and heralding a radically new beginning in the total human situation. Whether the condition of theology today marks the extinction of a dinosaur or the emergence of a new life-form, that which theology has been, is, can be, and should be, must be explored, at least to extend our knowledge of the human experience.

The issue, therefore, is to come to a definition of theology, not simply as an abstraction but as an expression of the human experience, as reality lived out by actual men, and thus as significant within the context of the human situation. Further, rooted to this extent and in this manner is man's awareness of himself and his universe, the definition of theology we seek must be extended maximally and not be derived from one tradition of religion or civilization. Therefore, we must turn to the most fundamental observations to be made of actual men to identify factors which would be basic to any theological tradition which could be formed.

I

The obvious and necessary place to begin is with man himself. Yet most older theological traditions do not begin with man at all, and indeed some seem never to reach man. Mas as the beginning point is obvious and necessary only if whatever theology is must be in the human life-situation. Typically, older western formulations of the nature and function of theology have presumed that the basic problem is that posed by the affirmation of divinity; the fact of humanity could be taken for granted, often enough because humanity was reduced to an idealization—an ideal human nature was substituted for actual men, as unreal as the "average man" of statistics. Thus the etymological formation of the word "theology" clearly indicates the evaluation of the issues: the central concern is divinity—*theos*—while man, the foundation of the proposed knowing—*logos*—is avoided. A situational approach to theology must challenge such an orientation. Whatever significance is to be given properly to the *theos*-category, it is the *logos*-category which must occupy first place in our exploration. And this cannot mean that we will be content simply with the pursuit of theories of knowledge. We must ask: What is the significance of *men in the process of knowing?*—the kind of knowing identified by the designation *theology*.

In attempting to deal with the theological situation in terms of historic actuality, we must seek our understanding of the human foundation in a full historic process. What we encounter in contemporary developments is in some sort of continuity with past developments, though of course this continuity may well be characterized as markedly antithetic. The historical perspective is not merely an additional aspect but is an essential factor in our problem, for without it we are not dealing with the actual human situation. Within the limits of this presentation we are forced to be very selective, and so to avoid culture-bound arbitrariness, let us begin to view the developmental process of theology from a most unlikely vantage-point: Confucius.

At first sight, to link Confucius and contemporary theology might seem meaningless, yet if they can be linked validly the combination could produce some unexpected insights. For if Confucianism is properly a religious tradition, what revisions in the western concept of religion must be made? Or, if Confucius is a proto-theologian, does he throw light on non-God-centered contemporary problems? Or, if Confucian concern for the values of civilization is a theological concern, what does the dichotomous structure religious/secular mean? Other questions of this type could be asked, all illustrating the implications of theology extended to include Confucius.

Whether or not we could see Confucius as a proto-theologian at this stage, there is no doubt that he addresses himself almost exclusively to the problem of man. His concern is not with a theory of man but with man in his real context. Thus, one of Confucius' personal goals, one in which he is to be bitterly disappointed, is to become the prime minister of one of the feudal states and thus be able to put into practice what he teaches. In fact, for Confucius the true teacher, the complete teacher, is one who is able to effect actual change in others and not remotely through ideas alone, but by practical accomplishment. (It is interesting to note in passing the concurrence with the Marxist concept of the theorist in which philosophy out of the context of socio-cultural action is a self-contradiction.) The inner reason why Confucius insists on the inseparability of thought and action is his recognition of *man as social*.

For the typical westerner, the phrase *man as social* actually means very little. This is a primary reason why Confucius with his profoundly social orientation is relatively ignored in the west. Over a period of several centuries, western man has lost sight of his very life-situation, and society has become a mere practical circumstance of human life in which the individual exists in near isolation, especially with regard to the deepest of human values. In medieval Christian spirituality we can see the emergence of what will be a continuing pattern of divisive tension between individual and society: the deepest religious relationship is viewed as the individual alone with God; Christian theology is conceived of as intellectual preparation of the individual Christian for the achievement of an essentially isolated mystical experience; the Christian Church ceases to be recognized as a body of people constituted by their out-reaching unity and instead becomes a jurisdictional autocracy and the psychologically introverted anarchy of incommunicable personal piety. Renaissance humanism extends this divisiveness further in individualistic intellectualism; renaissance nationalism and despotism destroy the socio-political patterns of the extended social consciousness called Christendom. And the Enlightenment enthrones individual Reason in that solemn isolation which must denounce all socially shared values and relationships as the ultimate enemies of man, tolerating those imposed by practical necessity in an uneasy coexistence. The present stage of western civilization has been formed by a generation raised in the ideals of extreme nineteenth century *laissez-faire* individualism, and has produced the paradox of totalitarianism with the one extreme of absolutizing the individual as society (Hitler's *fuehrerprinzip*) and the other of absolutizing society as the individual (the Marxist *collectivity* prepared for by the Leninist *dictatorship of the proletariat*).

II

Yet in the very crisis of the twentieth century we find signs of a new emergence of a social consciousness, still only in its beginnings, but of great potentiality for the future. In the very area thought individualistically sacrosanct, heretofore, human moral conscience, we find significant social stirrings. Is there a social responsibility reaching all of us for the murder of millions of Jews? Does such a social responsibility implicate us all in the centuries of exploitive colonialism and imperialism? What is the social responsibility for war and peace, killing and life-giving, enslavement and freedom? Perhaps most significant of all in current western society is the unrest in the Christian church with the growing recognition of the absolute necessity for involvement in the total situation of man and a consequent painful judgment against institutional irrelevance.

Rousseau established an irreconcilable dualism of individual and society:

> "Man's first feeling was that of his own existence, and his first care was that of self-preservation..."

> "If we compare the extraordinary diversity which occurs in the education and manner of life of the various classes of men in the state of society with the uniformity and simplicity of animal and savage life,... it is easy to conceive how much less difference there must be between man and man in a state of nature than in a state of society, and how greatly the natural inequality of mankind must be increased by the inequalities of social institutions."

> (*Discourse on the Origin and Foundation of the Inequality Among Men.*)

However recently this characterized the western attitude, such an evaluation of what the human condition is today is not only meaningless, in its implications it is repulsive. On the other hand, Confucius proposes that the central concept in our understanding of man is *jen*—man related to man, mankind together (expressed in written form by the combination of the characters for *man* and the numeral *two*, hence *man as social*). Although twenty-five centuries, language, civilization, and entire life-patterns separate us, we find a responsiveness to his insight. If we are concerned with the human situation, *man as social* is at the center of any valid understanding.

Confucius discovered that he knew nothing at all about man as an abstraction; he could say nothing at all of Human Nature. He also recognized he did not and could not understand the foundation of man's reality, that although he could speak of man and the universe in terms of ultimacy, an Ultimate as such could be named (Heaven) but could not be known. What Confucius could study and come to know was man as he lived, the works of man. Thus, in the *Analects* we find a disciple saying:

> "... We are permitted to hear the Master's views on culture and the manifestations of *jen*. But he will not speak to us at all on the Nature of Man and the Way of Heaven." (*Analects*, Book V : 12)

Confucius does not deny Human Nature, a real basis for the commutuality of man and for the recognition of that commutuality, nor does he deny the Way of Heaven, the Ultimate of Reality, Ultimacy. Confucius studies man as man manifests himself, the human phenomenon, that which phenomenal knowing is capable of studying, and he necessarily discovers that individual men are always social.

Theology today, or, more properly, current theological systems and traditions are caught in the tensions of contemporary civilization discovering the positive fact of man as social. This will not mean a return to the primitive consciousness of man as almost exclusively social. We cannot expect the reemergence of the archaic orientation of individuality to family, clan, tribe, or nation. Although we have many vestiges of this earlier state with us still, and certain of the characteristics of twentieth century totalitarianisms are at least reminiscent of the psychological dominance of the group, it does not seem possible that the recognition of the individual self, once achieved, can be eradicated. Rather we seem to be observing the development of a two-fold integrative awareness, both individual and social. This poses the general problem of establishing the means of integrating these two dimensions of consciousness—heretofore we have been witnessing their divisive tension.

This general problem is also a particular problem for theology. All too many theological systems have been structured along lines which have at least tended to overemphasize the individuality of man, even where the religious tradition they seek to represent has a social center. Thus, the typical pre-modern Christian theological system has so downgraded the social character of Christianity that the discovery of the centrality of the *koinonia* comes as a revolutionary shock calling into question the function and relevance of many institutional forms of Christianity. Even for those who recognize the centrality of *koinonia*-awareness, there is the Herculean task of transforming their recognition into the awareness, not simply the idea or conceptualization of the awareness. And, still further, there is the corresponding necessity of developing new theological systems as adequate expressions of the awareness.

Other religious traditions will face the same or related challenges. Although many non-western traditions were not seriously affected on the popular level by the development of western ultra-individualism, nonetheless they are drawn into the general problem of the emergence of the new twofold individual-social awareness characteristic of the coming worldwide civilization. For some traditions the issue is actually the reverse of that facing the west, since they must move from a context dominated by social values which allow little place for individuality; for them the tension arises in the increasing discovery of individuality-awareness modifying social-awareness. Still other traditions are embedded almost completely in language and culture systems which are disappearing with the growth of a more universal civilization, or they are integral to a cosmology or anthropology which must give way to the reconstructed universe of the new science. In these cases the two-fold individual-social awareness of man forms an image of humanity so different from the old that we cannot expect the religious tradition intimately linked with such an image to survive it.

III

The emergence of a new human awareness, then, must effect fundamental changes in theological systems as these are the intellectual expressions of religious traditions, and religious traditions necessarily reflect human reality. However, the new human awareness has even wider effects, not simply on particular theological systems but on the constitution and function of theology in general. Particular systems must devise appropriate formulations of relationships expressive of what man is in a religious awareness both individual and social. But, even more profoundly, we must recognize that this type of awareness insists that theology as such come to grips with the reality of actual men as they are and not be content with mankind in general or man in the abstract.

When we deal with man conceived of primarily according to individuality we inevitably fall into a paradox: individuality, or the basis for it, is of necessity incommunicable—no matter how closely two individuals resemble each other, actually share characteristics, one individual as such is not in any way convertible into another; hence, there is nothing to say about one individual as such which would be significant to another individual as such—we name or identify the individual and that is all. Therefore, we find ourselves actually unconcerned with the real human individuals and instead speak of abstractions, ideal patterns, unreal men. In all of this we soon forget the actual individual men who supposedly preoccupy us from the beginning. Theology structured according to radical individuality inevitably goes to extremes both ludicrous and horrifying—thus, classic western scholasticism, concerning itself with "universals," could produce such elusive concepts as *dogness* to categorize the nature of dogs, and Nazi racist ideology with the absolutized individuality of the *fuehrerprinzip* could produce the anti-human concept of the *Untermensch* to render real human beings unreal and hence objects of liquidation rather than murder.

When we deal with man conceived of primarily according to society we fall into the same paradox but with the context reversed. Society conceived of as apart from real individuals does not exist, nor can there be any social awareness except insofar as individuals who are conscious share or intercommunicate their separate consciousnesses; hence there is no one to whom one can say anything about society if the individual is not addressed, and whether each individual is addressed singly or simultaneously with others, each must be addressed or none is. Therefore, in a primarily social orientation we find ourselves actually unconcerned with society as it really is and instead speak of something composed of non-individuals, which thus is not composed of men at all and so cannot be real society. The self-contradiction of a theology structured according to society as an abstraction is well illustrated by the concept of the Marxist *collectivity,* a society to be produced by the self-contained dynamics of the dialectic process of history but which will have no significant individuality within it and hence will destroy the dialectic process and become static, futureless, and absolutely opposed to the immutable laws which are to create it, a human society without real names, that is, without humans as we experience them—the only kind we know and thus the only kind about whom we can speak meaningfully.

If theology is to be situated in the actual condition of man, and if the *logos*-category of theology is to reflect adequately man's experience in knowing, then the central recognition of theology must be *jen*: man both individual and social, man communicating, man in an ultimately significant relationship. Thus, seen from this orientation, theological knowing does not consist in abstract formulas, whatever their derivation, but rather must be the meaningful analysis of the truly significant relations of human experience. Such an orientation in no way compromises the actual commitments proper to any religious tradition. As a system of analysis, theological knowing can be developed around any tradition of human experience. If, for example, the experience occurs because of the manifestation of divinity—revelation —that experience as it occurs in man must have proper human significance, both individual and social, and hence at least something of it must be communicable. The development of a theological system takes place in response to the attempt to come to grips with the experience in every communicable dimension.

In the *logos*-category theological knowing is always the same as the attempt to analyze and thus communicate actual religious experience. Differences occur in terms of the content of the experience, the type of effect the experience has upon the individual and hence upon his communication group. The variety in theological systems is expressive of the variety of approach made historically to the content of the *theos* category. In the study of specific religious traditions, the content of the *theos*-category is determined and articulated according to the insight of communities sharing concrete commitments. However, for theology in general, an understanding of the *theos*-category cannot be attempted in terms of one specific religious tradition. Yet it is the *theos*-category which specifies theology as a particular kind of knowing, which attempts to analyze and systematize a particular kind of human experience.

Returning once again to our first emphasis, that is, theology in terms of the human situation, a significant functional relationship for the *theos-* and *logos*-categories can be established in the very process of theological knowing. The Confucian concept of *jen* focuses attention on religious experience as both individual and social. However, against our usual western tendency, *jen* insists that we see the experience as a basic interhuman relationship rather than as an isolateable phenomenon of consciousness. In other words, conscious religious experience occurs insofar as a fundamental human relationship exists which constitutes man what he is. This relationship not only allows for communication, it makes communication inevitable. Thus, a knowing process of analysis, systematization, and articulation is integrally part of what it means to be human.

As Confucius observes man actually living out this process, he finds that there is something about it which extends beyond momentary experience, transitory relationships, and the simple appearance of things. *Jen* expresses a necessary relationship which constitutes the very condition of human existence and also expresses the further significance of man and his world. Man is constituted in an all-embracing relationship of individuals, and this relationship is definitvely significant in the most profound sense.

In any theological system, or approach to the meaning of theology in general, we can recognize that the *logos*-category expresses a definitiveness for man somehow located in the *theos*-category, however the content of the latter may be conceived. Although a theological system may be primitive, poorly systematized and badly articulated, it never fails to express a call for commitment. Theological systems are never indifferent theories of religious knowledge. They come into existence for the very purpose of formulating an understanding of religious conviction so that commitment can be specified and made concrete and practical.

It seems clear that one of the basic reasons why the *logos*-category should always be social in its extension is that the human experience in religion always has a characteristic absoluteness about it, and hence cannot be confined to the individual without self-contradiction. The urge to communication which gives rise to concrete theological systems is not simply the result of gregariousness or of the psychological need to stimulate others to pursue common interests. The religious experience seems always to insist upon an absolute involvement of everything which actually constitutes man, and hence man's social situation precludes a purely individualistic significance for religion. Thus, theological systems inevitably express involvement of man in the broadest possible terms, reflecting an irreducible human interrelationship which somehow has ultimate significance.

The *theos*-category is the structural element in theology in which concrete conceptualizations of the ultimacy in the religious relationship are attempted. The various theological traditions differ radically in the conceptualizations proposed for the *theos*-category. However they are in complete agreement in the general affirmation that there is a basis in reality for the definitiveness experienced in the religious relationship.

IV

Although it is true that theological systems typically specify a conceptual content for the *theos*-category, even the slightest acquaintance with the historic religious traditions reveals an apparent contradiction. For while each theological system does propose a *theos*-category conceptualization, at the same time each theological system inevitably asserts that that which constitutes this category is in itself absolutely unknowable, and thus ineffable.

The oldest texts of Confucianism affirm over and over the paradox of man in a definitive relationship which orients him to an unknowable. Confucius sees man and everything which man does as immediately reflective of the Principle or *Tao* of existence. But although this direct reflectivity of things manifests the *Tao*, the *Tao* in itself remains unknowable. And so Confucianism concentrates man's attention upon what can be known: the outward appearance of things, on-going human relationships, and the works of man. But this is not simply a devotion to culture or an ethical discipline; by involvement with all that can be known, man can reach the unknown—a harmony of life lived here and now is the mysterious image of a total Harmony in all of reality.

Hence when Tzu-kung says,

> "... we are permitted to hear the Master's view on culture and the manifestations of *jen*. But he will not speak to us at all on the Nature of Man and the Way of Heaven...,"

we are being told two things. First, the Way, or *Tao*, of Heaven and the ultimate significance of man are unknown. But second, to know human culture and the manifestations of *jen* is to reach into the ultimate mystery of man and *Tao*.

Another important text of the *Analects* points up Confucius' recognition of the paradox.

> "Someone asked the meaning of the Great Sacrifice. The Master said: I do not know; anyone who knew its meaning could deal with all that is under Heaven as easily as he could look at this (and he pointed to the palm of his hand)." (*Analects* Book III : 11)

The central concern of Confucius as a scholar and teacher was the study of culture and the manifestation of *jen*. For him the most important subject of study was the complex of ritual and ceremony whereby human relationships, and hence man himself, were most formally expressed. Outstanding among the cultural rituals was the Great Sacrifice which summed up all that constituted society through the affirmation of the continuity of the human community in spite of the barrier of death. The Great Sacrifice ritually united ancestors and descendants in the timeless mystery of family. Yet Confucius cannot say what the inner meaning of the Great Sacrifice is. It is not simply that he does not know.[1] Rather, as the central image of man in his ultimate relationship, the meaning of the Great Sacrifice is the ultimate meaning upon which all of reality is founded. It is the *Tao,* the Principle of Reality itself. And this in the religious experience of Confucius is completely unknowable.

There is a peculiar subtlety in the thought of Confucius, especially if we view him as a proto-theologian. The *theos*-category is recognized as unknowable, and Confucius never is tempted to propose any concrete conceptualization for it. He identifies it, affirms it, and recognizes its absolute significance for all that he does attempt to know. The only positive identification he can give it is as the *Tao,* the Principle.

This designation affirms that there is a further significance for the *logos*-category beyond the mere description of human activity. Confucius sees the destiny of each man in the achievement of harmony with other men through life in accordance with the essential social condition of human relatedness, and this human harmony extended to the cosmos which it mirrors. This complete harmony of the *logos*-category, both knowable and achievable, is the image of a further Harmony, the foundation of all reality, which can be reached but which must remain a mystery.

---

[1] It should be noted, however, that some Neo-Confucianist scholars interpret this passage in the sense that the full ancient meaning of the sacrifice is no longer known or understood.

As a proto-theologian, Confucius starts with man and remains with man—yet this is expressive of a mysterious ultimacy which exceeds what man is and what man does but which gives all that is human a value beyond the passing moment.

In Taoism, China gives us another outstanding example of the attempt to formulate man's significance in the religious experience. While Confucianism concentrates on the *logos*-category in its full social extension, Taoism attempts to look within the individual consciousness to discover what happens to man that makes him commit himself absolutely. While highly individualistic, Taoism is nonetheless not anti-social for it presumes that all men have a common origin and destiny though each must walk the path of return alone. Taoism concentrates on the paradox of individual mysticism. To pursue the *Tao* as the Principle of Reality one must wait for it rather than seek it, be passive rather than active, and prefer unknowing to knowing. Thus, in Chapter 47 of the *Tao Te Ching* we read:

> "Without going outside his door, one understands everything under the sky. Without looking out from his window, one sees the Way of Heaven. The further one goes out from himself, the less he knows. Therefore the sages achieved their knowledge without travelling, gave the right names to things without seeing them, and accomplished their ends without any purpose of doing so."

Taoism does not look to things for the manifestation of *Tao*, but calls upon the individual consciousness to empty itself so that the *Tao* can fill it in the situation of personal mysticism. Taoism constantly views the human commitment to ultimacy through a symbolic reversal of value. We see this in the water image of the Taoist mystics. In contrast to the heat of the sun and the force of the wind which seem to dominate the world, it is water flowing into the crevices of stone that has the irresistible power when it freezes to break apart the earth and split open mountains. And the Taoist mystic asks what constitutes the usefulness of a bowl—is it its solid sides and bottom or is it the interior emptiness which waits to be filled?

In seeking to express what man is, Taoism is not concerned with impotence, inaction, or passivity. Rather, it affirms that all that is apparently negative is actually the positive of reality, intensely active and powerful. Confucianism sees man and his works as manifesting the ever mysterious *Tao* which remains behind them at their foundation. Taoism attempts to look within, directly at the mysterious foundation. Hence, Taoism accepts what man is and what man does but is only interested in the reversal of all of this. Yet, however much Taoism may stress the immediacy of the ultimate Principle to man, it nonetheless affirms that the *Tao* remains unknowable. Thus Chapter One of the *Tao Te Ching* opens with the mysteriousness of the *Tao*:

> "The *Tao* that can be trodden is not the enduring and unchanging *Tao*; the name that can be named is not the enduring and unchanging Name."

Chapter Fourteen provides us with an extraordinary insight into the Taoist coordination of the function of the *logos*-category and the *theos*-category. What is the mystic doing as he approaches the unknowable *Tao* in the situation of human consciousness, what understanding is there, and, hence, what interhuman communication can take place?

> "We look at It and we do not see It, and we name It the Equable. We listen to It and we do not hear it, and we name it the Inaudible. We try to grasp It and we do not get hold of It, and we name It the Subtle. With these three qualities It cannot be made the subject of description and hence we blend them together and obtain the Oneness."

The same chapter later refers to the form of the Formless, the semblance of the Invisible, the Fleeting and the Indeterminable.

Although Taoism reverses the evaluation of man made by Confucianism, the problem remains the same when the attempt is made to determine what it is that makes the religious relationship somehow ultimate and definitive. Even diametrically opposed visions of man and hence of the *logos*-category allow for no difference in the attempt to give content to the *theos*-category. The category is affirmed and it is affirmed as profoundly significant for man. Man's relationship to it is seen as real in every sense. Yet, whatever words are used to designate the *theos*-category and however much they may seem to give positive conceptual content to it, it is declared to be simply unknowable, a complete and permanent mystery.

V

As we extend our range of comparison further to observe the occurrence and treatment of the paradox in other areas of major religious development, we find a consistent similarity in the articulation of the basic problem. Whatever the conceptualization of man and the phenomenal universe, and whatever meaning the particular religious tradition gives for man involved in the religious relationship, the theological systems [1] as the formal articulations of the religious traditions uniformly assert the ineffability of the *theos*-category. If we look to the development of the two major religious traditions of India, Buddhism and Classic and later Hinduism, we find two closely related yet quite distinct approaches to the formulation of the paradox. Hinduism and Buddhism share a basic orientation towards man and the universe which, from the popular western point of view, "devaluates" the entire phenomenal order. In the extreme school of metaphysics, man, everything that is like man, and the whole context of human life, are ultimately substanceless, without reality, simply illusions. Phenomena as appearings only seem to appear. There are a great many variations proposed for the understanding of the fundamental transitoriness of things according to the many widely differing schools of metaphysics, but the basic orientation of Indian thought is that man and all that man can know are, in some sense, illusions: both the knower and known are "unreal." The religious traditions of India, therefore, must face unique problems as they approach the religious issue of the full significance of man.

All of Indian thought influenced by the structure of relationships given in the *Bhagavad-Gita* proposes that man's significance is not to be found in the illusory self which he seems to be nor in the equally illusory world in which he seems to exist, but in One Absolute, the Only Real, that which alone can be the True Self, totally singular Being opposed to the multiplicity of illusions. The significance of the religious relationship is conceived of as the One Unmanifest Real being manifested through many appearings which themselves are not the Real. Thus, in the Vedantist interpretation, that which appears, which is manifested, is the only Reality existing, and, insofar as the various appearances are seen to differ, these individuations are illusions and cannot be the Real. That which appears is consistently the One Reality while the many ways of appearing are outside that Reality. The Indian religious tradition draws upon many elements in its attempt to express the proposed relationship between the manifest and the Unmanifest. Mythological figures from the prehistoric era come to constitute a rich variety of vehicles for symbolization of the Abso-

---

[1] Properly speaking, theology as such has been a western religious development (of Judaism, Christianity, and Islam); this consideration of theology in relation to non-western traditions is here intended as an extension and new development in the context of religious convergence.

lute. The One Real thereby is personified in many different ways, expressive of the many types of response made by man to the life situation. Abstract philosophical elements provide another form of expression outside of the context of cultic involvement. Other elements drawn from the experience of mysticism allow for an approach through the most impressive phase of personal consciousness in spite of the characterization of consciousness as illusory.

Yet with all the varieties of expression, the tradition consistently undercuts any attempt to resolve the paradox of ineffability. Perhaps the most eloquent example of this is to be found in the *Bhagavad-Gita,* in the presentation of the two visions of the Absolute. In one vision the Absolute is presented in images of splendor, majesty and awe. He is glorified by a series of comparisons in which the greatest things known to man, the most beautiful and pleasing aspects of existence, are made the bases for divine analogies. In each instance, however great or beautiful the object is for man, the Absolute is proclaimed still greater, still more beautiful. The second vision of the Absolute is a total reversal of the first. In place of the images of beauty and inspiring glory the Absolute appears in a nightmare of horror repelling the terrified beholder. We see the image of a fire-breathing monster with blazing eyes, jagged teeth, and tusks dripping with blood, hundreds of hands reaching out for victims who are thrust into the awful mouth and whose flesh sticks between the teeth of the divine destroyer. These two totally contrasting visions presented one after the other lead the beholder dramatically into the paradox of ineffability. Both images are drawn from human experience: man's fulfillment and man's nightmare. These are images of man, and, as man himself is unreal, the images must be illusions. Whatever the manifestation may seem to be, the Unmanifest must remain unmanifest.

The *Bhagavad-Gita* clearly affirms the paradox in a statement reminiscent of Taoism:

> "One looks upon It as a wonder; another speaks of It as a wonder; another hears of It as a wonder; and even after having heard of It no one really does know It." (Chapter II)

And to prepare us for the understanding of the two visions as the contradictory symbol of the paradox, the Absolute is addressed as Divinity:

> "You only know Yourself by Yourself." (Chapter X)

Of all the major religious traditions Buddhism most radically asserts the ineffability of what is ultimate for man. With the common Indian heritage of the approach to the phenomenal world as transitoriness, Buddhism, unlike Hinduism, attempts no analogy derived from man's experience, which can only speak of transitoriness and the unreal. Man senses mysteriously some total contrast to his own existence, a contrast to illusion. He sees himself as completely unsubstantial, properly characterized by transitoriness. Mysteriously, he realizes that as his fulfillment cannot be found in this, there must be changelessness.

Whatever images and symbols are developed, Buddhism will always be centered upon this changelessness—Nirvana. To the question, what is the ultimacy of changelessness, Buddhism will give only the answer of the mystical experience. Language and concept as human and hence as illusory can do no more than designate man's ultimacy by a negation: changelessness as the denial of transitoriness. The ineffability of this ultimacy is not thought of in terms of a relative limit to human knowing—human knowing is simply irrelevant. Yet, of course, the human side of the paradox asserts itself in the Buddhist consciousness *to seek.*

In the *Manual of the Heart of the Perfection of the Wisdom of the Other Shore,* the meaning of the paradox is presented as the process of life symbolized by the passage over the sea from the shore of illusion and unknowing to the Other Shore.

> "All the Enlightened Ones of the past, present, and future cleaving to the Wisdom of the Other Shore have awakened to the highest, perfect, complete awakening. Therefore, one should know the Wisdom of the Other Shore is the great mystic formula, the mystic formula of great Wisdom, the most excellent mystic formula, the peerless mystic formula capable of allaying every suffering. It is truth because it is not falsehood. A mystic formula has been given in the Wisdom of the Other Shore. It sounds as follows:
>
>> O you who are gone, who are gone,
>> who are gone to the Other Shore,
>> who have landed on the Other Shore,
>> O YOU ENLIGHTENMENT, HAIL!"

The ultimacy proposed for man by religion is here not known or knowable; the Wisdom of the Other Shore is the State of Changelessness, existence, which cannot be properly named. In the last analysis, the ultimacy is not the "Other Shore," but the "Wisdom," not Ultimate Being, but Ultimate Truth.

VI

As we shift our attention westward for further comparative material, the theological paradox of the content of the *theos*-category is highlighted in an extraordinary manner because of the dominance in most western religious traditions of proposed historic revelation made by divinity to man. In the religious traditions of Judaism, Zoroastrianism, Christianity, and Islam, we have a common fundamental structure in the paradox of Divinity, mysterious and unknowable, being revealed to mankind so that man can respond to the reality of God with a new and significant awareness.

For Zoroaster, the cleavage between matter and spirit makes impossible the reduction of Divinity to any image of man's phenomenal experience. The cult symbol of light or fire does not show what God is like, but points to the enlightenment man must seek if he is to reach God. God reveals a pattern of life which man must lead, a way of righteousness, so that man can survive the Day of Judgment coming at the end of time—but man cannot truly know God until after the Judgment and his transformation, when he as spirit is freed from matter. Thus, God, the Wise Lord, remains a mystery, yet is somehow revealed through the happenings of existence.

> "O Wise Lord, I recognized you as the Holy One,
> When I saw you at the beginning, at the birth of life,
> Establish a recompense for deeds and words:
> Evil to the evil and good to the good,
> Through your Wisdom at the last crisis of creation."
>
> (*Gathas,* Yasna XLIII : 5.)

God is revealed, is recognized as the Holy One, insofar as man is transformed by knowing the Law of life, by knowing the Judgment is coming, by giving worship appropriate to spirit, by following unquestioningly the dictates of Divine Will, by knowing the value of existence, by the renunciation of evil. (*Gathas,* Yasna XLIII: 5, 7, 9, 11, 13, 15).

For Judaism the entire significance of human history is bound up with the fact that God reveals himself in an on-going process of human fulfillment. God is the Lord-of-people whose lives are bound up with Him through the Covenant, and whose every act constitutes either a manifestation of the dominion of the Lord in this world or a rebellion whose punishment will further reveal God in history. God enlightens man with the Law, the way of life which he is to live, and the awareness of this revelation is deepened by the actual historic process in which the Law is obeyed or not.

In every era of the development of Judaism, the paradox of God as unknowable yet known in a tradition of revelation asserts itself. Israel at Sinai receives the Law and enters the Covenant pledging its observance, and God remains hidden and remote:

"No man can see Me and live." (Exodus 33 : 20)

As Israel is formed into a nation, God is totally present in every act of his elected people, yet there can be no image of him, anything attempting a representation of him must be cast aside. The succession of prophets bears constant witness to the intimacy of relationship between Israel and its Lord, proclaiming his Will in every event of importance, yet always insisting on the awe-inspiring remoteness of God from sinful man—the God whose ways cannot be known, who cannot be counseled, whose very name must not be uttered.

Later, as the systematized analysis of formal theology is developed within Judaism, the mystery of God as totally unknowable but revealed in the Law as his Will, inevitably becomes a central area of inquiry. The paradox is also found in the development of the several mystical traditions of Judaism. Here we find patterns of expression and modes of approach reminiscent of the mysticism of India and China. God cannot be reached by human knowledge, but somehow in a process of ultimate unification man can be enlightened, can achieve a wisdom which is not human knowledge, and in this wisdom be involved in God as God is. The Kabala, though so often reduced to the crude abuses of divining and sorcery, expresses the mysterious distinction between knowledge and wisdom in a striking manner. And the effect of the Kabala tradition on Jewish folklore testifies that this distinction as an attempt to express the theological paradox is one which can be popularly grasped to some extent.

With roots deep in the prophetic tradition of Israel, the vitality of Islam is founded upon a dialectic of Divinity revealed dramatically in his own Words, yet remaining totally mysterious. In the Qur'an the Will of God for man is made manifest as Divine Compassion so that man will turn to God in the complete surrender of faith, worshipping that which remains beyond him by a life of grateful and joyous submission to the Absolute. The acceptance of the Qur'an as the ultimate manifestation of Divine Will leads Muslim thought inevitably to an elaboration of the dialectical tension in which the very words and language of the Qur'an are sacred—are God's not man's—and further that the Qur'an given to man, though complete and final as revelation, nonetheless is but a small portion of a Heavenly Qur'an, the infinity of Divine Wisdom itself. Through the historic Qur'an man can know who he really is, can know the meaning of creation and the world as it develops throughout time, can know his relationship to God, and, most important of all, can know through his loving faithfulness his own creatureliness in the face of the absoluteness of Divine Majesty. Islam effectively translates the fundamental theological paradox from an intellectual problem to the awareness of the everyday, moment-to-moment living out of the religious situation.

The Muslim prays in the words of the Qur'an, hearing his own voice speak the words of God. What happens to him each day, his success and his failure, are all the concrete realities of the Divine Will, and yet they are also always man's own realities. Destiny is the absoluteness of what is decreed, but it is also the fulfillment of selfhood from deep within the individual, since the Will of the Compassionate is a calling to faithfulness rather than a deterministic imposition.

The dynamics of the paradox have their most forceful expression in the development of Sufi mysticism. Sufism recognizes in the Qur'an both the manifestation of God and the call to approach the unknowable God through mystic union. Though God speaks in the Qur'an to reveal his Will to man, the mystic also finds in the Qur'an the *ayah,* or sign, of the interior mystery of the Presence of God. The Qur'an not only reveals, but it also contains hidden mystical meanings to be approached through contemplation.

Sufism identifies a number of passages as signs of the mystery:

> "Wherever you turn yourselves to pray, there is the Face of God." (Q., 2: 109)
> "Say: God! and leave them to their vain amusements." (Q., 6: 91)
> "They do not make a proper estimation of God." (Q., 6: 91)
> "God knows, but you do not know." (Q., 3: 91)

The popular mystic devotion of the litany of the Ninety-Nine Most Beautiful Names of God is another demonstration of the paradox. There are several traditional lists of names, and the limitation to ninety-nine is symbolic and not intended as a definitive number. But all the variations share the same structure, a series of names designating divine attributes, referring to God as Creator, Protector, King, Merciful, Generous, Strong, Glorious Eternal but subtly opposed to these attributive names is the One Hundredth Name, *Allah,* called the Essential Name—the name of revelation in the Qur'an, the mysterious unexplained sound which is the proper identification of Divinity. Thus, on the level of popular mysticism, the Ninety-Nine Names proclaim that God is known while the One Hundredth Name calls upon the believer to surrender himself to the mystery of faith.

VII

The place and function of the paradox within the Christian tradition have always been involved in a peculiar ambiguity. Christianity, like Islam, has deep roots in the prophetic tradition of Israel. From this source the recognition of God as unknowable in himself is therefore an element to be found in the earliest documents. If anything, the Christian conviction concerning the nature and manner of revelation should tend to heighten the importance of divine ineffability. For revelation as historic incarnation emphasizes God as knowable in himself and known in the sense of experienced insofar as one knows or experiences the historic man who, as a man, is in total union with the Godhead. Incarnational revelation thus is centered upon a medium, a human being who is completely a human being and who always remains such and yet is so united to Divinity that to experience this man is to experience God fully.

Since Christianity affirms that this incarnational revelation is a historic reality, necessarily many historic events or elements must be accounted for implicitly or explicitly in anything approaching a full statement of the mystery of God revealed. But the core of Christian revelation is not to be identified with the events as such or with any particular teachings or understandings of man in his religious relationship, important as these are. Christianity ultimately is the recognition of the historic reality of Christ: who and what He actually is, and who and what man must be as a consequence. For the Christian, the issue of revelation in terms of the human situation is clear. If man seeks fulfillment, and if this fulfillment is not simply from within himself as he is, then the basis for the fulfillment as real must somehow "come into" the process of human existence. If there is to be fulfillment it necessarily must be real for man as man is, and hence it must be an actual historic fulfillment taking place in a human manner. In other words, human fulfillment in an Absolute must take place through a human. And if this has not taken place through Jesus of Nazareth, then it must take place through someone else, some real human being, if it is to take place at all. Christianity sees itself as a historic religion not simply in the sense of being founded within a period of recorded chronological history but as historic in the ultimate meaning that man as he really is can have.

This Christian consciousness of revelation as theophany calls for a continuing dynamism in the affirmation that God as He is in Himself is always unknowable but in Christ is known through the *human* reality of Jesus. In the historic development of Christian thought, especially in the formal theological traditions, the full impact of the paradox tends to be lost. Sometimes the paradox is simply ignored, and the crucial balance in the insight of the primitive period is all but forgotten. And popular Christianity in almost all of its many forms has little or no awareness of this central ambiguity. In the context of certain contemporary theological developments and their popularization it is interesting to note how often an almost violent reaction occurs against the serious proposal of ineffability especially when there is the further proposal to carry the implications to their logical conclusions. With the present popular reemphasis on Scripture and the new attempts being made to develop a complete Scriptural theology, the serious assertion of the ineffability of God is even countered with the criticism that the assertion is not itself biblically based! There is no doubt that the strong statement of the paradox can be quite disturbing especially for a simplified theological approach, systematic or popular. Yet even a rather superficial acquaintance with Pauline or Johannine literature should be sufficient demonstration of a Scriptural basis for the problem as one which must be faced within the Christian tradition.

The principal developments of systematized Christian theology have always expressed the paradox, however they have treated its implications. In the Eastern tradition the so-called negative theology of John Chrysostom takes up the paradox boldly, and simply does not allow for an undercutting of ineffability by denying the possibility of any positive conceptualization of Divinity. Chrysostom's intellectual commitment has a profound influence on all future development of the Eastern tradition, even though the full impact of his so-called negativism is often somewhat obscured. Of the Eastern Fathers, Chrysostom is the most cited in the west, his negative theology is known, but for the most part westerners tend to ignore what Chrysostom recognized.

If we look to Thomas Aquinas as the western theologian most

committed to the development of systematized thought prior to the Renaissance, we will find an enlightening but all too often ignored dimension of his insight. He is keenly aware of the intellectual problem raised by the assertion of ineffability. But he wishes to achieve a balance between this and the western intellectual heritage of positive philosophical statement. Thus, rather than following the technique of negative expression characteristic of Chrysostom, Thomas uses positive expression but carefully establishes a proper negative norm for the evaluation of theological language.

In the opening sections of the *Summa Theologiae* Thomas sets forth several principles for the interpretation of the conceptual structure he will use in systematizing the Christian tradition. He proposes these considerations as derived from reason and hence as providing a proper key for the meaningful use and understanding of language. Whatever one might think of the derivation of these principles philosophically, they provide us with a fairly clear understanding of his insight into the limits of religious knowledge.

Enunciated as a fundamental principle Thomas asserts without reservation that what God is is unknowable:

> "The Nature of God, however, cannot be seen by any created similitude (that is, concept) representing the Divine Nature itself as it really is." (S. Th., Pt. I, Q. 12, A. 2)

If he follows this principle rigorously, then the many concepts he advances concerning divine nature are simply positive statements used to express a negative theology. If a concept cannot represent the divine nature as it is then, logically, theological concepts of God are advanced to represent the divine nature *as it really is not!*—and hence actually to represent man related to God, the human and hence knowable dimension of religious knowledge. Some object to this interpretation of Thomas' principle as too rigorous, but other related texts from the early sections of the *Summa* carry forward its logical implications. Thus, Thomas identifies Divinity as existence, asserting that in God the Divine Nature is the Divine Existence. (S. Th., Pt. I, Q. 3, A. 4). To emphasize this assertion he makes explicit the absoluteness intended in the term *Divine Existence* with the statement, "God is not a being but being itself." (*Liber de Causis*: VI). This is further extended by the meanings given to other possible attributions. Thus, not only is the Divine Nature the Divine Existence, but the Divine Intellect and the Divine Will are also completely identical in themselves with the

Divine Existence. Hence Thomas has radically altered a previous pattern of western language by reducing four vocabulary elements to one meaning: Existence, Nature, Intellect, and Will mean *Existence*. (*S.Th.,* Q. 19, A. 1).

If we proceed on the basis of these fundamental statements through the development of the *Summa,* the theological system will be observed to be completely consistent in elaborating the implications of its first principles. In terms of language and its use in interpretation in theology, Thomas attempted and achieved the development of a conceptually positive expression of a negative theology. For the theological historian, however, the general failure of Thomists to recognize this is perhaps more remarkable than the system itself. And so at the Reformation Period, for example, the later Scholastics became embroiled in the famous Grace Controversy with two opposed factions explaining human election to Salvation as determined either by an act of the Divine Will or by an act of the Divine Intellect, apparently forgetting that Thomas' identification of Intellect and Will with Divine Existence reduced both positions to linguistic nonsense.

As a final example drawn from western Christianity, the theological developments of the Reformation Period bring a new emphasis to the paradox as a central issue. Calvin's biblically oriented theology, to cite but one of the several major creative theologians of Protestant Christianity, places a strong emphasis on the recognition of God as completely mysterious and yet as revealed through his Word. When Calvin speaks of the Divinity as such, it is always in terms of the Divine Majesty. This designation is the insistence of the Absoluteness of God, the trancendence with its infinite gulf separating man. For Calvin, we can speak only of the "infinite fullness of God" (*Institutes,* Book I: 1: 1). In thus speaking, we are not expressing knowledge of God but rather we "acknowledge that in the Lord alone are to be found true wisdom, solid strength, perfect goodness and unspotted righteousness" (*ibid*). The reflection of the Divine Majesty is to be found throughout the universe in that all things as creatures bear the imprint of the Creator. However, knowledge of God through creatures does not reveal what God is in Himself, but reveals the relationship of total subjection of creature to Creator. This is, again, an acknowledgement rather than knowledge.

Yet this is not even possible for man as he is due to the depravity of man's fallen nature. The revelation of God in Christ as Redeemer enables man to acknowledge the relationship of creature to Creator and, of course, further enlightens man as to God's will for him and the way of life for the elect. For our purpose the important point to note is the prominence given to the assertion of God as unknowable. This particular approach has insured only a formal theological place for the paradox but generally not popular awareness on the level of individual religious consciousness.

VIII

This review of some of the major areas of man's religious development has taken up only one issue in a highly simplified (but, hopefully, not oversimplified) manner. Although this issue is of great importance in the consideration of several fundamental questions facing the study of religion today, such as that of convergence, the purpose of the review in the present context of theology is to delineate a crucial area of data which must be taken into account in any attempt to formulate a meaningful definition of theology and an understanding of the function of theology in the overall process of knowing. Hence this review is not designed to "prove" anything, but it does lay the groundwork for a structuring of theology which can overarch the boundaries separating most systems of theology and religious traditions.

Working solely from what we can observe in the continuing paradoxical treatment of the *theos*-category on the part of actual systems, we must come to the following conclusions, subjectively independent of the various separate traditions in which we as individuals stand.

First, the variety in the conceptualizations proposed comes from a wide range of factors in the individual tradition. Although the concepts proposed are proposed *because of religious experience*, the particular characteristics of the concepts do not derive from the experience itself (inevitably described as mysterious) but from the context in which the experience occurs, the context which necessarily embraces the entire range of our consciousness. Thus, the actual conceptual content being proposed is not valid simply because the religious experience is valid. The variety in theological expression must be accounted for by the range of materials which go to form the consciousness of the individuals who become involved in what they identify as unknowable. Theological content must pass the same judgment we make in all the areas of our consciousness: how realistically does it express a human relationship which is real, which occurs in a real context, and which must be really communicable if it is to be thought of as meaningful?

The second conclusion is intimately related to the first, namely, that the validity of the religious experience and hence of the recognition of mystery, ineffability, does not depend upon the way in which it is conceived. If the religious experience occurs, it occurs whether or not we have any way of accounting for it afterwards. If it is an actual experience then we can attempt to understand it or explain it but this can never "explain it away." Thus, if we say that the religious experience is expressive of one or another psychic need, this might well give some understanding of the context of its occurrence, but it cannot deny the occurrence as such. Ultimately the question comes down to one facing all scientific inquiries: human experience of something takes place, the data to be studied; observable characteristics of the experience are analyzed and we attempt to establish relationships with other areas of our experience; but the conceptual representation of the experience and the formulated relationships are not the experience. Put another way, a theory advanced to provide an understanding of observed experience cannot be valid if it first calls for the denial of the data supposedly being studied.

Therefore we must make an adequate distinction between the problem of conceptualization and the inner experiential factor which together form the paradox of the *theos*-category. And as in the case of every paradox both components must be adequately maintained in the same context of their occurrence, lest we do the impossible and resolve the paradox.

There is a third and most important conclusion drawn from the first two taken together. Theology as a process of knowledge dealing with the religious experience in the context of an identifiable tradition does not deal with the *theos*-category directly but only relationally. That is, because of a particular kind of human experience, a complex of relationships arises and is conceptualized within an actual historic setting. But our observation shows us that that towards which the relationship is oriented is unknown—unknowable—in terms of the actual knowing process, and hence a theological system, as a system of knowing, does not actually take account of the terminus of the orientation. Implicit in this recognition is the judgement that theology cannot even deal with the religious relationship as terminating in an object, an entity, an item of any sort. If it were to do so then we would be faced with a clear contradiction rendering all theological language nonsense, namely, in asserting that that which the *theos*-category stands for is genuinely unknowable, there would have to be the simultaneously contradictory assertion that it is nonetheless known to be an object in a human subject-object relationship or an entity, whatever kind, or an item among items. The assertion *ineffability* admits of no degrees.

Theology deals with a human subject in a particular kind of relationship. Because the human is in a line of experience we identify as religious he relates himself in a particular way to everyone and everything else. The consciousness of the religious experience terminates in the affirmation of *unknowing,* but this must not be violated by transforming the termination of the *consciousness* into an object corresponding to a subject.

Perhaps it is in this consideration that the real significance of the so-called negative theology can be seen when it insists on the assertion of the Sacred and refuses all conceptualizations. Here also we can see something of the proper impact intended by Aquinas in the statement "God is not a being but being itself."

If we accept the logic which insists that the *theos*-category does not represent an object of any sort, then what is it for theology, what is it that specifies theology as a discipline? According to what has been developed above, the *theos*-category is expressive of a particular kind of relationship of which man is conscious and which he attempts to conceptualize. The universal effect of the experience upon man is that he sees himself in a particular kind of relationship with other men and his world. He specifies this relationship in two ways. On the one hand he relates the content of his entire life to whatever ultimate significance the experience of the sacred may have. On the other hand, in the mysteriousness of the Sacred, he perceives that the religious relationship is somehow *definitive*—definitive in the impact of what the Sacred is upon his consciousness and definitive in contrast to all other relationships. Both dimensions of definitiveness are rooted in the same experience but concentration upon that which reflects the Sacred in consciousness leads to mysticism, while concentration upon that which expresses the correlation of human relationships leads to theology. The former calls for the continuing assertion of ineffability in religion, while the latter allows man to attempt to relate the significance of religion as experiential to everything else in his life, hopefully to find a meaning for each area of relationship and an overarching meaning for the entire process of existence.

IX

At this point it is at last possible to offer a definition of theology. It must be born in mind, of course, that this definition is formulated within the orientation developed here and thus is valid for that orientation if it is self-consistent, regardless of the judgment passed on the orientation itself. Also this is proposed as a general definition of theology and thus any one theological tradition would require particular specification of historic context if this definition is to be applied meaningfully. Within these limitations, theology can be defined as *the systematization of man's experience of definitive relationship.*

Systematization presumes that the theological enterprise is basically intellectual. It is concerned with man as religious, but it is not itself a religious act. As a specified area in the knowing process it must reflect adequately the characteristics appropriate to knowledge. Rigorously pursued, this should itself guarantee the continuity of theology with the other branches of knowledge, a continuity often sacrificed or ignored in the past and whose restoration has become such a contemporary preoccupation.

It is the systematization of man's experience, and therefore it must deal with man as he actually is. Thus the struggle to establish our full recognition of man as individual and social, and the realization that these two dimensions constitute a dynamic complementarity rather than a tension threatening one or the other are issues proper to theology itself. Theology must reflect the on-going character of man's experience and not be caught in the error of presuming that experience from the past can be transmitted adequately to the present or future. Theology must deal with the perplexing fact that meaningful continuity is possible since the understanding of experience is communicable, yet change must occur in the very communication, and further experience precludes any closed system.

In the systematization of man's experience of definitive relationship theology at all times must deal with the fundamental paradox so often stressed here by limiting its attempts to systematize to the observable relationship which actually occurs in men. It is the definitiveness of this relationship as contrasted with the relativity of all others which guarantees that theology will remain oriented towards the full reality at the root of the experience even though it is inconceivable. Focused upon the definitiveness of the relationship, theology will also remain in communication with the rest of knowledge built around the attempt to articulate man's meaning.

Specific theological systems, since they reflect the religious traditions which give rise to them, embody the particular characteristics of these traditions as well as reflect a wide range of factors operative within the socio-cultural context. Religious traditions heavily dependent upon historic personages and events will necessarily be represented by theological systems which emphasize concepts relating the definitiveness of the relationship as concretely experienced. Traditions centered upon symbol and myth involvement will develop theological systematization appropriately ignoring narrative history. The specific characteristics of each theological system will be understood properly only in terms of the total religious tradition in which it arises. Regardless of conceptualization, however, we will observe, as a basic unitive factor among them all, the insistence that man recognize that there is a type of relationship in his life which overrides all others, which represents ultimate values and which somehow embodies his own real significance and that of everything else, and thus is ineffably "other."

If our concern for the nature and function of theology calls for a traditional evaluation of theology as a science, we must insist on a formulation which is continuous with the other varieties of knowing designated sciences. Although this might seem obvious, at least in the west, we have witnessed a long and meaningless struggle between theologians and scientists accidentally, but effectively, cut off from one another. Theologians too often have insisted that theology is some sort of super-science overriding the other, lower sciences and that theology is called to sit in judgment upon their findings and very principles. Conceived of as the *science of God,* the scientist has been called upon to submit to a higher authority of theological judgment in virtually every apparent conflict. On the other side, scientists have all too often lost sight of the fact that science is not an abstraction and cannot be hypostatized, but must always be recognized as the on-going process of human knowing. As such, science must be seen as continuous with all other aspects of knowing, including the systematized attempt to know something of the significance of religious experience in both the individual occurrence and the continuing and elaborated occurrence of historic social religion.

Only insofar as theology is recognized as a systematization of human experience can it be thought of as a science among the other sciences. There is no other basis for the scientific character of theology (even for those who would insist that theology must be the "queen of sciences"). The continuity of theology with the other sciences is not to be *achieved* or *restored,* it is simply a self-demonstrated fact if it shares the characteristics which constitute any branch of learning as a science. On this issue a comparison of apparent extremes will provide sufficient demonstration. Are theology and physics sciences together? Although he does not address himself to this question, the renowned physicist Niels Bohr in the introductory essay in *Atomic Theory and the Description of Nature* (1961, Cambridge Edition) clearly stands in the affirmative if the fundamental structure of theology is a systematization of human experience.

He says, first of all,

> "The task of science is both to extend the range of our experience and to reduce it to order, ... Only by experience itself do we come to recognize those laws which grant us a comprehensive view of the diversity of phenomena. As our knowledge becomes wider, we must always be prepared, therefore, to expect alterations in the points of view best suited to the ordering of our experience .... all new experience makes its appearance within the frame of our customary points of view and forms of perception." (p. 1)

Science, thus, is both an ordering and extension of experience. Investigation of the experience results in a recognition of patterns allowing us to erect a structure, theory, and law. However this itself extends the pattern of experience, and hence new experience occurs within the framework developed for previous experience, and this in turn brings about changes in that framework.

This process occurs in physics and clearly is the same process occurring in theology: individual religious experience and the complex traditions of such experience with their full historic contexts are brought into order, and theory and law are formulated—and always within the thrust of the on-going human historical situation.

Next Bohr States,

> in a consistent manner essential aspects of the phenomena." (p. 12)
> "... we are concerned with expedients which enable us to express

Theological systems, as in the case with physics, have taken up a variety of instruments ("expedients") in the attempt to give meaningful expression to the happenings which constitute a religious tradition. In fact, the schools of theology (or the equivalents) of all traditions are identified primarily by the type of expedient which they employ, such as the intellectual structures of philosophical systems, structures drawn from evaluations of sacred writings proper to the religious tradition, and so forth. In other words, theological systems develop around the use of *models* employed to elaborate analogies which interconnect a wide variety of experience, in much the same way that physics uses models drawn from mathematics.

Finally, Bohr adverts to the crucial problem of expression which occurs for physics in the discovery that subject and object cannot be distinguished unambiguously.

> "The impossibility of distinguishing in our customary way between physical phenomena and their observation places us, indeed, in a position quite similar to that which is so familiar in psychology where we are continually reminded of the *difficulty of distinguishing between subject and object.* It may perhaps appear at first sight that such an attitude towards physics would leave room for a mysticism which is contrary to the spirit of natural science. However, we can no more hope to attain to a clear understanding in physics without facing the difficulties arising in the shaping of concepts and in the use of the medium of expression than we can in other fields of human inquiry." (p. 15)

For theology the comparable problem is the one we have viewed at some length: the meaningfulness of proposing conceptual content for the *theos*-category while experientially negating the category as knowable.

Whatever other issues may be raised by formulating theology directly in terms of human experience in which the human can be studied in the individual and social contexts with all their ramifications, and the relationship experienced as definitive can also be studied within the context of concrete traditions, while an object as such corresponding to the human subject cannot be studied, such a formulation of theology demonstrably establishes it as a science in the same sense that other fields of knowledge are so categorized; yet it also establishes the basis for both its distinctive disciplinary requirements and its natural autonomy. Theology, thus constituted continuous with the other sciences, needs no defense for existence and needs no reconciliation. With regard to the process of the continuing convergence of knowledge, the only problem remaining for theology as such is the development of a consciousness on the part of theologians and other scientists of the *fact* of continuity, overcoming the all too understandable prejudices of the past.

X

All of the above brings us to a concluding consideration: the dynamics of theology today and for the future.

The formulation developed here for theology in its broad disciplinary meaning has been seen in terms of two complementing categories—the *logos*-category and the *theos*-category—designated according to the two elements composing the word "theology" itself. The use of these two categories has not been determined simply because of the presence of two elements constituting a time-honored word. Actually the principle factor favoring theorizing in terms of two categories is the present and predictably the future state of the other sciences in the light of their use of mathematical models. In one way or another these models are ultimately binary in character, their usefulness being determined by the dynamism set up by this bipolarity. This model structure, classically associated with modern physics, has been extended to the other natural sciences, recently and most dramatically to biology through the advances in genetics correlated with the development of computers; the binary model plays an essential role in the social, cultural, and psychological disciplines; and with the emergence of cybernetics its effects can be extended throughout the full range of human knowledge.

We have yet to explore in any depth the extension of the use of mathematical models to theology. The very suggestion of it might appear not only preposterous but also offensive to many. But insofar as theology is approached as a science in continuity with the other sciences this development seems inevitable. And it is not as untraditional as it might seem. If we think back for a moment to Aquinas' adaptation of the Aristotelian structure of hylomorphism, it is impossible to escape the recognition that this is a primitive use of a binary model. And the *Yin-Yang* Theory of ancient China is an even more striking example.

While being able to sketch only the barest outline, the structure proposed for theology in the interrelated *logos*- and *theos*-categories sets up a dialectic as a dynamic mathematical model. Further, the extension of the model into each of the two categories sets up a further dialectic. The dynamics of the *logos*-category occurs in the relationship of man as an individual to man as social, the basis for the singularity of the religious experience as it actually occurs within any one person and the unity of the effects of such singular experience in the development of the religious tradition in which many individuals participate as socially united, communicating and evolving the meaning of the experience. Within the *theos*-category there is a dialectical relationship between the proposition of concrete conceptual content and the experiential recognition that that which this category embraces is unknowable, dynamically allowing and calling for a wide range of meaning, ultimately the basis for religious communication and convergence on any level—including the universal convergence towards which we now seem to be drawn.

The effects of this complex dialectical process are yet to be explored. The exploration has begun, commonly spoken of as the dialogue situation, and yet we must be frank in recognizing that it is still at its most primitive stage. As a socio-cultural phenomenon of religion, dialogue up to this point has meant primarily the very important but only preparatory phase of social interchange whereby, emotionally, theological interchange could take place. From the vantage point of this presentation of the situation of theology it is evident that the word "dialogue" has two quite different meanings. Dialogue, as used up to this point, designates the attempt of men to talk *to* one another. Communication in this instance is basically informational, an exchange of previously derived meanings, derived in isolation, not experientially shared, and therefore not fully communicable.

Dialogue can also mean talking *with* one another—a situation of *community* in which individuals are already constituted in a social relationship and hence are undergoing new experience in which they are further formed and which becomes the basis for completely open communication. If religious convergence is to occur it will do so only insofar as united experience occurs. If theological interchange is to be significant it will be so as it systematizes this united experience. The new experience and the new meaning will not be brought about by a fusion of the past experiences of isolation. Recalling again the expressions used by Bohr, the old isolated experiences constitute the framework of our customary points of view and previously established forms of perception; the new experience makes its appearance here and not only must not be identified with it but also must be recognized as the very force of change.

It seems self-evident to say that the dialogue situation for the convergence of the religious traditions and hence the formation of theological systems reflecting this new experience is still confined to the preliminary interchange—we are at most talking *to* one another, not *with* one another. It also seems clear that this preliminary phase has accomplished all that it can apart from further popularization. If religious convergence is an historic process moving towards fulfillment, the new unified experience must now begin to take place. This suggests a question which must be asked and faced seriously by individual men and their institutional forms of religious and theological tradition: are we truly serious about the process of convergence as a reality; do we seek this new dimension of experience?

Of the many hundreds of institutional forms of religion, hardly any as yet are consciously prepared for the full meaning of convergence, and of course none are provided with leadership whose thinking has been formed within this experiential unity. As yet the intellectual institutions directly related to the religious traditions as the formative agents for intellectual leadership have not moved into the mature dialogic situation. Interchanges of great importance take place between individuals and on a limited basis within the framework of the intellectual institutions. Conferences to promote exchange are important sources of stimulation but cannot themselves form on-going communities of knowledge. And this is precisely what must occur for the revolutionary new stage to take place.

Theological knowledge like all knowledge occurs within community, that is, occurs as individuals undergo shared experience, find ways to articulate this experience, and settle upon patterns expressive of mutual understanding. This process is not one of the exchange of ideas but of the shared formation of ideas. If a situation of unity is to develop the intellectual leadership, both technical and popular, must be formed in the same experience.

All of this means much more than the grouping of individuals representing the wide range of differing traditions. It must also involve significantly the convergence of the major areas of our knowing. It is not accidental, for example, that some of the most controversial developments taking place currently in western religion should derive from sources not usually associated with scriptural, patristic, or theological foundations. The influences coming to bear most vitally have their origins in social and cultural change, the deepening of insight into the human psyche, involvement in the existential community, and so on. As always, anything happening in human experience happens within the full context of that experience. If something new is now happening, it must be met institutionally as well as individually on its own terms. If it is to be understood, it must be known from the *inside,* that is, it must be experienced. We must therefore look forward to the coming revolution not as an abstraction but as an involvement. And the intellectual breakthrough whereby the involvement can take place will occur when an institution sees itself in terms of the community of experience—the actual origin of every institutional form we now have—and commits itself concretely to its real situation.

Confucius as a proto-theologian spoke with great meaning for our time. In the concept of *jen,* he saw the dynamism of what man does and what man is, the dialectical complementarity of individual and society, and the manifestation of what is definitive in individual relativity. The *Tao* of Heaven and the *Tao* of Man constitute the unknowable and yet there is a reflectivity in man's consciousness of relatedness. The full significance of theology seen as completely within the human community—*the situation of theology*—is perhaps best expressed by Confucius' teaching on the nature of the Great Learning:

> "What the Great Learning teaches is: to manifest illustrious virtue, to renew the people and to rest in the highest excellence. The point where to rest being known, the object of pursuit is then determined and, that being determined, a calm unperturbedness may be attained. To that calmness there will succeed tranquil repose. In that repose there may be careful deliberation. And that deliberation will be followed by attainment." (*The Great Learning,* text)

EPILOGUE

These concluding paragraphs will hardly claim the right to summarize the matchless intellectual harvest so bountifully displayed in the preceding chapters, nor do they aspire to crystallize the lively conference discussion that followed in the plenary sessions. The intention at this final stage is a modest one. It draws attention to three major categories of the anthology in its direct bearing upon treatment of the subject.

Emphasis is to be laid, firstly, upon certain salient vistas of understanding toward which the history of religions seems to draw our attention. The object lesson is unmistakable that the status of world scholarship in the field will never be the same again.

Secondly, in a more verifiable fashion, an appendix is presented for conceivable use as an integrating format. The plan of operations proposed is obviously subject to drastic revision and critical comment. Yet reproduced in facsimile is an outline of what was actually presented for discussion at the conference table. Attached are names of persons who concerted their efforts in an organized endeavor under formal stipulations of an agenda. A methodology is thus interposed. It emerges as a possible channel of discourse among members who informally represent a plurality of cultural opinions and a diversity of religious beliefs. Hence the setting for imaginative involvement culminating in a unique experience of convergence. Such a gathering of scholars figuratively takes on certain attributes of religious pluralism and world community.

Thirdly, several crucial facets of this creative interchange are set forth. Meaningfully interwoven in each instance are the norms, criteria, and findings of theology and the history of religions. Unresolved hermeneutical issues are at least braved if not transcended. New strategies of contact and conversation spur exploration. A more catholic phase of theological reform and rehabilitation begins to take visible form.

I

New horizons beckon as modern man revises former conceptions of his manhood and the world he lives in, of his faith and the theogonies he once tenaciously held. Alfred North Whitehead said in *Adventures of Ideas* [1], "Progress of religion is defined by the denunciation of gods. The keynote of idolatry is contentment with the prevalent gods."

More meaningful episodes are currently in progress as strides are taken toward affirmation of the goals of being and becoming. Minds are troubled for dearth of freedom. Theirs is a keen option for liberation, among other things, from a redundantly drab traditionalism and the insidious temptation to embroider embroidery. [2] They yearn to be rid of an incestuous obsession with the wearisome routines of myth, cult, and rite.

Demand for reform steadily mounts. At times it acquires the dimensions of a ruthless bellicosity. The call is blatant for an order of rationality and credibility that carries greater conviction. In their own style, modern humanism and secularism promise to make all things better and more pleasant. Measures are taken that seem refreshingly justified. They vie with the once heralded patterns of traditionally redemptive grace. In their disavowal of sham and pretension, the new vogues stand resplendent in their integrity.

Evidence meanwhile piles up to prove a contrary viewpoint. After all repetitious and silly patter has subsided, an abiding faith remains. It is resilient as man's solitary focus of religious enthusiasm. It mellows and deepens across the years. Whereas many a myth and symbol, shrine and temple, have fallen into lamentable disarray, faith has built its stately mansions. It has not wavered in urging the believer to climb every mountain and to vanquish every foe of the spirit and truth. Faith defies reductionist postulates. It outlives dialectical verbosity. It is a light which steadily shines brighter unto the more perfect day.

Such a deep-seated faith sharpens in man an eagerness for involvement. This is primarily a passionate attachment to whatever he deems ultimate and indubitably final in its claims as well as absolute in its impact and sovereignty. Here is the groundwork of man's unerring partiality to this or that idol before which he bends the knee. Yet he is patently torn asunder by a dreadful insecurity. Concern over his fate leaves him utterly helpless. Consisting in both physical and mental anguish, such a malaise will at times worsen into crushing hysterical and suicidal syndromes. Harvey Cox [3] sees, however, in the events

---

[1] New York, 1933, p. 12.

[2] Samuel H. Miller, *The Dilemma of Modern Belief: The Lyman Beecher Lectures*, Yale Divinity School, New York, 1963, p. 102.

[3] *The Secular City: Secularization and Urbanization in Theological Perspectives*, New York, 1966, pp. 225, 233.

that would take place in the future a metaphysical answer to the problems of the modern world. There have always been important similarities, he reminds his reader, between biblical faith and atheism as contrasted, for example, to belief in demons and spirits.

Beyond the varieties of religious experience cited by William James, and others, there is a candid yet persistently critical voice. It arises to challenge the truncated and rickety structure of any incoherent faith. James himself formulated a rather comprehensive conception of religion: "The feelings, acts, and experiences of individual men in their solitude so far as they apprehend themselves to stand in relation to whatever they may consider the divine. [1]

But the challenge confronting religion is by no means an outcome of the permissive/inclusive definition advanced by William James. A formidable stricture is rather inherent in the resolve to test and reject every unwarranted caricature of religious reality. Even more vigilantly, the modern mind sets up standards of historical criticism sharpened by the cutting edges of agnosticism and skepticism.

Hence the drastic evaluations of what constitutes genuinely "religious" phenomena and unalloyed faith. The depth psychologist must insist on a reckoning with the conscious: religious faith must manifest evidence of an encounter with and a response to ultimacy in psychoanalytical terms. Such a requirement has in fact been validated and made explicit in the concreteness of persons reborn and in character formation. It is made palpable in the objectively studied experience of the person attesting that for him all things have been made new.

Such an objectively studied experience is for the man of faith climaxed in victory over anxiety, suffering, and the fear of mortality. Faithfulness in this sense is a power that will match the sting of death and defy the inroads of an ironical tragedy. It is vibrant in the courage to be. In the drive to become something more distinctive than ordinary mundane humanity is capable of, it adds a crowning dimension to the personality. Thanks to this conception of faith, personality adds up to something infinitely more significant than the aggregate of scientifically computed traits. More than environmental forces apparently mold homo sapiens.

If he conducts his research with circumspection, the historian of religions will render a contribution of first magnitude as he reckons with man and ponders his faith. While extremely sensitive to theolog-

---

[1] William James, *Varieties of Religious Experience,* New York, 1911. p. 34.

ical responsibility, his is an independence from provincialism and a forthright enmeshment in the faith of other men. With a little luck, he might offer a possible alternative to theology. This is never merely a matter of operational techniques. Both minimally and maximally, it demands taking the mystery of faith seriously—in all its cosmic connotations and theological implications.

This is the new emphasis and these are the suggestive vistas, providing the historian of religions with his strategic key. Although bound by his own confessional bias, as are all men of faith, the historian of religions breathes the fresh air of openness and subjective/objectivity. He sets dogmatics and apologetics, systematics and polemics where they belong—within the framework of every faith known to him, where they exist, and therefore in the context of the truth itself wherever accessible.

II

In order to set the record straight, identities of those who staged this encounter of cultures and faiths are reproduced below. They symbolize in miniature a world come of age. Also personified are certain implications of religious pluralism and world community. Cited hereunder is (a) the primary cadre of personnel, (b) as members of the advisory and administrative committees, and (c) as participants in program development.

(a) The Second Edward F. Gallahue Conference on World Religions, Princeton Theological Seminary, May 4-11, 1966.

Participants:

Andrew L. Alföldi
Institute for Advanced Study

Philip H. Ashby
Princeton University

John S. Badeau
Columbia University
New York, N.Y.

Shojun Bando
Otani University
Kyoto, Japan

C. J. Bleeker
University of Amsterdam
Amsterdam, The Netherlands

Samuel W. Blizzard
Princeton Theological Seminary

S. G. F. Brandon
University of Manchester
Manchester, England

Wing-tsit Chan
Dartmouth University
Hanover, N. H.

Kenneth Ch'en
Princeton University

Kiyoko Taketa Cho
Princeton University

Bernard J. Cooke
Marquette University
Milwaukee, Wisconsin

Gerald Cooke
Bucknell University
Lewisburg, Pennsylvania

Bayard Dodge
The American University
Beirut, Lebanon

Howard R. Dressner
The Ford Foundation
New York, N.Y.

Abdul M. El-Biali
The Islamic Center
Washington, D.C.

Ismail Faruqi
Syracuse University
Syracuse, N.Y.

Louis Finkelstein
Jewish Theological Seminary
New York, N.Y.

Charles T. Fritsch
Princeton Theological Seminary

H. C. Ganguli
University of Delhi
Delhi, India

George S. Hendry
Princeton Theological Seminary

Norvin J. Hein
Yale University
New Haven, Connecticut

Seward Hiltner
Princeton Theological Seminary

Philip K. Hitti
Princeton University

Marius B. Jansen
Princeton University

K. N. Jayatilleke
University of Ceylon
Peradeniya, Ceylon

Edward J. Jurji
Princeton Theological Seminary

Ali Abdel Kader
The Islamic Center
Washington, D.C.

Hugh T. Kerr
Princeton Theological Seminary

Joseph M. Kitagawa
University of Chicago

James Kritzeck
Secretariat for Non-Christian Religions
Vatican City, Rome

Richard Lancaster
Meridian Street Methodist Church
Indianapolis, Indiana

James N. Lapsley
Princeton Theological Seminary

James E. Loder
Princeton Theological Seminary

William Loos
Council on Religion and International Affairs
New York, N.Y.

James I. McCord
Princeton Theological Seminary

Vincenzo Miano
Secretariat for Non-Believers
Vatican City, Rome

Kenneth W. Morgan
Colgate University
Hamilton, N.Y.

William C. Mounts
Westminster Presbyterian Church
Knoxville, Tennessee

Robert P. Murray
The Aquinas Institute
Princeton, New Jersey

K. Srirama Murti
Member of the Legislature
State of Andhra Pradesh, India

K. S. Murty
Andhra University
Waltair, South India

Hajime Nakamura
University of Tokyo
Tokyo, Japan

Willard G. Oxtoby
Yale University
New Haven, Connecticut

Charles Pellat
University of Paris
Paris, France

Fazlur Rahman
Central Institute
of Islamic Research
Karachi, Pakistan

Richard C. Raines
Bishop of the Methodist Church
Indianapolis, Indiana

Annemarie Schimmel
University of Bonn
Bonn, Germany

Albert L. Schlitzer
University of Notre Dame
South Bend, Indiana

Huston Smith
Massachusetts Institute
of Technology
Boston, Massachusetts

Jonathan Z. Smith
Dartmouth University
Hanover, N.H.

Wilfred Cantwell Smith
Harvard University
Cambridge, Massachusetts

Donald K. Swearer
Oberlin College
Oberlin, Ohio

Arend T. van Leeuwen
Kerk en Wereld Institute
Driebergen, The Netherlands

G. E. von Grunebaum
University of California at Los Angeles
Los Angeles, California

Charles C. West
Princeton Theological Seminary

Robley E. Whitson
Fordham University

E. David Willis
Princeton Theological Seminary

Robert C. Zaehner
Oxford University
Oxford, England

(b) Conference Committees

Advisory

James I. McCord, chairman
Andrew L. Alföldi
James E. Andrews
Philip H. Ashby
Bayard Dodge

Seward Hiltner
Philip K. Hitti
Marius B. Jansen
Edward J. Jurji
Hugh T. Kerr

Administrative

James I. McCord, chairman
Edward J. Jurji, director
Seward Hiltner,
Hospitality chairman
James E. Andrews,
administrative assistant

Mrs. John E. Roberts, secretary
Willard G. Oxtoby, aide
Theodore G. Belote,
radio and television

(c) *Program* (Papers and discussion followed a sequence of practical convenience rather than the logical order represented in the table of contents of the book reflecting more strictly a history of religions approach and inquiry.)

Public Lecture: Wednesday, May 4, 1966, 8 : 00 p.m.
Religious Pluralism and World Community, Huston Smith, Massachusetts Institute of Technology, Campus Center Auditorium, Princeton Theological Seminary.

Conference Sessions (Participants only)

Wednesday, May 4
9.00 a.m. "A New Awareness of Time and History." Speaker: S. G. F. Brandon; Chairman: Wilfred Cantwell Smith; Commentator: Hajime Nakamura.
2.00 p.m. "The Historic Chinese Contribution to Religious Pluralism and World Community." Speaker: Wing-tsit Chan; Chairman: Philip H. Ashby; Commentators: K. S. Murty, Fazlur Rahman, Huston Smith.

Thursday, May 5
9.00 a.m. "Methodology and the Science of Religion." Speaker: C. J. Bleeker; Chairman: Joseph M. Kitagawa; Commentators: Kenneth Ch'en, W. C. Smith, R. C. Whitson.
2.00 p.m. "The Jewish Vision of Human Brotherhood." Speaker: Louis Finkelstein; Chairman: James I. McCord; Commentators; Bernard J. Cooke, H. C. Ganguli.

Friday, May 6
9.00 a.m. "The situation of Theology." Speaker: Robley E. Whitson; Chairman: Robert C. Zaehner; Commentators: Wing-tsit Chan, K. N. Jayatilleke.
2.00 p.m. "The Islamic Involvement in the Process of History." Speaker: A. H. Abdel Kader; Chairman: John S. Badeau; Commentators: Arend Theodore van Leeuwen, Charles Pellat.

Monday, May 9

9.00 a.m. "The Indian and Buddhist Concept of Law." Speaker: Hajime Nakamura; Chairman: Kenneth Ch'en; Commentator: Norvin Hein.

2.00 p.m. "Buddhist Relativity and the One World Concept." Speaker: K. N. Jayatilleke; Commentator: Kenneth Ch'en.

Tuesday, May 10

9.00 a.m. "Islam and Modern Culture." Speaker: Annemarie Schimmel; Chairman: Bernard J. Cooke; Commentators: Shojun Bando, R. E. Whitson.

2.00 p.m. "Religion and the Population Explosion." Speaker: H. C. Ganguli; Chairman: Norvin Hein; Commentators: Joseph M. Kitagawa, R. C. Zaehner.

Wednesday, May 11

9.00 a.m. "The Impact of Modernity on Islam." Speaker: Fazlur Rahman; Chairman: James Kritzeck; Commentators: Philip Ashby, W. C. Smith.

2.00 p.m. "History, Historical Consciousness and Freedom." Speaker: K. S. Murty; Chairman: R. E. Whitson; Commentators: S. G. F. Brandon, Hajime Nakamura, W. C. Smith.

"By Way of Summing Up." Speaker: W. C. Smith; Chairman: G. E. von Grunebaum.

III

Informed by this involvement of the several faiths and cultures, and enlightened by their projected guidelines for desegregation, the history of religions establishes an interdisciplinary juncture with theology. Illustrative of the new trend is a hermeneutical development. It gravitates toward four principal objectives where radical change is in the offing. These are the objectives of ultimacy and ecumenicity, of transcendence and incarnation.

1. On ultimacy, a dire need arises for what is identifiable as a cosmic rather than particular concern with finality. The reason is not far to seek why change in our conception of ultimacy is mandatory. It stems in part from the fact that atheism is here to stay as are the closely related phenomena of secularism and demysticizing. Since these

press a worldwide thrust, response to them must embody the universal spirit of mankind rather than a limited western outlook.

International democracy and emancipation of men and peoples await observance of certain pertinent criteria. These embrace the apprehension of religious phenomenology that the dimension of ultimacy encompasses not just the faiths of the western world but those of the East and of the rest of the planet too. Another criterion is derivative from the very concept of world community. It seems to be contingent in part upon an idea of God commensurate with the universal gospel of reverence for reverence. A third criterion is implicit in a reciprocity which takes into account this selfsame variability in notions of ultimacy—current among followers of many creeds or none—and seeks enrichment thereby.

2. An ecumenicity rightly so called is a longing for togetherness on a world-community basis. Derived from the Greek oikos, house, the word designates the "inhabited world" as if it were one great "household." In this sense, oikoumenē occurs in many New Testament passages. But this luminous objective encounters stubborn resistance of those who deprecate measures that might resolve the problem of the one and the many.

Whereas this age generally depreciates theological polemics, modern hermeneutical revival looks to theological dialogue for potent reenforcement. More vibrantly articulate, however, in dealing with the intricacies of the one and the many is engagement in authentic deliberative meditation. By now, interfaith communication is a well-established activity. It is a by-product of the historical study of religion spearheaded by the scientific methods of phenomenology. But its profound relevance awaits the perfection of more adequate techniques in the advanced stages of meditative partnership. When the ineffability of the truth draws men, different in religious and social backgrounds, its anthropological manifestation in man and community becomes irrationally rational.

In the light of this genuine meditative ecumenicity, coercive apologetic modes of interpretation prove counter-productive. They fail to yield a meaningful result in the contemplation of the one and the many. Such a futility is somewhat comparable to that of the medieval crusades. The latter failed to provide at the point of the sword a commonground of East/West interchange and creative involvement. The nineteenth-century missionary enterprise, although altruistic in fundamental motivation, perhaps unwittingly identified itself with an antithetical western exploitative machinery. What collapsed eventually was this false image rather than missionary love itself.

Certain contemporary strategists of evangelism are unduly carried away, nonetheless, by modern eficiency and secularism, technology and science. So enamored are they by these things that they advocate their deployment as vehicles of Prophetic proclamation. [1] Such a proposal seems to miss the point of an ecumenicity aware of the importance of the one and the many as the primary item of business in this interfaith and intercultural realm. [2]

3. As for transcendence, a postulate that is self-explanatory might serve as a point of departure: the autonomy of a faith in solid rapport with culture, science, and philosophy cannot be exaggerated. James B. Conant, [3] in company with William James and Sir Arthur Eddington, argued for a synthesis in the realm of culture. He was persuaded that more adequate understanding was attainable through three channels: scientific, philosophical, and religious. Those are the principal avenues of vitality for the sensitive seeker after a lofty view of transcendence.

Inevitably, however, religious anthropology confronts a human faith transcending any such cultural and societal perception of reality. Under exhaustive inquiry, the history of religions yields keen insight into the ineffability of the objects of faith. The idea of the Holy is simply irreducible to scientific, philosophic, or theological laws and concepts.

Above all else, faith breaks through involvement. Thereby new resources of interpretation are released. A world perspective is projected which ineluctably distinguishes between means and ends. On life's arduous trails, it holds out the promises of a purposeful ascendancy of meaning, hope, and joy. Those are the irreducible solvents of a transcendence attaching a sui generis character to religion and faith.

4. A final hermeneutical item is expository in nature. It centers in the theme that for those who see the light of truth in the Incarnation, interfaith solidarity and intercultural involvement appear as bits of corroborative evidence. The crux of the matter hinges on a principle enunciated by Jesus of Nazareth. The pure of heart, he

---

[1] See Arend Theodoor van Leeuwen, *Prophecy in a Technocratic Era,* New York, 1968.

[2] Cf. Wilfred Cantwell Smith, *Questions of Religious Truth,* New York, 1967, pp. 31-32.

[3] *Scientific Principles and Moral Conduct,* Cambridge, 1957.

taught, shall be blessed. They shall see (the truth of) God. Insofar as the finite intellect perceives it, such a truth is invariably relative. The truth will not disclose itself to all men in equivalent fashion, uniformly and identically.

The reality beyond our grasp is ever shrouded in obscurity. Indeed the very fact that the unfolding of religious novelty is fragmentary is because it must be gauged to the limitations of our human capacity to perceive. Yet with every purifying token of ultimate reality an element of rapturous blissful surprise accentuates man's awareness of the unknowable. Progressively and intuitively, personality is thrilled with deep emotional serenity and delight as a consciousness of quasi-ultimacy becomes real, garbed though it be with the mantle of ambivalence and beset by an elusive fluidity.

In thus elucidating the cardinal doctrine of the Incarnation, involvement merits something more than personal assent and mathematical calculation. Before the mental eye it unfurls an impulsive logic supportive of the secret intimations of a vibrant consciousness. It exhibits a compassion resonant in the self and joining in the free, untrammeled celebration of life.

Such a transcendence translating itself through incarnation is a proclamation of good news. For our time and generation, the Word becomes flesh and dwells among men—superbly in the act of faith involving us all in each other's predicaments of misery, doubt, and distance no less than in prospects of splendor, good cheer, and love. "If any man will do his will, he shall know of the doctrine (John 7: 17)." This will to be involved is symbolically the wine of brotherhood which all drink who join together in joyous expectancy. It is also figuratively but accurately the eucharist chant that lifts up the heart in a festive mood. Those are the emblems of a radical Prophetic conquest over the hosts of alienation and darkness threatening to undermine the very edifice that harmony built.

In short, victory is climaxed in resurrection—constituting man's equilibrated balance of redemptive opportunity and powerful coexistence. That is, men shall finally discover access to unfathomable resources of comfort. They shall have the benefits of revolutionary courage It is a trait born out of the gift of grace which in faith fulfills man's deepest longings—for liberation from ignorance and pride, for deliverance from the evils of lust for power. And this is what glorifies man's gallant, selfless adventures. It is a marching out toward penitence and the forgiveness of sins, made explicit in settlements of feuds and wars both at home and abroad, so that men and nations shall walk together as brothers awakened to the strength and vision of a new order of the ages.

Those are but theological trains of thought which will suffice in an epilogue dedicated to the truly elevating contributions of esteemed friends and erudite colleagues.

INDEX

ibn-ᶜAbd-al-Wahhāb, Muhammad, 249
Abdūh, Muhammad 250-262
Absolute, the 38, 41
Adam 71
adharma 135
Advaita Vedanta 147
Adventures of Ideas 298
al-Afghani, Jamaladdin, 176, 186, 250
Africa 186, 189, 191
Agha Khan 189
Ahimsa 25, 141
Ahmadiya 184, 191
Aitareya aranyaka 35
Akiba 84-89
Alföldi, A. L. 300, 302
Ali, Ameer 184, 189, 252 *sqq.*
Allah 175-192, 249-262, 282 *sqq.*
Ambedkar 47
Amitābha 57, 59
Amos 6
Analects 267 *sqq.*
Anatolia 190
Andhra, 4
Andrews, J. E. 302
Antonius Pius 85
Apocalypse of John 234
apologetic 19
Apter, D. 30
ibn-Arabi 175-176
Arabia 7, 92, 100, 187, 249, *sqq.*
Arabic 179, 182, 187, 249
Arabs 21, 93-109, 175-192, 249-262
Arab states 2, 21, 176
Arameans 6
Archbishop Michael Ramsey 214
Arjuna 230
artha 131, 134
Ashby, P. H. 300, 304
āśrama 145
Asia 10, 131-174, 195-221
Asoka 149-174
Assumption 257
Atatürk 175, 190
Ātman 159
Atomic Theory and the Description of Nature 291
Austin, J. 151
Avatar 68

Ayah 281
Ayer, A. J. 69
Ayub Khan 186, 261
Azhar 192

Babel, 20
Badeau, J. S. 300, 304
Baljon 177
Bando, S. 300, 304
al-Bannā 190
Bazzaz 186
Ben Azariah 90 *sqq.*
Ben Azzai 90 *sqq.*
Belote, T. 303
Bengal 189
Bhagavadgītā 131-174, 230, 173 *sqq.*
Bhakti 168
Bharat 186
El-Biali, A. 1, 301
Bible 182, 232
Bleeker, C. J. 13, 237-248, 300, 303
Blizzard, S. W. 300
Bodhisattva 53, 61
Bohr, Niels 291 *sqq.*
Book of Changes 121
Book of the Dead 229
Bosporus 189
Bowen, H. 96
Brahmā 161, 164
Brahmanism 144, 158
Brahmavedanam 36
Brandon, S. G. F. 13, 225-236, 300, 303, 304
British 186
Buddha 30, 43-78, 131-177
Buddhism 5, 16, 23, 43-78, 105-130, 131-174, 239, 276 *sqq.*
Burma 140

Caitanya 38
Calvin 285 *sqq.*
Carlyle, T. 184
Catholicism 18, 114-130, 263, 296
Cayce, E. 69
Ceylon 2, 77, 140
Chan, Wing-tsit 8, 9, 113, 130, 300, 303, 304
Chandrasekhar, S. 202

INDEX

Chang Jung 115, 123
Chantepie de la Saussaye, P. D. 15, 241
Ch'en, K. 300, 303, 304
Ch'eng I 124
Chiao 121
Chin dynasty 122
China 9, 10, 113-130, 149-174
Cho, K. T. 301
Chosen People 232-233
Christianity 14, 16, 113-133, 164, 212, 216, 229-236, 239, 263-296
Chrysostom, John 283 *sqq.*
Chu Hsi 124, 125
Chuang Tzu 121, 123
Church, 263-296
City of God 235
Classic of Filial Piety 115
Clive 40
Code Napoleon 106
collectivity 270
Communist 44, 113-130
community 263-296
Conant, J. B. 306
Confucianism 16, 113-130, 265-296
Confucius 113-130, 138, 265-296
Congo 237
Cooke, B. J. 11, 298, 304
Cooke, G. 301
Cox, H. 302
Cragg, K. 177, 190-191
Cromer, Lord 175
Crusades 104
Cyprus 82

Damocles 237
Dartmouth
Darul Harb 96-108
Darul Islam 96-108
dawlah 10, 177
Delhi 200, 203
Devas 142
Dhamma 49, 56, 61-78, 131, 174
Dhammapada 131-174
dharma 9, 10, 131-174
Dialogue 263-276
dīn 10, 177
Doctrine of the Mean 121
Dodge, B. 301, 302
Dōgen 155, 156
Draz, M. H. 192

Eastern Fathers 283 *sqq.*
Ecumenism 27, 305, 306

Eddington, A. 306
Egypt, 13, 186, 228-229, 250-262
eidetic 15, 242
Eliezer 90-92
Eliot, C. 49
Enlightenment 14
epoché 15, 242
Ethical Study Society 119
Ethiopians 6
exegesis 101
Exodus 232

Faruqi, I. 301
al-fatḥ al-mubīn 190
Finkelstein, L. 1, 4, 6, 79-92, 301, 303
fiqh 255
Fordham 263
Four Noble Truths 165
Frazer 225
Freud 225
Fritsch, C. T. 6, 301
fuehrerprinzip 266, 269
Fung Yu-lan 125
Fuqahāʾ 261-262
Fyzee, A. A. A. 175, 182, 191

Gallahue, E. F. 1, 18, 21, 300 *sqq.*
Gandhi 11, 40, 47, 209-221
Ganguli, H. C. 8, 11, 12, 193-221, 301, 303, 304
Ghana 22
Gibb, H. A. R. 96
Ginzberg, L. 80
Gnosticism 230
God 3, 14, 20, 56-78, 139, 164, 243, 248, 263-293
Goldziher, 100, 185
Greek 24, 191
Grotius, H. 144
Grunebaum, G. E. von 19, 302, 304

hadīth 185
Hakuin 156
Halachah 80
Hamidullah, M. 184
Hammurabi 185
Hanyü 128
Hanafi 255
Harappa 4, 39
Harvard 236
Hein, N. 301, 304
Hendry, G. 301
Heraclitus 139

hermeneutics 101
hijra 186
Hillel 80, 92
Hiltner, S. 301, 302, 303
Hinayana 46-78
Hinduism 2, 16, 21, 131, 174, 176, 193-221, 229-230, 276 *sqq.*
History 225-236
Hitler 80, 266
Hitti, P. K. 301, 302
Hiuen-Tsiang 46
Hobbes, T. 151
Hokke Sūtra 155-162
Holy War 181
hsing 123
Hsiung Shih-li 125
Hsüang-tsang 127
Husserl, E. 241-248

ᶜ*ibādāt* 182
ijmā 103
ijtihād 182, 253
Imam 186
India 2, 13, 131, 174, 176, 186-188, 193-221, 33-262
Indo-Europeans 10
Indus 39
integrity 19
intentionality 18
interpenetration 18
Iqbal, Muhammad 177-179, 183, 184, 188, 190, 195, 249-262
Iran 13, 186, 187, 189
Isaiah 6, 79-83
Īsvara 58
Isis 228
Islam 2, 7, 14, 21, 93-109, 175, 192, 211-212, 232, 239, 249-262, 80 *sqq.*
Islamic Literature 177
Islamic Research Institute 261
Ismailiya 189
Israel 6, 82-95, 233
ithna-ashariya 189

Jains 68, 143-174
Jamāᶜat-i-Islāmī 60
James, W. 299, 306
Jansen, M. 301, 302
Japan 9, 149-174
Japanese Religions 25
Javidname 188
Jayatilleke, K. N. 4, 5, 43-78, 301, 304
jen 271 *sqq.*

Jesus Christ 136, 137, 139, 163, 234, 257, 307
Jewish (Jews) 6, 16, 79-92, 233-234, 266
jihad 182, 190
Jinnah, M. A. 189
jinns 183
Johanan 91
Jomier 190
Jordan 2, 21
Joshua 91
Judaism 2, 14, 18, 79-92, 119, 234, 239, 280 *sqq.*
jumhuriya 186
Jurji, E. J. 1-20, 297-308
jus naturale 144
Justin 140

Kaᶜba 186
Kader, A. H. A. 3, 7, 93-109, 301, 304
Kaivalya
Kali 229
Kamakura 155
karma 69, 207-211
Kautilya 40
Kerr, H. T. 301-302
Khadduri, M. 96, 97
Khān, Ahmad 250-262
Khāravela 134
Kitagawa, J. 12, 301, 303
koinonia 268
Koran (al-Quran) 7, 10, 16, 95-109, 175-192, 249-262, 281 *sqq.*
Kristensen, W. B. 15, 242-248
Kritzeck, J. 301, 304
Ku Huan 122
Kumārajīvā 126

laissez-faire 266
Lambeth 214
Lancaster, R. 301
Lao Tzu 114-130, 138, 288
Lapsley, J. 301
Lebanon 216
van Leeuwen, A. T. 7, 302, 304
Legge, J. 127
Lehrbuch der Religionsgeschichte 241
Leviathan 151
Leyden 15, 241-248
Loder, J. 301
Logical Positivists 43
logos 16, 17, 20, 139, 140, 263, 296
logos spermatikos 140

INDEX

Loos, W. 301
Lotus Scripture 115
Luther, 30

Mahāvīra 143-174
Mahayana 5, 46-78, 147-174
Maimonides 83-91
Mālik 103, 255
al-Manār 182
Manchester 225
Manichaeanism 117
Manu 133-174, 208
Manual of the Heart 278
Manusmrti 40, 133-168
Marcus Aurelius 85
Marx, Karl 3
Marxism 25, 106, 265-296
Marxist 3, 4, 44
Masao, Abe 25, 26, 27
maṣlaḥa 103
Matter and Spirit 26
Maulana Azad 185
Maulana Mawdudi 188, 190
Max Müller, F. 225
McCord, J. I. 301, 303
Mecca 186
Meditation 124
Meir Simhah 83
Mencius 138
Messianic 84-92
Methodology 237-248
Miano, V. 301
Middle Ages 238
Mīmāmsā
Ming, Emperor 126
Miᶜrāj 257
Mirza Qalich Beg 188
Modernity 249-262
Mohenjodaro 4, 39
mokṣa 134
Mongol 104
monologisch 19
Morgan, K. 301
Moses 83
Mounts, W. 302
Muhammad 93-109, 183-192, 249-262
Mukti 42
Mullas 175 *sqq.* 260
Munir Report 191
Murray, R. 302
Murti, K. S. 302
Murti, T. R. V. 50
Murty, K. S. 4, 35-42, 302, 303, 304

Muslim Brethren 182
Muslim Marriage law, 261
Muslims 7, 10, 93-109, 113-130, 175-192, 249-262
Müspet Maneviyat etüdleri, 182
Muᶜtazilite 178

Nāgārjuna 155
Nakamoto Tominaga 157
Nakamura, H. 8, 9, 10, 131-174, 302, 304
naql 192
Nara College 25
nāstika 161
Nawwab Salimullah 189
Near East (Middle East) 185, 188, 249-262
Nehru, Jawaharlal 210
Neo-Taoists 117
Nestorian 117
New Testament 230 *sqq.*
New York Post 30
Newman, Cardinal 2, 21
Nichiren 155-162
Nietzsche 164
Nirvāna 51, 55, 78, 125, 138, 149-174, 275 *sqq.*
Nizamiya 190
Nkrumah 22
Nomocracy 176
Northrop, F. S. C. 131-174

oikos 305
oikoumenē 305
On Jewish Law and Lore 80
One-World concept 43-78
Origen 140
Osiris 228
Otto, R. 225
Oxtoby, W. G. 12, 302, 303

Pakistan 2, 12, 21, 175-192, 249-262
Pali 146
Pan-Islam 176, 186
Parsons, T. 207, 220
Parwez 185
Pellat, C. 302, 303
Pentateuch 83
Phenomenology 241-248
Philistines 6
Pirism 175-176, 189
Platform Scripture 124
Pluralism 113-130, 246-248

INDEX

Population explosion 193-221
Pope John 31
Pope Paul VI 11, 31
Pope Pius XII
Population 193-221
Princeton Theological Seminary 1, 17-18, 300 sqq.
Le Prophète de l'Islam 184
Protestantism 16, 18, 215, 221
Punjab 191
Pure Land 57
Purgatory 234
Pyramid Texts 228-229

Qadiani 184
Qāsim Amīn 188

Radhakrishnan, S. 27, 213
Rahman, F. 12, 13, 15, 16, 185, 302, 303, 304
Raines, R. C. 302
Ram Rajya Parishad 26-27
Ramadan 180-181
Ramakrishna Mission 27
Rāmāyana 135
Record of Buddhist Kingdoms 127
Reformation 285 sqq.
Relativity 43-78
Religion 193-221, 234-245
Ribā 261
Ricci, Matteo 128
Ridā, Muhammad Rashid 251
Roman Catholic 11, 12, 16, 17, 31, 159, 204, 221
Roman law 24
Rousseau 163-164
Rudra 229
Russia 113, 237

Sacred 288-296
Sadettin Ervin 182
St. Augustine 235
St. Paul 229, 235
Samudragupta 40
Saṅgha 150-174
Sankara 168
Sanusi 249
Satan
Satyagraha 40
Schaeder, H. H. 191
Schimmel, A. 8, 10, 11, 175, 192, 302, 304
Scripture in Forty-two Chapters 126

Shafāʿa 257
Shafei 101, 102
Shammai 80-92
sharīʿa 177, 182, 185
shaykh 176, 189
Shiʿa 182-192
Shihtsung, Emperor 117
Shingon 60
Shinran 155
Shinto 157-174
Śiva 159, 224-230
Shōtoku 150-174
Sibling 79 sqq.
Sikhs 160
Smith, H. 3, 21-31, 302, 303
Smith, J. Z. 302
Smith, W. C. 3, 61, 302, 303, 304
Smṛti 144, 146
Society of World Religions 118
Soka Gakkai 27
Spengler, O. 237
Spirit of Islam 252
Stoic 151
Sufism 189, 191
Sunnah 16, 189, 253-262
śūnyatā 50, 147
Suzuki, W. 27
Swearer, D. 302

Tagore, 302
Taḥrīr al-Marʾah 191
T'ai-wu, Emperor 117
Taika 150, 172
talfīa 255
Taʿlīmāt-i-Islāmīya 260-261
Talmud 81-92
T'ang 117
Tao 113-130, 148, 171, 269 sqq.
Tao-te-ching 115, 123, 274 sqq.
Taoism 16, 105-130, 274 sqq.
taqlid 182
tasavvuf 189
tathatā
tawakkul 176
tawḥīd 176
Tendai 60, 155-162
Texas 18
Theodorus 163
theology 263-296
theos 16, 17, 263-296
Theravāda 53-59, 64, 165
Thomas Aquinas 284 sqq.
Tibet 47, 154

Tillich, P. 21, 48-54, 243-248
Time 225-236
Tokyo 2, 8, 9, 10
Torah 83-84
Toynbee, A. 21
Transcendent 4, 36, 41, 42
Troeltsch, E. 16, 17
Truth 20
tulūᶜul-Islām 185
Tunisia 181
Turkey 15, 175-192, 249-262
Turks 175-192, 258
Tylor, E. B. 225

U Thant 31
Ulama 249-262
Underdeveloped 196 *sqq.*
United Nations 17, 21, 31, 43
Untermensch 269
Upanishads 168

Vaisnavite 47, 68
Varna 145
Varuna 133, 229
Vatican II 11, 16, 28
Vedas 146, 164
Vedānta 168
Vietnam 23, 31, 238
Vinaya 137, 140
Vishnu 159, 168, 229, 230

Wahhabi 182
Wang Fu 115
Weber, M. 76, 220
Wechsler, J. 31
Weltanschauung 184, 235
West, C. 302
Whitehead, A. N. 14, 27, 302
Whitson, R. E. 13, 16, 17, 263-296, 302, 303, 304
Willis, E. W. 302
World War I 237
World War II 12
Wu, Emperor 116

Yahweh 232, 233
Yale 12
Yatīm 255
Yeats, W. B. 227
Yin-yang 293 *sqq.*
yoga 146, 148
yugas 153

Zaehner, R. E. 3, 26, 302, 304
zakāh 254
Zen 27, 49, 63, 124, 149, 174
Zia Gökalp 188
Zoroaster (Zarathustra) 185, 245, 279 *sqq.*
Zoroastrian 16, 117, 229, 245, 279 *sqq.*
Zurvān 229